D0983053

STUDIES IN
CHRISTIAN ANTIQUITY

STUDIES IN CHRISTIAN ANTIQUITY

RICHARD P. C. HANSON

T. & T. CLARK LTD
59 GEORGE STREET, EDINBURGH

Copyright © T. & T. Clark Ltd, 1985

Typeset by C. R. Barber and Partners (Highlands) Ltd,
Fort William, Scotland,
printed and bound by Billing & Sons, Worcester,

for

T. & T. CLARK LTD, EDINBURGH

First printed in the U.K. 1985

British Library Cataloguing in Publication Data

Hanson, R.P.C.
    Studies in Christian antiquity.
    1. Church history—Primitive and early church.
    I. Title
    270.1   BR165

    ISBN 0-567-09363-8

CONTENTS

PREFACE

Anyone who brings before the public articles and essays which have already appeared in print in other publications should recognize the duty of explaining to his readers why he thinks himself justified in bringing to light again what he has written in the past. I feel obliged to set forth briefly here why I have agreed to the inclusion in this book of seventeen pieces of work, all of which, except one, have already been printed.

In the first place it should be made clear that these seventeen are a selection, made with some care, out of a considerably larger list. I am not in this volume scraping the barrel. Each chapter can in itself be regarded as a study in Christian antiquity. This applies even to the chapter on the *Filioque* Clause, which is the only chapter which has not been printed before. It originally was written as a paper for the Joint Doctrinal Conversations which are taking place between the Anglican and the Orthodox Churches, and was chosen because this subject is in Orthodox minds one of burning importance and one which has been for a long time a stumbling-block in the way of the Orthodox understanding of Anglicans. But though it has this clear contemporary relevance, the *Filioque* Clause, if it is to be properly considered, leads directly into the subject of the doctrine of the Trinity in the fourth and fifth centuries, as anyone who reads my essay on it will perceive. One cannot, in short, discuss it intelligently without studying Christian antiquity.

Each of these essays is intended to be a positive contribution to the subject concerned and not merely a survey of recent treatment of the subject by other scholars nor a review of a particular book or books on the subject. I was indeed tempted to publish one or two reviews which I have written on books of particular interest, but came to the conclusion that I have not sufficient nerve, or self-confidence (or perhaps impudence) to bring these before the public again. None of the contents of this work represents a major discovery, but some may be thought to have established historical probabilities which had not been perceived, or not soundly based, before. Of these are the essay on the provenance of the interpolator in the 'Western' text of Acts (No. 3), the attribution to the original text of Origen's *Contra Celsum* of the passage marked *Unde?* by Robinson (No. 5), and the exploration of the Rule of Faith of the ancient British Church (No. 14).

In one case I was particularly anxious to make again a point which I then believed not to have been sufficiently appreciated by others. Historians and archaeologists concerned with Roman and sub-Roman Britain continue from time to time to conjecture that various sites may represent a pagan temple transformed into a Christian Church. Chapter 16 is intended as a warning against such temerarious conjectures. It was originally published in a journal which has indeed a deservedly high reputation in its own field, but that field is not one likely to be of interest to historians and archaeologists of Roman and sub-Roman Britain.

Here we meet one more justification for producing *Studies in Christian Antiquity*. Several of the articles reproduced here appeared originally in journals which do not have a wide circulation among the English-speaking public, though they are in themselves very reputable journals. Two (Nos. 4 and 14) appeared in two different examples of that tomb for learned works, the *Festschrift*, a form of publication which is admirable for the eminent man to whom the contents are dedicated but calculated to bury these contents in a deeper obscurity than that offered by most periodicals, because they are usually miscellaneous in character. This volume gives them an opportunity of reaching a rather wider public.

The contents of this book, of course, to some extent reflect the particular interests which have claimed my attention during the last twenty years or so, Origen, St. Patrick and the Early British Church, the Arian Controversy, and are by no means intended to represent an even coverage of the whole field of Christian antiquity. They are, however, placed in a chronological order, and if the reader will make his way through all of them he will be led from the New Testament itself on to the collapse of the Western Roman Empire in the fifth century and some of its sequels. They are primarily historical, though some of them (such as Nos. 6, and 10–14) deal with the history of thought rather than that of events.

Finally the question may be asked, why trouble ourselves about antiquity, pagan or Christian? What can events, the latest of which occurred more than fourteen centuries ago, have to do with us? One answer to this question is that as Christianity is still relevant to many societies throughout the world, it may be of interest and importance to learn as much as possible about the origins of Christianity. Again, several of these essays touch on points which are of considerable interest, and indeed constitute subjects of controversy, among contemporary Christians, such as the form of the eucharist (No. 7), the nature of the ministry (No. 8), eucharistic doctrine (No. 6), the doctrine of the Trinity (Nos. 10 and 11), the *Filioque* Clause (No. 12), and the nature of dogma (No. 13). But apart from any other argument, ancient history, both the history of the rise of Christianity, and the history of that remarkable period when paganism was dying, and, in death, was bequeathing a large legacy to the Christianity which was taking its place, is in itself of perennial and fascinating interest. The study of it needs no further justification.

I want here to acknowledge my gratitude to the firm of T. & T. Clark for undertaking the publication of this book.

R. P. C. Hanson.

ACKNOWLEDGEMENTS

Chapter 1, 'Are We Cut Off from the Past?', was originally published in *The Continuity of Christian Doctrine* by R. P. C. Hanson (*c* 1981 John Carroll University); the publisher was the Winston Press (formerly the Seabury Press). Chapter 7, 'The Liberty of the Bishop to Improvise Prayer' appeared in *Vigiliae Christianae* (published by the North Holland Publishing Co., Amsterdam) Vol. XV, No. 3 (1961), and chapter 17, 'The Church and the Collapse of the Roman Empire', in the same journal Vol. 26, No. 4 (1972). Chapter 2, 'The Journey of Paul and the Journey of Nikias', appeared in *Studia Evangelica* IV (ed. F. L. Cross), 1968, and chapter 13, 'Dogma and Formula in the Fathers' in *Studia Patristica* XIII, II (ed. Elizabeth A. Livingstone) 1975, both volumes published by Akademie-Verlag, Berlin. Chapter 3, 'The Provenance of the Interpolator in Acts', appeared in *New Testament Studies* Vol. 12 (1966), and chapter 15, 'The Church in Fifth-Century Gaul', appeared in the *Journal of Ecclesiastical History* Vol. XXI, 1 (1970), both volumes published by the Cambridge University Press. Chapter 4, 'Did Origen apply the word *homoousios* to the Son?', appeared in *Epektasis* (Mélanges Patristiques offerts au Cardinal Daniélou) published by Edition Beauchesne, Paris, and edited by Jean Fontaine and Charles Kannengiesser. Chapter 5, 'The Passage Marked *Unde?*', appeared in *Origeniana Secunda*, edited by Henri Crouzel and Antonio Quacquacarelli, published by Edizioni dell'Ateneo (Rome 1980). Chapter 6, 'Eucharistic Offering in the Pre-Nicene Fathers', appeared in the *Proceedings of the Royal Irish Academy* Vol. 76 (C) 4 (1976) and was also reproduced in *Eucharistic Offering in the Early Church* by R. P. C. Hanson (Grove Books, No. 19, 1976 and 1979). Chapter 8, 'Office and Concept of Office in the Early Church', is the original English of an article which appeared in a German translation *sub voce* 'Amt/Amster?Amtsverstandnis' (V Alte Kirche), in *Theologischee Realenzyklopädie* Bd. II, Lief, 3/4 (1978), published by Walter de Gruyter, Berlin. Chapter 9, 'The Christian Attitude to Pagan Religions', appeared in *Aufstieg und*

Niedergang der Römischen Welt II (Principat), Bd. 23 (2), edited by Hildegard Temporini and W. Haase, also published by Walter de Gruyter. Chapter 10, 'The Doctrine of the Trinity achieved in 381', appeared in the *Scottish Journal of Theology* Vol. 36, published by the Scottish Academic Press (Journals) Ltd. Chapter 11, 'The Transformation of Images in Trinitarian Theology', appeared in *Studia Patristica* XVII (alternatively numbered XVIII) Part I (1982), edited by Elizabeth A. Livingstone and published by the Pergamon Press. Chapter 12, 'The Filioque Clause', was originally a paper read to a meeting of the Anglican Orthodox Joint Doctrinal Commission and published with the agreement of its Co-Chairman, the Rt. Revd. Henry G. Hill D.D., LLD. Chapter 14, 'The Rule of Faith of Victorinus and of Patrick', appeared in *Latin Script and Letters A.D. 400–900* (Festschrift presented to Ludwig Bieler), edited by John J. O'Meara and Bernd Naumann and published by E. J. Brill of Leiden. Chapter 16, 'The Transformation of Pagan Temples into Churches', appeared in the *Journal of Semitic Studies* Vol. 23, 2 (1978).

Thanks and acknowledgements are due to all the publishers of these articles and are here offered.

R. P. C. Hanson.

Part I
The First Three Centuries

ARE WE CUT OFF FROM THE PAST?

I

At no point in the whole history of civilization has as intense and widespread a scrutiny of the past been made as today. At no point has skepticism about the possibility of our knowing the past been so emphatically expressed as today. Before we consider the question of the continuity of Christian doctrine we must first examine, however briefly, the question of whether any historical knowledge of the past, and especially of the remote past, is possible.

As historians have pushed their investigation of the past further and further, using new techniques and aiming at an ever more exact imaginative reconstruction, so they have become more conscious of the enormous difference of outlook which separates us from almost all past ages. Let me give a concrete example. If any of the audience had lived in Constantinople in the year 530 A.D. they might easily have heard one educated man saying the following sentence to another: *ho archimandrites ton akoimeton apologian poiei huper tou kephalaiou tou kai ek tou huiou*. This sentence has first to be translated out of ancient Greek for most people to understand it today. Translated it would run, 'The archimandrite of the Sleepless defends the Filioque clause'. But that does not tell us much. What is an archimandrite, and who are the Sleepless, and what is the Filioque clause? Well, we can duly learn that an archimandrite is the head of the ancient Greek monastery, that the Sleepless were an order of monks in Constantinople who maintained by relays a round-the-clock routine of worship, and that the Filioque clause is the expression 'and the Son' added by many Western churchmen in the sixth century to the term in the original Creed of Nicaea and Constantinople applied to the Holy Spirit 'who proceeds from the Father'. But even after his explanation most moderns would be quite unaware of the significance of the defense of this clause by the archimandrite, of all the theological, ecclesiatical, and political, consequences and nuances involved in this defense.

Above all, most modern readers would find it very difficult to envisage a society in which the opinion of the head of a monastery about an apparently abstruse and minor expression in a creed should be regarded as a matter of the greatest importance. How remote from us, how alien to us, seems such a situation! What chance could we have of understanding the minds of people in Constantinople in A.D. 530? They spoke a language quite different from ours. They lived in a pre-scientific age. Their ideas of the physical universe, of the origin of mankind, of the functioning of the human body, of the manner in which spiritual and divine agencies—if there are any—operate, of art, of history, of literature, of government, of pyschology, of technology, were utterly different from ours. If we tried to reconstruct their total world-view we would have to abandon large parts of the enterprise through lack of evidence. A vast avalanche of events, of history, has fallen between us and them, permanently cutting off communication. And if this is true of situations as comparatively recent as the sixth century A.D. how much truer must it be of situations much earlier than that, in the first century A.D.., in the second millenium B.C., and earlier than that at the beginnings of civilization in Sumeria and in Egypt! The mists of history quickly thicken and surely we must admit that for the greater part of its extent they are virtually impenetrable, even though we may deceive ourselves into thinking that we can occasionally and fleetingly penetrate them. How can we then have the presumption to imagine that it is possible seriously to reconstruct the minds and intentions of people who believed and wrote about Christian doctrine long, long ago?

Such are the arguments being widely canvassed among theologians, philosophers, and scholars today. To deal more concretely with a representative (certainly not an exhaustive) list of authors; we have to face the argument of men like Dennis Nineham, who in a recent book[1] denies any continuity at all to Christian doctrine, refuses to believe in the possibility of the past providing us with any viable norm for doctrine, does not believe in the survival of a fixed quantum of truth from the first

[1] Dennis Nineham, *The Use and Abuse of the Bible* (London, 1976).

century A.D. or in the possibility of finding an authoritative and consistent core of doctrine in the New Testament, sees little chance of the ideas of one culture surviving intact and comprehensible into the age of another culture, and seriously doubts whether the reliability of any historical account before about 1720 can be trusted. This is to revive, in a totally different form, the contention that Christianity has no essential connection with history, first put forward in an extreme form by Søren Kierkegaard and since adopted with various modifications by Paul Tillich and Rudolph Bultmann.

Another writer, much used by Nineham, is the eminent Cambridge historian J. H. Plumb whose book *The Death of the Past* conveys its own message in its title. For Professor Plumb the past is dead, though history is not. By 'the past' he means 'a created ideology with a purpose, designed to control individuals, or motivate societies, or inspire classes'.[2] Until the advent of modern scientific historical investigation, all account of the past was apparently motivated ideologically, even the works of nineteenth-century historians such as Thomas Macaulay and John Motley and William Stubbs, though the eighteenth-century Edward Gibbon is exempted from this judgement whereas contemporary Marxist historians are not. The true purpose of history, which has only recently been discovered, is 'to understand men both as individuals and in their social relationships in time', and this includes not only finding out what happened (which Plumb apparently thinks to be generally possible), but 'why things were so and why they changed'.[3] Further, the historian works with a purpose, 'in the hope that a profounder knowledge, a profounder awareness will help to mold human attitudes and human actions'.[4] And finally one principle or lesson can be derived from history 'that the condition of mankind has improved, materially alas more than morally, but nevertheless both have improved', and this truth in its turn impresses on us the value of rationality.[5] Finally we can refer to the well-known work by the American scholar

[2] J. H. Plumb, *The Death of the Past* (London, 1969), p. 17.
[3] *Ibid.*, p. 105.
[4] *Ibid.*, p. 106.
[5] *Ibid.*, pp. 136–142, quotation from p. 142.

Van A. Harvey, *The Historian and the Believer*.[6] This is a powerful argument for the view that no conviction or belief can be proved from history, and that the Christian believer is positively handicapped in approaching the task of investigating history because his convictions are likely to disturb the delicate balance of historical judgment. I have no opportunity at this point of referring to the works of many other authors who have written in support of some of these arguments, *e.g.*, of Maurice Wiles, of John Hick and the other authors of the famous or notorious book, *The Myth of God Incarnate*, nor of doing more than the scantiest justice to the arguments even of those authors whose views I have attempted to summarize.

II

It would be disingenuous of me to pretend that I agree with these arguments, for I would hardly have undertaken to write on the subject of the continuity of Christian doctrine if I thought that no such thing existed. Let me begin the process of countering them by referring to a subject which seems quite irrelevant. At Paestum on the western coast of Italy several miles south of Rome there have survived a number of ancient stone temples. They were built by Greek immigrants to Italy, perhaps in the fifth or fourth centuries B.C., much more than two thousand years ago. They did not arouse much comment until, during the last few decades of the eighteenth century, a number of British architects 'discovered' them, as it were, and were greatly impressed by them. The influence of these temples can be distinctly discerned in some surviving examples of architecture in Britain, especially in the work of Sir John Soane. Here is an example of apparently dumb buildings—for there are no inscriptions on these temples—still retaining the capacity of exercising influence in a totally different situation and culture thousands of years after they were first built. Hans-Georg Gadamer, in his magisterial work *Truth and Method*, has these words to say about buildings and statutes: 'As long as they still fulfill their function, they are contemporaneous with every

---

[6] Van A. Harvey, *The Historian and the Believer* (London, 1965).

age'.[7] Here is an example in which the remote past may be said to speak directly to each age in its surviving monuments. Every sensitive person must have experienced a similar communication when gazing at the Parthenon in Athens, the Hagia Sophia in Constantinople, at a great mediaeval cathedral in Europe, or even at the remains of the pre-Columbian civilizations in the continent of America. These monuments do not indeed give us an exact transcript of the psychological state of their creators, nor inform us much about the significance which those who built them attached to them. They do not tell us 'exactly what happened'. But, as we shall see, this is not the only criterion of historical effectivenss. It is enough for the moment to note that works of art such as we have been considering constitute an example of authentic communication in spite of the mists of history.

Let us now turn from ancient monuments to ancient historians. Dr. Nineham gives the impression that all ancient historical accounts are to be classed as equally unreliable from the point of view of the modern investigator. I think that he is here reproducing his own version of Professor Plumb's idea that all historians until very recently were so much obsessed by one ideology or another that, compared with the historian of today, they cannot be thought to be dealing with history proper but only with a more or less imaginary past. I do not for a moment believe that Plumb's distinction between the past and history will hold water or will be respected by future writers on the subject. It must at once occur to any intelligent reader of Professor Plumb's little work that, after dismissing almost all historians of previous ages as the victims of ideology, he himself betrays his own adherence to a very promising ideology. Why should any historian wish to advance the cause of humanity either morally or materially, and why should he value highly the exercise of rationality among historians or others? What does Professor Plumb mean by moral advance anyway? He would, I suspect find it impossible to give a non-ideological answer to that question.

[7] Hans-Georg Gadamer, *Truth and Method* (English translation, 1975, of original German edition, Tübingen, 1960), p. 108.

But let us return to the subject of the reliability of ancient historians. That very many annalists, chroniclers, and historians of antiquity and of the mediaeval period accepted legend and myth as true history and were to a greater or less degree uncritical in their use of sources, every student of history must admit. Anyone who, like myself, has had any acquaintance with mediaeval Irish hagiography will admit this more readily than most. But to use this general observation to condemn all ancient historiography as unreliable is itself a very uncritical procedure. When I was studying classics in Trinity College, Dublin, more than forty years ago, I was encouraged to think of the ancient Greek historian Herodotus as an untrustworthy source of information, one who too credulously took myth, legend, and hearsay to be equivalent to historical fact; but scholarly opinion has shifted, and I think rightly shifted, since then. Herodotus is now regarded as a good historian in his own right. An eminent American student of ancient history, Truesdell S. Brown, in his book *The Greek Historians*,[8] regards him as an historian as great as Thucydides, and describes him as 'the embodiment of historical curiosity'.[9] It was indeed this wide-ranging and versatile curiosity which apparently constituted the main motive for Herodotus in investigating history. Does this count, we may ask, as 'ideology' in Plumb's sense of the word? It looks remarkably like the motive which, according to Plumb, impels most modern historians, *i.e.*, 'to understand men both as individuals and in their social relationships in time' and to find out not only what happened, but 'why things were so and why they changed' (see above, p. 5). Indeed, by chance, Herodotus' accuracy has recently been remarkably vindicated in two separate instances. His description of the various ways in which the ancient Egyptians embalmed the dead has been shown to be substantially true by modern research done on mummies.[10] And his account of the complete disappearance of an armed expedition sent by the Persian King Cambyses on a journey across the desert has been substantiated by the discovery of the

---

[8] Truesdell S. Brown, *The Greek Historians* (Lexington, Mass., 1973).
[9] *Ibid.*, p. 152.
[10] Herodotus, *Histories* II.86–88.

remains of their bodies, arms, and equipment.[11] I may perhaps draw attention to another incident in Herodotus' *Histories*.[12] Darius, the successor of Cambyses, is campaigning in Scythia and has crossed the Danube, leaving his allies from the Greek Ionian islands and coastal area to guard the bridge over the river while he attempts to find a route back to Persia round the Black Sea, whose size Darius had grossly underestimated. The Scythians evade Darius' army and reach the bridge before he can discover that his search is vain and return to the river. They invite the Greeks to break down the bridge and leave Darius and his army to inevitable destruction. Now, we might think that the Greek generals had at this point only two choices. Either they could refuse the Scythian request and remain honorably faithful to their promise to support Darius. Or, they could break down the bridge, return to their homeland, and encourage the movement of emancipation of the Greek Ionian cities from Persian rule, which breaking away was in fact destined to begin soon after. But Herodotus records that they did neither. Histiaeus of Miletus reminded the other leaders that they were all tyrants or despots in their native Greek principalities and that if the Persian power was impaired their chances of survival would be slight. So they decided to do no more than make a token destruction of the bridge in order to get rid of the Scythians. Darius and his army were saved. Not only is it likely that Herodotus was here relying on the work of an earlier historian, Hecataeus, who may actually have been present on this occasion, but the unprincipled realism of the Greek leaders' conduct has a ring of truth about it which we cannot miss.

I do not, of course, argue that Herodotus was as painstakingly accurate or as critical of his sources as a modern historian would be. I only maintain that it is very unwise to dismiss all ancient history as equally unreliable, or hold that we can see a common fault in all ancient chroniclers in the motives that impelled them to write and so conclude that it vitiates their historical judgment and puts them in a different class from modern historians. 'Thucydides' says Truesdell S. Brown, 'is often wrong, that was

---

[11] Herodotus, *Histories* III.26.
[12] Herodotus, *Histories* IV.135–139.

inevitable, but he thinks in historical terms'.[13] One should perhaps note in addition that there were historical skeptics in the ancient world as in the modern. Pytheas, a famous mariner who lived in the last quarter of the fourth century B.C., was the first to bring to the learned world of ancient Greece the news that Britain was an island to the far west. He claimed to have sailed round it. Some ancient historians believed him. But, others, Dicaearchus and Polybius among them, regarded him as a liar. They could estimate confidently the unreliability of ancient historical tradition and knew that Britain could not be an island.[14]

Again, the whole question of the possibility of people in one culture understanding people in a quite different culture is not as easily solved by a negative conclusion as Nineham thinks. Gerald Downing, in a penetrating review article devoted to Nineham's book,[15] has pointed out that it is an illusion to imagine that people absorb a single total culture and find themselves confronted by the totality of other cultures which are wholly alien to them. People live in a plural situation as far as cultures go, and are compelled constantly to switch from one to another and reconcile each with the others, and the first and second centuries A.D. in the Roman Empire offered as good an example of the existence of many cultures interpenetrating each other as one could wish. I may perhaps be allowed to illustrate this point by a more modern instance. I recently saw a good television program on the painter Rubens, the four hundredth anniversary of whose birth occurred in 1977. The commentator remarked that the outlook and background of Rubens differed completely from ours, and indeed seems alien to ours. And as we look at his elaborate mythological scenes representing people in violent motion, his historical tributes to the ruling classes of Italy, Spain, Flanders, and England, his large-bosomed, fleshy nudes, and the products of his rhetorical style, we can agree with this verdict. But the same commentator remarked that Rubens was also utterly different from his

[13] Brown, *Greek Historians*, p. 133, n. 40.

[14] *Ibid.*, pp. 157, 158.

[15] Gerald Downing, 'Our Access to Other Cultures, Past and Present', *The Modern Churchman*, vol. 21, no. 1 (Winter 1977), pp. 28–42.

younger contemporary Rembrandt. Rembrandt, however, living in much the same age and society as Rubens, we regard as a supreme genius and we fully appreciate his introspective, quiet, melancholy art, full of depth and dimness. This does not at all support the view that distance in time inevitably means distance in sympathy, nor that any culture can be so homogeneous and self-consistent as necessarily to be wholly alien to us if any part of it is.

Again, there are undoubted instances of people in a later age being able to understand phenomena in the past better than an earlier age did. Two instances will suffice here. The book of Job we now acknowledge to be one of the profoundest, most important, and most moving documents in the Old Testament. We perceive that the author, though he never doubts the existence and sovereignty of God, discusses with astonishing freedom the problem posed by man's suffering and man's finitude, dismisses contemptuously conventional solutions to the problem and challenges God to vindicate his providence, and in the course of his dramatic exposition of the subject produces some of the finest poetry and most searching thought to be found in the Hebrew Scriptures. Almost all of this was lost on the Jews of the Rabbinic period and on the Christians of the early and mediaeval periods. To the author of the Epistle of James, Job was simply an example of patience (James 5.11), as he was to all the Patristic writers. Those who write commentaries on the book of Job, such as Didymus the Blind, the Arian Julian, and Gregory the Great, exhibit an almost complete misunderstanding of the purpose and character of the book. They sympathize with the conventional doctrines paraded by the author only to be condemned by him, and they tend to be rather shocked at the daring nature of Job's accusations against God and attempt to explain them away. They read a thousand other meanings into the book which are certainly not there, but they fail to see its main point. They seem to be wholly unaware of its literary splendor. Here undoubtedly the advancing years have brought a new and richer understanding of an ancient document. An increasing distance of centuries from its composition has brought increasing light. Cultures separated by twenty-one centuries have understood each other better than cultures separated by a mere six or seven hundred years.

The other example is provided by the anthropomorphisms of the Old Testament, those passages where God is represented in a human way, as baring his arm or changing his mind or sleeping or grieving, and so on. This troubled the Rabbis, but it gave much greater embarrassment to the Christian Fathers. The Greek philosophical thought in which they were steeped rejected such, as it seemed to them, all-too-human language about God, and they took a great deal of trouble to explain it away. Most theologians of today, on the other hand, are not troubled by this at all, having an understanding of, and even admiration for the vivid, personalist language of Hebrew religion and piety in treating God, and appreciating the advantage it has over the cold formal language of philosophy. Here once more antiquity, distance in time, has brought, not a fainter, gradually diminishing, but a greater and stronger insight and sympathy for the memorials of the remote past.

It has been suggested by several writers that the one basic factor which we have in common with the men of the past, whatever their age and culture, is that we share human nature with them. We can recognize them as human as we know ourselves to be human. This looks like an incontrovertible fact, but it has been denied or at least doubted by some, among them Dr. Nineham, who darkly hints that some sociologists are beginning to suggest that we have no right to assume, and no proper evidence for assuming, that there is such a thing as a recognizably common human nature in this case. The argument depends, of course, on what is meant by human nature. If we mean what the ancient Greek theologians meant by the word they used for it, *anthropotes*, that is an externally existent intellectual universal inadequately represented by particular instances of it who are called persons, then we may indeed cast doubt on the concept. But if we mean that it is possible that the men and women of, say, two or three thousand years ago who lived in Greece or Israel or China or Palestine may have belonged to a race or breed which was not human as we are human, but was sub-human or para-human, or that their psychological or nervous systems, their unconscious and conscious minds, were differently constituted or worked differently from ours, so that we have no right to argue from our reactions and feelings to theirs, this is indeed a very serious matter. If it means that they would not, for instance, be afraid of a charging tiger, love their children, wish to avoid economic destitution, be jealous of the success and popularity of others, desire to satisfy their physical appetites, and feel in certain circumstances moral obligation, then indeed we could not conduct any historical inquiry at all.

The investigation of history largely depends upon estimating the motives and intentions, the thoughts and desires, of people in the past. If we have no means of doing this because they were psychologically constituted quite differently from us, we cannot possibly reconstruct their actions, and past history becomes an indecipherable chaos. But much past history can be reconstructed; the known facts are very largely consistent with each other and fit into place, whether the historical investigation is being conducted by a Mexican, a Russian, or a New Yorker. It is inconceivable that all the attribution of motives, intentions, and desires to the people of the past are just bad guesses (though some of them may be), or are a phantasmagoria more like an opium dream than a genuine account of past events. To take this view would be to indulge quite gratuitously in despairing nihilism. The Stoic philosophers of the last two centuries B.C. and the first A.D. developed an elaborate, rational, and in some ways impressive account of human psychology, that is, the psychology of the men and women of two thousand years ago. It was based largely on empirical evidence. It can be to a large extent reconstructed. Modern scholars may not agree with this account of human psychology. But they can and do recognize it as a study of the same phenomenon as contemporary psychologists study—*homo sapiens*. The subject, though differently analyzed by the Stoics, manifestly displays much the same behaviour as the subject does today. Indeed, this assumption underlies all study and appreciation of all culture, all art, the literature, philosophy, science and religion of all ages. Skepticism about this principle is a skepticism which destroys itself.

III

Let us here turn aside for a short time to consider the relation of faith to history. It must first be realized that the truth of Christianity cannot be proved from historical data alone. It was the task of Kierkegaard to make this quite clear in an age which tended to be intoxicated with idealist philosophy. This philosophy claimed that, once history was viewed in the correct philosophical light, it could be demonstrated on historical grounds that Christianity was true, or at least as approximately true as any religion could be. Against this Kierkegaard declared passionately that apprehending the truth of Christianity involved the personal concern and commitment of the believer who believed the truth, and could not possibly be a matter of objective philosophical or scientific observation. He maintained that Christian faith needs no historical evidence at all, or only the barest minimum. In this conclusion he was followed for varying motives by both Tillich and Bultmann; they held that Christian faith is completely independent of history. Van Harvey, as we have seen, maintains that faith has no right to seek for proof in history. 'No historical event, especially if assertions about it can elicit only a tentative assent, can as such be the basis for a religious confidence about the present'.[16] We recall G. E. Lessing's famous dictum that 'accidental truths of history can never become the proof of necessary truths of reason', which has recently been re-examined and to some extent reaffirmed in an essay by my colleague at Manchester University, Dr. David Pailin.[17]

In this chapter, I shall make only three points about this much debated subject. First, Kierkegaard was undoubtedly correct in maintaining that Christianity cannot be *proved* from historical (or philosophical or scientific) data alone. The truth of Christianity is known through making a decision, the decision and commitment of faith. This excludes the possibility of proof in a scientific, mathematical, or even perhaps a philosophical sense, because it is impossible for anyone to commit himself to

[16] Harvey, *Historian*, p. 283.

[17] David Pailin, 'Lessing's Ditch Revisited', in *Theology and Change*, ed. R. H. Preston (London, 1975), pp. 78–103.

something which is logically clear and true beyond contradiction, like a geometrical proposition or a demonstration that the earth goes round the sun and not vice versa. Van Harvey's argument will certainly hold against anyone trying to find proofs for Christianity in history. But that does not say very much, as the truth of Christianity is not discovered, and should never have been commended as discoverable, by that sort of proof. The second point, however, is that though faith does not operate with proofs, it does work according to *motives*. Nobody can have faith without having some motives for faith. If a housewife trusts a recommendation by a consumer magazine of a washing machine and buys it, her purchase is an act of faith in its reliability and the recommendation has awakened her faith.

Further, faith necessarily takes it character from the motives or reasons from which is springs. If I believe that the world is going to end in a fortnight because a passage in the Revelation of St. John the Divine says so, this kind of belief is different from the kind of belief that thinks the world is going to end because a nuclear war between two major powers has broken out. That history can and does provide motives or reasons for faith is so obvious that is scarcely needs arguing, even if we abandon the field of religious belief altogether. If a statesman pursues a foreign policy designed to secure the balance of power in Europe, he does so because his belief in the necessity of preserving this balance of power has been aroused by his consideration of what happened in the past when the balance of power was disturbed. Men and women join movements of protest, of rebellion, and take part in crusades for justice because of beliefs drawn from history. Nationalist movements rely largely on faith which is of a similar character. Half the participants and most of the propagandists in the English Civil War in the seventeenth century and the American Civil War of the nineteenth were similarly motivated by reasons drawn from history. Harvey in fact makes the admission—which seems to me a damaging one—that a fact can awaken faith or provide the symbol that faith can use.[18] If events in history can in these

---

[18] Harvey, *Historian*, p. 284.

varied ways provide motives for faith in secular contexts, I cannot see why they cannot do so in religious contexts. There is nothing in religious faith which places its motives in a different class from those which supply secular faith.

Thirdly, both the sides of Lessing's famous dictum have recently been questioned. We have seen that the 'accidental truths of history' (which incidentally is a very curious way of stating the subject) are not required by faith to become the *proof* of necessary truths of reason, nor anything else, because faith does not deal in proofs but in reasons for decision. And, on the other side, the concept of the necessary truths of reason, at least as far as truth as the object of religious belief is concerned, involves, as we shall see, an impossible attempt to emancipate the human mind from the historicality of its existence.[19]

IV

To deny that we can establish communication and at least a limited understanding with the men and women of the past, where we have any sufficient evidence of their existence and activity, is therefore unnecessary. Indeed, it is contradicted by evidence which should be plain to any person capable of understanding the methods of historical investigation. And whereas history cannot be asked to produce proofs of the truth of Christianity in the formal sense, it may legitimately be expected to supply motives for faith. Let us now move on to consider the subject of objectivity in writing history. This subject is brought forward by Harvey's objection that Christian belief upsets the delicate mechanism of historical judgment, and by Plumb's doctrine that all historians until very recently have been writing ideology and not history.

Van Harvey seems to me to have an exaggerated idea of the

[19] I do not deal here with Dr. Pailin's appeal to the impossibility of achieving a correct perspective for appreciating events from a study of events put forward in his essay in *Theology and Change*. Perhaps what is said in the next section will sufficiently indicate that nobody ever does attempt to achieve such a correct perspective for appreciating events from a study of the events *alone*, but that this does not preclude the possibility of understanding history, and therefore, of course, of history's providing a motive for faith.

impartiality of historians. Indeed at times in his book he almost appears to write as if facts were small hard balls which historians have to find and arrange in patterns, and he seems to be quite unaware that knowledge of the past is affected by the knower. I am not, of course, arguing for complete historical relativism. This is a position which Nineham in his curious book at times seems to be nearing. It must be obvious to the meanest intelligence that if we are wholly bound by our cultural context, and can neither make generalizations about history nor enjoy any continuity of truth in history, then we cannot make the generalization that there are no universal truths surviving through history. But it can be stated with entire confidence that complete historical impartiality (which, incidentally, Plumb seems to think he has achieved) is impossible. Whether it would be desirable if it were capable of achievement I will consider shortly.

In fact by the nature of things no historian can be completely impartial. I will develop this idea first by an example.J B. Bury was an eminent historian of the ancient world, one of the most eminent of his day, who first occupied a chair in Trinity College, Dublin, and later became Professor of Modern History at the University of Cambridge. He wrote a magisterial history of ancient Greece which is still useful. He edited Gibbon's *Decline and Fall* with notes. He wrote a number of weighty works on the Byzantine Empire. And then, in the year 1905, he published his *Life of St. Patrick*.

Scholarly work on Patrick had up to that point tended, as everything else in Ireland has tended, to run along denominational lines. Catholic scholars usually belonged to the maximizing school, accepting a great deal of later tradition about Patrick; Protestant scholars took the minimizing line, rejecting much of the later tradition. Bury was the son of an Irish rector, but had become a freethinker and agnostic. He was determined to show himself impartial, and in order to do so he came out on the maximizing, one might say the Catholic, side. His deserved reputation caused his views on Patrick to prevail for nearly fifty years. But now we can look back and realize that in his study of Patrick Bury made a number of errors which no historian of the ancient world ought to make. He spoke confidently about sources in a language—old Irish—which he did not know; he accepted as reliable very late and untrustworthy sources about Patrick, such as the *Annals of the Four Masters*, and he failed to notice a vitally important piece of evidence about Patrick, the quality of his Latin. His very desire for impartiality led him into grave historical blunders.

Harvey's warnings to the Christian historian are misplaced. They amount to a kind of psychological blackmail, and they should be rejected, as all blackmail should. Of course, the Christian believer must not allow his Christian beliefs to distort his view of historical evidence. But it is equally true that the non-believer must now allow his disbelief to distort his view of the facts either. One cannot deny, for instance, that Gibbon's dislike of Christianity distorted his view of some of the events of the early Roman empire. His unjustified reductions in calculating the numbers of Christians killed for their faith in the first three centuries is one example. His outrageous assertion that the Arian controversy turned on a single iota is another. Harvey has no more right to warn the believer off the field of historical investigation than a Christian has to warn off a non-Christian.

The fact is that every historian uses as part of his technique in pursuing historical investigation a stock of general ideas, some of which he must have derived from other sources than his historical work, but some of which have been derived from or influenced by his study of history, and without these he would not be an historian nor find it possible to investigate history at all. He employs these ideas in making sense of the subject which he is studying, and they are inseparably bound up with the more exact and quasi-scientific techniques and judgments which have so much impressed Harvey. Harvey suggests that the orthodox believer brings faith to history.[20] But this is a false antithesis. Faith in the case of a believer represents something that in one form or another is part of an historian's activity. He can perhaps be a man without prejudices, but he cannot be a man without beliefs, and those beliefs will necessarily and rightly dispose him to make judgments not only about what should have happened or what could have happened, but about what did happen. His

[20] Harvey, *Historian*, p. 283.

beliefs will even affect his attitude about 'facts'. This is not a matter of different historians giving different interpretations of commonly acknowledged 'facts'. It concerns whether facts are recognized as facts or not. Why do different historians estimate evidence differently, even to the point of whether facts are facts? Because they have different minds preoccupied with different collections of ideas, and there is nothing a priori to preclude Christian belief from being included in these ideas, and therefore conceivably influencing the historian's mind to recognize or not to recognize facts. The orthodox believer is not disqualified from writing history because he is an orthodox believer, any more than the non-believer is disqualified because he is a non-believer. Faith is not necessarily a state of mind alien to and inconsistent with the writing of history.

The whole subject of objectivity in writing history has been illuminated and placed in a new perspective by the weighty work of H. G. Gadamer already mentioned, *Truth and Method*. This scholar, who displays a range of learning which even a fellow-German might envy, argues not only that complete impartiality in historical writing is impossible, but that it is undesirable. This apparently shocking thesis he advances with great cogency and persuasiveness in his work of 600 large pages. It has been the error of the human sciences too long to emulate the method of the natural or 'exact' sciences. 'The world of physics cannot seek to be the whole of what exists. For even a world formula that contained everything, so that the observer of the system would also be included in the latter's equations, would still asssume the existence of a physicist who, as calculator, would not be an object calculated'.[21] Further, the method used by the natural sciences excludes the possibility of history affecting it, what Gadamer calls 'the historicality of experience',[22] and yet this is an essential and inalienable part of historical investigation. Our own historical circumstances and the tradition which we inherit is a necessary part of our understanding of evidence from the past. We can never place

[21] Gadamer, *Truth and Method*, p. 410.
[22] *Ibid.*, p. 310 *et alibi*; *cf.* Nicholas Lash, *Change in Focus* (London, 1973), pp. 168–175.

ourselves, unencumbered by any presuppositions, exactly in the mental position of some person in the past, because we cannot know him without judging him by, or at least from, our own contemporary situation. A lengthy quotation will perhaps make this clearer:

> A person who imagines that he is free of prejudices, basing his knowledge on the objectivity of his procedures and denying that he is himself influenced by historical circumstances, experiences the power of the prejudices that unconsciously dominate him as a *vis a tergo*. A person who does not accept that he is dominated by prejudices will fail to see what is shown by their light ... A person who reflects himself out of a living relationship to tradition destroys the true meaning of this tradition. Historical consciousness in seeking to understand tradition must not rely on the critical method with which it approaches its sources, as if this preserved it from mixing in its own judgments and prejudices. It must, in fact, take account of its own historicality. To stand within a tradition does not limit the freedom of knowledge, but makes it possible.[23]

As Gadamer puts is epigrammatically, all that the historian who searched for complete impartiality gains is to incur the prejudice of being free from prejudice. One of the main arguments of Van Harvey's book, if we accept Gadamer's thesis, was cut away from under him five years before he published *the Historian and the Believer*.

As far as Christianity is concerned, it can be demonstrated with some ease that it stands or falls by historical continuity. I do not gather from Nineham's book in what sense he can continue to believe in Christianity once he has abandoned belief in the validity of its continuity. Presumably devotees of Christianity today claim to be in contact with some form of truth. Presumably they are not simply playing an enjoyable game or telling a pretty story or indulging in a comfortable form of self-delusion. Whether this truth is envisaged as consisting of communication with God, who must be true, or knowing the gospel, or even just finding a true paradigm or example, it must have some form. It cannot be completely formless nor wholly

[23] Gadamer, *Truth and Method*, p. 324.

inexpressible. That form must have some relation to Jesus Christ, an historical personage, or at least a character believed to be historical. The form therefore must be related to the period in history when Jesus Christ appeared. Contemporary Christianity can only vindicate itself as authentic if it can show that it is related to this historical event. The subject of continuity cannot be evaded. Tillich and Bultmann misled us at this point. It may well be that contemporary Christianity has many other tasks and obstacles in order to authenticate itself. But this is a basic, preliminary, indispensable demand. Nineham denies that a fixed quantum of truth can have survived the centuries. This is a very curious and misleading way of referring to truth; it would be misleading even if it were applied to the development of scientific truth; truth cannot be weighed and measured. The question which has to be answered is, does contemporary Christianity encounter or reflect or express the same communication with God, or the same gospel, or the same paradigm or example as primitive Christianity did? Or has the process of transmission so altered the original that it can no longer be recognized? In this chapter I have attempted to clear away some of the immediate obstacles to answering this question. I have tried to make it clear that it is mistaken to discredit all ancient records; that it is possible for us to understand and reconstruct the past; that the type of objectivity demanded by Plumb and Van Harvey is not only impossible but positively misleading, that past situations and cultures are not necessarily forever alien to us, and that though we cannot prove the truth of Christianity from history, our faith can and does and should receive strength and encouragement from history. But the question of the development of Christian doctrine remains.

2

THE JOURNEY OF PAUL AND THE JOURNEY OF NIKIAS

An Experiment in Comparative Historiography

This brief paper is written in response to the treatment meted out in his recent Commentary on Acts[1] by H. Conzelmann to Luke's account in the 27th chapter of Acts of Paul's journey from Caesarea to Malta and his shipwreck during the course of it. Conzelmann does not deny that the journey described by Luke was a real journey undertaken at some time by somebody, but he gravely doubts if it was ever undertaken by St. Paul. He points out that Paul's part in the story, at least as far as Malta, can be easily detached from the rest. He reminds the reader that several stories of sea voyage and shipwreck were current in literature roughly contemporary with Luke or in a period not long after his. In an Appendix to his Commentary he reproduces parts of some of these by way of comparison. His theory is that Luke has used a popular contemporary story of a shipwreck in order to lend interest and excitement to his narrative and has rather clumsily inserted into it some fictitious anecdotes about Paul in order to connect the story of shipwreck with the rest of his narrative. This theory enables him to maintain the thesis which appeals to him, namely that the sources upon which Luke relies for the greater part of the book of Acts are late and unreliable and that the book is rather a piece of imaginative reconstruction that a sober narrative, even judged by the canons of ancient history-writing.

I must confess to finding Conzelmann's whole approach to the book of Acts unconvincing and indeed often unscientific. But it is almost impossible to prove negations from history; it is not open to those who disagree with Conzelmann to prove that his scepticism is incorrect. One experiment can, however, be made by way of demonstrating that my belief in Luke's substantial accuracy is not subjective prejudice and credulity and that Conzelmann's methods are at fault. This is to take a parallel

[1] Die Apostelgeschichte (1963), pp. 141–147.

piece of ancient history-writing and to subject it to the same critical methods as Conzelmann uses and—as one must in any experiment—see what happens. This is the purpose of this paper. I have chosen as the subject of experiment a similar journey taken more than 400 years before the journey described by Luke, in roughly the same direction, a description of which also survives in Greek. I refer to the journey of Nikias the Athenian general from Athens to Catana in Sicily described in the first 61 chapters of the sixth book of Thucydides' *Peloponnesian War*.[2] Imagine for a moment that this journey was described not by Thucydides but by Luke. What would Conzelmann make of it?

In the first place, the story begins with a gross improbability. We are expected to believe that the Athenian Assembly voted the man who was the chief opponent of the plan for sending a naval expedition to Sicily into the position of leading general of the expedition (8.2 and 9.14). Thucydides was certainly not in Athens at the time that he relates this unlikely story. The expedition took place in the year 415 B.C. Thucydides had been exiled in 424 B.C. and did not return to Athens until 404, during the whole period of the sea voyage which he purports to describe. His sources for this extraordinary tale must be unreliable and legendary. In the course of the narrative he gives us a number of alleged speeches; those made in the Athenian Assembly for and against the despatch of the expedition; the speeches made in the Assembly at Syracuse when the people of that city learnt that they were to be made the object of an Athenian attack; the different suggestions about the right strategy to be adopted put forward by the different generals, including Nikias, when the expedition had reached Rhegium. All these speeches are in exactly the same style, the style which Thucydides uses for all his speeches throughout his work. We may dismiss them all, as Thucydides was not present at any of them, and it is wholly unlikely that any written record of them was made, far less that, if it was made, it survived.

The narrative of the voyage from Athens to Catana itself is

[2] The text followed here is that of J. Classen (1876), revised by J. Steup (1963).

full of suspicious features. There is no mention whatever made at any point of winds nor of the state of the sea, nor of any of the nautical movements of the fleet—details which Luke has at least included in his borrowed narrative in Acts. The account of the journey consists simply of a bare list of names, which any intelligent historian could have imaginatively reconstructed with the aid of such maps as were in existence in those days. We may dismiss the suggestion that Thucydides was relying on the reports of eyewitnesses. The ancients were not interested in the scientific collection of historical evidence, and anyway the period of time elapsing between the alleged events and Thucydides' reporting of them—at least ten years and probably more—would ensure that all oral tradition on the subject would have been corrupted by the ideology of those who were transmitting it. The account of the voyage does not even include 'we' passages—a feature which Luke either found embedded in his narrative when he took it over or which he added when he re-wrote it. Thucydides does not even claim that he was present at the events which he relates.

In his alleged journey of Nikias with the Athenian fleet to Catana there is at least one manifestly legendary story, about how the people of Egesta, whom the Athenians were ostensibly coming to help, had tricked the Athenian ambassadors sent to them at an earlier stage by putting all their goods in the shop window. When they entertained the Athenian deputation they borrowed valuable vessels and plate and passed the same set on from household to household, thus creating a false impression of opulence (46.3–4). This is a well-known motif in folk-stories. It is reminiscent of the legendary story of how the men of Gibeon tricked the Israelites, only here the impression to be created was one of poverty and distance, not of opulence (Joshua 9.3–27). The story of Alcibiades being sent off as one of the three generals and then being recalled as soon as he reached Sicily and then escaping and being condemned to death in his absence is a most unconvincing one (27,28,53). Can we imagine an Athenian assembly doing anything as rash as this? The legend about Alcibiades manifestly has no connection with the rest of the story and originally circulated quite independently. Here we have a piece of imaginative reconstruction by Thucydides designed to support his well-known anti-democratic prejudices. Its main function was probably to give the author an opportunity of introducing (very clumsily, to be sure) his version of the story of Harmodius and Aristogeiton (54–59). This story is totally irrelevant to his narrative, as he virtually admits when he begins the next chapter with the words ὁ δῆμος ὁ τῶν 'Αθηναίων καὶ μιμνησκόμενος ὅσα ἀκοῇ περὶ αὐτῶν ἐπίστατο (60.1)—as if the Athenian Assembly would recall at this point a minor incident alleged to have happened nearly a hundred years before! Thucydides introduces this piece of tradition here simply because it contributes to his anti-democratic ideology by throwing discredit upon the early heroes of democratic freedom. The story of Harmodius and Aristogeiton must of course have been circulating so long in oral tradition and have become so much open to alteration in the interests either of democratic or anti-democratic ideas as to be historically worthless.

Most suspicious of all is the fact that it is perfectly possible to detach all the incidents in which Nikias figures and still to leave the account of the expedition quite intact. We have already dismissed the account of his speeches in the Assembly and his recommendations about strategy at Rhegium. There remains only one more mention of him, and here the marked abruptness and awkwardness of his introduction betrays the work of a later editor. Thucydides has described (46.1) how three ships which had been sent on ahead returned to Rhegium to announce that the people of Egesta were much less well supplied with money than had been expected. Then he goes on (46.2) καὶ τῷ μὲν Νικίᾳ προσδεχομένῳ ἦν τὰ παρὰ τῶν 'Εγεσταίων, τοῖν δὲ ἑτέροιν καὶ ἀλογώτερα. There is no reason whatever why Nikias should be mentioned here and it is impossible to conceive that Thucydides could have known the state of his mind at this juncture. We may dismiss this as an insertion of the author's designed to show the superiority to the other generals of his anti-democratic hero, Nikias, and his power of foreseeing the future. There follow the unlikely story about the Egestan deceit (46.3–4), a general, editorial, passage recounting how the ambassadors were blamed for being deceived (46.4–5), and a reconstruction of the views of each of the three generals about what should be done (47–49). Nikias is not mentioned again for another 20 chapters (not until 67.3). In short, it is highly probable that Thucydides is here reproducing an account of a naval expedition made, no doubt, at some point by an Athenian fleet, an account which he picked up from somewhere, but one wholly unconnected with Nikias.

This essay in comparative historiography has been indulged in simply to show how easy it is to apply historical criticism of the type employed by Conzelmann to a narrative of a sea-voyage which every historian of the ancient world admits to be reliable, not only in substance but in detail. Yet the story of Nikias' voyage from Athens to Catana does not on the whole give as vivid and authentic an impression of historical truth as does the story of the voyage of Paul from Caesarea to Malta. Indeed Nikias' voyage may be said to make rather less claim to be historical, in so far as it is not written in the first person plural. We may reasonably ask, how in the circumstances could any mention of Paul have been made, supposing Luke's story of his voyage to be true, without such mention being 'detachable'? Paul was neither captain, ship-owner, nor member of the crew but a passenger, and passengers are by definition detachable. I therefore offer this little essay as an experiment in how not to conduct historical criticism.

3

THE PROVENANCE OF THE INTERPOLATOR IN THE 'WESTERN' TEXT OF ACTS AND OF ACTS ITSELF

First of all, the title of this paper needs justification.[1] Why should we assume that anyone ever made interpolations in the text of Acts? Ropes, who is still the most considerable authority on this subject, spoke of the 'Western' text all through his work on the Text of Acts in *The Beginnings of Christianity* as if it gave evidence of the work of a reviser of the text, not of an interpolator, and many scholars before him had the same opinion. On the other hand, very recent scholarship has tended to the opposite view, that it is wrong to hold that 'Western' readings in the New Testament necessarily represent a single continuous revision done at one particular moment in the history of the text. Professor G. D. Kilpatrick, for instance, in a recent article[2] suggests that every reading in Acts has to be considered on its merits, independently of speculation about whether it represents a revision or a recension or a 'good' MS tradition. He believes that the 'Western' readings often do not represent a revision or recension, but are single examples of original, correct readings preserved in this particular MS tradition. In his view, word order, orthography, and grammatical, syntactical and philological considerations applied *de novo* to each reading should be paramount in attempting to discover correct readings. The wisdom of this approach has been confirmed by the careful scholarship applied to the subject by M. Wilcox in his book *The Semitisms of Acts* (1965). He has shown reasons for concluding that several

[1] In determining the text of the 'Western' tradition in Acts this essay has followed A. C. Clark's text which he printed in his book *The Acts of the Apostles* (1933). In this edition he printed the 'Western' peculiarities in the text in black type; acceptance of Clark's text does not of course imply belief in the existence of his 'Z Text' as the original text of Acts. When this article refers to the 'B Text' or 'the text of the great uncials', it means to use these terms as a convenient abbreviation for the text of Acts as given in Nestle and and Kilpatrick's text of the New Testament (2nd edn, 1958).

[2] G. D. Kilpatrick, 'An Eclectic Study of the Text of Acts', in *Biblical and Patristic Studies in Memory of R. P. Casey*, ed. J. N. Birdsall and R. W. Thomson (1963), pp. 64–77.

'Western' readings in Acts witness to passages where an original Aramaic influence may be detected surviving in Luke's Greek rendering of an earlier source (oral or written) which may have been in Greek, but, if so, in Greek influenced by Aramaic. Other 'Western' readings represent a different version of the Old Testament from the LXX, resembling the Samaritan Pentateuch or early Aramaic Targums. That the 'Western' text preserved a number of correct readings has usually been acknowledged by scholars who have turned their attention to this subject, though their estimates of the number have varied greatly, from those who regarded the 'Western' text as originating from a second-century revision (who usually reckoned the number to be small) to A. C. Clark, who regarded the 'Western' text as the original and all other traditions as later. Ropes, for instance, was confident that three well-known apparent additions by the 'Western' group of MSS in the second half of Acts preserved in fact original words which had disappeared in other MSS, viz. Acts 20.15 καὶ μείναντες ἐν Τρωγυλίῳ; 21.1, καὶ Μύρα, and 27.5, δι' ἡμερῶν δεκάπεντε.[3] But if we accept the views of Kilpatrick about the proper way to approach 'Western' readings it is possible to regard as genuine and correct a number of readings which earlier scholars had attributed to a 'Western' reviser. Some of the passages which Ropes adduced as evidence that the 'Western' reviser knew Hebrew, and perhaps therefore worked in Syria or Palestine, may seem more plausible if regarded as survivals of the original text; e.g., the form of the name Bar-Jesus where it appears at Acts 13.6 may preserve in the form given by the 'Western' group of MSS a Greek transliteration of the Semitic ayin (Βαριησοῦαν, in contrast to Βαριησοῦς), and the 'Western' text's version of the name Silas whenever it appears, Σίλεας, may be an attempt to reproduce a Semitic guttural.[4] The

---

[3] *The Text of Acts*, by J. H. Ropes (vol. III of part 1 of Foakes-Jackson and Lake, *The Beginnings of Christianity* (1926), pp. 238–239). Reproduced in A. F. J. Klijn, *A Survey of Researches into the Western Text of the Gospels and Acts* (1949), p. 76.

[4] Ropes, *op. cit.*, pp. 243–244. Ropes also adduces here 13.33 πρώτῳ ψαλμῷ, read by the 'Western' tradition, whereas B has δευτέρῳ. But this may be regarded as an original reading also.

instances given originally by Ramsay of accuracy in describing places and other details in Asia Minor in the 'Western' text can also now be recognized by a less complicated process of argument as genuine and consistent with Luke's accuracy, visible elsewhere, about details such as these. They are Acts 13.14 where D reads εἰς 'Αντιόχειαν τῆς Πισιδίας which is more correct in describing Pisidia in a wider context than B's reading εἰς 'Αντιόχειαν τήν Πισιδίαν; 14.2 where D more accurately describes the opposition to Paul and Barnabas at Iconium as οἱ ἀρχισυνάγωγοι τῶν 'Ιουδαίων καὶ οἱ ἄρχοντες than B's reading at this point, οἱ ἀπειθήσαντες 'Ιουδαῖοι; 14.13 where D's phrase τοῦ ὄντος Διὸς προπόλεως, using προπόλεως as an adjective immediately after the name of the deity, is more correct than the τοῦ Διὸς τοῦ ὄντος πρὸ τῆς πόλεως read by B; and finally 19.28 where D's μεγάλη Ἄρτεμις is proved by inscriptions to be more accurate than B's μεγάλη ἡ Ἄρτεμις.[5] It is not irrelevant to the argument of this article that in recognizing these readings of the 'Western' tradition as original we are destroying much of the evidence that a 'Western' reviser worked in Asia Minor.[6]

But when we have made all possible allowance for readings in the 'Western' group of MSS being more correct than those of B and the other uncials associated with it, we are still left with a large number of 'Western' readings in Acts which cannot be explained by this hypothesis. We shall look now at a list of these readings, but the list is by no means exhaustive. We can begin with six texts chosen by Dibelius[7] as the clearest examples of the 'Western' MSS' tendency to provide readings which are intended to smooth over difficulties and inconsistencies or to

---

[5] These examples are reproduced by Klijn from Ramsay, *op. cit.*, pp. 19–21.

[6] One of the most commonly quoted examples of an apparently original reading in the 'Western' tradition is at Acts 20.4, where Δουβ(ε)ριος is attached to the name Gaius. Doberus is a town in Macedonia south-west of Philippi. But against this is the argument that the men who accompanied Paul to Jerusalem probably represented different areas of the Church, in which case Aristarchus and Secundus from Thessalonica would represent the Church in Macedonia, and Gaius and Timothy the Church in Lycaonia (Derbe). Timothy certainly came from Lystra or Iconium (16.1, 2).

[7] M. Dibelius, *Studies in the Acts of the Apostles* (1956), pp 85–86.

explain obscurities in an existing text, and which therefore cannot possibly be original. The first of these six is Acts 3.11, where the 'Western' text reads 'as Peter and John went out he [the man whose paralysis had been healed] went out with them holding on to them'. The B text says nothing about Peter and John going out. Several scholars have thought that this is a proof that the reviser in the 'Western' text knew the topography of the Temple area better than Luke did, because in order to reach the Porch of Solomon from the Beautiful Gate it would have been necessary to move out of the court to which the Gate gave access. But Dibelius points out that the real motivation of the 'Western' reading here is the roughness left by the conclusion of a typical healing-story at v. 10 and the awkward attachment to it of Luke's introduction to Peter's speech which follows. In either case the 'Western' text is clearly explanatory and not original. The next example occurs at 10.25 where for the great uncials' brief statement, 'when it happened that Peter came near, Cornelius met him and fell at his feet and worshipped', the 'Western' text reads 'And when Peter drew near to Caesarea, one of the slaves ran ahead and indicated that he had arrived. And Cornelius started up ...', *etc.* This, Dibelius holds, is because Luke had set out to tell the story of how Cornelius was moved by a vision to send for Peter in order to hear his message, but Luke, in introducing vv. 27–29 at this point of the narrative, was threatening to reduce its effect by the story of how Peter was moved by a vision to preach to Cornelius. The 'Western' text evades this danger by adding a very emphatic account of the move of Cornelius towards Peter. The next example is at 14.6–8 where Luke tells us that under pressure of persecution Paul and Barnabas fled to 'Lystra and Derbe and the surrounding countryside, and there they were evangelizing'. Then he proceeds to relate the story of the healing of the crippled man at Lystra. But before this account the 'Western' text insists, 'and the whole population was amazed at the teaching. But Paul and Barnabas remained in Lystra', manifestly to correct the impression left by Luke's text that at the point where the next incident begins Paul and Barnabas were in Derbe. Next at 14.18, 19 Luke leaves a strong impression of abruptness in transition. The people of Lystra have been so favourably impressed by Paul and Barnabas that it is only with difficulty that the apostles restrained them from sacrificing to them as gods. 'But Jews from Antioch and Iconium arrived and persuaded the crowds and stoned Paul and dragged him out of the city imagining him to be dead.' The 'Western' text (represented here by h and the Harklean Syriac) removes this impression of abruptness by rewriting the passage. 'By these words they just managed to restrain the crowds from sacrificing to them, and persuaded them to go each to his own home. But when the two remained and were engaged in teaching, some Jews arrived from Iconium and Antioch and by bold contradictions persuaded the crowds to desert their cause, alleging that nothing which they said was true but all was fiction.' Then the text describes the stoning. The next example is found at 16.35, where Luke causes considerable difficulty by omitting to connect the action of the magistrates in freeing the prisoners Paul and Silas at Philippi with the earthquake, probably because the story of the imprisonment and liberation and the story of the earthquake were originally two unconnected narratives. The 'Western' text repairs this omission: 'But when daylight came the magistrates convened a meeting in the market-place and recalled the earthquake and became very apprehensive. So they sent the police', *etc*. Finally at 20.12 the 'Western' text supplies another transitional phrase, 'When they had bidden us farewell', to smooth over another abrupt change of subject in Luke's text.

These six examples must make it clear that some readings in the 'Western' tradition are intended to smooth over roughness or explain obscurities and cannot therefore be original. Once this point is admitted, a very long list of such secondary readings can be compiled. At 8.1 the 'Western' text labours to make even clearer the point that the apostles did not leave Jerusalem at the time of Stephen's death. At 14.2–5 it alters a rather confused account of persecution at Iconium into an account of two clear-cut periods of persecution interrupted by a period of peace. At 14.25 it supplies a reason for the visit of Paul and Barnabas to Attalia, which is left unexplained in Luke's text. Its well-known transposition of the demands of the 'Apostolic Decree' at 15.20, 29 from the ceremonial sphere to the moral is wholly likely to

be secondary.[8] At 15.34 it manifestly corrects an inconsistency
between 15.33 where Silas is reported to have left Antioch with
Judas and 15.40 where Paul later leaves Antioch with Silas, by
inserting 'But Silas decided to remain and Judas set out alone'.
At 18.7 the 'Western' text explains an obscurity by causing Paul
to leave, not merely the synagogue at Corinth which he had
been attending, but the house of Aquila where he had been
staying. At 18.25 it attempts to relieve a little the obscurity of
Apollos' origins by suggesting that he had learnt the Christian
message in his native city of Alexandria. Two verses later it
brings precision into Luke's language which is vague at this
point by connecting Apollos' movements definitely with
Corinth, in preparation for the reference to him in 19.1. And at
19.1 it explains why Paul did not visit Jerusalem at this period,
unaware apparently that ἀναβάς at 18.22 probably implies that
he did. At 19.5 it illuminates the obscurity of Luke's account of
Paul's dealing with some disciples of John the Baptist
encountered at Ephesus by suggesting that Paul baptized them
(and perhaps also laid his hands on them) 'for the remission of
sins'. At 20.3, 4 where Luke wrote that Paul intended to go from
Greece to Syria and decided to return through Macedonia,
which is far from being the obvious route, the 'Western' text, as
so often, supplies a motive: 'the Spirit told him to return'. At
21.16–17 it usefully articulates what Luke clearly meant to
convey, but did not in fact express, that Paul and his party stayed
a night at an intermediate place on the journey from Caesarea to
Jerusalem, and that this was the occasion of their meeting
Mnason, a primitive disciple. At 22.29 it has transferred the
action of the commandant in releasing Paul from his chains
from early in the next day where Luke had somewhat oddly
placed it to a point immediately after the commandant's
learning that Paul was a Roman citizen. At 23.24 the 'Western'
text has supplied a motive for Claudius Lysias' surprisingly
elaborate precautions in escorting Paul from Jerusalem to
Caesarea 'because he was afraid that the Jews might kidnap Paul
and kill him and he himself might be accused of taking a bribe'.
It also rounds off Tertullus' speech at Acts 24.6–8 by a well-

[8] Cf. Klijn, op. cit., p. 19.

timed reference to Claudius Lysias, which however betrays its secondary origin by its assumption that Claudius Lysias was present during the speech. At 27.15 it adds the details that when the ship was running before the wind the sails had been furled; and at 28.29 it characteristically provides a fuller and more elegant ending for the account of Paul's encounter with the Jews in Rome by adding 'and when he had said thus the Jews departed having a lively discussion among themselves'.

These seventeen examples, added to the six already discussed, should convince anybody that some agency has been at work on an earlier text of Acts in order to introduce order and clarity into that text. What the agency should be called is a difficult question. 'Reviser' suggests a wholesale re edition of the text; but this is a question which this article wishes to leave open. 'Interpolator' is perhaps the best word to use because it implies that the characteristic readings attributed to it are secondary without implying that they emanate from an editor of the text. It seems reasonable to conclude that the type of interpolation which we have been considering derives from a single hand, rather than from a number of hands working necessarily over a considerable period of time. Such bold and extensive alterations in the text must have taken place at an early period while the text of Acts was fluid, before the book was regarded as sacrosanct and not open to addition or subtraction; this period cannot have lasted long. 'To suppose', says Ropes, 'that the bulk of the variations proceed not from one but from many hands is a wholly unnecessary complication and multiplication of hypotheses, and runs counter to the clear indications of unity furnished by style and method in each text.'[9] We can, more modestly, presume that what Ropes says of the whole can at least be applied to the work of a single interpolator. Presumably he was an interpolator whose work became somehow incorporated in the type of text witnessed to by those MSS which scholars have agreed to regard as representing the 'Western' tradition, even though we may not conclude that he was the only contributor to this tradition. Klijn, indeed, speaks with good reason of 'the differences between the groups within

[9] Ropes, *op. cit.*, pp. 222–223.

the "Western texts" ',[10] reminding us that we must not assume that we have in the 'Western' text a single homogeneous production deriving from a single hand at a single period. All that is being claimed here is that the work of the interpolator, as far as we have traced it, appears to be a single phenomenon within the whole composition which we call the 'Western' text.

Upon the conclusion that the 'Western' text must bring us back to a very early date all scholars seem to be agreed. Corssen had shown that readings characteristic of this text must go back to before the time of Cyprian, for readings in the Fleury palimpsest characteristic of the 'Western' text have striking similarities with the text of Acts used by Cyprian. Rendel Harris showed that the same text could be detected in Tertullian. Further, Irenaeus, quoting Acts 16.8, says, according to his Latin translator, 'Separatis enim, inquit, a Paulo et Barnaba et Johanne qui uocabatur Marcus, et cum nauigasset Cyprum, *nos uenimus in Troadem*', apparently reading κατηντήσαμεν εἰς Τρωάδα, for he regards this as a 'we'-passage and proceeds to base an argument on this fact.[11] Though D here reads κατήντησαν, yet Irenaeus may have had a copy which read a first person plural, as Codex D does in an addition to 11.28. Harris concludes from this that the 'Western' text cannot be later than the second century.[12] Ropes agrees that Irenaeus used a Greek MS for Acts which was of a thoroughly 'Western' character. His translator closely followed the original but may at times have used an Old Latin Version to aid him.[13] The use of the 'Western' text by Irenaeus, and its appearance in the African Old Latin Version (which Ropes believes to have had some considerable history before it was used by Tertullian), convinced Ropes that the date of the 'Western' text must be brought back to 150 at the latest. He believed, too, that Marcion and Tatian show signs of using a 'Western' type of text in their

[10] Klijn, *op. cit*, p. 74.

[11] Irenaeus, *Adversus Haereses* 3.14.1. It is generally agreed that the Latin translator of Irenaeus is an unusually faithful one, though the date of the translation is disputed. See Klijn, *op cit*, pp. 83–84.

[12] J. Rendel Harris, *Four Lectures on the Western Text of the New Testament* (1894), pp. 64–66.

[13] Ropes, *op cit.*, pp. 187–188.

quotations of the Gospels. His final opinion is that the origins of the 'Western' text must be sought as early as the first half of the second century.[14]

Enough reason has perhaps now been given to show that a good case can be made for assuming that the 'Western' text of Acts gives evidence of the activity of an interpolator, though we need not assume that he was the editor or originator of the 'Western' text, which may indeed be composite and contain contributions made by several textual traditions, and that this interpolator must have been at work very early indeed, as early as 150 or even earlier. Let us now turn to see whether we can learn anything from this man's work about his date, interests and origins. We shall have to be careful to use only evidence which looks as if it is the work of an interpolator and is not original nor derived from some other and irrelevant source.

The first point to be noticed is that this interpolator has no special knowledge of Judaism nor of the topography of Palestine. We have already suggested that the rather more accurate transliteration of the names Bar-Jesus and Silas are more likely to be correct readings than secondary ones, and have shown that it is not necessary to assume better knowledge of the topography of the Temple at Jerusalem in the 'Western' text than in Luke at Acts 3.2. The 'Western' addition at 12.10, 'they went down the seven steps', throws no light on anything, because Luke does not tell us in what part of Jerusalem Herod Agrippa had imprisoned Peter, and no one has ever been able to explain this enigmatic sentence satisfactorily. It has been thought that the 'Western' text betrays a better knowledge of the geography of Palestine than Luke does when at 21.16 it causes Paul and his party to spend a night on the road between Caesarea and Jerusalem. But in the first place it is pretty clear that this is what Luke meant at this point, though he expressed himself badly, and in the second place the interpolator in the 'Western' text, who certainly had scrutinized carefully the text of Acts which he had before him, could have learnt from Acts 23.31, 32 that a journey from Jerusalem to Caesarea necessitated stopping for the night at Antipatris on the way. Against this we

[14] *Ibid.*, pp. 223–224.

must set the fact that the interpolator entirely misunderstood the ritual significance of the articles of the 'Apostolic Decree' at Acts 15.20, 29, fashioning them in a moral or spiritual sense to become a list of prohibitions, of idolatry, or unchastity generally, and of murder, and adding the 'Golden Rule', an entirely general guide for conduct. In fact he took those regulations quite out of their original intensely Jewish context. At Acts 17.4 the 'Western' text alters τῶν τε σεβομένων Ἑλλήνων πλῆθος, γυναικῶν τε τῶν πρώτων οὐκ ὀλίγαι into πολλοὶ τῶν σεβομένων καὶ Ἑλλήνων πλῆθος πολὺ καὶ γυναῖκες τῶν πρώτων οὐκ ὀλίγαι, apparently on the incorrect assumption that οἱ σεβόμενοι meant Jews. At 19.9 the 'Western' text reads ἐνώπιον τοῦ πλήθους τῶν ἐθνῶν, where the B text has ἐνώπιον τοῦ πλήθους, meaning the majority of the Jews. This suggests that the interpolator was not interested in the Jews nor in Paul's relation to them. The 'Western' text makes no attempt to correct Luke's chronological mistake concerning the order of the rebellions of Judas and of Theudas at 5.36, 37, nor does it try to elucidate the rather obscure reference to the Nazirite vow (if this is what is indeed intended here) at 21.22–26. We may safely conclude that our interpolator had no special knowledge of nor interest in Jews, Judaism or the topography of Palestine.[15]

Next, we may observe that the interpolator was used to an invariable connexion between baptism and the reception of the Holy Spirit and endeavoured to make his text of Acts witness to this too, and that he expected baptism to be accompanied by the baptized person's profession of an interrogatory creed. At 8.37 the 'Western' text interpolates the well-known words, 'And Philip said, If you believe with all your heart, it is permitted (to be baptized). And he answered and said, "I believe that Jesus Christ is the Son of God".' The formula of belief given at Acts 11.17 and 16.31 (though not in a directly baptismal context) is different (but *cf.* 9.20). Two verses later, the 'Western' text, instead of 'but when they came out of the water, the Spirit of

---

[15] E. J. Epp has argued in an article entitled 'The "Ignorance-Motif" in Acts and Anti-Judaic tendencies in Codex Bezae' (*Harvard Theological Review*, LV (1962), 51–62) for an anti-Jewish motive in the interpolator's work. His arguments are slight, but they may convince some.

the Lord snatched away Philip', reads 'but when they came out of the water, the Holy Spirit fell upon the eunuch and the angel of the Lord snatched away Philip'. And at 11.17 to the sentence 'If therefore God gave to them the same gift as to us when they believed in the Lord Jesus Christ, how was I able to prevent God?', the 'Western' text adds 'so as not to give them the Holy Spirit when they believed in him'. At 19.5 the 'Western' text adds to the sentence 'and when they heard this they were baptized into the name of the Lord Jesus Christ' the words 'for remission of sins'. In the next verse (v. 6) the B text reads 'when Paul laid his hands upon them the Holy Spirit fell on them and they began speaking with tongues and prophesying'. The 'Western' text adds an 'immediately' before the phrase 'the Holy Spirit fell on them' and between the speaking with tongues and the prophesying it interpolates 'and they were intelligible to each other so that they interpreted the tongues to each other'. It may be that the interpolator thought of the laying-on of hands as a sign of the forgiveness of sins, as it appears to be at 1 Tim 5.22. The impression is created that the interpolator lived at a period when the rite of Christian initiation was more formal and more regulated than it was in Luke's day, when the profession of an interrogatory creed was an invariable accompaniment of baptism, and when the speaking with tongues was a rare phenomenon, rather frowned upon.[16]

Slight indications of the interpolator's date may be provided by three more texts. The addition at 18.7 ἀπὸ τοῦ ᾽Ακύλα indicating that Paul left the house of Aquila and Priscilla (which we have noticed already) may betray the fact that the interpolator knew 1 Cor 16.19 ἀσπάζεται ὑμᾶς ἐν Κυρίῳ πολλὰ ᾽Ακύλας καὶ Πρῖσκα σὺν τῇ κατ᾽ οἶκον αὐτῶν ἐκκλησίᾳ, as it suggests that where Aquila and Priscilla resided Christians came to worship. At 18.25 the 'Western' text represents Apollos as having learnt Christianity in his native city, Alexandria, thus implying that at the time the interpolator wrote Christianity had reached Alexandria. There is an

---

[16] There does not seem to be any substance in the theory that this writer's references to the Holy Spirit betray Montanist sympathies.

extraordinary lack of information about the origins of Christianity in Alexandria. *Egerton Papyrus 2*, a fragment of an unknown Gospel from Egypt dating from some time before 150, suggests that some form of Christianity had reached Egypt, and therefore no doubt Alexandria, before the middle of the second century. Basilides taught a Gnostic form of Christianity there *c*. 130 and Valentinus the Gnostic came from Alexandria, but we do not know that he learnt his Christianity there, for he taught in Rome. Irenaeus mentions that there were Christian churches in Egypt.[17] In fact this reference to Christianity in Alexandria in the 'Western' text of Acts may well be the earliest testimony to its having reached there that we possess. It we can accept the margin of the Harklean Syriac version of Acts alone as a competent witness to the 'Western' text, we have a faint indication at Acts 24.10 where this reading describes Paul as 'taking on an inspired appearance'.[18] This would imply that enough time had elapsed for Paul to be thoroughly idealized and treated as a θεῖος ἀνήρ—an interpretation of him which Luke avoids (*pace* certain commentators).

The indications which we have so far reviewed are far from definite and tell us very little except that the interpolator should be placed in the second century, which we might have guessed already. We reach more interesting material when we observe that there are some signs in the work of the interpolator of a special interest in magnifying the role of Peter and the possession of information which would have been most readily available at Rome.[19] At 1.23 the 'Western' text reads ἔστησεν δύο thereby causing Peter to choose Joseph Barsabbas and Matthias as the two between whom the choice of apostle shall be made, whereas the B text reads ἔστησαν, assigning this

---

[17] *Adv. Haer.* 1.3. For a summary of the evidence concerning the origins of Christianity in Alexandria see R. P. C. Hanson, *Tradition in the Early Church* (1962), pp. 166–167.

[18] Latin tr. *statum assumens divinum*, which A. C. Clark, *loc. cit.*, in his edition of Acts ventures to render as σχῆμα ἔνθεον ἀναλαβών, But these words appear to be purely Clark's conjecture.

[19] J. H. Crehan had independently set out much of the evidence to support this point given below, with some additions, in 'Peter According to the D-Text of Acts' (*Theological Studies* 18, no. 4 (Dec. 1957), 596–603).

function to the apostles as a whole. Again the interpolator at 11.1, 2 inserts a large addition designed apparently to give Peter more activity and perhaps more authority. He tells us that Peter had been anxious for some time to go to Jerusalem (perhaps this was inserted to make it clear that Peter chose to go of his own accord and was not ordered to Jerusalem by the church authorities there), that he summoned the local Christians (presumably at Caesarea) and strengthened them, then made many speeches (πολὺν λόγον ποιούμενος) 'through the districts', teaching them, and then went down to them (presumably in Jerusalem) and declared to them the grace of God. A rather similar attempt to avoid the suggestion that a church founded by Peter owes allegiance to Jerusalem may be detected at 15.1–7. The B text relates that some people came from Judaea to Antioch and began teaching that only those Christians who are circumcised and keep the traditional teaching (ἔθος) of Moses can be saved, and that after some discussion these same people ordered Paul and Barnabas to go to Jerusalem, and that when they reached Jerusalem a different group, 'some believers from the sect of the Pharisees', renewed these demands. The 'Western' text identifies the two groups of supporters of the Law and sharpens the contrast between Paul and his supporters on the one side and the champions of the Law on the other; it enlarges the reference to Paul 'for Paul maintained resolutely (ἔλεγεν διϊσχυριζόμενος) that they should remain as they were when they believed', and it describes his opponents as coming not merely from Judaea but from Jerusalem. And when Peter comes to make his speech, justifying the attitude hitherto taken towards the Gentiles, it enhances the effect of it by adding that he rose up to speak 'in the Spirit'. We may, I think, see in this a desire to keep the authority of Peter and Paul, and perhaps of the church of Antioch with which they were so much associated, free from any obligation of obedience to the church of Jerusalem. Then at 8.24 we find a curious addition to the story of Simon Magus' discomfiture at the hands of Peter; referring to Simon, the 'Western' text interpolates 'and he did not leave off weeping greatly' (ὃς πολλὰ κλαίων οὐ διελίμπανεν). Why should the interpolator desire to emphasize Simon's dismay? Probably because he was aware of the later greatly elaborated body of legend about Simon Magus, traces of which can be found in Justin Martyr, who wrote in Rome about the middle of the second century; Justin places Simon's activity in Rome.[20] The Pseudo-Clementine literature, part of which probably derives from the second century, uses and elaborates this legend, and it too places much of Simon's activity, and Peter's counter-activity against him, in Rome. The interpolator wishes here to drive home the lesson that the great sorcerer Simon, whose disciples in his day are disseminating doctrine which rivals that of the Catholic Church, was utterly discountenanced in his first encounter with Peter, the great apostle associated with Rome. It is not fanciful to envisage a cult of Peter—or better perhaps of Peter and Paul—already in existence in Rome in the middle of the second century. Excavation under St Peter's in Rome has established that there was a memorial shrine to him in the place of his martyrdom as early as 160. Both *I Clement,*[21] and Ignatius[22] at an earlier date than this associate the martyrdom of Peter and Paul with Rome. The Pseudo-Clementine literature is evidence that legend had been busy with Peter's association with Rome at an early period, perhaps as early as the middle of the second century. Irenaeus regards the connexion of Rome with Peter and Paul as one of the chief reasons for the leadership which he ascribes to the church of Rome[23] and after him we have the testimony of Tertullian,[24] of Gaius[25] and of the *Epistola Clementis*. Again, the addition of the 'Western' text to the statement at 19.9 that Paul disputed daily in the school of someone called Tyrannus, 'from the fifth to the tenth hour' (*i.e.*, from eleven to four), might be interpreted as evincing a desire to present Paul as a conventional philosopher—like Justin Martyr, who also taught daily, or his opponent Crescens—to a Roman public which would be accustomed to such figures. It is possible, of course, that this

[20] Justin Martyr, *Apology* 1.26.2, 3; 56.1, 2; *Dialogue* 120.6.

[21] *I Clement* 5.1–7.

[22] *Romans* 4.1–3.

[23] *Adv. Haer.* 3.3.1.

[24] *Adversus Marcionem* 4.5.1; *De Praescriptione Haereticorum* 36.2.3; *Scorpiace* 14.3.

[25] Eusebius, *H.E.* 2.25.5, 6.

reading may be an original one; but it is hard to see why it should then have been omitted. It is perhaps worth noting that the phrase in the passage in the 'Western' text as Acts 10.25 'when Peter came near Caesarea one of the slaves ran on ahead' probably implies that Peter, in this writer's view, was wealthy enough to own slaves. Of course the slave might have been one of the party that originally visited Peter from Cornelius, but the balance of probability is against the view that this is what the writer meant. In either case we are safe in concluding that the writer came from a class which was used to owning slaves, and was therefore fairly wealthy. He must too have had a good education and a capacity for appreciating clarity and consistency in a written narrative, for these are the qualities which he so often tries to import into the text of Acts. Next, at Acts 24.24 the margin of the Harklean Syriac Version, which, Codex Bezae being deficient here, is usually regarded as representing the 'Western' text, after the words 'Drusilla was a Jewess' adds 'who was anxious to see Paul and hear him speaking; therefore, desiring to please her, he sent . . .'. And three verses later (v. 27) MSS 614, 2147 and the margin of the Harklean Syriac add to the end of the verse the words 'but he (Felix) left Paul in custody because of Drusilla'. Felix, later procurator of Judaea, had in fact enticed Drusilla, the sister of Herod Agrippa II, away from her first husband, Aziz King of Emesa. It looks very much as if this last addition was intended to convey that Paul's discourse on 'righteousness and self-control and judgement to come' (24.25) had been thought by Drusilla to refer too pointedly to her case and that she had consequently conceived a grudge against Paul. Now these apparent additions are most unlikely to be original because they hang together and while we might imagine one to have been omitted accidentally it would be too great a coincidence to imagine that the other had been omitted by accident too. We may therefore with confidence attribute them to the interpolator and conclude that he was surprisingly well informed about the family of the Herods; he knew Drusilla's history. For reasons which we have already considered, we may exclude the likelihood of his having learnt this knowledge in Jerusalem or in Palestine. The other obvious place to learn gossip or fact about the Herods was Rome, where the Herods were very well known, and where presumably Felix had first met Drusilla and exercised his attractions upon her.[26]

The suggestions that the interpolator lived in Rome about the middle of the second century, hitherto faint and uncertain, receive strong confirmation from the last piece of evidence from 'Western' additions to Acts, and the most important one, which we are going to consider. At Acts 28.26 most MSS read 'but when we came to Rome Paul was permitted to remain by himself with the soldier who was guarding him'. But the MSS which are usually allowed at this point (Codex Bezae being deficient) to represent the 'Western' text[27] read 'but when we came to Rome ὁ ἑκατοντάρχης παρέδωκεν τοὺς δεσμίους τῷ στρατοτεδάρχῃ, but Paul was allowed to remain by himself ἔξω τῆς παρεμβολῆς with the soldier who was guarding him'. What official is intended by the use of this word στατοπεδάρχης? It is certainly not the *praefectus urbi*, because the word does not directly translate this title, and because the interpolation refers to Paul being allowed to stay 'outside the camp', thereby associating the official named with a camp. The Codex Gigas (which is of the thirteenth century) translates the title *princeps peregrinorum*, and A. C. Clark confidently identifies the στατοπεδάρχης with this official.[28] This particular title is well attested for an official whose duties included those of police-work, but he is not known to have functioned in this capacity until late in the second century. The word στατοπεδάρχης is in fact applied quite widely in Josephus, in

---

[26] The very curious addition at 11.28 ἦν δὲ πολλὴ ἀγαλλίασις συνεστραμμένων δὲ ἡμῶν, remains an enigma which does not seem to cast light on our investigation. That it is an addition and not original seems certain because of its use of the genitive absolute construction which is typical of additions in the 'Western' text and is not a Lucan characteristic. The least improbable suggestion to account for it is that the interpolator wanted to associate Lucius of Cyrene (who is mentioned in 13.1 as among the 'prophets and teachers' at Antioch) with the author of the 'we' passages (whose significance was noted as early as Irenaeus), and therefore in effect to identify Luke as the author of Acts.

[27] 383, 614, Codex Gigas and Codex Perpinianus, the Book of Armagh, Codex Parisinus 343, Codex Wernigerodensis, the Philoxenian Syriac and the Sahidic Vulgate version.

[28] *The Acts of the Apostles*, pp. 386–388.

Eusebius, and in inscriptions to a variety of military officers. Sherwin-White[29] rules out the *princeps peregrinorum* as the correct official here on the grounds of date. He points out that the word στατοπεδάρχης could translate 'praetorian prefect', but that this prefect was too exalted an officer for a comparatively unimportant prisoner like Paul to be directly entrusted to. He much prefers as the original title translated by this word that of *princeps castrorum* (which is, it may be pointed out, the literal meaning of the Greek word). This officer was 'the head administrator of the *officium* of the Praetorian Guard'. Sherwin-White admits, however, that the existence of such an official on the staff of the Praetorian Guard at Rome is not attested until about A.D. 120. A little further information can be added to this stock.[30] Every legion in the first and early second centuries had an official called the *princeps praetorii legionis* on its staff (a phrase which could also be translated στρατοτεδάρχης). But about the year 120, probably as a result of the reorganization of the Roman army by the Emperor Hadrian, the title of this official was in all legions changed to that of *princeps castrorum*. We may therefore reasonably conclude that the word στρατοτεδάρχης in the 'Western' text at Acts 28.16 translates either the *princeps praetorii legionis* of the Praetorian camp in Rome before *c.* 120, or the *princeps castrorum* of the Praetorian camp after *c.* 120, with probability strongly inclining to the latter alternative in view of the evidence which we have reviewed suggesting that the interpolator's work should be dated in the middle of the second century, or a little before that time. We can rule out the reading here being an original one, both because of the difficulty of accounting for its omission had it been in the autograph and because the title *princeps castrorum* would not have been applied to an official of the Praetorian Guard at Rome as early as the time that Acts was written. It has indeed recently been maintained[31] that Acts was written as late

[29] A. N. Sherwin-White, *Roman Society and Roman Law in the New Testament* (1963), pp. 108–110.

[30] I owe the following information on this subject to the kindness of my colleagues, Mr G. R. Watson and Mr W. R. Chalmers, who are on the staff of the Department of Classics of the University of Nottingham.

[31] By J. C. O'Neill, *The Theology of Acts in its Historical Setting* (1961).

as the year 130, but in view of other arguments this theory can be discounted. The most important point to notice, however, is that this phrase in the 'Western' text of Acts at 28.16 creates a strong presumption that the man who wrote it was well acquainted with the different functions of the officers of the Praetorian Guard at Rome, and we may probably add, after about the year A.D. 120. Only one who knew the Praetorian camp at Rome fairly well could have produced such an interpolation here; it locates its author at Rome and combines with the other evidence which we have surveyed to produce a probability, perhaps a strong probability, that we can identify one of the contributors to the 'Western' text in Acts as working in Rome some time between *c*. A.D. 120 and *c*. 150.

It must be repeated that this hypothesis does not claim that the 'Western' text originated in this place at this time. This would be a much larger claim and would hardly be justified on the basis of the evidence reviewed hitherto or in view of the present state of scholarly opinion about the 'Western' text. All it claims is that it is likely that an interpolator was at work on the text of Acts some time between A.D. 120 and 150 approximately, in the city of Rome. He was a Christian of some wealth and education with no strong connexions with Judaism. His additions to and alterations of the text somehow became incorporated in the MS tradition which we call the 'Western' text and which originated somewhere about the middle of the second centry.[32]

We must now ask whether this discovery (if discovery it be) throws any light on the place of origin of the book of Acts itself. Even if we were to regard the case for the Roman origin of the interpolations in the 'Western' text of Acts as proved, we should still not have proved that Acts originated in Rome, because these interpolations appear only in the 'Western' tradition and not in that of the great uncials. Unless we are to assume, as Clark did, that the great uncials represent a text from which these interpolations have been deliberately excised, it is impossible to argue that these interpolations were interpolations in the

---

[32] Perhaps it is worth noting that Blass held the theory that the 'Western' text of Acts originated in Rome; but he believed that this text represented an earlier rough draft of Acts made by Luke himself.

autograph of Acts. But the probability that these interpolations were made in Rome between 120 and 150, at a time when the book of Acts was not yet regarded as sacrosanct and inspired, is suggestive. It suggests, among other things, that the interpolator may have been, so to speak, preparing the work for canonization, as Ropes believed that the 'reviser' was doing. He knew that the book would have a large circulation and would be widely read in the Christian churches, and he did his best to make it more fitted to perform this role. If the book of Acts had been known hitherto mainly in the church of Rome, though some copies of it had penetrated further afield, but was in the interpolator's view likely to be much more widely known in the future, this would account both for his activity and for the existence of uninterpolated texts of Acts. At least the theory makes it worth while examining the evidence for placing the origin of the book of Acts in Rome.

The fact that the story related in Acts leads up to the arrival of Paul in Rome constitutes quite a strong argument. Acts is not the story of how Christianity reached Rome, for not only do we know from the Epistle to the Romans that there were Christians in Rome before Paul reached the city, but Acts itself betrays the author's knowledge of this fact when it tells us that Paul in Corinth met Aquila and Priscilla who had recently arrived from Rome and were clearly already Christians (18.1–4), and when it recounts how 'the brethren' from Rome came out to meet Paul as far as Appi Forum and Tres Tabernae (28.15). Acts is the story of how Christianity originated, how it passed from the Jews to the Gentiles, and how Paul, the great symbol of that movement, came to Rome. It has been noted that the topographical and local details which Luke provides in great abundance in other parts of his book seem to be lacking as Paul approaches Rome.[33] Places like Syracuse, Rhegium, Puteoli, Appi Forum and Tres Tabernae are mentioned without any explanatory additions such as we find in 'a city of Galilee named Nazareth', 'Capernaum a city of Galilee', and in Luke's description of Emmaus, Fair Havens, Philippi and several other places. There are no references in Acts to forums, temples or

[33] H. J. Cadbury, *The Making of Luke–Acts*, pp. 241–242 and *The Book of Acts in History*, p. 60; J. Dupont, *The Sources of Acts*, p. 160.

synagogues in Italy nor in Rome. This suggests that Luke was writing for a public whom he knew to be so well acquainted with Rome and the area for some distance round it that it was unnecessary for him to furnish such details. It is, in fact, worth considering the hypothesis that the book of Acts was written for the church of Rome.

If we raise this hypothesis we are at once plunged into the dark and thorny question of why Acts ends where it does. Why does it not go on to describe the rest of Paul's career, his later evangelism (if he carried out any), his visit to Spain (if he made it) and his return to the Aegean littoral (if he did return), and finally his death at the hands of Nero during that Emperor's persecution of the church after the fire of Rome in A.D. 64 (if this was indeed the occasion upon which Paul met his death)? One quick and ready answer to this question has been that Luke did not describe these events because when he wrote Acts they had not yet happened. But this answer is altogether too glib and raises more problems than it solves. It would entail assuming that Acts was written before Luke's Gospel and that later when Luke produced the Gospel he merely tacked on to Acts a preface, also addressed to Theophilus, linking it with his other work which was later in time but prior in order. But if Luke was capable of tacking on a preface, surely he was also capable of tacking on an epilogue describing what had happened to his hero. Further, there are some passages in Acts which suggest that Luke knew that Paul was dead when he wrote and that Paul would never again return to the Aegean littoral (20.22–25, 38; 21.11–13; 23.11). And this theory is difficult to reconcile with the evidence that Luke was writing his work at a period removed by several years—at least one decade and perhaps two—from the main events of Paul's career.

Another theory which has found support in very recent times among New Testament scholars is that the people of the time at which Luke wrote would not feel any curiosity about the details of Paul's career. We in the post-renaissance world characterized by individualism, an intense interest in events and in facts, and a concentration upon psychological observation, cannot imagine a reading public which did not want to know the historical details of the life of men in whom they were interested. But the ancient world—at least the ancient Christian world of the first century—had no concern with biographical details. Christians of that period wanted to know about the development and expansion of the faith which meant everything to them; they were interested in the Holy Spirit but not in the details of the lives of the agents of the Spirit in as far as they were irrelevant to His activity. Consequently they would have been quite content with Acts ending where it does. The movement of the Spirit had reached Rome. His great instrument or vessel (σκεῦος, Acts 9.15) had been allowed to preach there unhindered (28.31). That was all they needed or wanted to know. In a milieu full of eschatological expectation, when many Christians believed that all human aspiration and achievements would soon be nullified in a final judgement, the facts of Paul's later career faded into insignificance. But this view meets equally intransigent difficulties. As has been pointed out, the story of Acts is *not* the story of how Christianity reached Rome, and if it is the story of how anything reached Rome we must say that it is the story of how Paul reached Rome. There is *a priori* no reason why the story should end there, if there were still sensational and interesting events in Paul's career to happen after that—and there certainly were. From the point of view of following Paul's career, Acts 28.31 is not a natural stopping-place. Again, we must view with great scepticism the idea that Christians at the time that Luke wrote Acts were not interested in the biographical details of famous characters. We shall not here go into the question of whether they were interested in the biographical details of the career of Jesus, though it is possible to question whether we need assume that Christians had no interest even here. But the Christians for whom Luke wrote were not the most primitive Christians of all. Their minds were not—as the work of Conzelmann and of Haenchen has shown—filled to exclusion of everything else with eschatological expectations. On the contrary, Luke wrote Acts for an audience of Christians who were beginning to be conscious that the Church was an institution which had to exist in the world with a possible future stretching before it and a Golden Age, the Age of the Apostles, behind it in the past. If they had had no interest in biography, Christians of Luke's day would have been quite unlike the ordinary educated men and women of their own day, and there is no ground at all for making this vast assumption. Biography was a lively and well-developed form of literature in Luke's day, and so was the travel narrative. The works of Strabo and Pausanias assure us of this, and very soon there were to appear the books of Josephus, of Tacitus and of Plutarch and later of Suetonius and of Lucian. Luke is clearly imitating models like these and regards himself as supplying his public with history, with biography and with a travel narrative. In the next century many other Christians were to supply their fellow worshippers with works of biography, the Acts of Martyrs, the Acts of Paul, the Acts of John. The Gospel according to the Hebrews may have been in existence before the end of the first century; other apocryphal Gospels followed in the next century, some of them designed expressly to meet the need for further biographical details about Jesus. Papias wrote about apostles and apostolic men. The Second Epistle of Peter and the Epistle of Jude may have been written to satisfy those who wanted to know more about the original apostles. The various endings supplied to Mark's Gospel suggest that people wanted to know what happened at the end of a story which seemed to break off short. If the twenty-eight chapters of the book of Acts are not designed to satisfy historical and biographical interest, what else are they designed to satisfy? And if they are, we are entitled to ask why they cease at a point where the interest in Paul's career must be at its height. The theory that Acts ends where it does because its readers could have no further interest in Paul's career after that point suffers from a plethora of unproved assumptions and a deficiency of concrete evidence.

There is one theory often produced to account for the fact that Acts ends where it does. This theory is quite congruous with the last one which we have surveyed and often goes along with it. This theory suggests that Acts ends where it does end not because Luke could not have carried on Paul's story, but because he dared not. Paul was condemned and executed when he at last was brought before the Emperor's court in Rome, and Luke dared not recount this, for it would have contradicted much of what he wrote in Acts. That Paul endured only one full trial in Rome and that he was not acquitted at it, as the Pastoral

Epistles imply (2 Tim 4.16, 17), but condemned and forthwith executed, has become almost an article of scholarly orthodoxy. Ever since the Pauline authorship of the Pastoral Epistles has been questioned, and has indeed been abandoned by a very large number of scholars, probably the majority, it has become customary to assume that this account of the events of Paul's career is true. It has the advantage of rounding off Paul's life cleanly and tidily without allowing room for any divagations back to the Aegean or on to Spain. It accounts for the absence of genuine Epistles of Paul dating from the last two years of his life (62–64) according to the old reconstruction. And, as we have seen, it provides a reason why Acts should end where it does.

But this theory turns out to be as open to objections as the others. It is very difficult indeed to assume that Luke wrote the book of Acts knowing full well that at the end of the two years mentioned in the last sentence of the book (28.30) Paul was brought to trial and condemned as guilty. Luke has in his narrative intimated again and again that Paul was not guilty (22.25; 23.1, 29; 24.13, 20, 21; 25.8, 10, 11, 18, 19, 25; 26.21, 22, 31, 32) and that the Roman government is neutral and just towards Christianity once it is fully apprised of the facts (18.12ff.; 25.15; 26.31, 32). Paul is treated with justice, indeed with liberality, by the Roman authorities (18.12ff.; 21.31–33; 25.15; 27.3, 43; 28.7, 16, 30, 31). It is almost impossible to believe that all this was the prelude to Paul's being unjustly condemned and unjustly executed by Caesar. When God in a dream tells Paul (27.24) that he must stand before Caesar, Καίσαρί σε δεῖ παραστῆναι, Paul is not told that he must witness with his life before Caesar; these words are more consonant with Paul's being acquitted than with his condemnation by Caesar's court. Compare Luke 21.36, σταθῆναι ἔμπροσθεν, where the thought certainly is of acquittal.

And when one has once questioned the view that Paul was condemned at this trial, it becomes obvious that it stands on very frail foundations. Indeed, it could be said to stand on no foundations at all. There is no single piece of positive evidence in its favour. For the alternative view, that Paul was acquitted at his first trial in Rome and condemned and executed at a quite different trial on a different charge, there is at least *some* evidence. Admittedly this is a question about which positive evidence is scanty, but what evidence there is is wholly on the side of the traditional view. There is the evidence of 2 Tim 4.6, 16–18. It is not suggested that this is the testimony of a genuine letter of Paul written shortly before his second trial and execution. But it does represent what the writer of the Pastoral Epistles thought had happened to Paul; it represents the tradition about Paul at about the year 100, and probably in the church of Rome. There is the evidence of *I Clement*, which was probably written in A.D. 96. Not only does this writer closely associate the deaths by martyrdom of Peter and Paul, but he describes Paul as having reached 'the terminus of the west' (τὸ τέρμα τῆς δύσεως).[34] This famous and ambiguous term could mean 'the end, that is the west', meaning Rome, or 'the extreme boundary of the west', meaning Spain. It would be curious for one who was writing in Rome, with a thousand miles of Roman Empire to the west of him, to describe his own city as 'the end, that is the west', and on the whole it is preferable to take this expression as referring to Spain, though the matter does not admit of dogmatic certainty. This would mean that Clement believed that Paul had visited Spain; Paul certainly had at one time hoped to do so (Rom 15.24, 28), and we must not arbitrarily rule out the possibility that he did so. The probability that he returned to the Aegean littoral, however, seems utterly remote. We have reviewed the texts in Acts which suggest that Paul never returned to the east; Clement apparently knows nothing of such a period in Paul's life; the texts in the Pastoral Epistles which suggest that he did are confused and uncertain. But the fact that the author of the Pastoral Epistles attempted to fill this gap in Paul's career with his work suggests that he knew that there was a gap to fill. The other evidence which we can offer for Paul having been executed after a second trial, in association with the persecution which accounted for Peter's death too, is the word of Ignatius, who associates Peter and Paul together in a context which is full of the thought of martyrdom at Rome,[35] and the fact that there did exist about the year 200, and probably a good deal earlier, memorial shrines to Peter on

[34] *I Clement* 5.7.
[35] *Romans* 4.1–3.

the Vatican hill and to Paul on the Ostian Way.[36] If Paul had been put to death after his first and only trial by the Emperor's court two years before Nero's persecution, on a charge of raising a riot in the Temple at Jerusalem, it is difficult to believe that this would have been regarded as a martyr's death or as deserving a martyr's commemorative shrine. If, of course, the charge upon which Paul was tried at Rome was not a capital one (and there is no absolutely clear proof that it was), then of course the whole theory that he was executed after only one trial collapses.

We have therefore so far found no satisfactory reason to account for the book of Acts ending where it does. I believe that the best reason that has ever been advanced to account for this puzzling fact is that his readers knew the rest of Paul's story.[37] This would fully and exactly account for Acts ending at that particular point. The Christians of Rome know, of course, what happened to Paul once he reached Rome, just as they know what happened to Peter after he had reached their city. What they want to know is, how did Christianity originate and how did it distinguish itself from Judaism (of which Roman Christians would of course know something) and what happened to Paul before he reached Rome? This is precisely the information which Luke supplies in the book of Acts. Luke did not describe the acquittal of Paul by the Emperor's court, though he led up to it in his book, because he knew that his readers knew of this already. He stopped where he did, not inelegantly nor abruptly in the circumstances, meaning to imply 'Your local tradition takes on from here'.

The only serious objection that can be brought against this solution of the question is that by its own admission Paul was put to death by the Emperor Nero anyway, though after his second trial, not his first. Would not this discountenance all Luke's protestations of Paul's innocence and of the impartiality of the Roman Government towards Christianity, and if so is it not more economical and realistic to agree that Paul was

[36] Eusebius, *H.E.* 2.25.5, 6.

[37] J. H. Crehan had independently advanced some interesting arguments to support this suggestion (*Studia Evangelica* II (ed. F. L. Cross, Berlin, 1964), pp. 354–358).

executed, and Acts proved unrealistic, at his first and only trial rather than indulging in the complicated hypothesis of a trial, an acquittal and another trial later? But it can reasonably be answered that Paul being executed on the charge of raising a riot in the Temple of Jerusalem after a long process of trial culminating at the Emperor's court is one thing, and Paul being sacrificed, with many other innocent Christians, to the desire of an angry and unpopular tyrant to find scapegoats for the disaster of the fire of Rome is quite another. Opinion in Rome by the time Luke wrote would have been strongly against Nero, who had been a few years before outlawed and declared a parricide by the Senate and forced into suicide in circumstances no less squalid than those which surrounded the suicide of Hitler in 1945. Nero had by then condemned to death many eminent and aristocratic Romans, among them Piso, Seneca, and Thrasea, and had executed his own mother. Tacitus, who had no liking whatever for Christians, said that Nero's treatment of the Christians after the fire of A.D. 64 evoked sympathy for them even from those who regarded Christianity as a vile superstition (*Annals* 15.2–8). Luke could very well have led up to Paul's acquittal by the Emperor's court, quite possibly without the Emperor presiding over it, and maintained that the Roman Government was impartial to Christianity whenever it knew the full facts about that religion, and at the same time know, and know that his readers knew, that Paul had been put to death by Nero in the persecution which he had directed against Christians after the fire of Rome. The first incident would be an instance of Roman justice, the second of the weakness of the Roman imperial constitution, a subject upon which Luke did not wish to comment.

It can then be shown that there are good reasons for thinking that the book of Acts was written for Christians in Rome and that Rome was the city in which the book originated. It is all the more interesting and suggestive that an early interpolator in the text of Acts whose work became incorporated in the textual tradition which we call the 'Western' text should apparently have worked in the city of Rome. The two sets of evidence are quite independent of each other and can be regarded as giving each other mutual support.

4

DID ORIGEN APPLY THE WORD
HOMOOUSIOS TO THE SON?

This essay will try to convince the reader that the answer to the question which forms its title must be a decided No. It is a source of satisfaction to the author that so great an authority as his Eminence Cardinal Daniélou, in whose honour these essays are gathered together, should have declared himself decisively in favour of this view.[1]

I

The question of whether Origen could have used the word *homoousios* of the Son, or would have used it, is one that has been much debated. On the affirmative side are H. Crouzel,[2] and J. N. D. Kelly,[3] on the negative (as has been already indicated) J. Daniélou and M. Simonetti.[4] Bethune-Baker appeared to incline to the affirmative.[5] This essay will confine itself to the strictly historical question as to the evidence, not that Origen could have used the term, but that he did use it. The case will here be argued that several prominent and able Origenists avoid the use of the term before the Arian controversy made it a controversial one, and that it is most unlikely that they should have done so had their master Origen used it in a Trinitarian context, even once. The argument will continue by examining the one alleged occurrence of the word in Origen's works and showing the extreme implausibility of the passage and

[1] J. Daniélou, *Origène* (Paris 1948), p. 258, 'Entre le Fils et le Père, il ne reconnaît pas seulement une différence de personne, mais de nature', which I take to be incompatible with the view that Origen could have used *homoousios* of the Son.

[2] *Théologie de l'Image de Dieu chez Origène* (Paris 1955), pp. 98–110.

[3] *Early Christian Doctrines* (London 1958), p. 130: 'Whether or not the term ὁμοούσιος is original in this passage (there seems to be no cogent reason why it should not be), the idea expressed is authentically Origenist'.

[4] *Studi sull' Arianesimo* (Rome 1965), p. 125, n. 76; and see the references to his comments in the Περὶ 'Αρχῶν below.

[5] *The Meaning of Homoousios in the Constantinopolitan Creed* (Cambridge, Texts and Studies, Vol. VII, No. 1, 1901), pp. 26–27.

suggesting that Jerome's explanation of how it came to be cited is in all probability substantially correct. It is the view of the author of this essay that the remarks upon the subject of the compatibility of Origen's views with the doctrine of the consubstantiality of the Son of M. Simonetti are most judicious. He points out that though the concept is not incompatible with Origen's ideas about the relation of the Son to the Father, the question is complicated by Origen's use of *ousia* to mean individual reality (elsewhere expressed by *hypostasis*), and that Origen preferred to describe the unity of Father and Son as a unity of love, of will and of action. There can be little doubt that Origen believed that the Son was of the same nature as the Father, but this would not have prevented him from saying that the Son's *ousia* is distinct from that of the Father. A further complication is introduced by the unreliability of Rufinus' translation of those passages in the Περὶ Ἀρχῶν which refer to this subjects.[6] This question cannot be decided simply from a consideration of the text, in original Greek or Latin translation, of Origen's surviving works. Apart from the one controversial passage where the epithet *homoousios* does appear to occur, Origen leaves the question quite undecided, except perhaps inasmuch as there is only this one Trinitarian use of the word.[7] Whatever else may be said, we can be sure that *homoousios* was not a favourite nor frequent term as applied to the Son in Origen's thought.

If we now follow the line of argument mapped out for this essay above, we shall examine the attitude of Origen's disciples and admirers to this word in the period before the outbreak of the Arian controversy had made it a word to which everybody was bound to refer. The first of these is Dionysius of Alexandria. The evidence concerning the attitude of Dionysius of Alexandria to the word *homoousios* as applied to the Son is scanty

[6] M. Simonetti, *I Principi di Origene* (Turin, 1968), pp. 139, n. 35, 154–155, n. 51, 156, n. 60, 542 n. 7, and *Studi sull' Arianesimo*, p. 125 n. 76.

[7] It is scarcely necessary to add that Origen uses the word in non-Trinitarian contexts, which do not in fact tell us much about the sense which he attached to it, *e.g. Commentary on John* (ed. A. E. Brooke, Cambridge 1896), 13.25 (272.(17),19), 20.20(64.3) and 24(70.16,19), all reproducing the use of the term by Gnostic heretics.

and in parts is quite obscure. The following facts, however, are clear. In a letter to bishops Euphranor and Ammonius of the Libyan Pentapolis, directed against the Sabellianism which was prevalent in those parts, Dionysius made use of the two expressions, comparing the relation of the Son to the Father to that of a vine to its planter and a ship to its builder, which aroused the alarm of Dionysius' namesake of Rome. His perturbation was increased by the fact that in this letter Dionysius of Alexandria had said that the word *homoousios* is found nowhere in the Bible, and had therefore presumably rejected it as an unsuitable word to use in Trinitarian contexts. As a consequence, Dionysius of Rome wrote two letters, one to the church of Alexandria expounding the correct attitude to Sabellianism, and another to Dionysius of Alexandria himself. In reply to the second letter Dionysius of Alexandria wrote a work called Ἔλεγχος καὶ Ἀπολογία parts of which are extant because Athanasius quoted them in his *De Sententia Dionysii*. The relevant passage in Dionysius' reply to his namesake of Rome runs thus:[8]

πλὴν ἐγὼ γενητά τινα καὶ ποιητά τινα φήσας νοεῖσθαι τῶν μὲν τοιούτων ὡς ἀχρειοτέρων ἐξ ἐπιδρομῆς εἶπον παραδείγματα ἐπεὶ μήτε τὸ φυτὸν <ταὐτὸν> ἔφην τῷ γεωργῷ, μητὲ τῷ ναυπηγῷ τὸ σκάφος. εἶτα τοῖς ἱκνουμένοις καὶ προσφυεσερτοις ἐνδιέτριψα καὶ πλέον διεξῆλθον περὶ τῶν ἀληθεστέρων, ποίκιλα προσεπεξεύρων τεκμήρια, ἅπερ καί σοι δι' ἀλλῆς ἐπιστολῆς ἔγραψα ἐν οἷς ἔλεγξα καὶ ὃ προφέρουσιν ἔγκλημα κατ' ἐμοῦ ψεῦδος ὄν, ὡς οὐ λέγοντος τὸν Χριστὸν ὁμοούσιον εἶναι τῷ θεῷ. εἰ γὰρ τὸ ὄνομα τοῦτό φημι μὴ εὑρηκέναι μηδ'ἀνεγνωκέναι που τῶν ἁγίων γραφῶν, ἀλλά γε τὰ ἐπιχειρήματά μου τὰ ἑξῆς, ἃ σεσιωπήκασι, τῆς διανοίας ταύτης οὐκ ἀπάδει.

A little later Dionysius says his opponents throw 'these two unsuitable expressions' (τοῖς δυσὶ ῥηματίοις ἀσυνθέτοις) at him like stones.[9] Dionysius is, of course, making the best of his case here; Athanasius in his *De Sententia Dionysii* tries to defend

---

[8] This passage is from Athanasius, *De Sententia Dionysii*, 18; it can be found conveniently printed in C. L. Feltoe, *The Letters and Other Remains of Dionysius of Alexandria* (Cambridge 1904), p. 188.

[9] Feltoe, *op.cit.*, p. 190.

him by the implausible suggestion that his doubtful expressions referred to Christ's human nature, not his divinity. A clearer light is cast on the matter, however, by Basil of Caesarea, who had read (as we have not) all Dionysius' letters and works in connection with the subject.[10] Basil is much more open and honest about the heterodoxy of Dionysius than was Athanasius. He accuses Dionysius of Alexandria of having sown the seeds of the doctrine that the Son is unlike the Father (*anomoion*). The reason for this, he says, was that Dionysius inclined too much in the opposite direction to that of the error of Sabellius. Dionysius, he says, desiring to demonstrate the success of his argument against Sabellius' view that the Father and the Son are the same thing,

οὐχ ἑτερότητα μόνον τῶν ὑποστάσεων τίθεται, ἀλλὰ καὶ οὐσίας διαφορὰν καὶ δυνάμεως ὕφεσιν (gradation) καὶ δόξῆς παραλλαγήν.

Consequently Dionysius lapsed into unorthodoxy. On the *homoousios*, Basil says that Dionysius takes different attitudes in his writings:

νῦν μὲν ἀναιρῶν τὸ ὁμοούσιον διὰ τὸν ἐπ' ἀθετήσει τῶν ὑποστάσεων κακῶς αὐτῷ κεχρημένον,[11] νῦν δὲ προσιέμενος ἐν οἷς ἀπολογεῖται πρὸς τὸν ὁμώνυμον.

In addition, says Basil, Dionysius used very unsuitable language about the Spirit, rejecting him from the Godhead and classing him lower, with the created and worshipping creation.

We must conclude from this testimony given without any ulterior motive that Dionysius distinctly taught the difference of *ousiai* in the Father and the Son and the Son's subordination and that at one point he definitely rejected the term *homoousios* as applied to the Son, even though, when taxed by his namesake of Rome, he admitted that it was a permissible word to use in a Trinitarian context. Clearly he was a consistent Origenist who, no doubt, believed that the Son or Logos was from God in the

---

[10] Basil of Caesarea, *Letters*, ed. Y. Courtonne (Budé Series, Paris 1957), I.9.2.

[11] 'because of the man who used the term perversely to deny the distinction of Persons' (*i.e.* Sabellius).

fullest sense, and, like Origen, subordinated the Son radically to the Father, reproducing Origen's concept of the Son as a *ktisma*.[12] It is clear that Dionysius knew Origen and was friendly towards him.[13] It is almost impossible to imagine that, had Origen applied the term *homoousios* to the Son, this disciple of his writing within a few years of Origen's death would have taken an attitude towards the word which, until he was strongly admonished by the bishop of Rome, was unmistakeably hostile. Certainly we can conclude that *homoousios* was not in the accustomed vocabulary of Origenists; if it was one of their distinctive views that the Son's *ousia* was separate, or even different, from the Father's, this would be understandable.

The next piece of evidence for the attitude of Origen's disciples to the word *homoousios* is provided by the document known as the *Letter of Hymenaeus*. This is a letter addressed by six bishops of sees in Palestine and its neighbourhood, led by Hymenaeus of Jerusalem, demanding from the person to whom it is addressed that he shall subscribe to the Christological doctrine expressed in it. Its doctrine has obvious affinities with Origen's teaching. It is reasonable to conclude that this letter is genuine and that it was addressed to Paul of Samosata during the controversy over his Trinitarian views.[14] The main opposition to Paul must have been Origenist in outlook, and it is not without significance that the synod which, after considerable controversy, condemned Paul of Samosata apparently condemned the use of the word *homoousios* in a Trinitarian debate and in some way associated him with its use.[15] Once again, we find Origenists hostile to the use of this word in a Trinitarian context, and once again it becomes wholly unlikely that Origen ever used the word in such a context.

The last, and most important, disciple of Origen whose

[12] Περὶ 'Αρχῶν 4.1, and see Simonetti's comment on this passage in his translation of this work cited above (p. 543 nn. 10 & 11). It is interesting to note that Origen quotes *Prov.* 8.22 in this context.

[13] See Feltoe, *op.cit.*, p. xxv.

[14] For the arguments for the genuineness of this document, the places where it can be found, and its character, see R. P. C. Hanson, *Tradition in the Early Church* (London 1962), pp. 82 & 83.

[15] The matter is very obscure; it is best treated in H. De Riedmatten, *Les Actes due Procès de Paul de Samosate* (Freibourg 1952).

attitude to the word *homoousios* we shall examine is Eusebius of Caesarea. Eusebius, of course, lived well into the beginning of the Arian controversy, and indeed outlived Arius himself. He had every reason to know the importance of the word *homoousios*, and we shall look at what he said about it immediately after the Council of Nicaea had adopted it into the Church's creed in 325. But Eusebius wrote two long and weighty works in the very early years of the fourth century, before the Arian controversy had broken out, known today as the *Preparatio Evangelica* and the *Demonstratio Evangelica*, and his views expressed in these about the relation of the Son to the Father deserve careful study for the light which they can throw on the subject of this essay. Eusebius, I need scarcely say, was a great admirer of Origen. The amount of space which he devotes to Origen in his *Ecclesiatical History* demonstrates this, as well as his references to Origen in his other works, and his friendship with Pamphilus, the martyr-scholar, who produced in prison, assisted by Eusebius, that very defence of Origen which, in Rufinus' translation, appears to represent Origen as using *homoousios* of the Son. Eusebius was very well acquainted with Origen's works, regarded himself as reproducing Origen's doctrines, and also knew what Dionysius of Alexandria had written both to reject and to accept the *homoousios*.[16] His views developed before the Arian controversy about the Father will be valuable for our enquiry.

One or two passages from his earlier work, which is less concerned with Christological doctrine, *Praeparatio Evangelica*, are relevant to our quest. In one place Eusebius compares the Son with the Father:[17]

> μετὰ τὴν ἄναρχον καὶ ἀγένητον τοῦ θεοῦ τῶν ὅλων οὐσίαν,
> ἄμικτον οὖσαν καὶ ἐπέκεινα πάσης καταλήψεως, δευτέραν
> οὐσίαν καὶ θείαν δύναμιν, ἀρχὴν τῶν γενητῶν ἁπάντων
> πρώτην τε ὑποστᾶσαν κἀκ τοῦ πρώτου αἰτίου γεγενημένην.

This is very nearly a contradiction of *homoousios*. A similar passage, in which Eusebius is reproducing a passage from a work

[16] Eusebius, *Historia Ecclesiastica* 7.26.

[17] *Praeparatio Evangelica* (*Eusebii Caesariensis Opera*, rec. G. Dindorf, Leipsig, Teubner Series, 1877, vols. 1–3), VII.12.1–2.

(no longer extant) of Philo, Ζητήματα καὶ Λύσεις, of which Eusebius approves, can be compared:[18]

ὁ πρὸ τοῦ λόγου θεὸς κρείσσων ἐστὶν ἢ πᾶσα λογιχὴ φύσις· τῷ δὲ ὑπὲρ τὸν λόγον ἐν τῇ βελτίστῃ καί τινι ἐξαιρέτῳ καθεστῶτι ἰδέᾳ οὐδὲν θέμις ἦν γέννητον ἐξομοιοῦσθαι.

Later, Eusebius declares that the *ousia* of the Logos comes second after that of Father, deriving its source from him and reproducing him in an image (πρὸς αὐτὸν ἀπεικονισμένη).[19] First is the *ousia* of the Father:

τῆς ἀνεκφράστου καὶ ἀπειρομεγέθους δυνάμεως τοῦ θεοῦ τῶν ὅλων, δευτερούσης δὲ μετὰ τὸν πατέρα τῆς δημιουργικῆς ὁμοῦ καὶ φωτιστικῆς δυνάμεως τον θείου λόγου.[20]

And Eusebius proceeds to distinguish the Persons of the Trinity according to consistently Origenist lines.[21] It is obvious that in many of his uses of the word *ousia* he is referring to the Person and not to the substance. Later still, he says that existent things are not ὁμοούσια with τὸ ἀγαθόν (which he identifies with God), but derive their being from him who is himself beyond things.[22] Presumably therefore the fact that the δευτέρα οὐσία in the Godhead derives his being from the πρώτη οὐσία does not make him *homoousios* with the first *ousia*.

There is much more Christological and Trinitarian material in the *Demonstratio Evangelica*. In this work Eusebius virtually describes the Logos as created. God, he says, the sole true ingenerate omnipotent God, desired to create a rational creation and determined to make ἀσωμάτους τινὰς καὶ νοερὰς καὶ θείας δυνάμεις, and also human souls who would have free will. For this purpose he thought it right that there should be ἕνα τὸν τῆς δημιουργίας ἁπάσης οἰκόνομον ἡγεμόνα τε καὶ βασιλέα τῶν ὅλων,[23] by which he clearly means the Logos.

---

[18] *Ibid.*, VII.13.1.
[19] *Ibid.*, VII.15.1.
[20] 5.
[21] 6–9.
[22] *Ibid.*, XI.21.6.
[23] *Demonstratio Evangelica* (rec. Dindorf, ut supra), IV.1.1–8, and here especially 4.

This supreme God is the fountain of all, above all being, ineffable, incomprehensible, exercising providence. What he wills comes into existence. It is wrong to think that God created anything out of nothing. His will is the material (*hyle*) for all created things.[24] Though Eusebius showers many high metaphysical titles upon the Logos, he also calls him τὸ τέλειον τελείου δημιούργημα, καὶ σοφοῦ σοφὸν ἀρχιτεκτόνημα, ἀγαθοῦ πατρὸς ἀγαθὸν γέννημα. He is called God because he is the *eikon* of the high God.[25]

Later Eusebius remarks that one modification of the model describing the Son's relation to the Father as a ray coming from light is that the Son is not simply the Father's *energy*, because ὁ δὲ υἱὸς ἕτερόν τι ἢ κατὰ ἐνεργείαν τυγχάνει, καθ' ἑαυτὸν οὐσιώμενος (having his separate existence).[26] It was the Father's will that produced the Son; and in effect Eusebius says that the Son is the image of the Father's *ousia* (τῆς οὐσίας τοῦ πρωτοῦ ... τὴν ὁμοίωσιν ἐπάγοιτο).[27] In the next book he describes the Logos as

οὐσιώδη τοῦ θεοῦ λόγον, δεύτερον τῶν ὅλων αἴτιον, ἢ οὐσίαν νοερὰν, καὶ θεοῦ πρωτοτόκου ἐναρέτου φύσιν, τὴν πρὸ τῶν γεννήτων θείαν καὶ πανάρετον δύναμιν, ἢ τῆς ἀγεννήτου φύσεως νοερὰν εἰκόνα.[28]

Later in the same book Eusebius discusses the generation of the Son.[29] His main conclusion is that the Son is the image or 'perfume' of the Father's *ousia* and can be described as ἐκ or ἀπὸ τῆς οὐσίας of the Father. But he never uses the term *homoousios*. He insists that we must not think that the Son came from the Father as our births take place, οὐσίαν ἐξ οὐσίας κατὰ πάθος ἢ διαίρεσιν μεριστὴν καὶ χωριστήν.[30] The Son is not ἀγέννητος ἐν τῷ πατρί, μέρος ὢν αὐτοῦ, so as to leave the Father deprived when he was produced, for this would mean

---

[24] 5–7.
[25] *Ibid.*, IV.2.1,2 γέννμηα is applied to the Son again IV.15.35.
[26] IV.3.4.
[27] 7,8.
[28] *Ibid.*, IV. Praef. 1; *cf.* V.44, ἢ πρὸ τῶν γεννητων θεία καὶ πανάρετος οὐσία, ἢ νοερὰ καὶ πρωτότοκος τῆς ἀγεννήτου φύσεως εεκών.
[29] V.1.1–24.
[30] V.1.8,9.

that there were two *agenneta*.[31] It is wrong to say that the Son
was generated out of nothing, for the generation of the Son is
different from the creation of things through the Son.[32] Eusebius
is unwilling to define how the Son is begotten, and this is a
reluctance which he voices more than once elsewhere. But if a
definition had to be given it would run like this:[33]

τάχα δ'ἄν <τις> εἴποι τῆς τοῦ ἀγεννήτου φύσεως καὶ τῆς
ἀνεκφράστου οὐσίας, ὥσπερ εὐωδίαν τινα καὶ φωτὸς
αὐγήν, τὸν υἱὸν ἐξ ἀπείρων αἰώνων, μᾶλλον δὲ πρὸ πάντων
αἰώνων ὑποστῆναι, γενόμενόν τε συνεῖναι, καὶ
συγγενόμενον ἀεὶ τῷ πατρὶ ὡς τῷ μύρῳ τὸ εὐῶδες καὶ τῷ
φωτὶ τὴν αὐγήν.

But the Son is not like light in that light co-exists
ontologically (οὐσιωδῶς συνυπαρχεῖ) with its source, ὁ δέ γε
τοῦ θεοῦ λόγος καθ' ἑαυτὸν οὐσίωταί τε καὶ ὑφέστηκε καί
οὐκ ἀγεννήτως συνυπαρχεῖ τῷ πατρί.[34]
If these words do not actually rule out *homoousios*, at least they
suggest unmistakeably that their author does not use a
vocabulary which contains that word. Eusebius goes on to say
that in another respect the Son's relation to the Father is not like
that of scent to its source (which is Eusebius' favourite analogy)
οὐδὲ γὰρ ἐξ οὐσίας τῆς ἀγεννήτου κατά τι πάθος ἢ
διαίρεσιν οὐσιώμενος, οὐδέ γε ἀνάρχως συνυφέστηκε τῷ
πατρί,[35] for this clearly could not happen to a father and son.
Eusebius then attempts an even more accurate description of the
relation of the Father to the Son:[36]

εἴη δ'ἄν ταύτῃ καὶ εἰκὼν θεοῦ, ἀρρήτως πάλιν καὶ
ἀνεπιλογίστως ἡμῖν, ζῶντος θεοῦ ζῶσά τις καὶ καθ'αὑτὴν
ὑφεστῶσα ἀΰλως καὶ ἀσωμάτως καὶ τοῦ ἐναντίου πάντος
ἀμιγῶς, ἀλλ'οὐχ οἵα τις πάλιν ἡ παρ' ἡμῖν εἰκών, ἕτερον μὲν
ἔχουσα τὸ κατ, οὐσίαν ὑποκείμενον, ἕτερον δὲ τὸ εἶδος,
ἀλλ, ὅλον αὐτὸ εἶδος ὤν, καὶ αὐτοουσίᾳ τῷ πατρὶ
ἀφομοιούμενος.

[31] 13.
[32] 15.
[33] 18.
[34] 19.
[35] 20.
[36] 21.

It is fairly obvious that this means that the Son is not a mere reflection of the Father, but reproduces in his own self-existence the self-existence of the Father. A little later,[37] Eusebius describes the Father and Logos as

μόνον ἀληθῶς ἀγαθόν, ἀγαθοῦ γεννητικόν, δευτερεύοντος δὲ καὶ ὡς ἂν ἀπὸ πρώτης καὶ ἡγουμένης οὐσίας ἐπιχορηγουμένου τοῦ υἱοῦ ὃς καὶ μόνος τῆς πατρικῆς οὐσίας εὐωδία τις ἡμῖν ἀνείρηται.

The conclusion to be drawn from all this material is clear enough. For Eusebius, the Son is ἐκ τῆς οὐσίας τοῦ πατρός, but not ὁμοούσιος. He is a complete reproduction in a begotten (*gennetos*) form of the Father, possessing his own *ousia* (meaning Person), which he derives from the Father. Formally speaking, the Son might he described as *homoousios* in the generic sense, for he is αὐτοουσίᾳ τῷ πατρὶ ἀφομοιούμενος, though this refers to his self-existence not to his substance. But it is very significant that Eusebius does not use the word *homoousios* for the Son, even though there had been before the outbreak of the Arian controversy speculation concerning the Son's relation to the Father's *ousia*. Eusebius knew that Dionysius of Rome insisted upon this term. He knew that Dionysius of Alexandria had reluctantly conceded it. Yet Eusebius did not use it. If Pamphilus, his great friend, really had not long before Eusebius wrote in his *Demonstratio Evangelica* produced in his *Defence of Origen* a passage from the master which used *homoousios* of the Son, it is very difficult to believe that Eusebius would have refrained (one almost says, carefully refrained) from using the term in this very detailed and meticulous discussion of the relation of the Son not only to the Father, but specifically to the Father's *ousia*. If Bethune-Baker was correct in thinking that before 325 *homoousios* in Trinitarian contexts always means 'of identical *ousia*', and not 'of generic *ousia*' (a thesis whose truth I gravely doubt), then certainly Eusebius' doctrine positively amounts to a denial of *homoousios*. In any case, I see no reason to doubt that Eusebius is correctly reproducing Origen's doctrine here, and in large part Origen's

[37] 24.

vocabulary (if we allow the substitution of εὐωδία for ἀτμίς). The fact is that Origen had no motive to use this term *homoousios* of the Son's relation of the Father. It did not consort naturally with vocabulary which he used for discussion of Christological and Trinitarian themes, nor did it readily express anything which he wanted to say on these subjects. It will become clear that Rufinus had, in contrast, every motive for representing Origen as using it.

Before we finish with Eusebius, we should note what Eusebius said to the people of his see many years later when as a result of the decision of the Nicene Council of 325 he found himself forced to accept the term *homoousios* applied to the Son.[38] Eusebius describes the Emperor as commanding the creed because it represented his own belief, with the sole addition of the word *homoousios*, and this was inserted, at the Emperor's insistence, not in any corporeal sense, not to suggest that God could be divided or a part of him separated, but it must be interpreted θείοις δὲ καὶ ἀπορρήτοις ῥήμασι. Later, after giving the creed, Eusebius explains what he means in much greater detail. He accepts *homoousios*, he says, for the sake of peace and harmony, and also for the sake of orthodoxy, just as he accepts γεννηθέντα καὶ οὐ ποιηθέντα to secure the entire distinction between the Son, through whom all things were created, and the things created by him; and Eusebius adds, characteristically, τοῦ τρόπου τῆς γεννήσεως ἀνεκφράστου καὶ ἀνεπιλογίστου πάσῃ γενετῇ φύσει τυγχάνοντος. He goes on to warn against misunderstanding the intention of the *homoousios*, and then describes its positive function:

> παραστατικὸν δὲ εἶναι τῷ πατρὶ τὸ ὁμοούσιον τὸ μηδεμίαν ἐμφερείαν πρὸς τὰ γενητὰ κτίσματα τὸν υἱὸν τοῦ θεοῦ ἐμφαίνειν· μόνῳ δὲ τῷ πατρὶ τῷ γεγεννηκότι κατὰ πάντα τρόπον ἀφωμοιῶσθαι, καὶ μὴ εἶναι ἐξ ἑτέρας τε ὑποστάσεως καὶ οὐσίας, ἀλλ᾽ ἐκ τοῦ πατρός.

And Eusebius goes on to support the *homoousios* with precedents:

---

[38] Socrates, *Church History* 1.8.

ἐπεὶ καὶ τῶν παλαιῶν τινὰς λογίους καὶ ἐπισκόπους καὶ
συγγραφέας ἔγνωμεν ἐπὶ τῆς τοῦ πατρὸς καὶ υἱοῦ θεολογίας
τῷ τοῦ ὁμοουσίου συχρησαμένους ὀνόματι.

In this last quotation Eusebius almost certainly has Dionysius of
Rome in mind, and just conceivably Dionysius of Alexandria.
The name of Origen, who was not a bishop, does not easily fit
the description, and it could be conjectured that had Eusebius
intended Origen here he would have invoked the name which
must still have been very influential among theologians in the
Eastern church.

It does not appear from this explanation given by Eusebius
that he believed that *homoousios* could mean 'of identical being',
'possessing an identity of being', with the Father. On the
interpretation which he gives here, Eusebius could still believe
that the Son was created and produced by the Father, though
not as the other creatures and productions. What is crystal clear,
however, from this letter is that the word *homoousios* is
unfamiliar to Eusebius, that the word does not belong to his
vocabulary, and that he regards it as calling for a long, elaborate
and slightly specious explanation. Since Eusebius was a devout
and lifelong Origenist, this is an emphatic indication that the
word, as applied to the Son, was not in Origen's vocabulary.

II

Having shown that the word *homoousios* as applied to the Son
was unaccustomed and even uncongenial to Origen's disciples
and champions as late as the first decade of the fourth century,
and that after the Nicene Council Eusebius, the great admirer of
Origen, accepted it only in terms which suggest that it was not
part of his ordinary vocabulary, we must now examine
carefully the single passage in which Origen apparently does
apply this term to the Son. It occurs in Rufinus' translation of
Pamphilus' work originally published in Greek, known as
Apologia Pamphili Martyris pro Origene, of which only the first
book survives and only in this version.[39] This work takes the

---

[39] Migne, *Patrologia Graeca* 17.580, 581; the passage which we are
considering is printed again in Migne, *PG* 14.1308.

form of quotations from Origen interspersed with remarks made directly by Pamphilus himself, each portion preceded by the name of either Origen or Pamphilus. To the work is prefixed a Preface by Rufinus himself[40] in which he is very careful to demonstrate his orthodoxy, even giving a kind of rule of faith, including a statement that the Holy Trinity is *unius substantiae*. Pamphilus begins by giving a little summary of Origen's doctrine, under various headings, illustrated by quotations from the master, and then undertakes to answer nine separate accusations which have been made against Origen. The first accusation[41] is *quod aiunt eum innatum dicere Filium Dei*. Pamphilus, having produced some extracts from Origen to counter this charge, goes on to say:

> *Pamphilus: De libris Epistolae ad Hebraeos, quomodo* ὁμοούσιος *est cum Patre Filius, id est, unius cum Patre substantiae, alienus autem a substantiis creaturae . . .*[42] *Et post aliquanta* [from the same work of Origen].
>
> *Origenes: Oportet autem scire nos quia per ineffabilia quaedam et secreta ac recondita quemdam modum sibi faciens Scriptura sancta conatur hominibus indicare et intellectum suggerere subtilem. Vaporis enim nomen inducens, hoc ideo de rebus corporalibus assumpsit ut vel ex parte aliqua intellegere possimus quomodo Christus, qui est sapientia, secundum similitudinem eius vaporis qui de substantia aliqua corporea procedit, sic etiam ipse ut quidam vapor exoritur de virtute ipsius Dei; sic et sapientia ex eo procedens ex ipsa substantia Dei generatur; sic nihilominus et secundum similitudinem corporalis aporrhoae esse dicitur aporrhoa gloriae omnipotentis pura quaedam et sincera. Quae utraeque similitudines manifestissimae ostendunt communionem substantiae esse Filio cum Patre. Aporrhoea enim* ὁμοούσιον, *videtur, id est, unius substantiae cum illo corpore ex quo est vel aporrhoea vel vapor.*
>
> *Pamphilus: Satis manifeste, ut opinor,* et valde evidenter ostensum est quod Filium Dei de ipsa Dei substantia natum dixerit, *id est* ὁμοούσιον, *quod est, eiusdem cum Patre*

---

[40] 539–542.
[41] 578.
[42] 580.

substantiae, et non esse creaturam, nec per adoptionem, sed natura Filium verum, ex ipso Patre generatum.[43]

We should first note the context of this use of *homoousios* which Origen is supposed to have made. Pamphilus is refuting the charge against Origen, *quod aiunt eum innatum dicere Filium Dei,* *i.e.* the accusation that the Son of God was ingenerate. It is certain that *innatum* translates ἀγέννητος and not ἀγενητός. No Origenist would seek to defend Origen against the charge of teaching that the Son was unaffected by becoming, had never experienced entry into existence, was *agenetos*, for Origen certainly had taught this and no disciple of his would want to deny that he had. But it would have been quite possible to misunderstand or misrepresent Origen as teaching that that the Son was unbegotten, had never been begotten. His doctrine of the eternal generation of the Son could easily lend itself, in an intellectual atmosphere in which economic Trinitarianism was the traditional theology, to this misrepresentation. We may take it that it was against such misunderstanding that Pamphilus wanted to defend his master at this point in his work. In that case, it is quite irrelevant to say that the Son is consubstantial with the Father. If anything, this argument would strengthen the view that Origen regarded the Son as ingenerate; certainly it does nothing to contradict such a view. Some of the material in the quotation from Origen supposed to have been brought forward by Pamphilus at this point might be said to answer the accusation which Pamphilus sets out to refute. It would be a possible answer to point out how the Son derives from the Father as a breath or emanation from its source. It might even be relevant to remind the reader that Origen had taught that the Son was ἐκ τῆς οὐσίας of the Father. But to point to Origen's having used the word *homoousios* of the Son's relation to the Father would not advance he argument an inch. This observation makes this alleged passage from Pamphilus doubtful to start with. One may also ask, what motive would

---

[43] 581. The Biblical reference is to *Wisd.* 7.25: LXX ἀτμὶς γάρ ἐστιν τῆς τοῦ θεοῦ δυνάμεως καὶ ἀπόρροια τῆς τοῦ παντοκράτορος δόξης εἰλικρινής. Vulgate *vapor est enim virtutis Dei et emanatio quaedam est claritatis omnipotentis Dei sincera.*

Pamphilus have had in stressing, and in dragging in an irrelevant argument to stress, that Origen had used the word *homoousios* of the Son? It was not a controversial word, a touchstone, in Pamphilus' day. But Rufinus had every motive to introduce this word into the work.

Next we must observe that the last two sentences of the quotation which Pamphilus is supposed to have given from Origen are easily detachable from the rest, the words which begin *Quae utraeque similitudines* and which end *aporrhoea vel vapor*. It could well be that Rufinus added these two sentences, perceiving that this was a passage where Origen had said that the Son was from the Father's substance and thinking this is a suitable place to furnish Origen with unimpeachable proofs of orthodoxy according to the standards of the end of the fourth and beginning of the fifth century, and added what was supposed to be a comment from Pamphilus both before and after the quotation to emphasize his point. What Pamphilus should have said at the end of the quotation was that this passage proves that Origen taught that the Son was generate, was begotten. What Pamphilus is represented as saying is that the passage proves that Origen taught that the Son was not a creature nor adopted as Son. This inconsistency suggests that Rufinus had doctored the passage.

That Rufinus was capable of doing such a thing is quite clear. He tells us himself that he had performed this operation on Origen's text as he translates it. Under the impression that heretics and malevolent people had tampered with Origen's works, he had not only suppressed certain passages as he translated,[44] but he altered the sense of others to accord with his

---

[44] Rufinus, *Liber de Adulteratione Librorum Origenis*, Migne *PG* 17, 615ff. & especially 619–632. It is worth noting that in this work Rufinus says that Origen's text both described the Father and the Son as *unius substantiae, quod Graece* ὁμοούσιος *dicitur* and in later chapters of the same work described him as *alterius substantiae et creatum* (619), thereby, in Rufinus' view, showing that the text was interpolated. Here Rufinus must be referring to the Περὶ Ἀρχῶν, where Origen describes the Son as from the *ousia* of the Father (not as *homoousios*) and also as a *ktisma*. This was quite possible in Origen's system, but Rufinus has inaccurately represented this as a contradiction between *homoousios* and *heterousios*. Probably Origen had said in this work that the Son is a different Person (*ousia* = *hypostasis*) to the Father. For the same argument

ideas of orthodox doctrine, and, most tactlessly, he instanced the practice of Jerome in this respect as his great exemplar and justification.[45] He said that this operation was particularly necessary in Origen's book Περὶ 'Αρχῶν:

> Sicubi ergo nos in libris eius aliquid contra id invenimus quod ab ipso in ceteris locis pie de Trinitate fuerit definitum velut adulteratum hoc et alienum aut praetermisimus, aut secundum eam regulam protulimus quam ab ipso frequenter invenimus affirmatam. Si qua sane velut peritis iam et scientibus loquens, dum breviter transire vult, obscurius protulit, nos, ut manifestior fieret locus, ea quae de ipsa re in aliis eius libris apertius legeramus, adiecimus explanationi studentes; nihil tamen nostrorum diximus, sed licet in aliis locis dicta, tamen sua sibi reddidimus.[46]

Scherer's edition of the fragments of the Greek of Origen's *Commentary on Romans* found at Toura show that Rufinus certainly filled out Origen's text in a verbose way,[47] but unfortunately the fragments do not cover any controversial passages. Other evidence does, however, show small but significant examples, where the original Greek survives, of Rufinus altering the text for doctrinal reasons.[48] In the passage from the *Defence of Origen* which we have been considering, Rufinus had a very strong motive to tamper with the text; it was his custom to do so; we need not doubt that we have, in the appearance of *homoousios* applied to the Son's relation to the Father, another instance of Rufinus altering Origen's text for doctrinal reasons, perhaps the most heinous instance of all.

A little further light can finally be thrown on this subject if we

advanced by Rufinus see also Rufinus, *Origenis Commentarium in Epistolam S. Pauli ad Romanos* (PG 24.831ff.), 831–832.

[45] Rufinus, *Prologus in Libros* Περὶ 'Αρχῶν *Origenis Presbyteri*, PG 11.111–114.

[46] *Ibid.*, 112.

[47] J. Scherer, *Le Commentaire d'Origène sur Rom. III.5–V.7* (Cairo 1957).

[48] See R. P. C. Hanson, *Origen's Doctrine of Tradition* (London 1954), pp. 40–42, where several unmistakeable instances are given of Rufinus tampering from his translations of Origen's Περὶ 'Αρχῶν, his *Homilies on Leviticus* and his *Commentary on the Song of Solomon*, and also from a passage dealing with the Holy Spirit in Rufinus' translation of the first book of Pamphilus' *Defence of Origen*, unconnected with the passage from that work which we have already cited.

examine what Jerome says about it. Though Jerome had in his earlier years been a great admirer of Origen, and had translated some of his works into Latin, by the closing years of the fourth century he had come to regard Origen as a dangerous heretic, and was furious with Rufinus when he held Jerome up as his great exemplar in translating and in editing Origen. Jerome denied that Origen's works were, or ever could have been, interpolated and corrupted. One of his arguments was that Eusebius, Origen's ardent admirer and disciple, reproduced in his own writings everything that Jerome and his contemporaries objected to in Origen.[49] Jerome had an unlikely theory that the work called Pamphilus' *Defence of Origen* was not by Pamphilus but by Didymus or someone of his school and period; he noted that Pamphilus' *Defence* reproduced (in a passage which is not extant today) about a thousand lines of the beginning of the sixth book of Eusebius' (no longer extant) *Defence of Origen*, and he thought that Didymus or his contemporary had under the name of Pamphilus copied this passage.[50] In a work specially written against Rufinus, Jerome accused him of having interpolated and altered Origen's text of the Περὶ Ἀρχῶν in translating it so as to make it yield orthodox sense.[51] In the same work he mentions Rufinus' translation of Pamphilus' *Defence of Origen*, and accuses Rufinus of interpolating, altering and suppressing here too.[52] In this work Jerome also deals with Rufinus' *Liber de Adulteratione Librorum Origenis* and discusses Rufinus' statement in this book that Origen's text contradicted itself in that in one passage it affirmed the *homoousios* of the Son and in another declared that the Son was of a different *ousia* from the Father. Jerome deals with this question by saying nothing at all about the passage where Origen is supposed to have applied *homoousios* to the Son but by declaring emphatically that Origen was heretical on the subject of the Son's *ousia*, that Eusebius' doctrine certainly was unorthodox on this point, and that Didymus, in his

[49] Jerome, *Epistulae* (PL 22.751) 84.1.
[50] *Op. cit.*, 11 (751–752). *Cf.* also Jerome's *Apol. adv. Lib. Rufin.* I.8 & 9 (PL 23.403–404).
[51] *Apologia adversus Libros Rufini* I.6,7 (401–402).
[52] *Ibid.*, I.8 (403) and 9 (404); see also II.11(434–435).

commentary on Origen's Περὶ Ἀρχῶν, admitted that Origen had been heretical on the Son's *ousia*.[53]

At first sight, it seems strange that Jerome says nothing about the passage produced by Rufinus, allegedly translating Pamphilus, showing that Origen had used *homoousios* of the Son. Surely if Jerome could have shown that in the original Greek of Origen's *Commentary on the Epistle to the Hebrews* or of Pamphilus' *Defence of Origen* Origen had not used the word *homoousios* of the Son, he would have done so? This omission by Jerome might be used to suggest that Jerome knew that Origen *had* used *homoousios* of the Son, because he does not directly deny this. But a passage to be found a little later in Jerome's *Apologia adversus Libros Rufini* clears up this difficulty. In this passage, while repeating his implausible theory that the *Defence of Origen* was not by Pamphilus, he reveals that he had never known this work in any other form than in Rufinus's translation.[54] Since presumably Jerome had not read Origen's *Commentary on the Epistle to the Hebrews*,[55] he could not directly prove that Rufinus had tampered with the text at this point. He could only strongly suspect that Rufinus had done so, and voice his suspicions. For all his malice and rage, Jerome was a good scholar with standards of scholarly integrity, so that he could not directly say that Rufinus had forged a passage here. The fact that Jerome writes with such distasteful gall and *animus* should not blind us to the truth that he had a very strong case in believing that Origen's works were not interpolated, that Rufinus was in the habit of irresponsibly editing and tampering with Origen's text for doctrinal reasons, and in suspecting strongly that Rufinus had introduced the word *homoousios* into Origen's text. We need not hesitate to come to the same conclusions as those reached by the best scholar in antiquity.

[53] *Ibid.*, 15 (438) and 16 (438–439).

[54] The passage is too long to quote here, but its meaning is unmistakeable. It runs from the words *me istum librum qui sub nomine Pamphili* to the words *sub persona martyris haeresim introducens*, 23 (446–447).

[55] It should be noted incidentally that Eusebius certainly had read this work (*H. E.* 6.25), and yet Eusebius never used the word *homoousios* of the Son before the Council of Nicaea!

5

THE PASSAGE MARKED UNDE? IN ROBINSON PHILOCALIA XV, 19, 84–86

In his useful article 'Particularités de la Philocalie' in *Origeniana*,[1] M. Eric Junod refers incidentally (p. 191) to a long passage which appears in the *Philocalia*[2] in the middle of a much larger extract from the VIth book of Origen's *Contra Celsum*. Robinson does not attribute this passage to the *Contra Celsum* but at the top of his page marks it as *Unde?* M. Junod assumes that it cannot be an original part of the *Contra Celsum*, but seems dissatisfied with the inconclusive situation in which it has been left by scholarship, and regrets that M. Eichinger in a recent study did not mention the subject. This paper is an attempt to deal with the curious problem raised by this passage, the first serious attempt, as far as I can discover, for over seventy years. It is a problem which has from time to time troubled and interested me ever since I first read the *Philocalia* some thirty-five years ago.

To put the matter in a nutshell, this passage does not appear in any other MSS of the *Contra Celsum* except those of the *Philocalia* which give extracts from this work, but it does appear in all MSS of the *Philocalia*, and the original compilers, Basil of Caesarea and Gregory of Nazianzus, give no indication that they are at this point introducing a new source into the extract. The *Contra Celsum* of Origen is known to us from three different sources; first those MSS which give the whole work, all of which are now known by scholars to derive from, and be dependent upon a single MS of the thirteenth century, the Vatican MS whose siglum is A; secondly, extracts quoted in the *Philocalia*; thirdly, some passages in Greek found among the MSS of the Toura find in 1947. These passages derive from the same line of tradition as that represented by MS A. They are confined to the early books of the *Contra Celsum* and do not

---

[1] *Origeniana, Quaderni di Vetera Christianorum* 12 (Bari, 1975), 181–198. I shall in this paper from time to time use the abbreviation *Philoc* for *Philocalia* and *CCels* for *Contra Celsum*.

[2] Ed. J.A. Robinson (Cambridge) 1893, XV.19.84–86.

contain the part in the middle of which the *Unde?* passage is found in the *Philocalia*. Robinson, editor of *Philocalia*, and Koetschau, editor in the GCS series of the *Contra Celsum*, agreed that all extant MSS of the *Philocalia* derive from an archetype of the seventh century which in its turn is dependent on a copy made, with a new Prologue, in the sixth century. The extracts from the *Contra Celsum* in the *Philocalia* were originally made by the compilers from a copy of the work made or at least used by Eusebius of Caesarea early in the fourth century to be employed in the *Defence of Origen* which he and Pamphilus made. His copy, of course, was ultimately based on Origen's original manuscript of the work which was in Eusebius' day preserved in the library founded by Pamphilus in Caesarea in Palestine. MS A also ultimately derived (though of course at many removes) from Eusebius' copy of the work. Thus the archetype of extant MSS of the whole work, which are called the direct tradition, is much later than the archetype of extant MSS of the extracts in the *Philocalia*, the indirect tradition. The MS from Toura consists of extracts made at the beginning of the seventh century by a monk who was transcribing passages of different length. His MS was contemporarry with the MS which was the archetype of the indirect tradition, and was six centuries earlier than the earliest extant MS of the direct tradition[3].

A fierce controversy raged between German scholars at the turn of the present century about the relative merits of the direct and the indirect traditions of the *Contra Celsum*. Robinson and Koetschau championed the direct tradition, though they were not unaware of the value of the indirect. Wendland, Preuschen, Winter and Stählin maintained the superior merit of the indirect tradition. In a long, extremely critical, indeed malevolent review of Koetschau's edition of the *Exhortatio ad Martyrium*, the *Contra Celsum* and the *De Oratione* of Origen for the GCS series which appeared in 1899, Paul Wendland denounced the whole project as ill-managed and declared his intention (which he never carried out) of editing at least the *Contra Celsum* anew

---

[3] *Extraits des Livres I et II du Contre Celse d'Origène d'apres le papyrus no.88747 du Musée du Caire,* par Jean Scherer (Cairo, 1956).

himself[4]. It might be thought that the discovery of the Toura MS would have decided the question of the relative superiority of the direct or indirect tradition, but in fact it can hardly be said to have done so. No confident conclusions can be drawn sufficient to rule out any passages which are found only in one or other of the traditions, even though the witness of this MS may on a general judgement be said slightly to favour the direct tradition[5].

The *Unde?* passage itself has been differently evaluated by different scholars. In his earlier treatise on the text of the *Contra Celsum*[6] which appeared in 1889, ten years before his edition of the work was published, Paul Koetschau treated this passage as either an ancient scholion or an addition by the anthologists[7]. He had just before, on the same page, noted that Basil and Gregory very seldom make any additions to or embroidery of the text; he gives four examples of their doing so, three of which are insignificant and one (which certainly is a manifest gloss) occupies five lines only[8]. The *Unde?* passage occupies 50 lines. When Koetschau produced his edition ten years later he had changed his mind. He had come to the conclusion that the *Unde?* passage was an original part of the *Contra Celsum*, and printed it as such, indicating his decision in the *apparatus criticus*[9]. Wendland, on the other hand, though he took Koetschau severely to task for relying too much on the direct tradition, believed that in this instance he had relied on it too little, and rejected the *Unde?* passage. When much later Koetschau

---

[4] See *Göttingische gelerte Anzeigen,* 161 Jahrgang, Nr.IV, April 1899, 276–304, the last-mentioned remark on p. 295.

[5] See Scherer, *op. cit.,* 38–42.

[6] Paul Koetschau, *Die Textüberlieferung der Bücher des Origenes gegen Celsus* (TU VI), i-vi, 1–157 (Leipzig, 1889).

[7] *Op. cit.,* 133.

[8] *Op. cit.,* 133–4; the last example occurs at *Philoc* XVIII.20.115, lines 1–5.

[9] *Origenes* 2, 148–9, at *Contra Celsum* VI.77. He referred to this in his Introduction, *Origenes* 1, LXXI, referring the reader to an earlier article in the *Festschrift des Jenaer Gymnasiums zur 350-jahrigen Jubelfeier des Eisenacher Gymnasiums am 18 October 1894* (Jena Neuhahn, 1894), 51–58. I have been unable to consult this work; perhaps the fact that even without it I have come to the same conclusion as Koetschau set forth in it makes the defect less important.

published a German translation of the *Contra Celsum* he omitted the *Unde?* passage without explanation. Most scholars have therefore concluded that he was in this particular convinced by Wendland's arguments, though he certainly never agreed that the indirect was preferable to the direct tradition. Virtually all subsequent scholars *e.g.,* H. Chadwick,[10] M. Borrett,[11] and E. Junod,[12] have accepted Wendland's conclusion about this passage, though one conjectures that they can hardly have examined this subject (admittedly a minor one) very closely.

Before we consider particular arguments concerning this *Unde?* passage, one general observation should be made. The great controversy between favourers of the direct and champions of the indirect tradition would seem to some extent irrelevant to modern exponents of textual criticism. Today scholars are much less inclined to bracket a whole group of MSS or a MS as 'good' and to be preferred to others, and to characterize others as 'bad' and inferior, unless in extreme and obvious cases; the policy of preferring 'good' families of N.T. manuscripts, for instance, according to their presumed place of origin which prevailed in the days of Streeter is now no longer greatly favoured. The tendency is, within reasonable limits, to take each reading of each MS on its own merits, without deciding in advance the merits of the MS as a whole. This means that the question of the alleged superiority of the direct or the indirect tradition is less important generally, and in fact in this case hardly applies at all, if only because there are no similar cases in the *Contra Celsum* to compare with the case of this *Unde?* passage. Scherer, after a careful survey of the significance of the Toura fragments, refuses to answer the question as to whether the direct or the indirect tradition is better, saying that the problem cannot be posed in such simple terms: 'il conviendra ... gardant son esprit libre, de prendre son bien où on le trouvera'[13].

[10] Origen: *Contra Celsum* tr. with introd. and notes (Cambridge, 1953) 391, n. 3.

[11] Origène, *Contre Celse*, Tome III (*SC* Paris, 1969), 370, 372, 374–5 (esp. n. 1).

[12] *Op. cit.,* 190–191.

[13] *Op. cit.,* 58.

We must consider Wendland's arguments for the inauthenticity of the *Unde?* passage before looking at the context more closely. He declares that the end of the paragraph just before the *Unde?* passage and the short concluding passage immediately after it fit well together; that the *Unde?* passage is an unnecessary diversion which does not assist the polemic against Celsus, as it does not refer to the attributes to be expected in a god incarnate mentioned by Celsus, μέγεθος, φωνή, ἀλκή, κατάπληξις and πειθώ (*Philoc*, XV.12.79; *CCels*, VI.77.146), whereas these attributes are generally discussed in the admittedly authentic passage before the *Unde?* passage. He admits that there are some resemblances in subject matter between the *Unde?* passage and some other passages in CCels, Book VI, but thinks that the introduction in the *Unde?* passage of the allegorization of Scripture weakens the argument against Celsus. Finally he suggests that it is much more likely that an interpolation has taken place in the *Philocalia* after it had left the hands of its compilers than that, as Koetschau conjectured, two pages should have been lost from a MS of the *CCels*, both of which began and ended with a pause in the argument, and he points out an irregularity in this part of the *Philocalia* chap. XV (the chapter in question), whereby short passages from the Books I and II of *CCels* have been introduced into the long extract taken from the Book VI without any intimation of this being given by the editors in their *tituli*, though they are usually very punctilious about giving such notice [14].

It is the intention of this paper to argue that the *Unde?* passage is an original part of *CCels*, and that Koetschau's opinion when he published the text of that work was the correct one. This case can only be made by a proper consideration of the whole chapter in the *Philocalia* which contains the *Unde?* passage. But before we engage in this task we can dispose of one or two of Wendland's arguments briefly. It is indeed true that the *Unde?* passage does not refer to any of the divine attributes which Celsus thinks that a god should exhibit, μέγεθος, φωνή etc. But then, neither does the unquestionably authentic part of this chapter. The nearest that Origen approaches to doing so is when

[14] Wendland, *op. cit.* 284, 285.

he speaks of ποιότητα . . . ἔνδοξον καί καταπληκτικὴν καὶ θαυμαστήν (Philoc. XV.14.82; CCels. VI.77.146). Origen makes no attempt to deal in detail with the other desirable divine attributes, μέγεθος, φωνή, ἀλκή, πειθώ. Again, though it is true that the compilers, Basil and Gregory, usually are very exact in giving beforehand in their *tituli* the provenance of their selection, there are exceptions to this rule. In chapter XXVII of the *Philocalia*, sections 1–9, the prefatory *titulus* (p. 242) supplies the Biblical passage commented upon (*Ex* 10.27), but not the work of Origen from which the extract is taken; later (XXVII.10.252) appears a *titulus* giving the work but not the number of the Book, in surprisingly vague language: καὶ πάλιν ἐν ἄλλῳ τόπῳ ἐν ταῖς αὐταῖς εἰς τὴν Ἔξοδον σημειώεσιν, and the only other indication occurs later (11.253) as simply καὶ μεθ᾽ ἕτερα[15]. The absence of indication in the *titulus* concerning the extracts from Books I and II of *CCels* in the fifteenth chapter does not compel us to make the drastic assumption of Wendland that these passages represent interpolations by a later hand in the MSS of the *Philocalia*. We shall presently encounter an alternative explanation for their presence.

Now let us look more closely at the contents of the XVth chapter of the *Philocalia* in which the *Unde?* passage occurs (XVI–20, 70–86). It begins with a *titulus* supplied by the compilers: πρὸς τοὺς Ἑλλήνων φιλοσόφους τὸ εὐτελὲς τῆς τῶν θείων γραφῶν φράσεως διασύροντας, καὶ τὰ ἐν χριστιανίσμῳ καλὰ βέλτιον παρ᾽ Ἕλλησιν εἰρῆσθαι φάσκοντας, καὶ προσέτι δυσειδὲς τὸ τοῦ Κυρίον σῶμα λέγοντας καὶ τίς ὁ λόγος τῶν διαφόρων τοῦ λόγου μορφῶν ἐκ τῶν κατὰ Κέλσον, τοῦ κατὰ χριστιάνων γράψαντος, τόμον ς [i.e. VI] καὶ ζ [i.e. VII].

In fact nothing at all is said about the Transfiguration between this and the next rubric (p. 79), but as a description of the whole chapter, including the *Unde?* passage, it is excellent. After this long *titulus* the first eleven sections of the chapter are

---

[15] P. Nautin (*Origène*, Paris 1977, p. 246), following C.H. Turner, has suggested that part of the *titulus* referring to the work from which the extracts here were taken has been lost; but even if this were so the vagueness attaching to the 'reference' would remain.

concerned with defending the vulgar style and expression of the Bible against Celsus' denigration of it and his accusation that the teaching of the Bible is plagiarized from the philosophers and especially Plato. Origen points to the effect of the Bible, vulgar though its style be, in converting and transforming the minds, not merely of the intellectuals, but of people of every sort. After section 11 occurs another titulus which runs thus: καὶ ἐν τῷ ς´ (VI) πάλιν τόμῳ, πρὸς τὸν δυσειδὲς τὸ σῶμα τοῦ Κυρίου λέγοντα Κέλσον οὕτως'. Section 12 quotes Celsus' accusation, tries to tone down the damning passage in Isaiah (51.3ff) and points to a passage in the contrary sense in another part of the Bible (Ps 45.4f). Section 13 refers to the Transfiguration, when the appearance of Jesus was the reverse of mean. Section 14 produces a theory known from other passages in Origen also that the solution of these apparently contradictory accounts for the appearance of Jesus lies in the fact that Jesus changed his appearance, indeed his nature φύσις, according to the needs of those who were hearing or seeing him. The passage ends (p. 82, lines 3–5) with these words, ἀλλ' ἐρεῖ ταῦτ' εἶναι πλάσματα οὐδὲν μυθῶν διαφέροντα ὡς καὶ τὰ λοιπὰ τῶν περὶ Ἰησοῦ παραδόξων. The text of CCels of course reproduces this passage, but here adds (147, lines 1–2) a sentence which runs πρὸς τόδε μὲν οὖν διὰ πλειόνων ἐν τοῖς πρὸ τούτων ἀπελογισάμεθα. Philocalia however at this point suppresses this sentence and instead introduces three passages from a much earlier part of CCels from I.42 (Philoc sec. 15) and 63 (Philoc sec. 16) and II.15 (Philoc sec. 17). The reference to an earlier argument for the historicity of the Biblical narratives, about which all these earlier extracts are concerned, preserved in the original text of CCels, would of course be useless in an anthology like the Philocalia; the compilers have instead given some examples of this earlier argument (as we today would add such material in a footnote), without indicating their provenance in their titulus, assuming that the reader would realize that they came from CCels. The insertion is an entirely logical one.

There next follow in both Philoc. and CCels the words ἔχει δέ τι καὶ μυστικώτερον ὁ λόγος (Philoc 83, lines 21ff, sec. 18; CCels VI.77.147, lines 2ff), and this 'more complex explanation' turns out in the subsequent argument to be a typically Origenist theory that the different μορφαί of Jesus represent different stages in an ascending apprehension of the Logos, with a direct reference to the Transfiguration. Next follows in the text of *CCels* a short paragraph (VI.77.149, lines 17–21), asking rhetorically, What is τὸ βούλημα τῶν διαφόρων τοῦ 'Ιησοῦ μορφῶν to Celsus and the enemies of Christianity? and Origen adds ἐγὼ δὲ λέγω καὶ ἡλικιῶν, καὶ εἴ τι πρὸ τοῦ παθεῖν αὐτῷ πεπραγμένων, καὶ τῶν μετὰ τὸ ἀναστῆναι ἀπὸ τῶν νεκρῶν.

Philoc. has precisely the same passage (XV.20.86, lines 4–8), but in between this and what immediately precedes it in the text of *CCels* occurs this long *Unde?* passage of 55 lines. It deals with the clothes of Jesus at the Transfiguration and suggests that they represent an ascending significance to be found in the words of the Bible, with a comparison between the Word clothed in flesh and the Word clothed in words, and a conjecture that the final point of this process is reached when what is apprehended is beyond words (*Philoc.* XV.19.84–86).

Let us first note that Wendland is quite mistaken in thinking that this *Unde?* passage is manifestly out of place. On the contrary, it precisely fits Origen's argument. Origen has really finished dealing directly with Celsus' accusations before he brings on the μυστικώτερος λόγος. This 'more complex explanation' is, if not exactly a digression, at least an additional excursus into one of Origen's more daring theories, which he admits could have little appeal to Celsus ('but Celsus will declare that these are inventions and no different from legends, like the rest of the extraordinary circumstances of Jesus' (*Philoc.* p. 82, lines 3–5; *CCels* p. 146, line 26 - p. 147, line 1)). It is wholly consistent that he should in the *Unde?* passage add his further speculative theory, well attested elsewhere in his works, concerning the inner significance of the words of Scripture and what might be called the 'Inscriptation' corresponding to the Incarnation, especially as he has been dealing with the subject of the style and expression of Scripture a few paragraphs before. Indeed, the *Unde?* passage could well be described as quite as relevant to Origen's argument against Celsus' disparagement of the style of the Bible as the argument of the passage immediately before it is to Celsus' criticism of the appearance of Jesus. The final short passage, 'But what is the intention of the different shapes of Jesus' to Celsus and the enemies of Christianity?' is both another admission that Origen has diverged a little from his direct answer to Celsus and a means of resuming the argument against him. It does indeed fit very well the passage which immediately precedes it in the text of *CCels*, for that passage has referred to τὰς τοῦ Ἰησοῦ διαφόρους μορφάς (*Philoc.* p. 83, line 22, *CCels* p. 147, lines 3–4). But then the *Unde?* passage also refers to Jesus as μεταμορφουμένον (*Philoc.* p. 85, lines 29 and 30), and to his μεταμόρφωσις once (*Philoc* p. 85, line 27). The closing short paragraph therefore could quite as well succeed the *Unde?* passage as the other. It is worth noting that Origen refers gratuitously in this last passage to the different ages (ἡλικιαί) of Jesus, as a subject which he would apparently like to expatiate upon if he had opportunity. Celsus in the passage quoted by Origen had referred neither to the μορφή nor to the ἡλικιαί of Jesus. Clearly, as we have seen, by this time Origen has ceased directly to answer Celsus and instead is following the bent of his own speculations which are suggested to him by the context of his argument even if they are not directly relevant to it.

It is therefore quite incorrect to say that Wendland 'demonstrated' or 'showed' that the *Unde?* passage is an interpolation. On the contrary, it is remarkably relevant to its context, so relevant that it is difficult to believe that it could have fitted in anywhere else.

I pass over any suggestion that the *Unde?* passage can be shown to be 'homiletic' in its style and so attributable to some homily of Origen which has not survived. I do not believe that the homiletic style of Origen can be satisfactorily distinguished from his 'commentary' style, and certainly this passage gives no evidence of such a distinction; Wendland did not in fact attempt to produce any evidence for this hypothesis. The thought, and to some extent the vocabulary, of the *Unde?* passage can be paralleled easily from Origen's *Commentary on Matthew* (e.g. *ComMt*, XII.38 (Klostermann p. 154.19–21) and *ComMt*, fragment 11 (Klostermann III (i) p. 19), on Mt 1.18). But none of the parallel passages is an exact reproduction of any part of the *Unde?* passage. Perhaps it is significant that we must place the composition of the *ComMt.* quite near in time to the writing of *CCels.* Such ideas were in Origen's mind at the time.

The only argument adduced by Wendland which seems to me to be of any weight is his appeal to the difficulty of supposing that the *Unde?* passage dropped out of the MSS of *CCels* at some stage when two pages were missed out, the whole omitted passage happening to coincide with a break in sense both at the beginning and at the end of the two pages. In fact even if we were to make this assumption, which Koetschau felt compelled to make, it would not be a very improbable one. A count made from page 200 to page 250 of Vol. II of Koetschau's text of *CCels,* showed that within these pages a new page of the MS coincided with a stop in the sense ten or eleven times.

But there is no need to appeal to this theory produced by Koetschau. A much simpler explanation has been offered us by a phenomenon noted by Scherer in his Introduction to the text of the Toura fragments of *CCels.* He notes [16] that the copyist of the Toura fragments of *CCels* follows the practice of sometimes leaving a blank space to represent the end of one passage selected for reproduction and another, and as he goes on these spaces become more frequent and finally altogether replace other ways of indicating a new passage. Now Koetschau noted that blank spaces play an important part in the system of punctuation of MS A (Vaticanus) of *CCels* 'Ils marquent', says Scherer, 'les articulations de la pensée, séparant et distinguant les différents points de l'argumentation'[17]. And although there are blank spaces in A which are not in the Toura papyrus, there are no blank spaces in the papyrus which are not in A. It is remarkable that before the words μέμνημαι δέ in the papyrus (33.20) there is a particularly large blank, and that a similar large blank can be found before these words in the MS A (*CCels* I.55.106, line 3). This means that this system of blank spaces was not due to the copyists of the MSS which are in our hands; it no doubt came from the archetype, and perhaps even from the original model, the *editio princeps* of Origen in the library at Caesarea. We do not therefore have to postulate the disappearance in the MS

[16] Scherer, *op. cit.,* 11–13.
[17] *Op. cit.,* 12.

tradition of *CCels* of two pages with a break in sense before and
after them, but simply the disappearance of a passage between
two of these blank spaces, without having to invoke any
calculation of pages. It is easily seen how much more probable
such an accident is when we are dealing with a MS tradition
which uses blank spaces to indicate pauses in the argument. No
such system of punctuation is known to have been used in the
MS tradition of the *Philocalia*. Later copies of *CCels* than the MS
A do not exhibit these blank spaces.

We are therefore faced with a situation in which we have two
separate MS traditions for the particular passage in Origen's
CCels with which we are concerned, both going back to a single
archetype, though the archetype is different in each case. We
should separate the presence of the *Unde?* passage from the
presence of the shorter extracts from Books I and II of *CCels* in
Philocalia XV a little earlier; they are two different problems.
The addition of the extracts from *CCels* I and II is a problem
concerning the *titulus*; they are unannounced, but there is plenty
of precedent for Basil and Gregory inserting earlier passages
from *CCels* into later passages from the same work. The *Unde?*
passage presents us with a different problem. If it is an addition
to the text of *CCels* it is an addition from another work of
Origen, not from an earlier part of the same work, and if so the
absence of a *titulus* announcing it presents a considerable
difficulty. We must choose. Basil and Gregory might have
inserted a passage from another work of Origen, unknown to us
and unannounced by them; this seems to me wholly
improbable, and is without precedent in the *Philocalia*. Or else a
later interpolator inserted this *Unde?* passage from some other
work of Origen, choosing an extract which precisely fitted the
context in *CCels*, at a period at which the MS tradition
represented by MS A and that represented by the *Philocalia* had
already diverged. We have no MS evidence for this: there are no
precedents for this in the *Philocalia* as we know it. The 'Eusebian
Extract' was included because though Basil and Gregory took
its text from Eusebius' *Preparatio Evangelica* they thought that he
was here reproducing Origen's text[18]; the extract from the

---

[18] Robinson, *op. cit.,* XIff; *Philoc* cap. XXIV, pp. 212–226.

Clementine *Recognitions*[19] was added by the compilers on their own authority because it aptly supported a point made by Origen in the preceding chapter, and they say so in the *titulus* which heads the extract. The theory of a later interpolation seems to me to be unsupported by any satisfactory evidence. The final alternative, which I believe, and Koetschau once believed[20], to be the correct one, is that at some point in the MS tradition represented by MS A a passage of 55 lines length in our printed texts was accidentally omitted, a contingency made all the more likely by the system of punctuation which we know to have been used by the copyists in that tradition. This means that the *Unde?* passage is an original integral part of Origen's *Contra Celsum* and should be restored to its proper position in future editions of that word.

[19] *Philoc* XXIII.22, pp. 210–212.

[20] He still believed this when he wrote *Kritische Bemerkungen zu meiner Ausgabe von Origenes' Exhortatio, Contra Celsum, De Oratione* etc (Leipzig 1899), an immediate reply to Wendland's attack. The very brief and condensed arguments which he used there (pages 38, 39) to defend his inclusion of the *Unde?* passage in the text of *CCels.* are scarcely worth recounting here.

6

EUCHARISTIC OFFERING IN THE PRE-NICENE FATHERS

I

This paper attempts to present the relevant texts so as to illustrate the development of its theme with the minimum of comment. The history of the doctrine of eucharistic offering in the pre-Nicene Fathers is the history of the development of two originally quite separate ideas, which run parallel to each other for some time, are joined by a third, and finally fuse in the process of creating another, quite new, idea. The first of these ideas is the concept of the 'pure offering'. This probably had no connection with the eucharist in its origins. It is the idea that Christians fulfil the statement of Mal (1.11): 'from the rising of the sun to its setting my name is great among the nations, and in every place incense is offered to my name, and a pure offering (LXX θυσία καθαρά, "pure sacrifice"); for my name is great among the nations says the Lord of hosts'. From a very early period Christian claimed that Christianity fulfilled this statement, which they took to be a prediction. In the previous verse (1.10) the prophet represents God as rejecting the sacrifices of the Jews: 'I have no pleasure in you, says the Lord of hosts, and I will not accept an offering from your hand'. The pure offering, in which God has pleasure, is that which is offered by the Christians. This is the claim made over and over again by writer after writer in the first three centuries of the church's existence with a quite exceptional unanimity. It often makes direct reference to the text in Malachi and usually accompanies a strong rejection of pagan sacrifices, as well as Jewish.

It is not altogether easy to determine the origins of this doctrine. St. Paul had urged the Christians of Rome to present their bodies 'as a living sacrifice, holy and acceptable to God, which is your spiritual worship' (θυσίαν ζῶσαν ἁγίαν εὐάρεστον τῷ θεῷ τὴν λογικήν λατρείαν ὑμῶν Rom 12.1), and had used sacrificial language to describe his own ministry (Rom 15.16 λειτουργόν ... ἱεσουγοῦντα ... προσφορά), and no doubt this contributed to the formation of this doctrine. As we shall see, the doctrine of the priesthood of all Christians

(1 Pet 2.5,9; Rev 1.6, 5.10, 20.6) must also lie behind this concept. It is even possible that the germ of this idea of a pure sacrifice can be found in Hellenistic Judaism. Book III of the *Sibylline Oracles*, which derives from a Jewish source, perhaps an Egyptian Jew, in one passage prophesies an age of prosperity, in which pious Jews will be rewarded; they will celebrate the sacrificial cult of the great God at his Temple lavishly; they will have nothing to do with idols or pictures; instead

ἀλλὰ γὰρ ἀείρουσι πρὸς οὐρανὸν ὤλενας ἀγνάς
ὄρθριοι ἐξ εὐνῆς αἰεὶ χρόα ἁγνίζοντες
ὕδατι.

And they will honour only the everlasting God and their parents, refraining from sexual immorality and homosexuality, unlike the Phoenicians, the Egyptians and the Greeks.[1] But there is no reference in this passage to the verse from Malachi. Its date is uncertain; some have placed it as early as 140 B.C. It must come from a period before the Destruction of Jerusalem in 70 A.D. That is all that we can say. Perhaps one may venture to think that the Christians derived their intense opposition to pagan sacrifices from Jewish precedents, though I know of only one piece of evidence that the Jews maintained, as the Christians consistently did, that pagan sacrifices were offered to daemons (Or. Sib. frg. 1.20–22).[2] This rejection of pagan sacrifices could have combined with the strong emphasis on a high morality to produce the doctrine of the 'pure offering'. But evidence is almost completely lacking.

The appeal to the verses in Malachi could only have been

[1] *Oracula Sibyllina*, III 573–600; quoted lines are 591–592.
[2] Evidence for Christian opposition to pagan sacrifices is overwhelming, and it would go beyond the scope of this article to give anything but a few references. See Ptolemy's *Letter to Flora*, PG 7: 1288B; Aristides, *Apol*, 1.5 and 13.4; Athenagoras, *Supp.*, 13.1, 2, Irenaeus, *Adv. Haer.*, 4.29.1ff; Minucius Felix, *Octavius*, 32:2,3; Tertullian, *Apologeticus*, 30:5–6; 42.7; *Adv. Marc.*, 2.18.3 & 22.3; *Ad Scap.*, 2.8; *De Orat.*, 28,29: *Or. Sib.*, 8.390–1; Clement of Alexandria, *Protrep.*, 3–42.1–43.4 Origen, *Contra Celsum*, 8.19,20; Novatian, *De Cib. Iud.*, 7 (PL 3.992); Arnobius, *Adv. Nat.*, 4.31; 7.2; 8.26, 36; Lactantius, *Div. Inst.*, 6.24,25; Eusebius Caes., *Praep Ev.*, III passim & esp. 13.24; IV.16.1–27; Athanasius, *Contra Gentes* 25. 1–25. The Christians had, of course, some support in pagan thought for opposition at any rate to animal sacrifices.

effective for Christians at a period when Christianity had left its Jewish matrix and Christians were contrasting themselves with Jews, as well as with pagans. The proper, acceptable and 'pure offering', according to this doctrine was the pure heart and good conscience of the individual who made it, and sometimes there is added to this the idea that praise and prayer is part of the 'pure offering'. The first examples of the 'pure offering' doctrine come from that obscure period which overlaps the time of the writing of the latest books of the New Testament and extends to the middle of the second century, which used to be called the sub-apostolic period and is now sometimes called the Judaeo-Christian period, whose rare documents are usually difficult to date with any exactness. The first instance to be cited comes from that curious production the *Odes of Solomon*. These were probably written originally in Syriac, though Greek and Coptic versions of parts of them are extant. The second century seems the most likely period for their composition,[3] and perhaps the most probable provenance is Antioch; anyone acquainted with Christian literature of the second century will agree with the verdict of a recent writer that 'the milieu certainly seems Judaeo-Christian, not sectarian-Gnostic'.[4] In the twentieth *Ode* the following passage occurs:

> I am a priest of the Lord
> And Him I serve as a priest;
> And to Him I offer the offering of His thought.
> For His thought is not like the world,
> Nor like the flesh,
> Nor like them who worship according to the flesh.
> The offering of the Lord is righteousness
> And purity of heart and lips.
> Offer thy inward being faultlessly
> And let not thy compassion oppress compassion.
> And let not thyself oppress a self.[5]

The next passage is from the *Didache*, a work no less difficult to

---

[3] See *The Odes and Psalms of Solomon*, ed. J. Rendel Harris and *The Odes of Solomon* ed. J. H. Charlesworth.

[4] Robert Murray, *Symbols of the Church and Kingdom*, p. 25.

[5] The translation is from Charlesworth, *op. cit.* Ode 20, p. 83, verses 1–5.

date than the *Odes of Solomon*; one can only say that plus or
minus 100 A.D. appears to be the least improbable date to assign
it. In a famous passage it directly invokes Mal 1.10, and does so
in a eucharistic context: 'On the Lord's Day come together,
break bread and hold eucharist, after confessing your
transgressions, that your sacrifice may be pure (ὅπως καθαρὰ ἡ
θυσία ὑμῶν ᾖ); but let none who has a quarrel with his fellow
join in your meeting until they be reconciled, that your sacrifice
be not defiled (ἵνα μὴ κοινωθῇ ἡ θυσία ὑμῶν)'. The next lines
actually quote Mal 1.11 and 14.[6] There can be little doubt that
the θυσία here is the Christian's offering of himself, his heart
and his conscience. Hermas has a similar expression applied to
almsgiving in a context not so clearly eucharistic 'your sacrifice
(*thysia*) will be acceptable with God' (*Sim.* V.3 (56.8)). A long
passage in the *Epistle of Barnabas* reproduces the 'pure offering'
doctrine, though the context is not eucharistic and there is no
reference to the passage in Malachi.[7] God does not require
material sacrifices, says this writer; sacrifices were abolished by
the 'new law of our Lord Jesus Christ' (6); what God required is
good conduct, repentance and a heart that glorifies God. The
same theme can be found in the writings of the Apologists. God
does not need sacrifice and libation, says Aristides.[8] Christians 'as
men who know God offer to him prayers which (unlike
sacrifices) are proper for them to give and for him to receive'.[9]
Justin Martyr reproduces this doctrine, though with a
development which we shall be considering presently: all
Christians are a priestly race (ἀρχιερατικὸν γένος) who offer
acceptable sacrifices to God, with a reference to Mal 1.11. God
accepts prayers as sacrifices (θυσίας), and prayers and
thanksgivings offered by those who are worthy are the only
perfect and pleasing sacrifices for God.[10] Athenagoras repeats
that God needs no material sacrifices; he is ἀνενδεής καὶ
ἀπροσδεής; what should be offered to him are 'bloodless
sacrifice, our spiritual service (ἀναίμακτον θυσίαν τὴν

---

[6] *Didache*, 14:1–2; the translation is that of Kirsopp Lake.
[7] *Epistle of Barnabas*, 2:4–10.
[8] Aristides, *Apologia* 1.5; 13.4.
[9] *Ibid.*, 16.1 (my translation).
[10] Justinus *Dialogus*, 116:3; 117:2.

λογικὴν λατρείαν)'.[11] Minucius Felix is particularly eloquent on this theme: to offer sacrifices and victims to God is to misuse his own gifts. *Ingratum est, cum sit litabilis hostia bonus animus et pura mens et sincera sententia. Igitur qui innocentiam colit, deo supplicat; qui iustitiam, deo libat; qui fraudibus abstinet, propitiat deum; qui hominem periculo subripit, optimam victimam caedit. Haec nostra sacrificia, haec dei sacra sunt: sic apud nos religiosior est ille qui iustior.*[12] The highly intelligent Gnostic, Ptolemy, in his *Letter to Flora*, has the same doctrine when he writes that the Saviour taught us to offer sacrifices, but not of irrational animals; we sacrifice 'by means of spiritual hymns and praises and thanksgiving and by comradeship towards our neighbour and acts of benevolence'.[13] If we agree with H. Chadwick that the Sextus who wrote the *Sentences* was a second-century Christian moralist much influenced by Stoicism, we can add to the list two of his sayings, ἄριστον θυσιαστήριον θεῷ καρδία καθαρὰ καὶ ἀναμαρτήτος and θυσία θεῷ μονὴ καὶ προσηνὴς ἡ ἀνθρώποις εὐεργεσία διὰ θεόν.[14] We may cite a passage from the eighth book of the *Sibylline Oracles* which was written as a piece of Christian propaganda and has been dated to about 200: God does not want from the pagans sacrifice or libation nor filthy smoke of sacrifice nor repulsive blood;[15] what he wants is works of corporal mercy: καὶ ζῶσαν θυσίαν ἐμοι τῷ ζῶντι πόριζε,[16] and here we find a direct reference to Rom 12.1. What Christians give to God are pure hearts and cheerful spirits and sweet psalms and songs.[17] Finally, it should be said that the references of Ignatius of Antioch to his being offered on an altar (Rom 2.2; 4.2) as a sacrifice are only an extension of the same doctrine.

II

We must now turn to the second idea on the subject of

---

[11] Athenagoras *Supplicatio*, 13:1,2 (my translation).
[12] Minucius Felix, *Octavius*, 32:2,3.
[13] Ptolemy, *Letter to Flora*, Migne *PG* 7: 1288 B (my translation).
[14] *The Sentences of Sextus*, p. 16, 46b and 47.
[15] *Or. Sib.* VIII.390–1.
[16] *Ibid.*, 408f.
[17] *Ibid.*, 496ff.

eucharistic offering which runs parallel with that of the 'pure offering'. It is originally the simple idea that in the eucharist the elements of bread and wine are offered to God by those who take part in the rite and/or by those who celebrate it. This is an idea which cannot be found in the few references to the eucharist afforded by the New Testament, though it is by no means contradicted by them. It is a development of eucharist thought of a very natural sort arising out of the very practice of the rite itself. It first appears in the forty-fourth chapter of the *First Epistle of Clement*, where the writer rebukes the Corinthian Christians, to whom he is writing in the name of the Roman Christians, for deposing from their office certain presbyters, or presbyter-bishops (for with him presbyter and bishop are plainly identical): 'For our sin is not small,' he writes, 'if we eject from the episcopate (τῆς ἐπισκοπῆς) those who have blamelessly and holily offered its sacrifices'.[18] The translation of the last expression is a tendentious one; 'offered' or 'presented the gifts' would be more accurate and more satisfactory; the Greek is τοὺς . . . προσενεγκόντας τὰ δῶρα. It is obvious that τὰ δῶρα refers to the bread and wine in the eucharist, and that the presbyters are thought of as presenting them to God in the eucharist for him to bless them. In the same passage the ministry of the presbyters is described once as λειτουργήσαντες (3) and thrice as λειτουργία (3, 4), but there is no reason to see in this any other meaning than Paul himself attaches to the word λειτουργόν when he uses it, with other sacrificial language, to refer to the whole of his ministry (Rom 15.16). *I Clement* is usually dated with some confidence to about the year 96, on the grounds that its author was a member of the household of Flavius Clemens who was put to death by the Emperor Domitian in that year. But a recent article has shown very good reason to doubt the connection of Flavius Clemens and his niece Domitilla with Christianity,[19] and a number of small points in the Epistle itself have for some time suggested to me, independently of this argument, that the year 96 is considerably

---

[18] *I Clement* 44.4. Lake's translation.
[19] P. Kerestzes, 'The Jews, the Christians and Emperor Domitian', pp. 1–28.

too early a date for this work. There is nothing in it to prevent us placing it twenty or thirty years later than 96.

We might of course associate with this idea of the bread and wine in the eucharist being offered the passage in the *Didache* (14:1, 2) which we have already considered, but I think that this would be unwise. The *Didache* does not mention the word προσφέρειν or προσφορά, but θυσία '(sacrifice),' and it does so with the direct invocation of the passage in Malachi, which does not seem to be in the mind of the author of *I Clement*. It is better to think of the *Didache* as the earlier work in which the identification of the 'pure offering' and the offering of the eucharistic elements has not been made.

But this identification has certainly been made by the time that Justin wrote, or rather he has juxtaposed the two types of offering. For him the Christian sacrifice is both the 'pure offering' and the offering to God of bread and wine in the eucharist. The cereal offering under the Jewish law (Lev 14.10) was a type of the bread of the eucharist (τοῦ ἄρτου τῆς εὐχαριστίας) which the Lord 'gave to make' (παρέδωκε ποιεῖν) in memorial of his saving passion. The prophet Malachi spoke of sacrifices offered throughout the world among the Gentiles: God then 'is predicting concerning the sacrifices offered to him in every place by us Gentiles, that is the bread of the eucharist and the cup likewise of the eucharist, saying that we glorify his name, but you (*i.e.*, the Jews) profane it'.[20] We have seen that in the same work (116.3) he describes all Christians as priests offering sacrifices to God, and in the next chapter (117.1–5) he defines this sacrifice as εὐχαὶ καὶ εὐχαριστίαι (2, 5) offered in memory of (ἐπ' ἀναμνήσει) the solid and liquid food in which remembrance is made of the passion which the Son of God endured (3), and again the text in Malachi is invoked. In the *Apology* in his description of the eucharist Justin uses language consistent with this view, though designed not, as in the *Dialogue*, for polemic with Jews, but for persuasion of pagans. This is how he describes the central part of the rite: 'Then bread and a cup of water and wine mixed are brought to the president of the brothers and he takes them and

---

[20] Justin *Dial.* 41:1–3, the quotation (my translation) from 3.

gives praise and glory to the Father of all through the name of the Son and of the Holy Spirit and makes thanksgiving for some time for their having been made worthy of those things by him' (*i.e*, God).[21] The next chapter (66) virtually identifies the 'eucharistised' (εὐχαριστηθεῖσαν) food with the body and blood of Christ, comparing the mysteries of Mithras. The chapter after that briefly repeats the description of the eucharist in a way which has puzzled scholars: here the central part of the rite is described thus: 'when we have finished our prayer, as I have said, bread is offered (προσφέρεται) and wine and water, and the president sends up, as well as he can, prayers likewise and thanksgivings' (67.5).

It is worth noting that in fact in both these descriptions Justin uses the word προσφέρειν not directly of the celebrant nor of the people offering the elements to God, but of the elements being brought to the celebrant for his eucharistic prayer. In fact Justin does not in these passages precisely use sacrificial language, even though he has described the whole rite in the *Dialogue* as a προσφορά and a θυσία '(sacrifice)'. One would think that there was nothing to stop him or his contemporaries, in view of the very 'realistic' account of the effect of the eucharistic prayer on the elements, from moving directly into the conclusion that in the eucharist Christ himself is offered. But, as we shall see, this development does not take place among Latin-speaking Christians for a century nor among Greek-speaking Christians for a century and a half. In his essential attitude to the eucharist, Justin has not moved very far from the concept of the people of God gathered together calling upon God in the name of Christ to bless the bread and wine.

III

Irenaeus' doctrine of eucharistic offering does not make any significant advance on Justin's, though it introduces a new

---

[21] *Apol* 65:3 ἔπειτα προσφέρεται τῷ προεστῶτι τῶν ἀδέλφων ἄρτος καὶ ποτήριον ὕδατος καὶ κράματος καὶ οὗτος λαβὼν αἶνον καὶ δόξαν τῷ πατρὶ τῶν ὅλων διὰ τοῦ ὀνόματος τοῦ υἱοῦ καὶ τοῦ πνεύματος τοῦ ἁγίου ἀναπέμπει καὶ εὐχαριστίαν ὑπὲρ τοῦ κατηξιῶσθαι τούτων παρ' αὐτὸν ἐπὶ πολὺ ποιεῖται (my trans.).

theme characteristic of Irenaeus and little reproduced elsewhere. For Irenaeus, not only the apostles but all disciples of Jesus were priests and to-day his disciples still are priests.[22] His argument is that Christians offer to God in the eucharist praise and thanksgiving, and also offer to him the bread and wine to be transformed by him into the body and blood of Christ so that Christians can have communion with Christ. God did not want from the Jews any sacrifice except that of a pure heart and a humble mind.[23] Our Lord confirmed this fact in his teaching:

> But he also advised his disciples to offer the first fruits of his creation to God, not as if God needed them but so that they should not be unfruitful nor ungrateful, and so he took that which is from the creation of bread and gave thanks, saying, This is my body. And similarly he declared the cup which is from the creation which is our environment (*quae est secundum nos*) to be his blood, and taught the new offering of the new dispensation; this the Church received from the apostles and offers throughout the whole world to God who provides us with nourishment, as the first fruits of his gifts in the new dispensation . . .[24]

There follows a quotation from Mal 1.10, 11. Shortly afterwards Irenaeus again emphasises that God does not need sacrifices but that it is fitting that men should offer to God the first fruits of his own creation, and do so gladly and willingly, as is proper to children and not to slaves.[25] Many Scriptural quotations are then adduced to show that it is not the offering that matters but the sincerity and singleness of heart of the offerer,[26] and Irenaeus again stresses that our offering should express our gratitude, faith, hope and love.[27] The next passage speaks of the consecrated elements and declares that the transformation of the elements in the eucharist is parallel to our bodies achieving immortality through the eucharistic presence of Christ in them; when the bread receives the invocation

[22] *Sancti Irenaei Libros quinque Adversus Haereses*, IV.17.

[23] *Ibid.*, IV, 29.1–4.

[24] *Ibid.*, IV, 29.5 (my translation of the early Latin translation of the original Greek which has disappeared).

[25] IV.31.1.

[26] IV.31.2.

[27] IV.31.3.

(*invocationem*) it ceases to be ordinary bread but is 'eucharist consisting of two things earthly and heavenly' εὐχαριστία ἐκ δύο πραγμάτων συνεστηκυῖα, ἐπιγείου τε καὶ οὐρανίου.[28] And Irenaeus concludes his remarks by repeating that God does not need our gifts, but just as the Word directed the people under the old covenant to make offerings so that they should learn to serve God, so 'he wishes us also to offer a gift at the altar frequently and unceasingly'.[29]

The new thought here is that in offering bread and wine in the eucharist we offer the firstfruits of God's creation. And though other writers before Irenaeus had said that God does not need any sacrifices, Irenaeus elaborates this thought and supplies new motives for man's offering the bread and the wine. In fact his almost apologetic attitude in advancing the view that man should make any offering to God save the 'pure offering' of a good character and of praise shows how far from his mind is the concept, which to us using hindsight seems so ready to hand, that Christians offer Christ in the eucharist.

Irenaeus returns later to his analogy between the eucharistic bread and wine being made life-giving by the action of God and our bodies being given life through eucharistic participation.[30] Irenaeus is arguing, as so many of the apologists of his day argued, in favour of a doctrine of the resurrection of the body, and presents his point thus:[31]

> And because we are his members and are nourished by what is created he who makes his sun rise on and rains on whomever he chooses provides us with a created thing when he declares the cup taken from created things, from which he causes our blood to flow,[32] to be his blood, and the bread taken from created things, from which he gives growth to our bodies, he affirms to be his body. Therefore when the wine mixed with water and the

[28] IV.31.4: Greek fragment from Johannes Damascenus; see *Irénée de Lyon, Contre les Hérésies Liv. IV*, Tom. II.610,612.

[29] IV.31.5.

[30] V.2.2,3 (for 2 a Greek fragment is available).

[31] The quotation from V.2.2, the translation is mine. I have relied on the Greek rather than the Latin in rendering the meaning which is sometimes not altogether clear.

[32] ἐξ οὗ τὸ ἡμέτερον δεύει αἷμα (Lat. *auget*, a mistake for *rigat*).

baked bread receive the Word of God and the eucharist becomes the body of Christ, and the substance of our flesh grows and is sustained from these elements, how can they deny that our flesh is capable of receiving the gift of God, which is eternal life, since it is nourished by the body and blood of Christ and is a member of his?

The whole emphasis here, as far as the treatment of the effect of the eucharistic rite upon the elements is concerned, is not upon offering but upon communion.[33] We may once more sum up Irenaeus' doctrine of eucharistic offering by saying that he teaches that Christians offer to God bread and wine so that at their prayer he may make them into the body and blood of Christ in order to enable the Christians to communicate.

Tertullian reproduces the doctrine of eucharistic offering which we may call by now the traditional one, though dwelling more confidently and with less air of apology upon the sacrificial aspect than Irenaeus. He is as strong a champion of the doctrine of the 'pure offering' as anyone; references to it occur throughout his works.[34] The sacrifice which he offers, he says, is 'prayer issuing from pure flesh, from innocent soul, from holy spirit'.[35] Towards the end of his book *On Prayer*, Tertullian describes the prayer (called *hostia spiritalis*) which Christians offer as a sacrifice:

We are the true worshippers and the true priests who sacrifice in the spirit prayer as a suitable and acceptable sacrifice (*hostiam*) of God, which of course he demanded, which he foresaw for himself. We are bound to offer at God's altar this prayer, dedicated with all the heart, nourished by faith, protected by truth, sincere in its singleheartedness, pure in its chastity,

---

[33] It is scarcely necessary to add that I do not take into account the highly 'Irenaean' Fragment XXXVI of Harvey's edition, which is among the pieces proved by Harnack to have been forged by the ingenious and enterprising Pfaff.

[34] Except where it is stated otherwise, all references to Tertullian's text come from the *Corpus Christianorum* edition of his works. All the translations are mine.

[35] Tertullian *Apologeticus* 30.5 (71).

crowned by love and accompanied by good actions along with psalms and hymns—and it gains everything for us from God.[36]

God did not need, he tells us elsewhere, the offerings and sacrifices brought to him by people like Abraham and Noah, but he valued 'the honest and God-fearing mind of those who offered them'.[37] Later in the same work Tertullian quotes Mal 1.10–11 and explains the 'pure offering' as 'the ascription of glory and blessing and praise and hymns'.[38] This emphatic statement of the doctrine of the 'pure offering' can co-exist with a very 'realistic' estimate of the nature of the consecrated elements.[39] Tertullian thereby reveals that his eucharistic doctrine, which no doubt he owes largely to Irenaeus, is innocent of any suspicion that Christians offer Christ in the eucharist.

On the other hand, Tertullian develops Irenaeus' doctrine in that he uses for the eucharist not only the word *oblatio*, offering, but also the word *sacrificium* familiarly and freely, much more freely than Irenaeus uses *prosphora* or *thysia*.[40] But even as he calls the rite a sacrifice he explains that it is a sacrifice only of prayers: *ascendet sacrificium tuum* means that your prayer shall mount up,[41] and he can write *non tamen sine sacrificio quod est anima conflictata ieiuniis*.[42] When he is speaking of the eucharist in the context of the killing of the fatted calf at the return of the Prodigal Son it is significant that he is silent about the sacrifice of Christ.[43] But we must note one significant advance in Tertullian on the language

---

[36] *De Oratione*, 28.1,3,4 (the quotation from 3 and 4).

[37] *Adv. Marcionem*, II.22.3, *cf. Ad Scapulam*, II.8; sacrifice is prayer, and God does not need any smell or blood.

[38] *Ibid.*, III.22.6: *cf.* IV.1.8, where the same 'pure offering' is described as *ipsorum sacrificiorum alia officia potiora* and as *simplex oratio de conscientia pura*; again IV.35.11, the grateful leper knew what the true offering was—*gratiarum actionem* etc.

[39] As at, *e.g.*, *Adv. Marc.*, IV.40.3 and V.8.3.

[40] Examples of *oblatio*: *De Praescr. Haer.*, 40.4; *Ad Uxorem*, II.8.6; *De Exhort. Cast*, 10.5; *cf.* 11.12; *De Corona* 3.3; *De Monog.*, 10.4; *De Ieiun. ad Psych.*, 15.2 (*offerimus deo* = 'we celebrate'); *sacrificium*: *De Orat.*, 18.5; 19.1–4; *Ad Uxorem*, 2.88; *De Cult. Fem.*, II.11.2, *sacrificium offertur*, *i.e.* the eucharist is celebrated.

[41] *De Exhort. Cast.*, 11.2.

[42] *De Ieiun. ad Psych.*, 16.1.

[43] *De Pudicitia*, 11 and 16.

of Irenaeus, an advance pregnant with important possibilities for the future. He refers to the Christian minister as a priest, a *sacerdos*, and he is, as far as we know, the first Christian writer to do so. He speaks of a husband praying at the eucharist both for his dead and his living wives (a practice which offends Tertullian's susceptibilities): 'and will you offer for both of them and will you commend both of them through the priest (*sacerdotem*)?'[44] Women, says Tertullian elsewhere, are forbidden to be clergy; they may neither preach (*loqui*) nor teach (*docere*) nor baptize (*tinguere*), nor celebrate (*offerre*) 'nor take upon themselves the task of any masculine function, far less the priestly office'.[45] He can summarise Christian observance as *altare et sacerdos*,[46] and in fact both these terms occur frequently throughout his writings. But in spite of this important development Tertullian's thought does not at any point approach a doctrine of Christians, either clergy or lay, offering Christ in the eucharist. The book *Adversus Iudaeos*, whose authorship has sometimes been denied to Tertullian, at least in part, reproduces the theme of the 'pure offering', with a reference to Mal 1.10, 11, as praise and a contrite heart.[47]

IV

Apart from what can be found in his *Apostolic Tradition*, Hippolytus gives us little or no information about eucharistic offering.[48] But in the *Apostolic Tradition* there is plenty of evidence, were we but sure how to reach the original text which contains it.[49] In reproducing parts of the text I have primarily

[44] *De Exhort. Cast.* 11.2.

[45] *Nec ullius virilis muneris, nedum sacerdotalis officii, sortem sibi vindicare, De Virg. Vel.*, 11.1.

[46] *De Ieiun. ad Psych.*, 16.8.

[47] *Adversus Iudaeos*, 5.5–7. In 6.2 Christ is described as *novorum sacrificiorum sacerdos* and one who *nova sacrificia offerat*.

[48] In his *Elenchos*, I Pref. 6, he describes himself in his capacity as bishop twice as enjoying a high-priesthood (ἀρχιεράτεια), and in VI.39.2 he shows that he is aware that there is an *epiclesis* in the eucharist (*i.e.* a prayer over the elements during which the Holy Spirit is invoked).

[49] For this essay I have used *The Apostolic Tradition of St. Hippolytus* ed. G. Dix, and two works by B. Botte *La Tradition Apostolique*, Latin Text, fr.

followed Botte's edition of 1963, though I have kept an eye on the text of Dix revised by H. Chadwick. It is clear beyond any doubt that Hippolytus in this work agrees with Tertullian in regarding the bishop as a high priest and his ministry as a highpriestly one. In the model prayer for the consecration of a bishop request is made to God that the bishop may 'feed thy holy flock and serve as thine high priest ... that he may unceasingly ... propitiate thy countenance and offer to thee the gifts of thy holy church'.[50] It may be that this highpriesthood refers particularly to the bishop's power of forgiving sins, a privilege mentioned again later in the prayer of consecration[51] The model prayer for the bishop to make in the eucharist thanks God 'because thou has made us worthy to stand before thee and minister as priests to thee',[52] but this may well refer to all the people present. It is directed that the bishop alone is to ordain the deacon; the presbyter cannot do so 'because he (*i.e.*, the deacon) is not ordained for a priesthood'[53] (suggesting that the presbyter is). And in the directions about sick-visiting the bishop is again referred to as 'the high priest'.[54]

There is plenty of reference to offering in the *Apostolic Tradition*, but nowhere is there any noticeable advance on the thought of Tertullian. We have seen that part of the bishop's duty is 'to offer the gifts', but part of his duty also is to please God in meekness and a pure heart and to offer to him a sweet-smelling savour,[55] so that the doctrine of the 'pure offering'

---

trans. and *La Tradition Apostolique de Saint Hippolyte*. For references I give the chapter and then in brackets the page of Botte's ed. of 1963, followed by Dix's numbers in square brackets (*i.e.* his chapter, his page in round brackets and then his section). The English translation of this text quoted here is from the translation in Dix's edition.

[50] 3 (6–10) [*iii* (4–5(3] Botte thinks that the prayer can be reconstructed in its original Greek: the relevant words are these: ἀρχιερατεύειν σοι ἀμέμπτως, λειτουργησάντα νυκτός καί ἡμέρας, ἀδιαλείπτως τε ἱλασκέσθαι τῷ προσώπῳ σου καί προσφέρειν τὰ δῶρα τῆς ἀγίας σου ἐκκλησίας καὶ τῷ πνεύματι τῷ ἀρχιερατικῷ ἔχειν ἐξουσίαν ἀφιέναι ἀμαρτίας.

[51] 3 (10) [*iii* (5) 3].
[52] 4 (16) [*iv* (9) 11,12].
[53] 8 (22) [*ix* (15–18) 1–11].
[54] 34 (80) [*xxx* (57)] the MS L (Verona Palimpsest) has *princeps sacerdotum*.
[55] 3 (10) [*iii* (5) 3].

appears here too. The bread and wine are more than once in this work called 'the offering' (prosphora).[56] The final petition in the model prayer for the bishop to make in the eucharist includes the words 'we offer to thee the bread and the cup making eucharist to thee',[57] but the prayer for the Holy Spirit does not mention any conversion of the elements. The directions about the Paschal Mass are confused and the textual tradition uncertain, but if we follow Botte we shall reconstruct them thus:

> Alors l'oblation sera presentée par les diacres a l'évêque et il rendra graces, sur le pain (qu'il soit) le symbole (ἀντίτυπος) du corps du Christ, sur le calice de vin mélange, pour (qu'il soit) l'image (ὁμοίωμα) du sang qui a été repandu pour tous ceux qui croient en lui.[58]

And finally in one passage in the work the eucharist is directly referred to as the body of Christ while the cup is called the *antitype* of the blood of Christ.[59] Perhaps it is worth noting that at no point in the *Apostolic Tradition* as far as can be ascertained is there any mention of an altar. Hippolytus' doctrine of eucharistic offering, in short, is as conservative as most of his other theology, and the fact that his doctrine of the episcopal ministry as a priesthood shows some development has had no effect upon his doctrine of eucharistic offering.

Much the same picture can be found in the *Didascalia Apostolorum*, a work coming probably from a period later in the third century than that of Hippolytus, originally written in Greek in Syria or Palestine. It survives only in a complete Syriac translation and a fragmentary Latin one.[60] In this work we find,

[56] (10) [iv (6) 2]; 10 (30) [ix (20) 1]; 20(44[32.xx.10]—prosphora; 4 (16)[iv (9) 12]; 10 (30) [x (19) 3–4]; 21 (54) [xxxiii, 40.1]; 25 (64,66) [xxvi (51) 23,29); 33 (78) [xxix (55) 1]-oblatio. This list takes no account of those places where prosphora or oblatio is used of a non-eucharistic offering.

[57] 4 (16) [iv (9) 11].

[58] Botte p. 55, translating the Verona Latin text at 21 (54) [xxii (40) 1].

[59] 37, 38 (84) [xxxii (59) 2].

[60] See *Didascalia Apostolorum*. The Latin MS. is the same as that which gives us our Latin version of Hippolytus' *Apostolic Tradition*. The author of the fourth-century *Apostolic Constitutions* used the *Didascalia* but though an occasional Greek word or phrase can be gleaned from him he has so thoroughly reworked his source here, as elsewhere, that he is of little use.

as we did in Hippolytus, a developed doctrine of Christian priesthood but little development in its thought about eucharistic offering. The doctrine that the Christian's true sacrifice is prayer and thanksgiving appears cheek by jowl with the ascription of the title of 'high priest' to the bishop.

> Instead of the sacrifices which then were, offer now prayers and petitions and thanksgivings. Then were firstfruits and tithes and part-offerings and gifts; but to-day the oblations (Lat. *prosphorae*) which are offered through the bishop to the Lord God. For they are your high priests, but the priests and Levites now are the presbyters and deacons, and the orphans and widows; but the Levite and high priest is the bishop.[61]

The author is quite clear that the Christian now has nothing to do with sacrifices, oblations, purifications, holocausts and all the apparatus of the Jewish cult.'[62] He can use the curious phrase 'eucharist of the oblation'.[63] He declares that a poor man praying for his benefactor will be esteemed as the altar of God and he calls widows and orphans 'the altar of Christ'.[64] He thus explains the meaning of Matt 5.23 ('If though offer thy gift upon the altar . . . go first be reconciled with thy brother, and then come, offer thy gift', in his version):

> now, the gift of God is our prayer and our Eucharist. If thou then keep any malice against thy brother, or he against thee, thy prayer is not heard and thy Eucharist is not accepted; and thou shalt be found void both of prayer and of Eucharist by reason of the anger which thou keepest.[65]

We are reminded of the words of the *Didache* concerning the danger of defiling the *thysia* which we have already considered. The same thought is reproduced in a manner even more

[61] *Did.*, IX p. 86 (Eng.), p. 87 (Lat.). Connolly (not *in loc*) points out that the phrase 'they are your high priests' is a direct borrowing from the *Didache* 13:3; he does not point out that the *Didache* applies it not to bishops but to prophets. In fact bishops are referred to as high priests throughout the *Didascalia*. It should be noted that in the *Didascalia*, as in the *Apostolic Tradition*, the word 'offering' can be used in a non-eucharistic sense.

[62] IX p. 86 (Eng.), 99 (Lat.).

[63] IX p. 100 (Eng.); but this may be due to a mistranslation or mistake.

[64] XVII p. 154 (Eng.); XVIII p. 156 (Eng.).

[65] XI p. 116 (Eng.).

reminiscent of the passage in the *Didache* a little later in the *Didascalia*: 'forgive thy neighbour, that thou mayest be heard when thou prayest, and may offer an acceptable oblation unto the Lord'.[66] Finally, we must note a significant passage towards the end of the work which perhaps suggests that a development in the doctrine of eucharistic offering is at least potentially present in the *Didascalia*. 'Offer an acceptable eucharist, the likeness of the royal body of Christ . . . pure bread that is made with fire and sanctified with invocations'.[67] The Latin word which corresponds to 'likeness' is *similitudo*, and we may here accept the *Apostolic Constitutions* as a reliable guide when it gives us ἀντίτυπος as the original Greek of this word. This is not a doctrine of the offering of the body of Christ, but the text does speak of the offering of the *antitype* of the body of Christ.

The doctrine of eucharistic offering in Christian Platonists of Alexandria, Clement and Origen, does not materially differ from that which we have already reviewed, except that Origen, predictably, gives it an idiosyncratic nuance. Clement uses the word θυσία several times to express the Christian's sacrifice, and always this sacrifice is one simply of prayers. In one fragment Clement states: 'This is true priesthood and sacrifice—prayer'.[68] He devotes more space to this in the seventh book of the *Stromateis* than in any other part of his work. Sacrifice, he says, is a humble heart with right knowledge, and we ourselves, once our old man has been mortified, are the best sacrifice.[69] Later this sentence occurs: 'And indeed the sacrifice of the Church is the word sent up as incense by holy souls while all their intention is manifested to God along with the sacrifice'.[70] God does not need material sacrifices, so we give him prayer, the best sacrifice, and for Christians the word 'altar'

---

[66] XI p. 117 (Eng.).

[67] XXVI p. 252 (Eng.), 253 (Lat.). Connolly *in loc* notes that Hippolytus has already used this word in a eucharistic context.

[68] *Clemens Alexandrinus*, III p. 227, 1.8: αὕτη ἐστίν ἱερατεία· καὶ θυσία ἀληθινὴ ἡ εὐχή.

[69] *Strom.*, VII.2.14.1,2.

[70] VII.6.32.4 καὶ γάρ ἐστιν ἡ θυσία τῆς ἐκκλησίας λόγος ἀπὸ τῶν ἁγίων ψυχῶν ἀναθυμιώμενος ἐκκαλυπτομένης ἅμα τῇ θυσίᾳ καὶ τῆς διανοίας ἁπάσης τῷ θεῷ.

(θυσιαστήριον) means the gathering on earth of those who are devoted to prayer united in a common voice and mind.[71] The sacrifices of the 'Gnostic' are prayers and praises and intercessions and Psalms and hymns before the shrine of the Scriptures.[72] Then there is 'the other sacrifice', the giving of both teaching and goods to those who need them.[73] Apparently Clement does not invoke the passage in Malachi for his doctrine of eucharistic offering. He uses the word *prosphora* for the eucharist without developing a doctrine of an offering of Christ in it.[74]

As far as the doctrine of the 'pure offering' goes, Origen is entirely traditional, though he does not make much of the passage Mal 1.10, 11. He replies to Celsus' objection that Christians have no temples nor altars by agreeing that they have no such material adjuncts to worship; but 'our altars are the mind of each righteous man from which true and intelligible incense with a sweet savour is sent up, prayers from a true conscience'.[75] God needs nothing: 'he who is doing his duty is really keeping a feast; for he is always praying, continually offering bloodless sacrifices in his prayers to God'.[76] Christians have nothing to do with material sacrifices.[77] Again, throughout his work Origen refers to bishops as priests or high priests, comparing them to the high priests of the Old Testament cult.[78] He can declare that the apostles were priests and offered sacrifices.[79] He is quite ready to endorse the 'realistic' account of

[71] VII.5.3.7.

[72] VII.7.48.4.

[73] VII.7.48.5.

[74] E.g., *Strom.*, I.19.96.1; VI.14.113.3. The comparison of Melchizedek bringing bread and wine to Abraham with the eucharistic food (*Strom.*, IV.25.161.3) probably means that Christ (=Melchizedek) supplies us with food rather than that we offer food to Christ (=Abraham).

[75] *Contra Celsum*, VIII.17 (Chadwick's translation).

[76] *Ibid.*, VIII.21; the whole passage 17–22 is relevant.

[77] *Comm. on Romans* 9:1 (*PG* 14:1203–7); *Comm. on Psalm* 4:5 (*PG* 12:1148); *Hom. on Numbers* 17:1 (*PG* 12:702–3).

[78] *Hom. on Jeremiah* 12:3; *Dial. with Heracleides* p. 131 (Scherer's ed.); *Hom. on Leviticus 3:6 (PG* 12:430–1); 6:3 (*PG* 12:469–70); *Hom. on Numbers* 11:1 (*PG* 12:640–4); *Hom. on Joshua* 4:1 (*PG* 12:842–3); 8:7 (*PG* 12:869–70).

[79] *De Orat.*, 28:9.

the consecrated bread and wine which the church of his day held. He describes how Christians carefully avoid dropping any crumb of the eucharistic bread when they receive 'the body of the Lord'.[80] And the following passage is characteristic:

> But we give thanks to the Creator of the Universe and eat the loaves that are presented with thanksgiving and prayer over the gifts, so that by the prayer they become a certain holy body which sanctifies those who partake of it with a pure intention.[81]

This is the conventional doctrine of the Church presenting or offering the gifts of bread and wine in the eucharist for God to bless in order that Christians may communicate.

But, as in so many other subjects, Origen imparted to the doctrine which he had inherited his own individual interpretation which in this case did not give rise to later development, as it did in other subjects, and so must be mentioned only briefly. The priesthood of the apostles, and of their successors consists in forgiving sins and knowing what sins to forgive.[82] Their offering for sins is their power to convert sinners from the evil way, and it is done by warning, exhorting, instructing, and so on.[83] There is more than a hint throughout his work that the Christian minister's efficacy in functioning is limited by his character and by his spiritual understanding. Origen is ready to place the sacrament of hearing the word on a level with the sacrament of the eucharist and describe it as equally drinking the blood of Christ.[84] In discussing the eucharistic words and actions of Jesus at the Last Supper he can say 'Let the bread and the cup be taken by the simpler sort (τοῖς ἁπλουστέροις) according to the more usual interpretation of the eucharist, but by those who have learnt a deeper understanding according to the diviner interpretation and as referring to the nourishing Word of truth'.[85] And he can even

---

[80] *Hom. on Exodus* 13:3 (*PG* 12:389–90).

[81] *Contra Celsum*, VIII:33; cf. VIII:57, and *Fragment on 1 Corinthians* 7:5.

[82] *De Orat.*, 28:9,10.

[83] *Hom. on Leviticus*, (*PG* 12:804–5).

[84] *Hom. on Numbers*, (*PG* 12:701–2).

[85] *Comm. on John*, 32:24. Origen goes on to a long exposition of this intellectualising interpretation which has caused scholars much interest and

allegorise in a non-eucharistic sense the accounts of the institution of the eucharist.[86] Origen's deviations from traditional eucharistic doctrine are not, however, as has been noted, significant for the future course of this subject.[87] Perhaps we should notice that the scanty remains of another Christian Platonist, Dionysius of Alexandria, permit us to observe that he does not hesitate to describe the consecrated elements as the body and blood of Christ but refers to the 'table' (ἡ τρατέζη) and not as an altar.[88]

V

When we turn to consider the eucharistic offering in Cyprian we find that he has made just that move which we have found virtually all our authors hitherto stopping short of. He unequivocally regards the eucharist as an offering of Christ by the celebrant. But we must first note that the old doctrine of the Christian sacrifice as consisting of prayers and praises is also well represented in Cyprian's work. In an early work which is little more than a pastiche of some material older than Cyprian's day, the *Testimonia ad Quirinum vel Adversus Iudaeos*, Cyprian gives plenty of quotations from the Old Testamant to show that the old Jewish sacrifices were to cease and new ones consisting only of praise and prayer and good conduct were to be instituted by the Christ: Ps 50.13f and 23 (the sacrifice of praise); Ps 4.6 (the sacrifice of righteousness) and (inevitably) Mal 1.10, 11 (the pure sacrifice).[89] In his book on the Lord's Prayer he can say 'the greater sacrifice to God is our peace and brotherly harmony and

---

concern. *Cf. Comm. on Matthew* 11:14 where a not dissimilar distinction is made; and *Comm. Ser* 85. Several other examples could be adduced.

[86] *Contra Celsum*, VIII:22; *Hom. on Jeremiah*, 19:13.

[87] Several other passages could also be adduced in both Clement and Origen where apparently or potentially eucharistic passages are treated in a non-eucharistic way.

[88] *The Letters and Other Remains of Dionysius of Alexandria*, V.5 (p. 58) and XIV (p. 103).

[89] *Test. ad Quirinum*, I:16. All quotations from Cyprian are taken from the edition of G. Hartel, except for quotations from his *Letters*, which are from the edition of L. C. Bayard. All translations of Cyprian are mine.

a people united in the union of Father and Son and Holy Spirit',[90] and also that Paul at Phil 4.18 speaks of 'the activities which become sacrifices to God' (*opera quae fiunt sacrificia Deo*), and that he who gives to the poor and the little ones 'spiritually sacrifices sweetly odours to God'.[91] Even at the very end of his life, Cyprian can comfort bishops who are suffering in the mines during the Valerian persecution with the thought that they need not hanker after the eucharist which they cannot celebrate because they are offering themselves as an acceptable sacrifice in substitution.[92]

In this early work *Testimonia* we can find the kind of traditional eucharistic doctrine which Cyprian has inherited and which he has not yet had time to modify. One of its headings runs *quod panem et calicem* (not body and blood) *Christi et omnem gratiam eius amissuri essent Iudaei nos vero accepturi*.[93] Another runs *sacrificia malorum accepta non esse*, and its proof-text is from Eccles 34.19 (23) *dona iniquorum non probat Altissimus*, which appears to reproduce the old theology of the eucharist as an offering of gifts. Another heading reads *surgendum cum episcopus aut presbyter veniat*, and the proof-text is in Leviticus: *A facie senioris exurges et honorabis personam presbyteri* (Lev 19.32).[94] This certainly seems to imply a doctrine of ministry which does not appeal for its Old Testament support to the precedent of the cultic sacrificing priest in the Law.

But once Cyprian had become bishop of Carthage he adopted the most advanced and sacerdotal doctrine of the ministry and, bound up with it, a correspondingly developed doctrine of the eucharist. He regularly describes bishops, and sometimes presbyters, as *sacerdotes*.[95] This is not a drastic doctrine in the middle of the third century. The bishops in the *Sententiae Episcoporum* use the word quite freely, and so does the

[90] *De Dominica Oratione*, 23.

[91] *Ibid.*, 33.

[92] *Letters*, 76.3.1,2.

[93] *Testimonia*, I:22; *cf.* II:2 where the word *craterem* which Cyprian never uses elsewhere betrays a source.

[94] *Ibid.*, III: 111; III: 85.

[95] *Letters*, 1.1.7 *Divino sacerdotio honorati et in clerico ministerio constituti* apparently applies to presbyters, and this is not the only example.

Vita Pontii of Cyprian.[96] But Cyprian makes it quite clear that he is not using the word *sacerdos* in any general or ill-defined sense. The same sacrosanctity applies to bishops as applied to the priests of the Temple cult at Jerusalem, so that it is a serious sin to attack them or hurt them. Death, and the kind of death meted out to Korah, Dathan and Abiram, is to be expected from the hand of God by people who sin in this way.[97] He closely connects the altar and the priesthood:

> God is one and Christ is one and one church and one chair (*cathedra*) has been founded on Peter by the Lord's utterance. Another altar cannot be set up nor a new priesthood come into being save the one altar and the one priesthood.[98]

Elsewhere Cyprian says that if Cornelius bishop of Rome were to give way to the followers of Felicissimus, nothing would remain but that images and idols should be set up among gatherings of the clergy 'with the priests retreating and removing the altar of the Lord'.[99]

With this doctrine of priesthood is associated Cyprian's doctrine of eucharistic sacrifice. His regular word for the eucharist is *sacrificium* or *oblatio*.[100] In this he is not moving significantly beyond the thought of Tertullian.[101] In his sixty-third letter, however, Cyprian enunciates at some length a doctrine of eucharistic sacrifice and offering which goes far beyond that of Tertullian. He is in this letter concerned to emphasise that both wine and water must be used at the eucharist. The bishops must do in the eucharist what Christ did

---

[96] *Vita Pontii* 3 uses it of the presbyterate, and even (9,11) calls Cyprian *pontifex*, a title he never uses himself.

[97] *Letters*, 3.1.1,2 and 2.1 and 3.1; 4.4.3; 59.4.1 and 13.5; 61.3.2,3; 65.2.1; 73.8.1.

[98] *Letters*, 43.5.2.

[99] *Letters*, 59.18.1; *cf.* 61.2.3.

[100] E.g., *Letters*, 1.2.1. *nec sacrificium pro dormitione celebraretur;* 1.2.2. *fiat oblatio.* There are many other examples.

[101] And we may notice the expressions *sacrificium offeret* and *altare et sacrificium constituat* in the letter of Firmilian of Cappadocia to Cyprian, *Letters*, 75.10.5 and 17.2, though I have long regarded this letter as suspiciously Cyprianic in its wording.

and taught.[102] Here the cup is offered (*calix offertur*) in commemoration of him and in this cup is 'his blood by which we were redeemed and quickened' (2.1, 2). Christ offered his body and blood as a sacrifice for us (4.1). Consequently:

> it is clear that the blood of Christ is not offered if the wine is not in the cup nor the Lord's sacrifice celebrated with a valid consecration unless our offering and sacrifice corresponds to the Passion.[103]

The next part of the letter is taken up with an exposition of the significance of the water in the cup which Cyprian takes to symbolise the presence of the people with and in Christ, and here Cyprian seems to retain some elements of the traditional doctrine of the offering of bread and wine made so that the people may communicate with Christ (11.1—13.4). Soon after he comes to this conclusion:

> For if Christ Jesus our Lord and God is himself the high priest of God the Father and first offered himself as a sacrifice to the Father and ordered that this should be done in commemoration of him, then of course that priest functions rightly in the place of Christ (*vice Christi*) who imitates what Christ did and offers in the Church the full and true sacrifice, if he so begins to offer according to what he sees Christ himself to have offered.[104]

And a little later (17.1) he explains that 'because we make mention of his passion in all our sacrifices, for the passion of the Lord is the sacrifice which we offer, we ought to do nothing else than what he did'; we are assured by Scripture that whenever we offer the cup in commemoration of the passion of Christ we are doing what it is agreed that the Lord did. Cyprian's doctrine of the priesthood and of the ministry have here joined to produce a new and startling doctrine of eucharist offering pregnant with important consequences for the future. The bishop, as a cultic sacrificing priest, offers Christ himself.

Two pseudo-Cyprianic third-century works composed in

[102] *Letters*, 63.1.1.
[103] 9.3 *unde apparet sanguinem Christi non offerri si desit vinum calici nec sacrificium dominicum legitima santificatione celebrari nisi oblatio et sacrificium nostrum responderit passioni.*
[104] 14.4.

Africa show the influence of this development made by Cyprian. The little tract *De Aleatoribus* three times refers to the eucharist as *sacrificium Christi*.[105] And the work *Ad Vigilium episcopum de Iudaea incredulitate* describes the episcopal office as *constituit altario sacerdotem* and *honorem sacerdotii caelestis*.[108]

On the other hand, it is remarkable to find Lactantius, who came from Africa and who lived fifty years after Cyprian's day, displaying no influence from Cyprian whatever. He is perfectly ready to call clergy *sacerdotes*, but this was by his time a commonplace. Lactantius reproduces the doctrine that the Christian offering and sacrifice is nothing but prayer and a pure mind in its strongest form. He says of pagan worshippers:

> They offer to their gods nothing suitable, not purity of mind, not reverence, not fear ... Our religion is stable in this ... that it has the mind itself as a sacrifice. With them nothing else is demanded beyond the blood of cattle and smoke and futile libation: with us, a good mind, a pure heart, an innocent life.[109]

Shortly afterwards he declares that 'This is the true cult in which the mind of the worshippers offers itself as a spotless victim to God'.[110] A little later in a fine rhetorical passage he defines sacrifice as works of mercy:

> Use the money with which you buy beasts for ransoming prisoners, use the funds for feeding wild animals for supporting the poor, turn the resources from which you support gladiators for burying the innocent dead ... Transform into a great sacrifice what is destined to perish miserably, so that in exchange for these genuine gifts you may have an eternal gift from God. The reward for compassion is great in the case of a man to whom God promises that he will forgive all his sins.[111]

[105] *De Aleatoribus*, 4 (96); 5 (97); 8 (101).

[108] *Ad Vigilium*, 9 (130,131); this work is really only a preface to the Latin translation of the *Dialogue of Jason and Papiscus*.

[109] *Div. Inst.*, V.19.27,30 (466-7) my translation as in all quotations from Lactantius. It should be noted that Lactantius does, however, describe the eucharist in the same passage as a *sacrificium*, but presumably just such a one as he has described.

[110] *Ibid.*, VI.2. 13 (484).

[111] VI.12. 39,40,41 (531–2).

Towards the end of this sixth book of the *Divine Institutes*
Lactantius sums up this doctrine in drastic and emphatic words:

> Whoever therefore obeys all these heavenly commands is a
> worshipper of the true God, whose sacrifices are gentleness of
> mind and an innocent life and good actions. Whoever manifests
> all these, sacrifices as often as he performs any good and pious act.
> For God does not want a victim consisting of a dumb animal nor
> its death nor its blood, but that of a man and his life . . . And so
> there is placed on the altar of God, which is really the Great Altar
> and which cannot be defiled because it is situated in man's heart,
> righteousness,   patience,   faith,   innocence,   chastity,
> temperance',[112]

Only two things can be offered to God who is incorruptible,
themselves incorruptible, *donum* and *sacrificium, donum* forever
sacrificum temporarily. Here the reader may think that at last he
will find a reference to the offering of the bread and wine in the
eucharist, but not a bit of it. *Donum est integritas animi: sacrificium
laus et hymnus* (25.7 (578)). And Lactantius adds to this
pronouncement some very curious details. 'We indeed worship
when we give thanks; for the sacrifice of this (worship) simply
consists in blessing (*huius enim sacrificium sola benedictio*). And this
is right, for sacrifice ought to be made to God by word, in that
God is the Word, as he himself has proclaimed'. All we need ask
of God is goodness and forgiveness, nothing else. God himself
knows what we want anyway. There is no need for a temple in
this worship which can be done just as well at home: *secum
denique habeat deum semper in corde suo consecratum, quoniam ipse est
dei templum*.[113] Here, most surprisingly, at the turn of the third to
the fourth century is a doctrine of offering which not only
excludes the possibility of men offering Christ in the eucharist
but appears to end in a completely non-eucharistic account of
the subject. Arnobius, though he makes it quite plain that any
form of material sacrifices are unpleasing to God, and indeed
insulting, has left us in his extant work no doctrine of eucharistic
sacrifice.[114] In the world of Greek theology a contemporary of

---

[112] VI.24. 27,28,29 (576–7).
[113] All these quotations and summaries come from VI.25. 16 (578–80).
[114] Arnobius *Adversus Nationes*, 4:31; 6:1; 7:4.

Lactantius and Arnobius, Methodius of Olympus, reproduces
the doctrine of 'pure offering', as far as can be determined from
the extant text, in a context which may be eucharistic but where
he clearly distinguishes between the eucharistic elements and
'the offering of the mind, a rational sacrifice, spiritual gifts'.[114a]

VI

We end this survey by looking at the doctrine of eucharistic
sacrifice in an author who devoted a good deal of attention to it,
Eusebius of Caesarea. We shall find that though his thought
represents a development he has not advanced the subject as far
as Cyprian had. On the subject of the 'pure sacrifice' Eusebius is
uncompromising and abundant. In his *Praeparatio Evangelica* he
declares that we are not meant to worship God with animal
sacrifices or wreaths or wooden idols, but on the contrary with
'thoughts that have been purified and right and true ideas . . .
with a soul free from passion' and with the greatest possible
virtue,[115] and later he says that in Christian church buildings
suitable sacrifices (θυσίας) are being offered to God, *i.e.* 'prayers
of holy men offered with a will cleared of all evil in calm of soul
and with the practice of every virtue', and these are the sacrifices
pleasing and acceptable to almighty God.[116] In his *Demonstratio
Evangelica* he expands this theme further. He quotes the
traditional text, Mal 1.11 and defines this 'pure offering':

> to offer up to the God of all the incense of prayers and the
> sacrifice not made in blood but what is called pure, consisting of
> pious actions.[117]

[114a] Uncertainty arises because the passage is only extant in an Old Slavonic
version, and what is here given is my English translation of the editor's
German translation of the Old Slavonic translation of Methodius' original
Greek (*De Resurrectione*, III.23, p. 422).

[115] Eusebius Caesariensis *Praeparatio Evangelica*, III.13.24. All translations
from Eusebius in this paper are my own.

[116] *Ibid.* IV.4.

[117] *Demonstratio Evangelica*, I.6.44 (29–30) τὸ δι' εὐχῶν θυμίαμα καὶ τὴν οὐ
δι' αἱμάτων ἀλλὰ δι' ἔργων εὐσεβῶν καθαρὰν ὠνομασμένην θυσίαν τῷ
ἐπὶ πᾶσιν ἀναφέρειν θεῷ; *cf.* I.6.50. (30).

And in a passage reminiscent of Lactantius he says that each man now offers, not in Jerusalem, nor with animal and bloody sacrifice, but 'at home and in his own place the unbloody and pure worship in spirit and in truth'.[118] And later still he claims that those among the Christians who renounce the world perform their sacred service (ἱερουργίαν) not by animal sacrifices, libations nor incense, but 'by right ideas of true piety, and with the soul in a purified condition and further by actions and words consistent with virtue'.[119]

But Eusebius does not neglect the subject of eucharistic sacrifice proper. He devotes a long section of the *Demonstratio Evangelica* to it (I.10.1–I.10.38 (43.49)). The ancients, both Hebrews and other nations, certainly did sacrifice from the beginning. But what they offered did not affect the reasoning and spiritual essence (λογικῆς νοερᾶς οὐσίας, 11 (45)) of men, only their physical life (1–ll (43–45)). Christ made the final and effective sacrifice, superseding all others (14–17 (45)), and this Christians rightly commemorate, 'celebrating daily the memorial of his body and his blood',[120] Christ was worthy alone to represent God to man and man to God and offered his human nature to God (23 (47)), and left a memorial to us to offer continually to God 'instead of a sacrifice'.[121] This was destined to supersede all the sacrifices of the Jewish cult, and we have now received the injuction 'to celebrate the memorial of this sacrifice at a table through the symbols (συμβόλων) of his body and of his saving blood according to the ordinances of the new convenant' (28 (47)). The 'holy sacrifices of Christ's table' (σεμνὰ θύματα) are those in which we offer 'bloodless and reasonable sacrifices appropriate to him through all our lives to the God of all', through our high priest Christ.[122] Eusebius

---

[118] I.6.57 (32); *cf.* 65 (33); and *Vita Constantini*, 1:48.

[119] I.8.2 (39); *cf.* III.3.8. (110–11), and the statement in *Laus Constantini*, 2:5 that Constantine offers the most acceptable sacrifice to God, his own soul and mind.

[120] τοῦ τε σώματος καὶ τοῦ αἵματος τὴν ὑπόμνησιν ὁσημέραι ἐπιτελοῦντες, 18 (46).

[121] ἀντὶ θυσίας 25 (47).

[122] 29 (48); *cf.* ταύτας τὰς ἀσωμάτους καὶ νοεράς θυσίας 33 (48) and θυσίας ἀναίμους, the eucharist, *Vita Constantini*, 4:48.

finally introduces again the concept of the 'pure offering' of a good character. We sacrifice 'the sacrifice of praise', the pure sacrifice of the new covenant, the 'contrite spirit' of Ps 51.17 (36 (49)) and we offer this through our prayers (37 (49)). And he summarises the whole matter concisely thus:

> therefore we both sacrifice and burn incense: on the one hand we celebrate the memorial of the great sacrifice according to the mysteries handed down to us by him, and we proffer thanksgiving for our salvation through pious hymns and prayers to God; on the other hand we dedicate ourselves to him alone and to his high-priestly word, devoted in body and soul (38 (49)).

And Eusebius returns to this theme once more when he says later: 'First our Saviour and Lord himself then all priests (ἱερεῖς) throughout all nations, deriving from him, perform their spiritual cultic service (ἱερουργίαν) according to the Church's regulations and accomplish their mysterious rites (αἰνίττονται τὰ μυστήρια) of his body and of his saving blood with wine and bread'.[123] This carefully formulated account is not the doctrine of the offering of Christ to God in the eucharist. At most it is the offering of the memorial or of the symbols of his body and blood.[124] Eusebius was a more careful and better educated theologian than Cyprian. He foresaw the embarrassment likely to arise in a doctrine which began by ostentatiously disavowing all sacrifice, including Jewish sacrifices, and ended by embracing something very like a Christianised version of the Jewish sacrificial system. He was aware, as was his master Origen, of the 'realistic' interpretation of the consecrated elements held by the Church of his day, and assented to it. But he realised that it must not be allowed, in combination with a strong and relatively recent doctrine of Christian priesthood, to overshadow the early, traditional doctrine of the 'pure sacrifice', and he made an intelligent attempt to hold these doctrines in a proper balance. Later ages were not to be so careful nor so nice.

---

[123] *Dem. Ev.*, V.3.19 (222).
[124] Cf. *ibid.*, VIII.1.80 (366): ἄρτῳ συμβόλῳ τοῦ ἰδίου σώματος.

LIST OF SOURCES

Aristides *Apologia*, ed. E. J. Goodspeed. Die Ältesten Apologeten (Göttingen 1914)

Arnobius *Adversus Nationes*, ed. A. Reifferscheid (C S E L ser Vienna 1875).

Athenagoras *Supplicatio*, ed. E. J. Goodspeed, *ut supra.*

Barnabas, Epistle of, ed. K. Lake, The Apostolic Fathers (Loeb ser London 1948).

Clemens Alexandrinus *Opera*, ed. O. Stählin (G C S ser Leipsig 1936).

Clement, First Epistle of, ed. K. Lake *ut supra.*

Cyprian Letters, ed. L. C. Bayard (Budé ser Paris Tom. I 1945, Tom II 1925); Other works *Opera Omnia*, ed. G. Hartel (C S E L ser Vienna 1868).

Didache, ed. K. Lake *ut supra.*

Didascalia Apostolorum, ET of Syriac version and Verona Latin fragments ed. R. H. Connolly (Oxford 1929).

Dionysius of Alexandria *Letters and Other Remains*, ed. C. L. Feltoe (Cambridge 1904).

Eusebius of Caesarea *Preparatio Evangelica*, ed. K. Mras (G C S ser Berlin 1945); *Demonstratio Evangelica*, ed. I. A. Heikel (G C S ser Berlin 1913); *Vita Constantini* and *Laus Constantini*, ed. I. A. Heikel (G C S ser Berlin 1902).

Hermas *The Shepherd*, ed. Molly Whittaker (G C S ser Berlin 1967).

Hippolytus *Elenchos*, ed. P. Wendland (G C S ser Leipsig 1916); *Apostolic Tradition*, ed. with E T, G. Dix (London 1937, rev. H. Chadwick 1968); also ed. with French tr. B. Botte (Liturgie-Wissenschaftliche Quellen und Forsch. Münster 1963).

Irenaeus *Libri quinque Adversus Hareses*, ed. W. W. Harvey (Cambridge 1859) and Book IV (Armenian and Latin texts) ed. A. Rousseau *et al.* (Sources Chrét. ser Paris 1961).

Justin Martyr *Dialogue*, ed. E. J. Goodspeed *ut supra.*

Kerestzes, P., 'The Jews, the Christians and the Emperor Domitian', *Vigiliae Christianae* 27 (1973) 1–28.

Lactantius *Opera Omnia*, ed. S. Brandt and G. Laubmann (C S E L ser Vienna 1890).

Methodius of Olympus *Opera*, ed. G. Bonwetsch (G S C ser Leipsig 1917).

Minucius Felix *Octavius*, ed. G. H. Rendall (Loeb ser London 1931).

Murray, R. *Symbols of the Church and Kingdom* (Cambridge 1975).

Odes and Psalms of Solomon, ed. J. Rendel Harris (Cambridge 1909), and also *Odes of Solomon*, ed. with E T, J. H. Charlesworth (Oxford 1973).

Oracula Sibyllina, ed. J. Geffcken (G C S ser Leipsig 1902).

Origen *Contra Celsum*, ed. P. Koetschau (G C S ser Berlin 1899); E. T. H. Chadwick (Cambridge 1953); *Dialogue with Heracleides*, ed. J. Scherer (Cairo 1949); *Commentary on John*, ed. A. E. Brooke (Cambridge 1896); *Commentary on Matthew* and *Comm. Series*, ed. E. Klostermann (G C S ser Berlin 1933, 1935, 1941–5); *De Oratione*, ed. P. Koetschau (G C S ser Berlin 1899); *Homilies on Jeremiah*, ed. E. Klostermann (G C S ser Leipsig 1901); *Commentary on Romans* Migne *Patrologia Graeca* 14; *Commentary on Psalms*, *Homilies on Leviticus*, *Homilies on Joshua*, *Homilies on Numbers*, *Homilies on Exodus*, Migne *PG* 12; *Fragments on I Corinthians*, ed. C. Jenkins J. T. S. OS IX (1908) 231–47,353–72,500–14; X (1909) 29–51.

Ptolemy *Letter to Flora* Migne *PG* 7.

Sentences of Sextus, ed. H. Chadwick (Cambridge 1959).

Tertullian *Opera Omnia* in Corpus Christianorum ser; *Apologeticum*, ed. J. P. Waltzing Budé ser (Paris 1961).

7

THE LIBERTY OF THE BISHOP TO IMPROVISE PRAYER IN THE EUCHARIST

The earliest clear indication that in the eucharist of the early church the bishop was at liberty to improvise in making the long prayer (later to be called the anaphora) after the offerings of bread and wine had been brought to him is perhaps to be found in Justin Martyr's *First Apology* (67.5). Here, in his description of the normal Sunday eucharist, Justin says: καὶ ὁ προεστὼς εὐχὰς ὁμοίως καὶ εὐχαριστίας, ὅση δύναμις αὐτῷ, ἀναπέμπει, καὶ ὁ λαὸς ἐπευφημεῖ λέγων τὸ'Ἀμήν. Here the phrase ὅση δύναμις αὐτῷ suggests that the contents and expression of the prayer of the 'president' (who is clearly the bishop) are determined by his ability. Next, Irenaeus in his *Adversus Haereses* (1.7.2) tells us that in his juggling pseudo-eucharist the heretic Marcus ποτήρια οἴνῳ κεκραμένα προσποιούμενος εὐχαριστεῖν, καὶ ἐπὶ πλέον ἐκτείνων τὸν λόγον τῆς ἐπικλήσεως. This suggests that the celebrant could decide the length of the great prayer, unless Marcus arrogated to himself the right of improvising prayer as well as the right of producing faked miracles during the eucharist. Not much later Tertullian says that Christians pray *manibus expansis, quia innocuis, capite nudo, quia non erubescimus, denique sine monitore, quia de pectore oramus* ('with hands outstretched because they are innocent, with head uncovered, because we are not ashamed, finally without a prompter because we pray from the heart'). In official ceremonies of the Roman religion, a prompter would be employed on public occasions to ensure that the proper formulae were correctly repeated. Tertullian is speaking of praying for the Emperor, and it seems likely that he is referring to Christian public prayer, i.e. the celebration of the eucharist, because nobody could imagine that a *monitor* would be required in private prayer (*Apologeticus* 30.4). The *Apostolic Tradition* of Hippolytus provides very clear evidence on this point (ed. and tr. G. Dix, 10.4, 5). It tells us: 'It is not altogether necessary for him (i.e. the bishop) to recite the very same words which we gave before as though studying to say them by heart (ἀπὸ στήθους) in his thanksgiving to God, but let each one pray according to his own ability. If indeed he is able to pray suitably with a grand and elevated prayer, this is a good thing. But if on the other hand he should pray and recite a prayer according to a fixed form, no one should prevent him. Only let his prayer be correct and right (ὀρθόδοξος).'

Perhaps thirty years later Origen gives us a particularly interesting piece of evidence. In the *Conversation with Heracleides*, which is the report by an eyewitness of a conference between Origen and some bishops in a town in Arabia, about the year 246, Origen is reported as describing the right formula for making the offering to God in the eucharist: ἀεὶ προσφορὰ γίνεται Θεῷ παντοκράτορι διὰ 'Ιησοῦ Χριστοῦ, ὡς προσφόρου τῷ Πατρὶ τὴν θεότητα αὐτοῦ· μὴ δὶς ἀλλὰ Θεῷ διὰ Θεοῦ προσφορὰ γινέσθω. τολμηρὸν δόξω λέγειν, εὐχόμενοι ἐμμένειν ταῖς συνθήκαις· ἐὰν μὴ γένηται, οὐ μὴ λήμψῃ πρόσωπον ἀνθρώπου οὐδὲ θαυμάσεις πρόσωπον δυνάστου (Lev 19.15). The text then becomes so corrupt as to be incapable of restoration (ed. J. Scherer, pp. 126 and 128). But it is clear enough that Origen is pleading with the bishops present, whose eccentric, if not heretical, views, had caused Origen's presence at the conference, not to introduce their own peculiar ideas into the prayer which they make at the eucharist. It is also clear that there were 'conventions' (σύνθηκαι) which the bishop was expected, but was not compelled, to use in composing his prayer.

About ten years later, in his *De Unitate Ecclesiae* (17), Cyprian denounces schismatics in general and Novatianists in particular because among them the bishop *constituere audet aliud altare, precem alteram illicitis vocibus facere, dominicae hostiae veritatem per falsa sacrificia profanare*. *Prex* with Cyprian very often means the anaphora prayer. *Illicitis vocibus* is not likely to mean that the schismatic introduces improvised prayer where fixed liturgical prayer was proper, but rather it suggests that he introduces into his prayer as he celebrates his own peculiar views. The letter of Firmilian, bishop of Cappadocian Caesarea, to Cyprian, a Latin translation of which appears as no. 75 among the letters of Cyprian, gives interesting details about a woman in his part of the world who, under the influence of Montanism, made herself a church leader and even celebrated the eucharist. She was so daring, says Firmilian, *ut et invocatione non contemptibili sanctificare se panem et eucharistiam facere simularet et sacrificium Domino non sine sacramento solitae praedicationis offerret, baptizaret quoque multos usitata et legitima verba interrogationis usurpans, ut nihil discrepere ab ecclesiastica regula videretur* (Letter 75.10.5). It seems likely that *invocatione non contemptibili* refers to the bishop's prayer of the anaphora, and that this woman could compose a prayer whose style and content were not discreditable. *Sacramentum solitae praedicationis* then would refer to the homily, and *ecclesiastica regula* would refer, not to the church's rule of faith, but to the church's custom in baptizing. It is remarkable to find here that the rite which by this time possesses a complete liturgy is the rite of baptism,—not of the eucharist (*usitata et legitima verba* might be translated 'customary and orthodox words'). Another letter of Cyprian's (70.2.1) in discussing the ceremony of unction after baptism uses the phrase *creaturam olei*, which suggests the archaic or elevated language of a fragment of liturgy; it is therefore not unlikely that a fixed form for administering baptism did exist by the middle of the third century.

Finally Dionysius of Alexandria supplies us with a small piece of evidence which may be relevant. In his *Examination and Defence* written against the imputation of heresy made against him by Dionysius of Rome, he describes how he ends his prayer in the eucharist: 'In consistency with all these arguments we also, having of course received a formula and rule from the men of old before us, harmoniously with them, when we end our eucharistic prayer προσευχαριστοῦντες—and here we are formally instructing you—terminate it: To God the Father, and to the Son our Lord Jesus Christ, with the Holy Spirit, glory and power for ever and ever. Amen' (*Remains of Dionysius of Alexandria*, ed. C. L. Feltoe, p. 198 (*Examination and Defence* 14), quoted from Basil *De Spiritu Sancto* 29 (73)). The fact that Dionysius emphasizes that he ends his prayer with a fixed formula may perhaps imply that the rest of the prayer is not fixed. The ending is perhaps among the 'conventions'.

It is therefore reasonable to conclude that at latest from the middle of the second century, and no doubt from the very beginning too, till at earliest the middle of the third century, and probably till a much later date than that, the celebrant at the eucharist was at liberty to compose his own anaphora prayer if he liked, though the reference from Hippolytus' *Apostolic Tradition* makes it clear that, at any rate in the third century, he could use a fixed form if he chose. But if he improvised, he was expected to 'keep the conventions'. There was a conventional structure for this prayer. We may guess that this structure included most of the subjects which later became essential parts of the anaphora, mention of the creation, the redemption, the resurrection and ascension, and a rehearsal of the words of institution. The early church, in fact, seems to have for a time worked out an attractive compromise between the use of free prayer and the use of fixed forms of prayer.

This liberty of the bishop to improvise may also, in part at least, account for the relative scarcity of copies of ancient liturgies. The earliest complete liturgy which survices the so-called Clementine Liturgy in the *Apostolic Constitutions*, which dates from the second half of the fourth century. Many liturgical fragments and isolated forms dating from an earlier period can be found, but no complete liturgy. The reason may well be that before the fourth century there were no complete liturgies, or almost none. Where it is perfectly legitimate for the celebrant to abandon fixed forms and, within discreet limits, improvise his own prayer at the most important part of the service, there is not much point in laboriously compiling copies of complete liturgies which can be no more than hypothetical or permissive.

8

OFFICE AND THE CONCEPT OF OFFICE IN THE EARLY CHURCH

I Introduction To The Problem

i. The problem of ministry regarded as an office in the early Church, as distinct from the problem of the form of the ministry itself, did not, owing to historical circumstances, present itself to the minds of theologians, apart from some of the radical Reformers in the sixteenth century and a few later groups, such as the Society of Friends, until the nineteenth century. But the thorough re-examination of all Christian orgins and institutions necessitated by the development of historical studies in the last century brought this subject to the fore. It was, of course, almost always associated with discussion of the development of the ministry and of the form of the ministry, but it was, and remains, formally and logically a distinct subject. Those scholars who in the second half of the nineteenth century devoted themselves to an examination of the development of Christian doctrine soon found themselves confronted with the need of explaining how and why an official, in contrast to an informal or sporadic or purely occasional and functional, ministry had developed in the early Church. By an official ministry, this article intends to denote a ministry in which the ministers are regarded as holding an office, that is a permanent function in which they can be succeeded by others and to which they are appointed or ordained by some ecclesiastical authority other than themselves. Appointment, continuity and succession are the essence of office. Historical investigation soon made it clear that such an official ministry could not at least be unquestioningly assumed to have existed from the earliest moment in every part of the Church. How far, if at all, it did exist from the earliest period, by what authority and deriving from what origins, or, if it represented a development, how it developed and whether it was a proper or a disastrous development, became a matter of serious investigation and debate.

To some scholars, such as Edwin Hatch and Adolf von Harnack, the development of an official ministry was regarded as a symptom of the Hellenization of Christianity. For Harnack in particular, who was greatly influenced by the discovery of the Didache, the emergence of the official ministry was the result of the victory of the local official concerned with administration and jurisdiction over the general, wandering, charismatic and unofficial apostle or prophet, who functioned, not because he had been ordained or appointed to an office, but because he had a gift or talent, a *charisma*, given him by God to exercise wherever he could. Out of this victory grew 'Frühkatholizismus', in which the place of charismatic lay teachers was taken by the norm of apostolic doctrine and of the apostolic canon of Scripture and by subjection to the authority of the apostolic office. Christian preaching was carried into the Hellenistic world of thought, worked into a philosophic body of doctrine, and subjected to the control of a hierarchy. The view of Rudolf Sohm were more drastic. His attitude can be summarised in a single sentence: 'Das Wesen der Kirchenrechts steht mit dem Wesen der Kirche in Widerspruch'. For him the Church was originally, and should always have been, a purely religious, purely spiritual organization. Legal authority contradicts spiritual authority. The only force that should work in it is *agape*, which confers charisms variously on various people so that no bearers of a spiritual gift have a right to office and no function can be permanent nor entail succession. The Church obeys a living, not a dead Word, and is therefore not bound to the past. Under various pressures—lack of charismatic leaders, increasing bureaucracy, needs created by the development of the eucharist, and by possession of church property and the existence of church discipline—there appeared permanent Church officials, the objectivisation of piety, legalisation, the emergence of a clergy contrasted with laity, the control of *charisma* by officials. But the chief cause of this development was original sin, lack of faith, the desire for supports, guarantees, infallibility, visible divine assurance, impressive ritual, a fixed body of doctrine explaining everything, in a word the system of Dostoievsky's Grand Inquisitor. 'The natural man is a born Catholic.'

These views contained much valuable criticism and permanent insight, and they were widely influential. Indeed from about 1880 to 1930 it was the assumption of a great many Protestant scholars that the organization of the Christian community was primarily political and human and not divine nor hierarchical. Many ideas dear to the heart of Liberal Protestantism were congenial to this outlook. The doctrine of 'the priesthood of all believers' was much favoured by this school of thought, and the nineteenth century idea of a democratic, bourgeois, free individualism played its part too. In English-speaking countries such ideas found particular support among scholars so diverse as W. R. Inge and John Oman. The outer form of the Church was regarded as unimportant, in comparison with its inner spirit. The relation of the individual soul to Christ was all that mattered. Some scholars (particularly Anglicans such as Hastings Rashdall and B. H. Streeter) regarded with favour the picture of Catholicism gradually developing during the early centuries. Others (particularly Lutherans) regarded the appearance of 'Frühkatholizismus' as a fall or corruption.

This account of the emergence of an official ministry had always been vigorously opposed in some quarters, notably, as was to be expected, by Roman Catholic scholars. Loisy had subjected it to powerful criticism and Batiffol had defended the traditional view with wide-ranging scholarship. And from about 1930 onwards a change came over scholarly opinion on the subject. A new emphasis in theology, influenced by the Liturgical Movement in the Roman Catholic Church and beyond its borders, and by contemporary collective, corporate and even totalitarian concepts of society, began to conceive of the Church as God-given, a part of salvation, organic not a mere aggregate of individuals, supernatural, eschatological, from above. Simultaneously the emphasis in New Testament study shifted to focus attention on the preaching of the primitive Church rather than on the words and deeds of the Jesus of history. The concept of ministry as an office was more congenial to this attitude; the individualism which appeared to be part of the concept of a purely charismatic or personalist Church was contrasted unfavourably with the Pauline and Johannine corporate or organic accounts of the Church. Not only Roman Catholics such as Emil Mersch but Anglicans such as K. E. Kirk (whose bulky symposium *The Apostolic Ministry* represented the last major effort of Anglo-Catholic scholarship), Leonard Thornton and A. M. Ramsey, and Methodists such as Newton Flew and the Scandinavian Lutheran Stig Hanson joined in this new approach to the subject. Some of them found it possible to defend with the apparatus of modern scholarship the view that ministry was an office originally instituted by Christ or his apostles.

More recently the subject has been treated, in accordance with the trend of most branches of scholarship, with greater academic rigour and precision, and two scholars in particular, the Swiss Edouard Schweizer and the German Heinrich von Campenhausen, have made major contributions to it. It remains a problem, that is a subject which has by no means been exhausted and which will continue for the indefinite future to present a situation where it seems almost impossible to reconcile all the facts in a single coherent and convincing account, and one which is by no means irrelevant to the theological issues of the present day. The problem as it appears in the New Testament has been dealt with in another article. But all students of the subject admit that the critical point for the development of ministry as an office occurred in the second rather than the first century. There is therefore justification for considering the subject as it develops during the second and third centuries, and this development will form the theme of the rest of this article.

ii. Certain assumptions underlie the treatment of the subject in this article, assumptions which are not arbitrarily chosen nor, it is to be hoped, dictated by denominational prejudice, but which are forced on the writer by the evidence itself. The first assumption is that the historic, traditional ministry of the Church is a development. It was not instituted by Jesus nor by his apostles. The witness of the earliest documents of the New Testament, the letters of St. Paul, is decisive here, as interpreted by E. Schweizer, by S. Hanson and above all by H. von Campenhausen. The other major assumption is that the fluidity and wide-ranging use and meaning of the terms chosen by the Church to describe its main official ministries make the search for predecessors of these ministries in Jewish institutions and in

Greek or other pagan society an almost completely futile one. Inspector (*episcopus*), assistant (*diaconus*), older man (*presbyteros*)—these are names of such wide use and general application that scholars ought to be convinced that they were chosen to describe new and untraditional functions rather than that they were modifications or re-interpretations of offices or functions already existing in Jewish or pagan society. The extraordinarily wide range of suggestions as to the origin of the office of bishop made by scholars in the last hundred years should be sufficient to convince readers of this point: financial officer (Hatch); exponent of the self-contained community (Harnack); understudy for the charismatic teacher (Sohm); the person chosen to lead prayer according to Jewish custom (Linton); the descendant of the *m*ᶜ*baqqer* (Josephus' *epitropes* or *epimeletes*) of the Qumran Community (Gaster and more cautiously Reicke); the Jewish *shaliah* (Dix); the Jewish High Priest (Ehrhardt); the Jewish *s*ᶜ*mikah* (Lohse and Campenhausen). Theories of the origin of an office as fluid and ductile as this one can never be more than theories. As far as the official ministries of the Church were concerned, the Church took whatever materials it found most suited to its purposes lying ready to hand, and that material carried with it no compelling theological tradition.

II   The Development Of The Ministry As An Office

i. It is generally agreed that the first document plainly witnessing the ministry of the Church being regarded is an office is I Clem. Indeed, to Sohm, this letter was the exemplar and originator of corruption. It may be disputed whether I Clem is in fact the earliest example of this phenomenon, because the date of this document is not as securely attached to the year 96 A.D. as has been hitherto assumed, and if it is placed rather later, in the second or third decade of the second century, the demands of its internal evidence are more satisfactorily met (see Paul Kerestzes, 'The Jews, the Christians and the Emperor Domitian'). But certainly Clemens does witness to an official ministry. His presbyter-bishops are regarded as successors to the apostles, occupy a station or office from which they can be ejected, and to which they have been appointed permanently. Their function is defined (44.3, 4) as 'ministering to the flock' and 'offering the gifts' (*i.e.* in the eucharist). It should however be noted that Clemens shows no tendency to trace their origin back to the priests of the Old Testament, as has too often been assumed by writers on this subject. His references to the cultic priesthood of the Old Testament (40–44) are made only to emphasize the necessity of order (*i.e.* orderliness) in the ministry. When he wishes to find a text in the OT to support the Christian ministry, he does not go to the priesthood of the Law but, characteristically of an early Christian writer, to the prophets; he cites (42.5) Isa 60.17 in a curious form unknown to LXX or MT but found in Irenaeus also (Adv. Haer. IV.41). He does not contribute towards the idea of a sacral order maintaining a cult.

Ignatius of Antioch, whose letters may ante-date I Clem, shows no interest in succession in the ministry. 'Ignatius experiences the contemporary Church just as it is, a living mystery' (Von Campenhausen, *Ecclesiastical Authority and Spiritual Power*, 107). He tends to relate the bishop, not to the apostles, but to God, and the presbyters to the apostles (though there are exceptions to this tendency, (Ign Sm 8.2), perhaps reflecting in this the knowledge that presbyters derived historically from an early period whereas monarchical bishops are of recent growth). He is very anxious to unite in the hands of the bishop authority of every sort, not only doctrinal, and liturgical (Ign Sm 8.1, 2), but also disciplinary (Ign Phld 8.1, Ign Pol 5.2). But it is clear from his letters that not all Churches yet possess monarchical bishops; he calls himself 'bishop of Syria' (Ign Rom 2.2) implying that he is the only bishop there, though there must have been many more Christian congregations in Syria besides that of Antioch, from which Ignatius hailed, and the only satisfactory explanation of his total silence in his letter to the Romans concerning a bishop there is that the Roman Church had not yet developed a monarchical bishop; his emphasis upon the Roman Church as 'presiding in love' (Ign Rom Pref) and his statement that in his absence from Syria the love of the Romans will be bishop to the Church in Antioch (Ign Rom 9.1) may support this view. The very insistence on order, subordination and unity under the bishop which rings so loudly through Ignatius' Letters inclines us to conclude that he saw the emergence of the monarchical bishop (which he knew to be a development) as a necessary remedy for a state of fluidity and even anarchy in the ministry.

II Clem refers to elders as having authority to teach (17.3, 5) and Hermas reflects the same assumption. The whole theme and concern of Hermas is, however, the moral discipline of the Church, how far and how long forgiveness can be extended. For this author, as for the Church generally throughout the second century, the discipline, *i.e.* the behaviour, of Christians was ultimately the concern of the whole local congregation, not simply of clergy as individuals or as a body, however ready the congregation might be to delegate its responsibility to officials. It was to the congregation that the sinner had to display his repentance, and it was in the presence of the congregation that he was reconciled when his period of repentance was over. The impression which we gain from the primitive Church, that the local Church is the dynamic source of Christian life and expansion, with an enormous potential for exerting authority, is not seriously impaired during the first half of the second century.

ii. From the middle of this century onwards, however, a new trend is observable. This is the tendency towards tracing all existing phenomena back to the Apostles. It is not difficult to account for this tendency. By the middle of the second century the Church was fully conscious of itself as an institution existing in history, with a past behind it and a future in front, free from its Jewish matrix, its different congregations, strung out over most parts of the Roman Empire, aware of their solidarity, its attention no longer absorbed by the dream of *parousia*, judgement and world ending, faced with tasks, responsibilities and problems such as all institutions had to face. In order to establish its identity it found itself obliged to endure the competition not only of attractive mystery religions and immemorial cults supported by the authority of the local government or of the Imperial Government, but of many Gnostic sects and schools whose doctrines and membership tended often to merge into those of the Church and who laid claim to a connection with the sources of Christian truth more direct and more interesting than that which apparently the Church could claim. The appeal to the apostles, whereby the Church turned to the most primitive period of its history as a Golden Age, tracing everything that it regarded as important in its own life to their original impulse and foundation, took several different forms. The later books of the NT which was in process of forming at the time are those which lay claim to apostolic authorship. The rule of faith of the Church was thought to have apostolic authority. Unwritten tradition or custom was unreflectingly ascribed to some famous apostle, as by both sides in the Quarto-Deciman controversy. The rudimentary creed was attributed to the apostles (as in the Epistula Apostolorum). And above all Churches began to trace back their foundation to an apostle by producing a list of bishops who consecutively occupied the see, the first bishop having been appointed by an apostle. The first person we hear of who interested himself in this form of apostolic succession is Hegesippus, in the middle of the century (Eusebius Caes. *HE* III.11 and 32.1, 2; IV.8.1 and 22.1–3). Irenaeus probably used Hegesippus' succession-list for his account of the see of Rome (*Adv. Haer.* III.3.2, 3) and elsewhere (III.4.2, 3 cf Eus. *HE* IV.11.1). He made a great point in his teaching of the continuity of the Church from the apostles, in doctrine, in faith, in structure, in the possession and exposition of the Scriptures (*Adv. Haer.* III.38.1; IV.53.2), and the sign and guarantee of this continuity is the apostolic succession of bishops in their sees; this is the great argument against Gnostic claims—*omnes enim ii valde posteriores sunt quam episcopi quibus apostoli tradiderunt ecclesias* ('these men are all later in time than the bishops to whom the apostles entrusted the Churches', V.20.1). Similarly Tertullian appeals on several occasions to the apostolic succession of bishops in order to demonstrate the priority and authenticity of the teaching of the Church in contrast to that of the Gnostic heretics (*De Praescr. Haer.* 32–38); and he links Church and Scripture very closely by means of this succession: *quod sumus, hoc sunt scripturae ab initio suo, ex illis sumus, antequam nihil aliter fuit quam sumus* ('We are what the Scriptures are from the beginning. We derive from them, the past was nothing other than what we are,' 38.5). Clement of Alexandria has one reference to this apostolic succession (Strom VI.7.61.3), Hippolytus two (Elenchus I. Pref. 6, and Apostolic Tradition 3 (Botte 8) where the ordination prayer for the bishop asks for the 'princely spirit which thou didst deliver to thy beloved Child Jesus Christ which he bestowed on thy holy apostles'), and Origen one (De Principiis IV.2.2). But it is clear that the great period of this type of appeal to apostolic succession was at the end of the second and the beginning of the third centuries. After that, it began to lose its point and power.

This is indeed an appeal to ministry as an office. Each bishop succeeds his predecessor in a permanent station and rôle, and without the office the appeal would be useless. It marks a stage of development in the establishment of an official ministry. But certain qualifying circumstances should be taken into consideration here. In the first place, strictly speaking the bishop is not necessary to this argument. The succession of any minister would suffice, and in fact Irenaeus sometimes refers to the succession of presbyters rather than of bishops (Adv. Haer. III.2.2; IV.40.1 and 49.2; Letter to Florinus (Eus HE V.20.4); Letter to Pope Victor (ibid V.24.14)), and what matters to Tertullian is not so much episcopal as structural succession, in fact 'the succession of one generation to the next' (Ellen Flessemann-Van Leer, *Tradition and Scripture in the Early Church*, 152). Next, the succession invoked here is not a succession of ordination but a succession of witness to tradition, a continuity of one teacher succeeding another in the place of teaching. Molland remarks that Irenaeus 'does not take any interest in the question of hierarchical degrees' ('Irenaeus of Lugdunum and the Apostolic Succession', *Jnl. Eccles. History* I (1950) 22–23). He does not, for instance, co-ordinate the Levitical priesthood of the OT and the ranks of the Christian ministry. For him Levites and priests are all the obedient disciples of the Lord (Adv. Haer. IV.17; V.34.3). The claim that a line of valid ordination of bishops guaranteed either the purity of the faith or the authenticity of the Church did not enter the head of any of the writers. Finally, the particular claims which they made for episcopal succession at least were highly uncertain and ambiguous. The claim to apostolic succession was largely a

schematization of history, however sound may have been the
appeal to a general structural continuity in the Church
(R. P. C. Hanson, *Tradition in the Early Church*, 157–168, H. J.
Lawlor and J. E. L. Oulton, *Eusebius: Ecelesiastical History*,
167–170).

iii. In Irenaeus there is one significant reference to the bishop's
ordination, which we shall consider later in another context, but
this is not a subject to which Irenaeus pays much attention.
Tertullian, on the other hand, has assimilated the concept of
ordination more fully into his thought. He regularly
distinguishes between *ordo* which means the clergy and *plebs*
meaning the people, and regards this distinction as already well
established. He regards it as a serious charge against heretics that
their ordinations are 'haphazard, irresponsible, inconsistent'
(*temerariae, leves, inconstantes*, De Praescr. Haer. 41.6). Even in a
work where (as we shall see) he most truculently asserts the
priesthood of the laity, De Monogamia, he can use the phrase
omne gradum ordinis meaning 'every rank of the clergy' (8.3). His
discussion of the proper minister of baptism reveals the same
concept: because all equally receive baptism, all equally, clergy
or laity, can, if necessary, confer it (though it is more fitting that
the bishop or one of the *ordo* should do so). We are meant to
infer that, conversely, only ordained men can confer ordination
(De Baptismo 17.1, 2). As he tells us what a woman, whom he
regards as incapable of receiving ordination, may not do, so he
informs us about the functions and privileges of the ordained :*in
ecclesia loqui* (preach), *docere* (teach), *tinguere* (baptise), *offerre*
(celebrate); in fact she must perform no male function, least of
all the priestly one (De Virg. Vel 8.4). The importance of
ordination is brought out much more strongly in the Apostolic
Tradition of Hippolytus. The task of the bishop in his
ordination prayer is described as 'to loose every bond according
to the authority thou gavest to the apostles', to 'forgive sins' and
'to assign lots'; that is to ordain (Ap. Trad. 3 (Botte 10)). The
distinction between the bishop and the presbyter is emphasized
strongly; the prayer for the ordaining of a presbyter makes no
mention of him as a priest and does not specify particular duties,
except sharing in the presbyterate and governing the people.

The type for the presbyter in the OT is the elders appointed by Moses (Ap. Trad. 7 (Botte 20)). Presbyters are to lay hands on at the ordaining of a presbyter because of the spirit common to all clergy, but the presbyter in doing this is not ordaining but blessing (σφραγίζειν); only the bishop can ordain (χειροτονεῖν) (8 (Botte 24)). The bishop alone is to ordain the deacon, not the presbyter, because the deacon 'is not ordained for a priesthood' (which suggests, a little inconsistently, that the presbyter is so ordained), and he is not appointed to be fellow-counsellor with the bishop nor to receive the spirit common to all presbyters (8 (Botte 22, 24)). We may contrast with this the attitude of Irenaeus, who does not distinguish between the bishop and the presbyter as a matter of order (Letter to Pope Victor Eus. *HE* V.24.14). Similarly in the Apostolic Tradition a widow is not to be regarded as ordained, because she does not offer the oblation, nor has she a cultic ministry (λειτουργία). Cultic ministry (λειτουργία) is for clergy (κλῆρος); the same conditions apply to virgins (10, 12 (Botte 30, 32)). :Paul had described himself as a *leitourgos* exercising a cultic ministry (ἱερουργοῦντα) by offering an oblation (προσφορά), at Rom 15.16. But his use of these terms was figurative, to describe his labours on behalf of the Gospel. That of Hippolytus is literal. This cleavage between clergy and laity and emphasis upon the importance of ordination is carried further in a work not unlike that of Hippolytus' Apostolic Tradition, the Syrian Didascalia Apostolorum whose exact date cannot be determined but which should perhaps be placed about the middle of the third century. The concept of the rôle of the bishop in this work is still in some respects fluid. He is compared to a King, with the passage 1 Sam 8.10–17 invoked (IX Connolly 94–96). The position of the bishop as the arbiter of forgiveness and of penance however is strongly emphasised throughout the work, though he is urged to be merciful (VI Connolly 44, 46, 48, 50). He is described as 'set in the likeness of God Almighty' and is holding 'the place of God Almighty,' and the promise in Mt. 18.18 of binding in heaven and in earth is applied to him (V Connolly 40). We shall see soon how this work develops the concept of priesthood.

This increasing emphasis upon the importance of ordination

finds its climax in the thought of Cyprian of Carthage. In his view bishops were directly instituted and consecrated by the apostles who were themselves bishops consecrated and instituted by Christ; indeed his succession is a succession of consecration, or rather of authority handed down by means of ordination: 'hence by means of a chain of succession through time (*per temporum et successionum vices*) the ordination of bishops and the structure (*ratio*) of the Church has flowed on so that the Church is built upon bishops and every act of the Church is controlled by these same superiors' (*praepositos*, Letters XXXIII.1.1); and he can refer to 'all the superiors who have succeeded to the apostles by a chain of ordination' (*vicaria ordinatione*, Letters LXVI.4.1). *Ordinatio* is what makes a bishop, and illegal or unauthorised ordination is invalid (Letters XLIV.1.1; XLV.3.1; XLVIII.3.1). What constitutes a bishop is his possession of the episcopal chair (*cathedra*), *i.e.* the office, and the existence of a flock (*plebs*) under his control (Letters LVII.1.2). To the argument of Tertullian (which we shall consider later) that the Church is not the list of the bishops, Cyprian almost answers that it is. To the plea that the Church is where two or three are gathered together in Christ's name (Mt 18.20) Cyprian replies that it is not numbers but concord that matters—*Non multitudini sed unanimitati deprecantium plurimum tribui* ('the greatest answer is not given to numbers but to the harmony of those who pray'. De Unitate Ecclesiae 12). The aspect of the bishop in his official character which is most prominent in Cyprian's account of him is that of a ruler. His business is to rule his flock under Christ, and to co-operate with all other properly constituted bishops who exercise their own authority over their own flocks. He must treat his presbyters as counsellors or assessors, and must take account of the views of his laity; perhaps he could be called a constitutional ruler, but still he is primarily a ruler.

iv. One important development in the official aspect of the ministry has still be be considered, the emergence of the concept of a Christian priesthood. This first appears in the work of Tertullian. Some have purported to see this idea in earlier writers, in Did. 13.3 ('you are our high priests', applied to *prophets*), in I Clem 40–44 (which has already been dealt with), and even in Ign. Phld. 9.1. But none of these passages will bear this interpretation. With Tertullian appears unexplained the practice of describing the bishop as a priest or high priest (*sacerdos* or *sacerdos summus*), and with Hippolytus, almost Tertullian's contemporary, the title 'high priest' (ἀρχιερεύς) given to the bishop. To the question, why this development should have taken place, no single answer can be given. Ehrhardt's theory that the Christians in effect took over the Jewish institution of a single high priest stationed in a single cult centre and multiplied it by hundreds all over the Roman Empire is quite untenable. Equally impossible is the view that the third-century bishop employed this device to increase his power; the early bishop was not a greedy grasper after power, rather he displays the opposite weakness of an irresolute uncertainty in his use of the power of the keys (Von Campenhausen *op. cit.* 329–330). Several different forces appear to have operated to produce this development. The concentration of the life of the early Church upon the eucharist must have been one, a concentration perhaps assisted by the fading of acute eschatological expectation. Here was a cult, and in the OT were several passages about priests of a cult, especially in Leviticus and Numbers, and one or two particularly suggestive passages in the prophetic books apparently predicting a priestly activity among the Messianic community, especially Zech 3. The Christians were anxious to show that every part of the OT witnessed to Christ and his Church, but there were large parts of the Pentateuch which seemed to be wholly irrelevant. If the regulations for the Levitical priesthood could be taken as laying down in advance a blueprint for a Christian priesthood, then the Law could take on a new relevance. The lengthening distance between the Church and Judaism must have been another factor, for as long as Christianity was in close touch with Judaism it would be bound to emphasize the difference on the one hand between the Jewish sacrificial cult and its ministers, who had taken their part in bringing Jesus to the Cross, and whose whole dispensation Paul had declared to be rendered obsolete and superseded by Christ's act of redemption, and on the other the modest and *ad hoc*

ministry of the Christian Church. Perhaps the strongest
influence producing this development, however, was the
example of pagan religion, in its social rather than its cultic
aspect. Christians would be wholly unlikely to imitate or
borrow features of pagan cults; but the title *archiereus* or *sacerdos*
was one which conferred a distinct social cachet. The official
archiereus of a city like Ephesus or Antioch or Alexandria was an
impressive figure, in favour with the authorities and wielding
considerable power. When asked by friendly pagan neighbours
what was the title of the local head of his cult, the second-
century Christian could only give the lame answer, 'the
inspector'. He may have begun to realize the advantage of
calling this inspector a 'high priest'. Finally, when the point is
reached that the bishop is regarded as standing permanently in
the place of or as expressing the activity of Christ, sooner or later
he will be thought of as an agent or representative of Christ's
high-priestly activity. This theological motive is often explicitly
stated by those who use sacerdotal language of the bishop.

Tertullian's use of *summus sacerdos* and of *sacerdotalis* to
describe the bishop and occasionally the presbyter also extends
throughout his works, but does not in fact have much effect
upon his doctrine of ordination; with him the innovation is not
much more than verbal, particularly as he has strong views (as
we shall see) upon the priesthood of all believers. But in
Hippolytus the idea undergoes perceptible development. In the
beginning of his Elenchos he gives his idea of what a bishop is
when he states his own claim to be a bishop: we are, he says,
successors of the apostles, 'and reckoned to be partakers of the
same grace and high priesthood and teaching and guardians of
the Church' (I Pref. 6). The prayer at the ordination of a bishop
in his Apostolic Tradition runs thus: 'Grant to thy servant . . . to
feed thy holy flock, to act blamelessly as thy high priest
(ἀρχιερατεύειν), ministering (λειτουργοῦντα) night and day,
ceaselessly to propitiate thy countenance and to offer the gifts of
thy holy Church and in the high-priestly spirit (τῷ πνεύματι τῷ
ἀρχιερατικῷ) to have authority to forgive sins according to
thy command' (3 (Botte 8), Greek reconstructed by Botte
mainly from the Epitome; cf. 34 (Botte 80)). The Didascalia
Apostolorum maintains this doctrine and strengthens it. It

invokes the analogy of the OT cult more than once, though in one place, in dealing with the necessity of the bishop acting through the deacon, it cautiously adduces the example of the pagan priesthood (IX, Connolly 90–92). It applies the text 'Thou and Aaron shall take upon you the sins of the priesthood' (Num 18.1) to the bishop (VII, Connolly 56). And it insists that the bishop must be unblemished in body like the OT priest, referring to Lev 21.17 (IV, Connolly 32). The propriety of the bishop being supported by the offerings of the flock is asserted by the example of the Levites, and this is followed by a passage in which a number of titles (prophets, princes, leaders, kings, mediators, preachers *etc.*) are applied to the bishops, including Levites and priests (VIII, Connolly 80). Later still this writer takes the expression of Did. 13.3, 'for they are your high-priests' (applied in Did. to Christian prophets) and applies it to bishops leaving the titles priests and Levites to presbyters, deacons, orphans and widows, but reiterating, somewhat confusedly, at the end that the bishop is Levite and high-priest (IX, Connolly 86). The writer in this and similar passages in his work is feeling after a definite and formal identification of NT ministerial offices with OT correlates, but has not yet formally reached such a position.

The doctrine of Christian ministry as a priesthood finds its strongest expression in the work of Cyprian. That he should in the middle of the third century call bishops and even sometimes presbyters (Letters I.1.1) *sacerdotes* is not very remarkable. But his definition of this priesthood is specific and goes beyond any such doctrine before him. Not only does the bishop enjoy the sacrosanctity of the Levitical priests in the Pentateuch (Letters III.1.1, 2 and 2.1 and 3.1; IV.4.3; LIX.4.1 and 13.5; LXI.3.2, 3; LXV.2.1; LXXIII.8.1), but he closely links this priesthood and the eucharistic altar: 'God is one and Christ is one and one Church and one chair (*cathedra*) has been founded on Peter by the Lord's utterance. Another altar cannot be set up nor a new priesthood come into being save the one altar and the one priesthood' (Letters XLIII.5.2). He strengthens and adds detail to his doctrine of priesthood by his doctrine of eucharistic sacrifice, set out extensively in his sixty-third Letter. The bishop as a sacrificing priest does in the eucharist just what Christ did at the Last Supper. He offers Christ's body and blood as a propitiatory sacrifice to God. Under Cyprian's treatment the celebrant, whom he usually assumes to be the bishop, becomes a cultic sacrificing priest after the manner of the OT, offering Christ to God. When the idea is allied to the Cyprianic concept of the bishop as a ruler deriving his authority from Christ in a succession initiated by the apostles, the foundations of the mediaeval doctrine of the clergy as a sacerdotal caste possessing authority independently of the rest of the Church are laid.

Cyprian's doctrine of episcopal priesthood was widely influential. The Vita Pontii of Cyprian appears to endorse it. The majority of the bishops in the Sententiae Episcoporum use his vocabulary. Even the later Latin author Lactantius, who in his doctrine of eucharistic sacrifice does not go as far as Cyprian, can call episcopacy *magnum sacerdotium* (Div. Inst. IV.30). Clement of Alexandria does not describe Christian clergy as priests but by the time Origen is writing the usage has become conventional, and he employs it without comment throughout his works, though we shall see that his attitude to clerical office is far from conventional. Eusebius of Caesarea uses unmodified sacerdotal vocabulary of the Christian clergy throughout his works. By his day such sacerdotal treatment of the clerical office had become entirely normal. The later doctrines of ordination as a sacrament and of the 'indelible character' conferred by orders have not yet appeared by the end of the third century.

v. We have traced the development within the comparatively short time of less than two hundred years of a very strong doctrine of the ministry as an office, not only a function but a permanent station and role with powers and capacities attaching to it to which men are appointed in succession. We must now consider briefly what were the forces which brought about this development. Clearly it was part of a general drawing together of the forces of the great Church which took place during the second century with increasing dynamic as the century went on. Ignatius saw the entrenchment in power of bishop, with presbyters and deacons under him, as a vitally necessary move for the preservation of the integrity of the Church. It was easy for Celsus about 170 A.D. to mistake Gnostic ideas and practices for Christian ones. The line between orthodox Christianity and Gnosticism was blurred even as late as the period when Theophilus of Antioch was writing his Three books to Autolycus and Clement his Stromateis. The Church emerged from the first century looking more like a medley of near-Jewish sects than a single unified body. The work of people like Irenaeus and Tertullian was necessary to preserve the Church's doctrine from being finally drowned in a confused sea of Gnosticism, Judaism and Hellenism. Parallel with the formation of the Canon of the NT, and the articulation of the rule of faith (of which the rudimentary creed was regarded as no more than a mere summary) went the flowing of the Christian ministry into the mould of a series of stereotyped officers with thc bishop at their head. This stereotyping of the ministry was not the successful capture of a charismatic, personalist, informal Christian gathering of spontaneously inspired people by a ruthless official bureaucracy, but a successful strategy designed to prevent the Church losing its identity altogether.

The placing of authority over discipline in the hands of the bishop rather than in those of the assembly of local Christians, which must have taken place at some time in the second century, undoubtedly gave impetus to the creation of his ministry as an office. Some may regret this development, but it was inevitable. Attempts at the Reformation to reverse this development made by many reformed traditions were uniformly unsuccessful. Once placed in a position of authority over matters of discipline, and, we may add, of worship, the bishop found power flowing towards him automatically, sometimes against his will. Another assistance in this direction must have been his control of finance. The first references to clergy being paid are to be found in fragments of writers quoted by Eusebius who are writing about the year 200; Apollonius says that Montanus in the last quarter of the first century paid his clergy a salary, and an anonymous author writes of a certain Natalius who was a salaried anti-pope in Rome a little later (HE V.18.2 and 28.8–12). Both writers appear to find this phenomenon shocking, not so much perhaps because the clergy exist on other people's money, for it must have been necessary for most of them to do so well before this date (*cf.* Tertullian De

Ieiun. ad Psych. 13.3), as because both cases involved a definite and organized salary rather than a reliance on the gifts of the faithful. But by the time of the author of the Didascalia it is clear that bishop, presbyters and deacons, as well as widows and orphans, receive regular subsidies from the laity (VIII, passim esp. Connolly 82–84; IX, Connolly 90), though it is not clear that these pass through the hands of the bishop. And in the African Church in Cyprian's time the bishop had charge of the finances of his see (Letters I.1.2; XXIV.4.1; XXXIX.5.2; De Lapsis 6). There is some evidence in Cyprian that deacons were part-time officials, and earned money by other means as well as in the ministry (Letters L.1.2 Nicostratus the deacon was in charge of finance for his *patrona* (woman employer); *cf.* the early career of Callistus). But the requirement in Hippolytus' Apostolic Tradition that the presbyters and deacons are to assemble daily with the bishop (39 (Botte 86)) in order to give instruction to the faithful does not suggest that they can have had much time for other occupations. Both orders from an early point in the third century must have been largely dependent upon the bishop for their finances.

We have already suggested one external example which may have influenced the development of the episcopal office, the pagan high-priest (see above, p. 129–30). Another may have been the Roman magistrate. The resemblance of the *ecclesia* to the *civitas* (town) and the clergy and people to the *ordo* and *plebs* of a Roman town has more than once been noticed; the reproduction in Tertullian of these terms *ordo* and *plebs* may be no coincidence. Certainly in the *gravitas* (dignified responsibility) of his behaviour and style and in his role as a ruler and judge of his flock Cyprian seems to have learnt something from the Roman magistrate; perhaps this is a legacy of his days as a lawyer before he became a Christian (*cf.* Letters LV.11.1. *sicut et antecessores nostri saepe fecerunt*, 'as our predecessors frequently did'). Finally, it is difficult to exclude from the concept of apostolic succession the influence of the example of pagan philosophical schools, where each head took his turn in maintaining the succession of teaching of the original master, and usually prided himself upon retaining intact the master's authentic teaching.

III   *Influences And Factors Modifying This Development*

i. So far, the picture of primitive simplicity and spontaneity giving way to a bureaucracy which finally becomes government of priests invoking sacral powers might be regarded as accurate. But the development of the concept of office in the second and third centuries was not as straightforward as this account of it suggests, and we must now examine those facts which modify and alter this picture.

The first fact to consider is that the doctrine of the priesthood of all believers, of the corporate priesthood of the whole Church, laity quite as much as clergy, such as we find witnessed to in the NT. (1 Pet 2.5–9; Apc 1.6; 5.10; 20.6) was by no means forgotten in the second and even in the third century. Clemens writes in the name of the whole church of Rome to the whole church of Corinth. Ignatius greets the whole of each local church in the person of its bishop (*e.g.* Ign Eph 1.3; Trall 1.1); all his letters, save that to Polycarp, are addressed to churches and not individuals, and the same appears to be true of Dionysius of Corinth in his letters mentioned by Eusebius (HE II.25.8; IV.23.1–12). Justin Martyr, in the middle of the second century says that all Christians are a 'highpriestly race' (ἀρχιερατικὸν γένος) who offer acceptable sacrifices to God, invoking the traditional texts for this argument, Zech 3.4 and Mal 1.11 (Dial 116.3). Irenaeus declares that the apostles were justified in plucking ears of corn on the Sabbath day (Lk 6.3, 4), because they were all priests and hence permitted to do this (1 Sam 21.4ff.), and that all their disciples ever since have been priests (Adv. Haer. IV.17). Referring back later in the same work to this passage, he repeats that the Levites and priests are all the disciples of the Lord (V.34.3).

Tertullian's views upon this subject are much more pronounced, even before he becomes deeply influenced by Montanism. In his Adversus Marcionem he says that one of the goats mentioned in Lev 16 represents the Second Coming of Christ at which 'when all sins have been expiated the priests of the spiritual temple, that is the Church, enjoy as it were a kind of public banquet (*visceratione*) of the Lord's grace, while the rest are fasting from salvation' (III.7.7), and later in the same work he declares that the words of Jesus, 'Let the dead bury their dead' (Lk 9.60) meant that the Lord 'was training (*destinabat*) for worship and priesthood the man whom he had apprenticed (*imbuerat*) by preaching the Kingdon of God' (IV.23.10,11). In his works on points of Christian conduct where his rigorism has a full opportunity to display itself, he recurs to this doctrine frequently, drawing drastic consequences from it. In his De Exhortatione Castitatis, though he clearly recognizes the existence of a clerical *ordo*, including *sacerdotes*, the strength of his feeling against the practice of Christians being permitted to marry a second spouse after the first had died leads him to insist that in an emergency all laity are priests, and apparently to reduce priesthood to sheer convenience (8.1–4). He defines the Christian activity of a layman, *si orationem fecit ad dominum* ('if he has prayed to the Lord') . . . *si scripturis incumbit* ('if he has studied the Scriptures deeply') . . . *si daemonem adiurat* ('if he exorcises a devil' De Exhort Cast 10.2, confirmed 11.7). Not only can a laymen exorcize, but in an emergency any three Christians, lay or clerical, can celebrate the eucharist (De Fuga in Persecutione 14.1). And his De Monogamia contains several vigorous assertions of the priesthood of all believers (7.7; 12.1–5); *cf.* Adv. Iud. 14.9.

Though Tertullian pressed this doctrine in the interests of promoting rigorism, he was not eccentric in using it, nor the last to use it. A sentence in the bishop's prayer in the eucharist at an ordination in Hippolytus' Apostolic Tradition runs 'we offer to thee the bread and the cup making eucharist to thee because thou hast made us worthy to stand before thee and minister as priests to thee'; it suggests, if we can trust the plural of 'priests', that it is not the bishop only but the people who are priests (4 (Botte 16)). Finally Origen, who has no difficulty in recognizing clergy as officials and as priests, teaches the doctrine of the priesthood of all believers without seeing any contradiction (see Vogt, *Das Kirchenverstandnis des Origenes*, 111–117, citing such passages as Hom. Jos. 7.2 (GCS VII.329.17), Hom. Lev. 4.6 (GCS VI.323.27ff.), 6.2, 5 (VI.360.21f. and 367.16)). As with most doctrines, Origen has his own peculiar interpretation of this concept; he moralizes, spiritualizes and subjectivizes it. But clearly he has inherited and accepted the traditional doctrine.

ii. There are several pieces of evidence which suggest that during the second century, and even during the third, the Church as a whole did not take the official authority of the clergy with complete seriousness. What Irenaeus sees as handed down partly by means of the succession of bishops is not official authority but Christianity considered as a consistent system and something that can be seen everywhere working in practice (see, *e.g.* Adv. Haer. III.38.1); he can even appeal to the incompetence of the clergy as an argument: 'those who abandon the preaching of the Church accuse the holy presbyters of incompetence (*imperitiam*), not considering how much more impressive a religious amateur (*idiota religiosus*) is than a blasphemous and impudent sophist' (Adv. Haer. V.20.2). Then there is the curious incident narrated by Hippolytus where the presbyters of (we presume) the Roman church excommunicated Noetus after a theological argument (Contra Noetum Nautin 1, p. 235–237, PG 10:805A), apparently exercising an episcopal function. There are the occasional references (usually made in a tone of shocked horror) to women performing clerical functions (Tertullian De Praescr. Haer. 41.5; Irenaeus Adv. Haer. I.13.2; Cyprian Letters LXXV.10.1–5). But Tertullian allows that while women may not speak in church, they may *prophesy*, presumably because this was the Holy Spirit speaking and not the woman. Well before he has become deeply committed to the Montanist cause he quotes with approval examples of women prophets uttering inspired words (Adv. Marc. V.8.11; De Anima 9.43 De Resurr. Mort. 11.2f.), as well as when he has become wholly a Montanist partisan (De Exhort. Cast. 10.5; De Fug. in Pers. 9.3). No doubt this is the last flicker of activity on the part of Christian prophets which had been so important about a century before when Did. had described Christian prophets as high-priests (13.3), but such an attitude must have acted as a check on clerical officiousness.

The widespread opinion that the Church's power to forgive sins was limited also must have played its part in circumscribing the authority of the bishop. Hermas had been more concerned about this problem than about anything else, and advocated the view, which may well have at that time represented the majority opinion, that some sins, or some sins once repeated, were irremissible. Tertullian found it necessary to struggle for his rigorous point of view, for the contrary opinion had been gaining ground since Hermas' day. The question of who is Tertullian's episcopal adversary whom he loads with opprobrious epithets in his De Pudicitia (1.6, 7; 16.22) is a delicate one, whether Callistus bishop of Rome or Agrippinus bishop of Carthage. On the whole it seems better to envisage Callistus as his opponent; if we combine the phrase *suscepit hanc causam adversus Spiritum Sanctum ut falsum testimonium recitet de Apostolo eius* ('he undertook this cause against the Holy Spirit so that he gave false witness against his apostle' 16.22, whether we take *eius* as referring to Peter, Callistus' apostle, or to Peter, the apostle of the Spirit, the argument is unaffected) with the high epithets heaped on St. Paul in 14.27, we may reasonably see behind this an appeal by Callistus to Peter and a counter-move by Tertullian in playing up St. Paul. Tertullian has no half measures in his opinions here: the reconciliation given to committers of grave sins by the Church is purely human and is not the forgiveness of God (3.3, 4); the bishop has no power to forgive the gravest sins (18.17, 18). The apostles originally had power (*potestas*) and moral authority (*disciplina*), the bishops only have *disciplina*, not absolute control (*imperium*; 22.1–4 & 6). The Church consists of spiritual men (21.9–17), not of 'a list of bishops' (*numerus episcoporum*, 17). Tertullian was of course an exceptionally violent and irresponsible partisan, but his protest was certainly not the last spasm of a dying cause. Hippolytus, his contemporary, is just as much shocked by the behaviour of Callistus (Elenchus IX.19), and Origen a little later undoubtedly believed that the powers of bishops in forgiving sins were limited (Contra Celsum 3.9, 30; De Princ. 28.10; Comm Mt Comm Ser 12; Hom Lev 12.3; Hom. Ez 12.2 *etc*; see Hanson, *Allegory and Event*, 331–332; Vogt *op. cit.* 128–155). The Novatianist schism showed that this issue was by no means a dead letter even as late as the middle of the third century.

iii. We should also consider the bishop's rivals in exercising authority in the early Church. One of these was the confessor. The Passion of St. Perpetua, which may have been written or edited by Tertullian, reveals that Perpetua, in prison in Carthage under sentence of death, with some of her companions was quite ready to give orders (not merely exhortations) to the bishop and presbyters about how to look after their flock. Tertullian takes the trouble to tell us in his De Anima that Perpetua received a special revelation about the time of her passion, in which she saw the martyrs in Paradise (55.4, 5). It is possible that Callistus may have encouraged confessors to remit grave sins and may have even claimed this right for himself as a confessor (Tertullian De Pudicitia (22.1–3)). Hippolytus' Apostolic Tradition lays it down that if a confessor has suffered severely, in chains or in prison, he is to be regarded as having the rank of a presbyter without ordination (though it is unlikely that he was expected to perform clerical functions); only if he is appointed bishop are hands to be laid on him (9 (Botte 28)). It is quite clear that there were some people in Rome in the time of Cyprian who thought that a martyr needed no bishop's pardon for sins committed before martyrdom (Letters LVII.4.1). Cyprian himself during the Decian persecution had to play his hand very cautiously because though the confessors both in Rome and in Carthage never directly claimed to forgive sins in entire independence from the bishop, some of them came very close to this point, constantly forced Cyprian's hand, and were themselves evidently under great pressure from those who had lapsed to extend forgiveness without any reference to official episcopal authority (Letters XXI.3.2; XXII.2.2; XXIII; XVII.2.2). Not only the history of the Decian persecution but that of the Diocletian persecution shows how readily an unscrupulous or over-enthusiastic confessor could attract authority away from the official clergy by the glamour of his suffering.

Another rival for the bishop's power was the gifted teacher. Justin Martyr is an example of such a man, and Pantaenus who was a teacher of both Clement of Alexandria and of Origen, and Clement himself, and above all Origen. When the Empress Mamaea wished to interview a distinguished representative of the Christian religion, she did not summon a bishop to an interview, but a philosopher and theologian whose fame was already widespread in the eastern Church, Origen. (Eus HE

VI.21.3). This interview of Origen with the Empress is
significant in more than one way. It shows the prestige of the
Christian teacher, but it also shows how unimportant the
Empress considered the local Christian high official, the bishop
of Antioch, who was not summoned. A later female ruler,
Zenobia, was to repair this omission. It is also significant that
Origen's fame and skill aroused the resentment of his local
bishop, Demetrius. By this time (about 230) bishops tended to
think that they were the greatest authority on doctrine in their
sees, and disliked the idea that learned laymen should
overshadow that authority.

iv. On the question of charismatic persons and gifts, the men of
the second and third centuries took positions which were not as
clear-cut and stereotyped as might be thought. We do not find
here a simple taking of positions on one side or the other
'between Rome and Sohm', in E. Schweizer's epigrammatic
phrase (*Church Order in the New Testament* 28f.). The churchmen
of these centuries were well aware of the existence of
charismatic gifts in the Church, and that they posed something
of a problem. There is a famous and significant passage in
Irenaeus, where he appeals for support for the presbyters
(whom here he seems to identify with bishops), on the grounds
that they 'have with the episcopal succession received a sure gift
of truth' (*charisma veritatis certum*, Greek original lost but
certainly it was χάρισμα ἀληθείας Adv. Haer. IV.40.2), and a
little later he says that 'where the gifts (*charismata*) of the Lord
are placed, there we ought to learn truth, with those among
whom is the succession of that Church which is from the
apostles, and there exists sound and unblamable behaviour and
the word is undiluted and incorrupted' (IV.42.1). This passage
has aroused much discussion; it has been taken as a claim that
ordination confers infallibility (Van den Eynde, *Les normes de
l'enseignement clrétien dans la litterature patristique des trois premiers
siècles*, 187), or as an attempt to combine the prophet and the
official (Ehrhardt, *The Apostolic Succession*, 113–114). But much
the most likely interpretation is that of Ellen Flessemann-van
Leer (*Tradition and Scripture* 119–122). Irenaeus means that the
Church guided by the Spirit chooses and ordains for its ministry

men who have a God-given gift for perceiving and teaching Christian truth. This implies that Irenaeus does not deny that the Holy Spirit gives charismatic gifts in the Church, not does he underestimate them. He just sees them as to a large extent channelled into the official ministry (see Hanson *Tradition* 159–162). Tertullian recognizes the existence of *charismata* in the Church, and, characteristically, attaches special value to the gift of prophecy, but does not associate these gifts specifically with ordination or with clergy (*Adv. Marc.* V.8.5, 8, 9; De Praescr. Haer 29.3; Adv. Val. 4.4; De Monog. 1.2; De Ieiun Adv. Psych. 8.4; 16.8). Novatian (De Trinitate 29) follows Tertullian in his recognition of *charismata* without attaching them to ordination. Clement of Alexandria has a remarkable sentence (first brought to notice by Harnack, *Constitution and Law of the Church*, 214) in Quis Dives 42, 'intending to ordain to the clergy (κλήρῳ κληρώσων) each one of those who are indicated by the Spirit', which precisely reproduces the view which we have attributed to Irenaeus. In a passage to which we have already had occasion to allude (above, pp. 129) Hippolytus, stating his credentials as a bishop, declares that he shares the same grace (*charis*, not quite *charisma*) as well as the high-priesthood and doctrine of the apostles (Elenchos I Pref. 6). Botte believes that the Apostolic Tradition followed on a treatise by Hippolytus (now lost), called On Charismata, though Magne denies this. In his *Apostolic Tradition* Hippolytus lays it down that if any of the laity appears to have had a *charisma* of healing given in a revelation, he is not to be ordained. The reason for this prohibition is not altogether clear, Dix giving one reading and translation and Botte another (14 Botte 32, Dix 22). But it seems likely that what Hippolytus means is that it must first become clear through experience whether the man really has this *charisma*. This would suggest that normally possession of a *charisma* should lead to ordination.

Two corollaries follow from this attitude towards the relation of *charisma* to office, both of which are endorsed by evidence from the second and third centuries. One is that, in the words of E. Schweizer, in one sense, 'all order is an "afterwards", and attempt to follow what God has already designed' (*Church Order* 102). The attitude towards *charismata* of

Irenaeus, Hippolytus and Clement of Alexandria reflects this conviction. The other corollary is a negative one. Ministers who fall manifestly short of the standard demanded by their assumed possession of *charismata* have not been chosen by God and are not ministers at all, ordination or no ordination. There is plenty of support for this 'Donatist' position in the early Church. Irenaeus says that proud, factious and self-indulgent presbyters are not to be obeyed (Adv. Haer. IV.41.1). If clergy run away during a persecution, says Tertullian, they automatically cease to be clergy (De Fug. in Pers. 10.3). This doctrine, surprisingly, appears most strongly in Cyprian. He insists that one of the most important elements in the proper choice of a bishop is the judgement of God (Letters LV.8.4; LXVI.1.1, 2), and at times he seems to associate this judgement of God with the people's approval of the chosen candidate, another essential element in the choice (Letters XLII.1.2; XLIV.3.2). Consequently if a bishop went badly wrong it must be assumed that the divine judgement had not approved of him and he must retrospectively be regarded as never having been a bishop. Bishops who have sacrificed during the Decian persecution have ceased to be bishops and their 'offering' (*i.e.* celebration of the eucharist) cannot be sanctified (Letters LXV.2.1 and 4.1). Basilides, who sinned in this way, is no bishop (Letters LXVII.5, 3, 4). People who choose bishops must choose irreproachable men of unblemished character, so that when they offer the sacrifice their prayers will be heard (Letters LXVII.2.2); people who communicate with a sinful bishop are contaminated by him (LXVII.3.1, 2). Origen reflects the same doctrine. The authority of the bishop to bind or loose depends upon his moral and spiritual character (Comm. Mt. 12.14). 'Man Könnte sagen, das Sollen und Dürfen sei mit dem Amt gegeben, das Können aber stammte nicht aus dem Amt, sondern aus der personlichen Vollkommenheit bzw, der Bemühing darum' (Vogt op. cit. 54). And conversely there are some people who are recognized by God as bishops; though they have not been ordained (Comm. Mt. Comm. Ser. 12). This does not mean either that ordained clergy should not perform their official functions, nor that unordained people can usurp the functions of the ordained clergy, but that Origen sees no *ex opere operato* link between the action of God and the official clergy. His speculative and mystical thought soars beyond the limits of an official ministry.

It is, in conclusion, therefore, fair to say that the Church of the second and third centuries, while it certainly developed the concept of ministry as an office, adding new and not always satisfactory theological interpretations to it, and finding new possibilities for exploiting it, did not allow its official ministry to become an intolerable burden and clog. By the year 300 the official ministry was still flexible, still to some extent fluid, still capable of functioning effectively in ministering that which alone can give such a ministry justification, the communication of the gospel of Jesus Christ.

9

THE CHRISTIAN ATTITUDE TO PAGAN RELIGIONS UP TO THE TIME OF CONSTANTINE THE GREAT

I   Polemic

This is an essay on the early Christian attitude to pagan religion, not to pagan culture nor to pagan philosophy. Both of these last two subjects will, of course, be mentioned, because they are relevant to the subject of religion, but only as far as they are involved in the Christian attitude to pagan religion. This essay will not deal either with the Christian attitude to Judaism, intensely interesting though this subject is, because it forms a markedly different theme from the Christian attitude to paganism; the Christians always distinguished the Jews from the pagans and their anti-Jewish polemic, fierce though it was, had little in common with their anti-pagan polemic. For the Christian attitude to Judaism the reader must be referred to the experts on these subjects, Schoeps, Parkes, Marcel Simon, and many others. This essay, also, will not, with a few exceptions such as the work of Firmicus Maternus, useful for illuminating earlier material, conduct the reader beyond the reign of Constantine the Great. His advent upon the scene of history marks a convenient watershed both for the history of paganism and for the history of Christianity's relationship with it.

Christianity certainly inherited from Judaism its basic attitude towards paganism. The earliest Christian denunciations of idolatry, for instance, are no more than continuations of similar denunciations in such works as Ps 115, the Wisdom of Solomon, Ecclesiasticus, Pseudo-Aristeas, the Letter of Jeremiah, Josephus and the Jewish parts of the 'Oracula Sibyllina'.[1] The treatment of pagan worship in Rom 1 and Acts 14 is in no essential respect different from the Jewish attitude to it. As we shall see, the Christian estimate of the possibility of pagans arriving at truth stemmed also from Jewish ideas on this subject. Christian discipline, while it did not take the Jewish

[1] *E.g.*, Oracula Sibyllina (ed. J. Geffcken [Leipzig, 1902], G.C.S. series) 3.29–35; frag. 1.20–22; frag. 3.20–33. But there are many other such passages.

position that touching an idol made one ritually unclean, strictly forbade any association with idols. A Christian was not allowed to pursue the trade of an idolmaker, nor even to sell incense.[2] We shall meet later the touching story of two Christians who suffered death rather than make an idol. And in ages later than that of the primitive Church Christian apologists and writers developed in some ways the early Jewish polemic against idolatry. They stressed the irrationality of worshipping man-made images,[3] as had Deutero-Isaiah long before. But they also propounded a theory not prominent in Judaism, of which we shall hear much later, that pagan idols were inhabited by evil daemons who manipulated them for bad purposes. This theory is universal in the Christian fathers.[4] Origen, who in spite of his great gifts in other directions was devoid of aesthetic or literary appreciation, produced the Puritanical sentiment that pure hearts and good characters are better images than any ever made by Pheidias, Polycleitus, Zeuxis or Apelles,[5] and he will not allow that the motives of those nations mentioned by Celsus who abjure idol-worship can be compared with the motives of the Christians.[6]

Christians had been from an early period accused by pagans that their religion lacked images of their gods, as well as altars and temples. Celsus had made this a reproach against them and said that it was a sign that they belonged to a secret society (Contra Celsum 8.17), and Porphyry had made the same charge in his book 'Against the Christians', as Arnobius reminded his readers (Adv. Nat. 6.1). But the effective reply was open to Christians, and was constantly voiced by them, that many pagan authors and philosophers had repudiated idol-worship both before and after the coming of Christ. Heracleitus of Ephesus had attacked the cult of statues, saying that people who

[2] Tertullian, Scorpiace 7.1, 2 and 11.7.

[3] E.g., Athanasius, Contra Gentes (ed. R. W. Thomson, [Oxford, 1971]) 13.1–34. Athanasius in fact is much more influenced by Wisd 14.12–21 than by any other part of the O.T.

[4] It is pointless to burden the text with a long list of references to so widespread a belief; two typical passages are Arnobius, Adversus Nationes 4.12 and Athanasius, Contra Gentes 1.28.

[5] Contra Celsum 8.17–18.

[6] Ibid., 7.63–65.

treat lifeless images as gods are like a man who holds a conversation with houses.[7] Zeno had declared that temples are superfluous because God's true temple was the human intellect.[8] Chrysippus thought it childish to represent gods in human shape.[9] Celsus comments upon the irrationality of the Egyptians in building magnificent temples and precincts but worshipping animals within them: 'we mock the Egyptians although they show many profound mysteries, and teach that such worship is respect to invisible ideas and not, as most people think, to ephemeral animals'.[10] As we have already noted, Celsus observed that several other nations dispensed with images, altars and temples—the Scythians, the nomads of Libya, the Seres, and the Persians.[11] Porphyry, the last great defender of all things pagan, had been disturbed by the contemporary cult of statues. In his 'Letter to Anebon' he had submitted it to sympathetic but trenchant criticism, intending not to abolish it but to purify it. Though at the beginning of his 'Philosophy of the Oracles' he had attacked the 'remarkably unsophisticated' (ἀμαθεστάτους) people who, as ignorant in the presence of a statue as an illiterate person in front of an inscription, see in it nothing except stone, wood or metal, he knew that this was a weak point, and felt uneasy about it.[12] J. Geffcken believed that evidence from inscriptions suggests that a decline in the cult of statues set in from the second half of third century.[13] W. H. C. Frend sees a

[7] Clement of Alexandria, Protrepticus 4.50.4 and Celsus in Origen's Contra Celsum 1.5; 7.62 (cf. also Clem. Alex., Strom 5.11.76 and Plutarch, Moralia 1034B).

[8] Stoicorum Veterum Fragmenta (ed. Arnim) I.14.6; cf. Origen, Contra Celsum 1.5.

[9] Stoic. Vet. Frag. II.1076. But the Stoics on the whole accommodated themselves to the cult of idols; cf. E. R. Dodds, The Greeks and the Irrational (London, 1951), p. 240.

[10] Celsus in Origen's Contra Celsum 3.17 and 19; the quotation comes from the second passage and is in the translation of H. Chadwick (Cambridge, 1953). In a note in loc. Chadwick refers to a similar passage in Sextus Empiricus Pyrrhoneiai Hypotyposeis III.19.

[11] Contra Celsum 7.62.

[12] Cf. P. de Labriolle, La Réaction Païenne. Étude sur la polémique antichrétienne du Ier au VI^{er} siècle (Paris, 1934), pp. 237–238, 293–294.

[13] J. Geffcken, Der Ausgang des griechisch-römischen Heidentums (Heidelberg, 1920), p. 89, quoted by de Labriolle, op. cit., pp. 239–240.

similar decline in pagan cults in rural Numidia after 360.[14]

It is worth enquiring whether Christians really were as unsophisticated in their estimate of the cult of statues as Porphyry thought them to be. Bishop Heber in his famous hymn wrote

> 'The heathen in his blindness
>   Bows down to wood and stone',

and since he wrote these words many have accused him of failing to realize that the heathen were not honouring the idols themselves but the deities or spirits which they were thought to represent. The Christians had to face exactly the same reproach. On the whole the writers of Christian polemic are aware that the idol is not theoretically supposed to be the actual object of worship. Clement of Alexandria, indeed, betrays no such awareness in the 'Protrepticus', which represents the weight of his attack on contemporary religion. But this is perhaps because the paganism which he is attacking tends to be paganism as represented in literary sources rather than the pagan cults which were being practised in his day. That the Christians attacked a paganism which had long ceased to exist is a charge which we shall consider later in this essay, but we must admit it to some extent in Clement. Celsus had written that only fools think that the images actually are gods rather than votive offerings and representations.[15] We have seen already that Porphyry described as theologically illiterate those who could see the statue only and nothing beyond it; in his Περὶ ἀγαλμάτων he appears to have advanced no claim that the gods were in any sense present in the images which symbolized them.[16] Athenagoras, Origen, Lactantius, Arnobius, Eusebius and Athanasius recognize clearly enough that educated pagans at least do not think that the statues are gods. But they regard this argument as an insufficient defence of idolatry. Their main reason is that, while the educated pagan does recognize the distinction between the god and the idol, the great majority of idolaters, the uneducated ones, do not. Minucius Felix says as

[14] The Donatist Church (Oxford, 1952), cap. XIV.
[15] In Origen, Contra Celsum 7.62.
[16] So Dodds, The Greeks and the Irrational, p. 294.

148 CHRISTIAN ANTIQUITY

much. Arnobius dismisses the plea—which in itself betrays the fact that the defenders of the cult of statues knew the cruder view was widespread—that idolatry was rightly instituted to preserve the ignorant and superstitious masses from immorality.[17] We may therefore on the whole acquit the Christian authors of displaying the same insensitiveness as is attributed to bishop Heber. After all, however much they may have been occasionally obsessed by the literature of past ages, they knew better than we can how ordinary people who practised pagan cults felt about them. Some of the Christians who attacked them had themselves formerly been idolaters.

The Christian repudiation of animal sacrifice was much more widespread and emphatic even than their repudiation of the cult of statues. Here they could not rely on Jewish antecedents, for the Jews never could nor would repudiate the animal sacrifices which had formed so large a part of the Temple cult at Jerusalem. A few passages in the Jewish parts of the 'Oracula Sibyllina' suggest faintly that the Christian emphasis on the contrite heart and pure character as the sacrifice most acceptable to God may have had some support in Judaism. An ideal age is in one passage pictured, when the Jews will have nothing to do with idols or pictures, but instead:

ἀλλὰ γὰρ ἀείρουσι πρὸς οὐρανὸν ὠλένας ἁγνάς
ὄρθριοι ἐξ εὐνῆς αἰεὶ χρόα ἁγνίζοντες.[18]

[17] Minucius Felix, Octavius 22.1–5; Origen, Contra Celsum 7.66; Arnobius, Adv. Nat. 6.17, 23; Lactantius, Divine Institutes 2.2, 3. Cf. Athenagoras, Supplicatio 18.1; Eusebius, Praeparatio Evangelica 3.7.1; Athanasius, Contra Gentes 19.22–37; the more learned and educated of the Greeks defend idolatry on the ground that these images of both rational and irrational things are made ἵνα διὰ τουτων τὸ θεῖον αὐτοῖς ἀποκρίνηται καὶ φαίνηται· οὐκ ἄλλως γὰρ αὐτὸν ἀόρατον δύνασθαι γνῶναι ἢ διὰ τοιούτων ἀγαλμάτων καὶ τελετῶν; these images are a kind of writing through which by means of messengers who appear in them God can communicate with men (19.25–27). Athanasius replies in a logic-chopping way: if it is the material of the statues that conveys knowledge of the divine, why not worship the formless material? If it is the form, why not worship the living things of which the statues are mere copies? If it is the art, why not worship the artificer? (20.1–27).

[18] Orac. Sib. 3.591–592; cf. 4.162–170. In another Jewish part of the work (frag. 1.20–22) it is declared that men now, ceasing to offer holy hecatombs to the only true God, δαίμοσι τὰς θυσίας ἐποιήσατε τοῖσιν ἐν Ἅιδη.

But a few lines earlier the lavish celebration of the cult of God in the Temple is predicted and a few lines later men are exhorted to sacrifice to the only true God. The Christians did, however, have considerable antecedent support in paganism in their opposition to animal sacrifice. The Pythagoreans by the time that Christianity began to emerge into the world of paganism were widely credited with having discouraged animal sacrifice, and there appears at least to have been a rule observed among them which explicitly forbade the sacrifice of cocks.[19] Plato tolerated sacrifice as part of the religious furniture of his day, but regarded the concept of it with distaste as suggesting a bargain with the gods.[20] In the 'Asclepius' of the Hermetic literature the concept of a spiritual rather than a material sacrifice appears.[21] According to Eusebius (who is quoting Porphyry), Empedocles and Theophrastus had both attacked the practice of sacrifice in their day.[22] Galen had said that real piety ($\dot{\eta}$ ὄντως εὐσέβεια) lay in praising the demiurge for his works and not in sacrificing hecatombs of oxen or burning countless talents of cassia.[23] Apollonius of Tyana, that disciple of Pythagoras, would not wear garments made from animals' skins, was a vegetarian, and refused to offer animal sacrifices, but only hymns and prayers. Eusebius quotes a passage from his Περὶ θυσιῶν opposing sacrifice.[24] Varro in the introductory book of his 'Divine Antiquities' had readily allowed that the gods did not require sacrifice, but approved of the practice as a useful illusion. But two hundred or so years later opinion had changed among some of the intellectuals at least. The authors of the Hermetic literature and Celsus regarded sacrifice as something coarse of which they would have been ready to divest pure philosophical

[19] So Dodds, Greeks and the Irrational, p. 291, quoting Iamblichus, Vit. Pythag. 147.

[20] Dodds, op. cit., p. 222.

[21] See A. D. Nock, Conversion. The Old and the New in Religion from Alexander the Great to Augustine of Hippo (Oxford, 1933, repr. 1961), p. 117.

[22] Eusebius, Praeparatio Evangelica 4.14.1, 2, 7.

[23] Galen, De usu partium 3.10; see R. Walzer, Galen on Jews and Christians (London, 1949), p. 24.

[24] Eusebius, P.E. 4.13.1; see de Labriolle, Réaction Païenne, pp. 175–176.

piety.[25] The Neo-Platonic philosophers took a detached view of the subject, and for some the sacrificial cult had only a symbolic meaning.[26] The attitude of Porphyry among these was equivocal. He was prepared to defend animal sacrifices, as he was prepared to defend most of the pagan practices of his day. But they formed no part of his system. Eusebius can quote extracts from his works both supporting and repudiating sacrifices.[27] Louis Robert has observed that the oracles at Didyma and Claros in the second half of the second and the beginning of the third century did not enjoin hecatombs or expensive outlay on rites from those who consulted them, though they did enforce customary sacrifices, and rather decreed the singing of hymns to Apollo, but that this is not a sign of decadence nor of poverty. 'C'est la marque d'une évolution de la pensée religieuse dans le grand sanctuaire oraculaire et de préoccupations répandues à cette époque dans la philosophie'.[28] It may perhaps be that Constantine in the early fourth century was able to forbid or discourage public sacrifices in the pagan tradition with greater impunity because he knew that there was a current of opinion against it or indifferent to it among educated pagans.

Certainly there is overwhelming documentation of Christian opposition to animal sacrifices. The earliest appearance of it is perhaps in Acts 14.15 and 17.25, but a curious passage in the 'Odes of Solomon' (manifestly one of those works which Cardinal Daniélou has taught us to call 'Judaeo-Christian') cannot be very much later. 'I am a priest of the Lord', the passage runs, 'and to him I offer the offering of his thought. For his thought is not the world nor the flesh nor like those who worship according to the flesh. The offering of the Lord is

[25] So Nock, Conversion, p. 224.

[26] See J. Straub, Konstantins Verzicht auf den Gang zum Kapitol, Historia 4 (1955), p. 306.

[27] Eusebius, P.E. 4.10.1, 11.1, 12.1, 13.3–9, 15.1, 2. See also E. R. Dodds, Christian and Pagan in an Age of Anxiety. Some Aspects of Religious Experience from Marcus Aurelius to Constantine, The Wiles Lectures 1963 (Cambridge, 1965), p. 118.

[28] L. Robert, Trois oracles de la théosophie et un prophète d'Apollon, Commtes rendus de l'Académie des Inscriptions et Belles-Lettres (1968), p. 597.

righteousness and purity of heart and lips' (Charlesworth's tr.).[29] This is a strange but not eccentric variant of the conventional Christian conviction that God does not need material sacrifice but desires only the sacrifice of a pure heart. It is repeated endlessly in subsequent writers. In the middle of the second century Ptolemy the Gnostic Christian writing to Flora teaches her that the Saviour did not ordain offerings of irrational beasts nor smoke offerings, but spiritual prayers, praises and thanksgivings.[30] The apologist Aristides declares that God does not need libation or sacrifice and that pagan sacrificial practice argues a lack or need in the deity.[31] Another apologist, Athenagoras, says that as God is ἀνενδεής and ἀπροσδεής he needs no material sacrifice nor whole burnt offering.[32] His contemporary, Irenaeus, echoes this sentiment.[33] *Hostias et victimas deo offeram quas in usum mei protulit*, writes Minucius Felix, *ut reiciam ei suum munus? Ingratum est, cum sit litabilis hostia bonus animus et pura mens et sincera sententia.* Justice and virtue are the best offerings to God. *Haec nostra sacrificia, haec dei sacra sunt: sic apud nos religiosior est ille qui iustior.*[34] Tertullian on many occasions rejects animal sacrifice of any sort. In one passage he quotes the Biblical text which is behind almost all Patristic thought upon this subject, Mal 1.10–11 (though he wrongly attributes it to Micah) *et in omni loco sacrificium nomini meo offertur et sacrificium mundum*, and comments *gloriae scilicet relatio et*

---

[29] Odes of Solomon (ed. J. H. Charlesworth, Oxford, 1973), Ode 20, pp. 116, 117, 1–3. I believe that this passage can explain a difficult earlier text (Ode 7, p. 98, 12), 'wherefore he pitied me in his abundant grace: and granted me to ask from him and to receive from his sacrifice' (Harris' tr.). The word 'sacrifice' in the Syriac here is odd; the Greek, however (recoverable here from the 'Pistis Sophia') has θυσίας. Nestle conjectured οὐσίας, citing a passage in 'II Clement' about our being ἐκ τοῦ μὴ ὄντος. But the parallel is not a parallel but (if we read οὐσίας here) a contradiction, declaring that we are made of οὐσία given by God, and how could any Jew or Christian or Greek conceive of the possibility of asking God so as to receive his οὐσία? The author of the 'Odes of Solomon' appears to think of God as giving us his thought as a sacrifice to offer, and this is identical with purity of heart etc.

[30] Ptolemy to Flora, Migne P.G. 7.1288B.

[31] Aristides, Apology 1.5 and 13.4.

[32] Athenagoras, Supplicatio 13.1, 2.

[33] Irenaeus, Adversus Haereses 4.29.1ff.

[34] Minucius Felix, Octavius 32.2, 3. *Cf.* 30.6.

benedictio et laus et hymni.[35] Elsewhere he writes, *offero opimam et maiorem hostiam quam ipse* (sc. *Deus) mandavit, orationem de carne pudica, de anima innocenti, de spiritu sancto profectam*, not incense nor wine nor the blood of an ox offered with a defiled conscience.[36] Christians do not use incense.[37] God did not need sacrifices.[38] The Christian parts of the 'Sibylline Oracles' reproduce the same conviction in hexameters. God does not want θυσίη or σπονδή from the pagans or filthy smoke of sacrifice or repulsive blood, rather καὶ ζῶσαν θυσίαν ἐμοὶ τῷ ζῶντι πόριζε, a reference to Rom 12.1.[39] What Christians give to God are pure hearts and cheerful spirits, sweet psalms and songs.[40] We have already seen that Origen regarded pure hearts as better images than statues or paintings. He goes on to say that the bodies of Christians are temples and that these are better than burnt offerings and bloody sacrifices.[41] Cyprian, significantly, pays little attention to this doctrine of the pure heart as a true sacrifice (except for one passage, in Ad Demetrianum 12, which contrasts the smoking altars laden with victims of paganism with the Christian shrines), because he has his own innovating doctrine of the bishop offering Christ in the sacrifice of the eucharist. But his contemporary and, in some respects, antagonist Novatian can insist that sacrificing to idols is forbidden to Christians.[42] Bloody offerings and animal sacrifices, Arnobius declares, are not suitable for human beings to offer: *cultus verus in pectore est atque opinatio de dis digna, nec quicquam prodest inlatio sanguinis et cruoris.*[43] Later he introduces a more drastic analysis of sacrifice. He queries the whole principle not only of animal but of material sacrifice: what is the connection, he asks, between killing an animal and placating a

[35] Tertullian, Adversus Marcionem 3.22.6.

[36] Apologeticus 30.5–6.

[37] *Ibid.*, 42.7. About 200 years later the pilgrim, Etheria, notes that incense is burnt in the cave of the Anastasis at Jerusalem on Easter Day (Peregrinatio 2.24.10). The wheel had come full circle.

[38] Adv. Marc. 2.18.3 and 22.3; *cf.* Ad Scapulam 2.8; De Oratione 28, 29.

[39] Orac. Sib. 8.390–391 and 408 (quotation from the latter).

[40] *Ibid.*, 8.496ff.

[41] Origen, Contra Celsum 8.19, 20.

[42] Novatian, De Cibis Iudaicis 7 (Migne P.L. 3.992).

[43] Arnobius, Adv. Nat. 4.31.

god?[44] He too repudiates the use of incense in worship, after a critical investigation of its use in antiquity.[45] Lactantius says that man is not meant to offer futile animal sacrifices; the only sacrifice is good deeds, *integritas animi* and praise.[46] Eusebius, at the end of a general exposée of Egyptian and Greek religion, summarily concludes that we are not intended to worship God with animal sacrifices nor wreaths nor wooden idols, nor even with temple buildings, but on the contrary λογισμοῖς δὲ κεκαθαρμένοις καὶ δόγμασιν ὀρθοῖς καὶ ἀληθέσι, with detachment of soul and virtue.[47] Just after Constantine's day Firmicus Maternus produces a curious variation on this theme. For him the *vera sacrificia* are the husbandman's toil varying with the seasons.[48] On the whole, however, there are few more impressive examples of Patristic unanimity in the first three centuries of the Church's existence than in this concept of the true sacrifice. It is doubtful if the relatively small number of scholars who have investigated eucharistic doctrine in the early Church have taken sufficient account of this fact.

Many Christian writers with their attack on pagan sacrifices associate an account of human sacrifice carried out in pagan cults, in order to discredit them further. Minucius Felix gives a list of these, partly drawn from his local knowledge of practice in his own Africa, partly from Roman cults and partly from literature.[49] Tertullian briefly summarizes much the same list.[50] Clement of Alexandria racks his literary sources to produce another, largely different, list.[51] Lactantius mentions that the Celts, before they were conquered by the Romans, practised human sacrifice, and appositely quotes the lines of Lucretius:

---

[44] *Ibid.*, 7, 2; *cf.* 15 and 35. This does not prevent him giving a detailed account of the various parts of the sacrificed animal, their treatment and cooking 8.24.

[45] *Ibid.*, 8.26, 36.

[46] Lactantius, Divine Institutes 6.24.26–25.17 (quotation 25.7).

[47] Eusebius, P.E. 3.13.24; *cf.* Laus Constantini 13.1–16.

[48] Firmicus Maternus, De Errore Profanarum Religionum 3.4. He appears to mean that the husbandman offers his toil to God.

[49] Octavius 30.2–6.

[50] Scorpiace 7.6.

[51] Protrepticus 3.42.1–43.4.

tantum relligio potuit suadere malorum.[52] Eusebius gives the most exhaustive list of all, ranging over the whole Graeco-Roman world in his account of human sacrifices and quoting Porphyry, Philo of Byblos, Clement of Alexandria and Dionysius of Halicarnassus.[53] Athanasius gives a briefer list, mentioning only the best known examples, the sacrifice of shipwrecked people by the Scythians, the sacrifice of prisoners of war (by which he is probably referring to the Celts), Egyptian, Cretan and Phoenician practices and the sacrifice of human beings to Juppiter Latiarius by the Romans.[54]

A number of Christian writers show a peculiar interets in the old Roman religion, the religion of Stone Age ceremonies, of a multitude of petty domestic deities who presided over almost every conceivable human action and experience, and even of personified emotions like Pallor and Pavor. Burckhardt remarked with justice that nobody believed in these gods any more at the time that the Christians were attacking them.[55] But this type of religion was part and parcel of the *traditio maiorum* which most Romans regarded as inseparably bound up with the welfare of the Roman Empire, and it was maintained, albeit as a pure formality, at the time that the Christians were being accused of attacking traditional religion, and were suffering for their rejection of it. We may reasonably say that this entirely petrified and formal part of contemporary religion was fair game to the Christians. Minucius Felix rejects it with contempt, but he notes that the gods whose cult it served were supposed to have ensured the greatness of Rome.[56] Tertullian makes merry with Varro's division of gods into *incerti* and *electi*, and with the petty Roman tutelary deities.[57] He believes that the carefully prescribed rites, the priestly privileges, the furniture and details of sacrifice ascribed to the institution of Numa Pompilius are a

---

[52] Div. Inst. 1.21.13, 14. Minucius Felix and Tertullian had also mentioned the Celts as practising human sacrifice.

[53] P.E. 4.16. 1–27.

[54] Contra Gentes 25.1–25.

[55] J. Burckhardt, The Age of Constantine the Great (E.T. by M. Hadas, 1948 of a re-ed., 1880, of the original work of 1852), p. 130.

[56] Octavius 25.8, 9.

[57] Ad Nationes 2.9, 10.

deliberate and diabolic imitation of *morositatem illam Iudaicae legis.*[58] The writer who shows the greatest interest in and knowledge of the old Roman religion is Arnobius. We have had already occasion to notice that he details the various parts of the sacrificial animal with their functions. His interest in this particular cult extends far beyond this part of it. He shows himself knowledgeable about the sacrificial ritual and about incense; he is aware that neither Romulus nor Numa nor Alba nor Etruria-*mater superstitionis*—used it.[59] One of his sources is Cornelius Labeo, an antiquarian neo-Platonist who wrote a work called 'De Oraculo Apollinis' and another called 'Dii animales' (*i.e.* the spirits of the dead), and who was particularly expert in the old Roman religion.[60] Divination of any sort was equally repellent to the Christians. The Jews too were strictly forbidden to dabble in it, and a Jewish passage in the 'Oracula Sibyllina' expressly denounces it.[61] Intellectuals, both Roman and Greek, had long derided the art of divination. We can recall Cicero's famous jibe, *mirabile videtur quod non rideat haruspex cum haruspicem viderit* (De Nat. Deorum 1.26). We can find this scorn reflected in Clement of Alexandria's sweeping dismissal of all diviners from grain, inspectors of entrails and pronouncers of oracles from the dead in the Egyptian or Tyrrhenian (*i.e.* Etruscan) tradition.[62] But other writers took the art of divination more seriously. They either, like Minucius Felix, laboured to show that those who disobeyed auguries did not encounter disaster thereby and that those who obeyed them were unsuccessful in spite of their piety,[63] or, like Origen, they admit that auguries are sometimes correct in their predictions but maintain that they were manipulated by evil daemons.[64] Johanna ter Vrugt-Lenz has examined this subject in an interesting article.[65] She shows that if we are to regard the

---

[58] De Praescriptione Haereticorum 56.
[59] Adv. Nat. 2.67, 68; 8.24, 26.
[60] De Labriolle, Réaction Païenne, pp. 298–299, 301.
[61] 3.221–230.
[62] Protrep. 2.11.1, 2.
[63] Octavius 26.1–4.
[64] Contra Celsum 4.90–98.
[65] Johanna ter Vrugt-Lenz, Das Christentum und die Leberschau, Vigiliae Christianae 25 (1971), pp. 17–28.

originally Etruscan art of *haruspicina* as an adopted part of the Old Roman Religion, then the judgment of both Cicero and of Jacob Burckhardt must be modified. It was not a mere piece of archaism by the time that Christian writers came to examine it. On the contrary, the art of the *haruspex* showed a surprising vitality and continued to be practised by Christians and pagans (and denounced by the authorities) long after even Constantine's day, right into the sixth and seventh centuries. The Greek tradition of the inspired *mantis* had collapsed, but the more technical, professional, pseudo-scientific art of *haruspicina* long survived. The Western fathers at least realized that they were here facing a very obstinate example of superstition.

Generally the Christians' attitude to pagan religion compelled them to detach themselves from a large part of the activity, especially the communal and public activity, of the society in which they lived. They abstained from joining in festivals, processions, the theatre, the circus, the amphitheatre, public holidays. This fact is so widely known that it scarcely needs illustration. Tertullian, who provides perhaps the best illustration of this point, even had serious doubts as to whether it was permissible for Christians to serve in the Roman army (voiced especially in his 'De Corona'). It is not at all surprising that considerable unpopularity attached itself to the Christians as a result of this aversion from joining themselves to pagan public occasions. Arnobius, with many other writers, testifies to the scandal which Christians gave by their boycotting of festivals and religious rites.[66] Celsus, as we have seen, declared that it meant that they must belong to a secret society.[67] He asks why should Christians not partake in public festivals. Origen replies that Christians keep perpetual festival in their hearts to God, and that they have their own festivals, the Lord's Day, Preparation, Passover and Pentecost.[68] Celsus goes further and points out that if everybody followed the example of the Christians, the whole Roman State would collapse and the Empire would be left defenceless. Origen's reply that Christians defend the Empire with their prayers cannot but appear lame.

[66] Adv. Nat. 6.1.
[67] Contra Celsum 8.17.
[68] *Ibid.*, 8.21–23.

'Accept public office!' says Celsus. 'We do—in the Church', replies Origen.[69] There is a curious anticipation here of what happened in the fourth and fifth centuries. There is a remarkable story to be found in Lactantius of how Christians, attending in accordance with their duty as officials of Diocletian's court at Antioch a pagan ceremony involving consulting the omens by *haruspicina*, crossed themselves, with the result that the entrails failed to provide any guidance.[70] It typifies that unyielding hostility to society which characterizes much Christian behaviour in the first three centuries, and which is exemplified by Lactantius himself as well as by any other writer. *Infatigabilem militiam Deo militemus*, he cries, *stationes vigiliasque celebremus, congrediamur cum hoste, quem novimus, fortiter, etc.*[71] We cannot help admiring this courageous defiance of Graeco-Roman society and of the power of the Roman Empire. But we cannot help observing how utterly unfitted were people who held such sentiments and who had been brought up in such a tradition to face the situation which arose when Roman Imperial policy, switching abruptly from violent hostility to warm friendship, decided in the fourth century to favour the Christian Church instead of persecuting it.

In attacking, not merely the cult of statues and animal sacrifices with all their accompanying ceremonial, but also the old myths, Greek and Roman, which were related as the explanation of much Greek and Roman pagan religion, whether Homer's stories of the gods or other myths about gods, earlier or later than Homer, the Christians, as they well knew, had been anticipated by the pagans themselves. The philosophers of the Academy who were the successors of Plato had developed a large range of arguments against the absurdity and immorality of these stories. Carneades in the mid-second

---

[69] *Ibid.*, 8.69–71, 73, 75.

[70] Divine Instit. 4.27 and De Mortibus Persecutorum 10. Eusebius' account in Vita Constantini II.50, 51 and 54 of Constantine's story of Diocletian having consulted the oracle of Apollo at Delphi and of the oracle refusing to answer because of people who were identified as Christians may be a muddled version of this, or may represent a genuine and distinct episode. See de Labriolle, Réaction Païenne, pp. 318–320.

[71] Divine Inst. 7.27.

century before Christ had been pre-eminent here. The story of
Zeus' tomb which was shown in Crete, for instance, had already
met the scorn of the Academics before the Christians produced
it in evidence. Heracleitus and Theocritus of Chios and
Musonius Rufus were supposed to have attacked the old stories
about the gods. Cicero in his 'De Natura Deorum' had, largely
through the mouth of the sceptic in his dialogue, Cotta, used the
immense number of different stories about Juppiter and others
to discredit the whole existence of gods. Lucretius had exposed
the immorality of the myth of Iphigenia and such stories in
tremendous hexameters (Lactantius quotes him once or twice).
Greek and Latin comedy had long made fun of the stories of the
gods. Lucian of Samosata in the second century A.D. had
satirized the traditional stories of the gods in his 'De Sacrificiis',
and his 'Menippus' as bitingly as any Christian writer ever did.[72]

When therefore the Christians attacked the old myths they
were following a much-worked vein. The long and rhetorical
attacks upon these myths such as we find in Tatian, in Clement
of Alexandria's 'Protrepticus', in Arnobius and in Athanasius'
'Contra Gentes' cannot have greatly impressed any pagans who
read them. They did not need Aristides to remind them that
myths cannot be historical and should not be deliberate
fictions,[73] nor Minucius Felix to point out that gods could not be
born and could not die and should not behave immorally.[74] And
on the rare occasions when we can see the pagans counter-
attacking, the Christian reply suggests that the writer is on weak
ground. Celsus had pointed to the stories of Adam and Eve, of

---

[72] The following authors call attention to this fact: Burckhardt, Age of
Constantine, pp. 131–133; H. Chadwick, Origen's 'Contra Celsum' in E.T.,
Introd. p. x note on 1.25 and 3.43; de Labriolle, Réaction Païenne, p. 100;
Nock, Conversion, p. 107; M. L. W. Laistner, Christianity and Pagan
Culture in the Later Roman Empire (New York, 1951), p. 52; P. Courcelle,
Anti-Christian Arguments and Christian Platonism: from Arnobius to St.
Ambrose, in: A. Momigliano (ed.), The Conflict between Paganism and
Christianity in the Fourth Century (Oxford, 1963), p. 155. Justin Martyr tells
us about Heracleitus and Musonius Rufus in Apol. 1.46; 2.8, and Clement of
Alexandria about Theocritus in Protrep. 10.97.1, cf. Tertullian, Ad Nat. 1.10.

[73] Aristides, Apology 13.7.

[74] Octavius 23.1–4; cf. Arnobius, Adv. Nat. 4.21; Origen, Contra Celsum
1.17, 25; Athanasius, Contra Gentes 10.30–37, 12.1–28.

Noah and the Ark, of the Virgin Birth of Jesus and of the resurrection appearances and had asked why these stories should be treated with greater respect than the Greek myths were.[75] What we know of Porphyry's 'Against the Christians' makes it quite clear that he followed the same line of argument effectively. A certain immaturity in the Christian apologetic makes itself felt in their tendency to blame the poets and artists for propagating the myths about the gods. It may be that this tendency has its roots in Jewish thought, for the wholly Jewish Book III of the 'Sibylline Oracles' has one passage in which the Sibyl predicts the appearance of a deceitful poet (ψευδογράφος πρέσβυς, 419) who will represent men like Hector, Priam and Achilles to be gods.[76] Athenagoras accuses the earliest Greek artists of having invented the gods of the Greek pantheon.[77] Minucius Felix declares that the poets were particularly responsible for spreading falsehood about the gods: *carminibus praecipue poetarum qui plurimum quantum veritati ipsi sua auctoritate nocuerunt.* Homer is the worst of this band of forgers, and Plato rightly caused him to be expelled from his ideal republic.[78] Tertullian regards Homer as the prince of poets, but remarks that he gave the first example of ridiculing the gods: *exinde quis non poetarum ex auctoritate principis sui in deos insolens, aut vera prodendo aut falsa fingendo?*[79] Clement of Alexandria, who has a larger acquaintance with Greek literature than most other Christian writers, surprisingly shows himself more Philistine than the others. He indulges in a long denunciation of the artists who contribute to idolatry and the obscenity associated with it. He reached the point of quoting the commandment against graven images (Exod 20.4 and Deut 5.8) and hurling it against the artists, mentioning by name Praxiteles, Lysippus and Apelles.[80] Athanasius lays the main blame for the corruption of pagan religion on the poets and chroniclers (συγγραφεῖς, 5.13)

---

[75] Origen, Contra Celsum 1.37; 2.16, 55–58; 3.22–33, 43; 4.17, 21, 38, 39, 41.
[76] Or. Sib. 3.419–433.
[77] Supplicatio 13.1, 2.
[78] Octavius 24.1, 2.
[79] Ad Nationes 1.10.
[80] Protrep. 4.57.1–62.3.

who represented the gods in their stories as immoral.[81] Some pagans may reply that these are only the inventions of poets whose practice and character it is τὰ μὴ ὄντα πλάττεσθαι καὶ ψεύδεσθαι περὶ μύθων εἰς ἡδονὴν τῶν ἀκουσάντων (16.3–4), but Athanasius goes on to argue that if the poets are untrustworthy in ascribing immorality to the gods then they cannot be trusted for any information about them.[82] A later generation of Christian theologians, under less stress and therefore broader in their outlook, was to do better justice to the Greek poets, in such works as Basil of Caesarea's Πρὸς τους νέους and the books of Gregory of Nazianzus.

It is certainly true that at the period when the Christians were attacking the Greek myths no educated man would have defended them as literally true. Cicero had described their literal sense as absurd, vulgar and unworthy.[83] A long tradition of allegorizing them had existed and continued to flourish from Pherecydes and Anaxagoras in the fifth and sixth centuries before Christ through the Stoics, Heracleides Ponticus and Plutarch to Porphyry.[84] Celsus himself, as Origen has occasion to note, was far from eschewing allegory in his handling of the Greek myths.[85] The Christian writers who attacked the myths were not so unsophisticated as to be unaware of this. They frequently allude to the pagans' attempts to salvage the religious value of their myths by allegorizing them. Tatian rejects the allegorizing of pagan myths, especially the allegorizing of Homer's stories of the gods by Metrodorus of Lampsacus; he

[81] Contra Gentes 15.12–22.

[82] *Ibid.*, 16.1–5. Athanasius refers to Homer (though not by name) as ὁ πάντων ἐξοχώτατος ποιητής, 18.33.

[83] Cicero, De Natura Deorum 2.28.

[84] For a succinct account of the history of allegorizing among the pagan Greeks see R. P. C. Hanson, Allegory and Event. A Study of the Sources and Significance of Origen's Interpretation of Scripture (London, 1959) pp. 37–39, 55–62. *Cf.* also H. de Lubac, Histoire et Esprit, L'intelligence de l'Ecriture d'après Origène, Théologie 16 (Paris, 1950); R. M. Grant, The Letter and the Spirit (London, 1957); J. Daniélou, Sacramentum Futuri, Études sur les origines de la typologie biblique, Études de théologie historique 19 (Paris, 1960).

[85] Origen, Contra Celsum 3.43 and 6.52. For other references to pagans allegorizing in this work *cf.* 4.17, 38; 5.29; 8.66–68.

changed them, says Tatian, into φύσεως ὑποστάσεις καὶ στοιχείων διακοσμήσεις.[86] Tertullian in characteristic style refuses to allow the plea that the repulsive story of Chronos, Saturn and Juppiter can be allegorized: *quid sibi vult intellectio ista nisi foedas materias mentitis argumentationibus colorare?*[87] Arnobius declares that the pagans enjoy reading stories of the gods fighting each other, but they defend them by allegorizing them.[88] He subjects this practice to a more radical critique than most other writers. The heathen defend these unworthy or salacious stories: *allegoricis sensibus et subditivis intelleguntur omnia illa secretis.*[89] He asks, how do we know that these incidents are to be allegorized?,[90] and he gives an admirable account of the incurable subjectivity of allegory:[91]

> *cum enim rebus de occlusis omnis ista quae dicitur allegoria sumatur nec habeat finem certum in quo rei quae dicitur sit fixa atque immota sententia, unicuique liberum est in id quo velit adtrahere lectionem et adfirmare id positum in quod eum sua suspicio et coniectura opinabilis duxerit.*

Eusebius gives many examples of pagan allegorizing of myths, and mentions especially Plutarch and the Neo-Platonists.[92] He mentions three types of religion: the μυθικόν which takes these myths as stories of gods and so involves polytheism, the φυσικόν which turns these myths into pseudoscientific statements about the elements, and the πολιτικόν, which assumes that divine intervention by oracles into man's affairs

---

[86] Oratio 21.2, 3.

[87] Ad. Nat. 2.12.

[88] Adv. Nat. 4.33.

[89] *Ibid.*, 5.32. The particular stories Arnobius has described with gleeful and not altogether necessary detail in 5.1–29. They include the story of Numa's discovery by trickery how to manipulate Juppiter's thunderbolt; the story of Attis from the mysteries of Magna Mater full of sexual detail; a traditional story of a phallus appearing on a hearth and begetting in a chosen virgin Servius, King of the Romans; various discreditable incidents connected with the Corybantes; salacious stories from the Phrygian mysteries of Juppiter's incest; the story of Demeter and Baubo from the Eleusinian cycle; and accounts of the use of the phallus in different rites.

[90] *Ibid.*, 5.33.

[91] *Ibid.*, 5.34.

[92] P.E. 2.6.6ff.; 3.1–15.

takes place.[93] Firmicus Maternus tells us that some have interpreted the ritual weeping of Isis for Osiris in Egypt and the accompanying myths so as to make Osiris stand for the seeds of the crops, Isis for the earth, Tyfo for heat and the whole rite to mean the breaking up of nature in winter and its restoration in spring.[94] The cult of Magna Mater and Attis at Pessinus in Phrygia is also, he says, given 'a scientific interpretation' (*physica ratio*) and made a description of the cycle of nature.[95] The stories of Liber and of the rape of Proserpina (for which, as we shall see, he has his own explanation) have given rise to two different explanations: Liber is the sun and Proserpina the moon, or the stories refer to *indivisam mentem et divisam, id est* τὸν ἀμέριστον καὶ τὸν μεμερισμένον νοῦν. Needless to say, Firmicus scouts both suggestions.[96] The Christian attack upon pagan allegorizing was, however, considerably weakened by the fact that all Christian authors themselves used allegory on both Old and New Testaments, and especially on the Old. Celsus is aware that Christians allegorize stories in the book of Genesis to make them more palatable; he knew that some simple Christians took all parts of the Bible literally whereas the intellectuals used allegory.[97] Here he had Origen, the great allegorizer, at a disadvantage. Porphyry, in defending the symbolic interpretation of the cult of statues, had pointed out that Christians allegorized anthropomorphisms, such as 'the finger of God' in the Bible.[98] The Christian authors show a surprising obtuseness here. Eusebius, not very long after castigating pagan authors for allegorizing the Greek myths, can claim that the life of Jacob as recorded in Genesis 'is open to allegorizing' (τὰ δὲ καὶ δι᾽ ὑπονοιῶν ἀλληγορούμενα) and attempts to defend the soundness of applying allegory to the Old Testament, calling in Plato's authority to support the argument.[99]

---

[93] *Ibid.*, 3.17.5.
[94] Firmicus Maternus, De Errore 2.6.
[95] *Ibid.*, 3.1, 2.
[96] *Ibid.*, 7.7, 8.
[97] Origen, Contra Celsum 3.18, 19; 4.38. See de Labriolle, Réaction Païenne, pp. 160–163.
[98] De Labriolle, *op. cit.*, pp. 273–274.
[99] P.E. 7.8.29 (from which the quotation is taken); 10, 11–17; 12.4–31.

Some authors[100] have suggested that much of the Christian attack on the Greek and Roman myths was an assault on a paper tiger. They were attacking something which nobody believed in, a religion which had been long dead, a literary reconstruction and not a living contemporary cult. It is true that nobody took the myths seriously as straightforward descriptions of the activities of divine agencies. It is true that in rejecting the attempt to make them relevant by allegory the Christians were unconsciously damaging their own very similar use of allegory on the Bible. But we must remember how deeply embedded these myths were in pagan culture and how constantly the pagans appealed in their opposition to Christianity to religion as a single whole handed down by immemorial tradition from a remote period which must be accepted as a whole so that the erosion of any part of it, however apparently absurd or meaningless or indecent, might affect the whole and with this violation bring incalculable disaster from the divine forces which guaranteed the security of the fabric of society and the permanence of the Roman Empire. This is the argument of the Roman official who examines Cyprian at his last trial, of the pagan Caecilianus in Minucius Felix's dialogue, of the prefect Aemilianus who questions Dionysius of Alexandria during the Valerian persecution. For better or for worse, these myths were part and parcel of Greek and Roman religion. The Christians advocated a clean break with that religion, and were on occasion ready to pay for their principles with their lives. The myths were a fair target for them, even though we may think that the Christians did not often hit the bull's eye.

II   Philosophy of Religion

It can loosely be said that Christian writers in attacking paganism formulated a philosophy of religion, in that they searched for consistent explanations of the origin and nature of

---

[100] *E.g.*, Burckhardt, Age of Constantine, pp. 131–132; F. Cumont, The Oriental Religions in Roman Paganism (anon.) (E.T. Chicago, 1911 of revised ed. 1911 of original work of 1909), pp. 202–204.

pagan religion and even occasionally of all religion. This philosophy of religion is worth examining.

We have already had occasion to note that they ascribed much of paganism to the activity of daemons. In accepting the existence of these beings as needing no demonstration nor argument they were simply reproducing one of the universally held beliefs of their time. Plutarch gives us much information about these daemons. He quotes the definition of Cleombrotus that they are:

φύσεις τινὲς ὥσπερ ἐν μεθορίῳ θεῶν καὶ ἀνθρώπων δεχόμεναι πάθη θνητὰ καὶ μεταβολὰς ἀναγκαίας.[101]

They act as agents and servitors to the gods, doing such services as inspecting sacrifices offered to the gods and participating in the mysteries; others punish the arrogant and those who are guilty of great crimes. They reveal greater or less traces of ἀρετή and of τὸ παθητικόν and τὸ ἄλογον. Our traditional sacrifices and rites and mythical stories show scattered traces and signs of them.[102] Sad, inauspicious feasts and fasts and ceremonies of orgiastic violence or disgraceful ceremonies belong to evil (φαύλων) daemons who have to be appeased. The same applies to divinities who demand human sacrifices or who pursue mortals with outrageous desire or inflict plagues or famines or who stir up war.[103] This kind is also responsible for any story or divine activities unworthy of the gods, such as tales recounting gods being concealed or exiled or put to service.[104] Daemons can die, and to prove this one of the characters in the dialogue 'De Defectu Oraculorum' tells the well-known story of the announcement of the death of Pan.[105] Celsus admitted the Christian view that idols are manipulated by daemons, but regarded it as part of the providential ordering of things.[106] Daemons do honour to the god who has appointed them.[107]

---

[101] Plutarch, De Defectu Oraculorum (ed. R. Flacelière [Paris, 1947]) 12.415.

[102] Ibid., 13.417.

[103] Ibid., 14.417.

[104] Ibid., 15.417.

[105] Ibid., 17.419.

[106] Origen, Contra Celsum 7.68.

[107] Ibid., 8.2.

Christians cannot evade daemons by avoiding pagan rites because daemons are present everywhere performing the tasks to which they have been appointed, and we should be grateful to them for looking after us in this way.[108] It would be unwise to insult the high officials of a king; it is therefore unwise to insult daemons.[109] If Christians take part in the ordinary experiences of life, its pains and pleasures, they should acknowledge that these are administered and supplied to them by daemons.[110] But Celsus goes on to point out, somewhat inconsistently, that some people hold that daemons are only concerned with corporeal and mortal affairs, with such things as sacrificial blood and burnt-offerings and magical enchantments, and we ourselves should largely ignore them and seek after higher things.[111] And he suggests that as those who are in authority only hold power with the help of daemons it is advisable to worship daemons.[112]

The Christian account of daemons is very similar except that they identify all daemons as evil and none as good. Clement of Alexandria explicitly says so.[113] They bring about human sacrifices and fatal events and they manipulate oracles.[114] They haunt tombs in the form of 'wraith-like appearances' (σκιοειδῆ φαντάσματα, Plato, Phaedo 81 CD).[115] They are neither immortal nor mortal, οὐδὲ γὰρ αἰσθήσεως, ἵνα καὶ θανάτου, μετειλήφασιν.[116] The healings done at the shrines of Asclepius, Origen tells us, are not due to a god but to an evil daemon called Asclepius.[117] A series of legends of people coming back from the dead produced by Celsus in the course of his argument were deliberately invented or caused by daemons in order to discredit the resurrection of Jesus in advance.[118] Minucius Felix appears to

---

[108] *Ibid.*, 8.28, 33.

[109] *Ibid.*, 8.35; Origen answers well: no wise man would want to harm anyone; if daemons want to harm us, they must be evil (36).

[110] *Ibid.*, 8.55.

[111] *Ibid.*, 8.60.

[112] *Ibid.*, 8.63.

[113] Protrep. 2.10.1–41.4.

[114] *Ibid.*, 3.42.1–43.4.

[115] *Ibid.*, 4.55.5–56.1.

[116] *Ibid.*, 10.103.2.

[117] Contra Celsum 3.24, 25; magi are in communication with them, 1, 60.

[118] *Ibid.*, 3.26–33.

regard them as fallen angels who have undergone a metaphysical transmutation: *postquam simplicitatem substantiae suae onusti et immersi vitiis perdiderunt.*[119] Socrates made important decisions on the advice of his daemon; the Magi used them; Plato recognised them and analysed their nature in his 'Symposium'. They lurk in statues, they cause people to have diseases and then cure them in order to advance polytheism, and under exorcism by Christians they will admit that they have engaged in such wiles and frauds.[120] That spirits good and evil were nourished by the smoke and smell of sacrifice is a very old and widespread religious idea, evidenced in Genesis 8.21.[121] The Christians reproduce this primitive idea in as far as they believe that the evil daemons are nourished by the pagan sacrifices.[122] Firmicus Maternus is one of the many who testify to this belief: *nihil operantur victimae et cruor ex assidua pecudum caede profusus nisi ut daemonum substantia qui diaboli procreatione generantur ex isto sanguine nutriatur.* Porphyry had admitted as much in his book on 'The Philosophy of the Oracles'. The daemon Serapis had on one occasion admitted this on being exorcised from a man's body.[123] Firmicus even gives us a description of a man undergoing exorcism:[124]

> *ecce daemon iste quem colis, cum Dei et Christi nomen audiuerit, contremiscit, et ut interrogantibus nobis respondeat, trepidantia verba vix colligit, adhaerens homini laceratur, uritur, vapulat et statim de commissis sceleribus confitetur.*

That the Christian writers did distinguish between different forms of pagan religion is shown by their singling out the mystery-religions for special mention. They were well aware of the resemblances between Christianity and the mystery

[119] Octavius, 28.8.

[120] *Ibid.*, 28.9, 10, 11, 12.

[121] Nock, Conversion p. 226, reminds us of this (without reference to Genesis); but many others, including W. W. Fowler, The Religious Experience of the Roman People (London, 1911) had already noted it.

[122] Origen Contra Celsum 3.28, 37, et alibi; Comm. on Matt 13.23. Chadwick gives many references to the universality of this belief in the third century in loc. Contra Celsum 3.28.

[123] Firmicus Maternus, De Errore 13.4.

[124] *Ibid.*, 28.11.

religions. Tertullian is even for the sake of argument ready to allow that Christianity can be placed in the category of mystery religion, along with the Samothracian and Eleusinian mysteries. It is their reticence that forms the common element.[125] He regards mystery religions as imitations of Christianity deliberately devised by the devil, specifically naming Mithraism, as indeed he also regards the ancient Roman religion (cf above, p. 154–5).[126] He mentions parallels to baptism in pagan religions, which he also regards as diabolical.[127] The insistence of some pagan religions in various rites upon some women taking part being *univira* is another example, *cum Dei sacramenta satanas affectat*.[128] Clement of Alexandria derides a long list of mysteries, those of Deo, of Dionysus, the Thracian, Phrygian and Greek mysteries, those of Dardanus, of the Mother of the gods, of Eetion, of Samothrace, of Midas the Phrygian, Cinyras' mysteries of Aphrodite.[129] But he is capable of trying to outbid them by using the vocabulary of mystery religions (specifically the purely literary religion of Euripides' 'Bacchae') in speaking of Christianity:[130]

δᾳδοχοῦμαι τους οὐρανοὺς καὶ τὸν θεὸν ἐποπτεῦσαι, ἅγιος γίνομαι μυούμενος, ἱεροφαντεῖ δὲ ὁ κύριος καὶ τὸν μύστην σφραγίζεται φωταγωγῶν, καὶ παρατίθεται τῷ πατρὶ τὸν πεπιστευκότα αἰῶσι τηρούμενον. ταῦτα τῶν ἐμῶν μυστηρίων τὰ βακχεύματα· εἰ βούλει καὶ σὺ μυοῦ, καὶ χορεύσεις μετ᾽ ἀγγέλων ἀμφὶ τὸν ἀγένητον καὶ ἀνώλεθρον καὶ μόνον ὄντως θεόν, συνυμνοῦντος ἡμῖν τοῦ θεοῦ λόγου.

Arnobius parades the salacious stories attached to the mystery religions with no less relish than he does those of other religions, but he realizes that not all nations indulge in these religions. The Romans, the Gauls, the Spaniards, the Africans, the Germans and the Sicilians are free of them.[131] Eusebius cites Philo of

---

[125] Apologeticus 7.6.
[126] De Praescr. Haer. 40.
[127] De Baptismo 5.1; cf. 5.4 *immundi spiritus aquis incubunt*.
[128] De Exhortatione Castitatis 13.2. Compare Firmicus Maternus' fulsome contrast of the eucharist with eating ceremonies in mystery religions, De Errore 18.2, *alius est cibus qui languentes relevat, errantes revocat, lapsos erigit*, etc.
[129] Protrep. 2.12.1–13.5.
[130] *Ibid.*, 12.120, 1, 2.
[131] Adv. Nat. 5.24.

Byblus to demonstrate that mystery religions were invented by Egyptian priests in order to give a spurious glamour to honour paid to Thoth, a purely historical character, the inventor of writing.[132] Firmicus Maternus mentions and reviles the contemporary practice of *taurobolium* and *criobolium*.[133] Mithraism seems to have been the mystery religion which caught the attention of the early Church more than the others. This is not surprising, as this religion seems to have made its impact upon the Roman Empire most prominently under Commodus, the Severi and the Gordians (182–244), and between 284 and 313, when it was given official recognition by Diocletian and Galerius, as well as in the last brief pagan revivals of the fourth century.[134] Tertullian, one of whose references to Mithraism we have noted already (see p. 167), speaks of the lions of Mithras as allegorized by contemporary philosophy,[135] and he notes that the followers of Mithras also refuse to wear a military crown, as Tertullian would like Christian soldiers to do.[136] Celsus gives an elaborate account of the Mithraic conception of the ascent of the soul through seven planets, apparently approving of this cult and regarding it as preferable to Christianity. Origen, in reply, plays down Mithraism. He gives a list of native Greek and Egyptian mysteries, remarking that the Greeks do not think that the mysteries of Mithras have anything remarkable in them compared with those at Eleusis or those of Hecate at Aegina, and he wonders that Celsus should have preferred these exotic Persian mysteries.[137] Here Origen is noting a genuine tendency in the religious history of his time. Mithraism, when it began to spread to the Roman Empire, made little appeal to the Greeks but was eagerly adopted by the Romans.[138] It is the Latin-speaking Fathers who show most

[132] P.E. 1.9.24–26.
[133] De Errore 27.8.
[134] Nock, Conversion, p. 132.
[135] Adversus Marcionem 1.13.5.
[136] De Corona 15.3.4.
[137] Contra Celsum 6.22; but in 23 he parallels the cult and symbolism of Mithras with Ezekiel 48, 31–35, Revelation 21 and Numbers 2. He does not claim that Mithraism is a devilish imitation of Christ.
[138] Cumont, Oriental Religions, p. 150.

interest in it. Firmicus Maternus mentions Mithraists as Persians who worship fire, and divide it into two powers, male and female, symbolized respectively by an ox and by intertwined serpents. They call the ox Mithras and worship him in caves and darkness.[139]

We may well ask, how well acquainted were the Christian writers with the mysteries which they derided and attacked? A few of them may have had first-hand acquaintance with mystery religions before they were converted to Christianity. Tatian says that he had investigated many cults and had even been initiated in the mysteries.[140] Most of those who attacked the mysteries knew the myths and cult-stories attached to them, but, at least in the case of the Greek mysteries, these would be easily accessible from Greek literature. Some authors quote formulae which they allege to be uttered by candidates for initiation during the enactment of the mysteries. Clement quotes ἐκ τυμπάνου ἔφαγον, ἐκ κυμβάλου ἔπιον ἐκερνοφόρησα, ὑπὸ τὸν παστὸν ὑπέδυν. He says that this comes from the Phrygian mysteries of Attis and Cybele and the Corybantes. Firmicus Maternus reproduces this formula, adding γέγονα μύστης Ἄττεως.[141] J. Burckhardt maintained that these formulae were in fact from the cult of Sabazius regarded as a personification of Dionysus.[142] Clement goes on to quote the formal statement of the initiate in the Eleusinian mysteries, ἐνήστευσα, ἔπιον τὸν κυκεῶνα, ἔλαβον ἐκ κίστης, ἐργασάμενος ἀπεθέμην εἰς κάλαθον καὶ ἐκ καλάθου εἰς κίστην.[143] Firmicius Maternus, who interprets all mystery religions as poor travesties of Christianity, quotes a few more fragments of ritual formulae[144] without mentioning the mysteries from which they come. He also relates that in one (again anonymous) mystery cult the image of a god is laid on a litter and a rhythmical lamentation-song is sung; then a light is

---

[139] De Errore 5.1, 2.
[140] Oratio 29.1.
[141] Clem. Alex., Protrep. 2.15.3; Firm. Mat., De Errore 18.1.
[142] Age of Constantine, p. 169.
[143] Protrep. 2.21.2.
[144] θεὸς ἐκ πέρας, De Errore 20. 1ff.; εὐοῖ δικέρως δίμορφε, ibid., 21.2; ταῦρος δράκοντος καὶ ταύρου δρακὼν πατήρ, 26.1.

brought in, the priest anoints the throats of everyone present with ointment, *quibus peractis sacerdos lento murmure susurrat*

θαρρεῖτε μύσται τοῦ θεοῦ σεσωσμένου·
ἔσται γὰρ ἡμῖν ἐκ πόνων σωτηρία.[145]

We may conclude that those Christian writers who attacked the mystery religions were not totally ignorant of them. They knew that these cults constituted a special group among contemporary religions and a group which more closely resembled Christianity than any others, both in the reticence with which the cult was surrounded and in the use of sacraments. They had picked up some phrases and formulae from the mystery-religions. They recognised that these cults were living religions and that they were Christianity's most formidable rival. But they had little or no genuinely inside knowledge of them and no serious understanding of them. Up to the age of Constantine the time had not yet come for Christianity consciously to imitate the mystery religions. It is only in the second half of the fourth century and later that we find the vocabulary of these cults deliberately introduced into Christianity on a large scale, when instruction before baptism can be called 'Mystagogic Catechesis', when mystery religion language can be used in speaking of the eucharist, when the *disciplina arcani* becomes effective, when bishops can be dignified by the title of *protomystes*, and can adopt the clerical tonsure from the priests of the mysteries of Isis. Christianity could then afford to spoil the Egyptians, for it knew then that the Egyptians had been defeated.

The mighty Gibbon maintained that Christianity made its way during the first three or four centuries of its existence largely by an appeal to miracles. It is certainly true that both pagans and Christians were ready on occasion to appeal to miracles to support their arguments. And from the second half of the fourth century onwards, miracles associated with saints' lives and saints' relics begin to proliferate greatly. But on a general view Gibbon's verdict cannot be sustained. There were two reasons why Christian apologists and writers of polemic

[145] *Ibid.*, 22.1.

were markedly chary of appealing to miracles to support their case. The first was that the market for miracles in the world of Christian antiquity was saturated. Everybody either performed miracles or claimed to do so, from the most despicable travelling charlatan to highly respectable philosophers like Apollonius of Tyana. A claim to perform miracles did little to advance anyone's cause in the eyes of educated people. The second reason is that miracles were associated with magic, and a charge of operating by magic was one which all well-informed Christians were anxious to avoid. They knew that one of the main charges against Christ was that he had been a magician and that magic, though universally practised, was usually disreputable and potentially treasonous. Porphyry had disparaged miracles.[146] Lactantius claims that Christ is superior to Apollonius of Tyana, not because he did miracles (Apollonius did them too), but because his advent was predicted in Scripture.[147] Arnobius insists that Christ healed directly, without medium or intermediary material, by touch or by word, unlike traditional and mythical healers, no doubt in order to avoid a suspicion of magic.[148] In all his vast output of theological writing Origen makes very little play with the miracles of Christ or his apostles, or even with miracles (apart from miracles of moral improvement) performed by the contemporary Church. He was too much of a rationalist to be impressed by miracles. But he was in this respect not far removed from educated opinion in the Church of his day.

Christianity indeed, in the course of its campaign against all forms of religion except its own and Judaism, deployed a radical destructive criticism which caused Christians to be widely regarded as atheists. Lucian, in his book 'Alexander the False Prophet', informs us that when Alexander had succeeded in establishing his oracle at Abounoteichos he instituted an annual festival as an attraction and at this festival criers warned off

---

[146] Against the Christians, frag. 4 (Harnack's enumeration). De Labriolle, Réaction Païenne, pp. 251ff. See also E. R. Dodds, Pagan and Christian, pp. 124–126.

[147] Div. Inst. 5.3.7–22.

[148] Adv. Nat. 1.48, 49; Arnobius (49) also points out that Christ healed both good and bad.

atheists, Christians and Epicureans. The reputation of Christians as enemies of all religions lasted into the fourth century. Arnobius tells us that pagans charged Christians thus: *religiones impias atque inauditos cultus terrarum in orbe tractatis*,[149] and later he says *infausti et athei nuncupamur*;[150] the pagans believed that Christ *ex orbe religiones expulit* and they called him *religionis extinctor et impietatis auctor*.[151] Eusebius says that in the eyes of the pagans the Christians have abandoned traditional religion in favour of a new, atheist one invented by the Jews.[152] The chief weapon of the Christians in this destructive rationalizing, almost modern, criticism of religion was the device of reducing what was claimed to be supernatural and divine to the human and historical. Octavius, in Minucius Felix's dialogue, sees the ancestral religion reverenced by his friend Caecilianus as a series of incredible unsophisticated legends about gods who are simply figments produced to meet men's needs.[153] Tertullian reduces the gods of the Greek and Roman myths to ordinary men deified after their deaths and insists that though the poets, in telling about them, exaggerated mendaciously, yet the subjects of their myths did exist and were historical characters.[154] He jeers at the concept which he finds in Varro of gods who are undefined (*incerti*) and others who are promoted (*electi*, see above, pp. 154, 161), and the idea of popular or adopted gods. These figures cannot possibly be gods but must be men.[155] We have seen how Arnobius applies robust common sense to the pagans' allegorization of myth (see above, p. 161). The copulation of Mars and Venus described by Homer cannot be interpreted as desire and anger being suppressed by force and the advice of reason; if that were so, why does not the poet say so directly without recourse to ambiguous allegory?[156] Arnobius also uses

[149] Adv. Nationes 1.25.

[150] *Ibid.*, 1.29.

[151] *Ibid.*, 2.2. P. Courcelle, Anti-Christian Arguments, in: Momigliano (ed.), Conflict, p. 153, notes Arnobius' evidence.

[152] P.E. I. 2.1–4.

[153] Octavius 20.5.

[154] Ad. Nat. 2.7.

[155] *Ibid.*, 2.9 and 2.8.

[156] Adv. Nat. 5.41.

his knowledge of comparative religion to disparage the use of incense (see above, p. 153) and insists, like Tertullian, that there are no gods who are not also men; only those deserve to be called gods who have achieved moral perfection.[157] Lactantius in his 'Divine Institutes' has an interesting critique of previous Christian writers. Tertullian's 'Apology' was a negative piece of work, purely defensive. Cyprian's 'Ad Demetrianum' relied too much on Scriptural proof texts though it was aimed at one who regarded the Scriptures as futile, fictitious, indeed a pack of lies; Cyprian should have refuted his opponent *argumentis et ratione* and especially with the words of pagan philosophers.[158] Lactantius' intention in his work, though he hopes to be more positive than was Tertullian, is rationalist destruction of religion and in order to assist his intention he quotes the poet Lucretius,

relligionum animos nodis exsolvere pergo.

His first book of the 'Divine Institutes' is designed to prove that all the gods with whom he deals were human beings, either deified after their deaths by their ignorant admirers or people who set up the worship of themselves in different places during their own lifetime.[159] Lactantius' work must have struck his contemporaries as an ably conducted rationalist and scientific critique of religion. To Athanasius, contemporary polytheism is essentially inconsistent, self-contradictory and irrational.[160] Firmicus Maternus attempts (with no great success) to explain away some of the gods by etymological arguments: *e.g.*, the Penates are simply daily food (*penus*) deified.[161]

In deploying this radical criticism of religion, the Christian authors do not stop short of criticizing the cult of the Roman Emperors which was so prominent a feature of the paganism of their day. On the contrary, they single it out for attack. Much of their argument seems to be deliberately designed to outrage the susceptibilities of patriotic citizens of the Roman Empire. Some of this certainly stemmed from Jewish thought. Anti-Roman

---

[157] *Ibid.*, 8.36.
[158] Div. Inst. 5.4.3–6.
[159] *Ibid.*, 1.23 (a summary); quotation from 1.16.3.
[160] Contra Gentes 23.1–47; 24.1–20.
[161] De Errore 14.1–3.

propaganda is to be found in some of the Jewish parts of the 'Sibylline Oracles'.[162] The first example of Christian polemic against Roman religious tradition is of course the book of Revelation. But later writers are more explicit and less symbolical. Minucius Felix declares that the argument that Rome's greatness was founded on its religion is worthless. The earliest founders of Rome were men of the vilest sort, criminals, outcasts, desperate scoundrels who indulged in wild and lawless actions; the Roman empire grew on rapine and unjust annexation and coercion: *quidquid Romani tenent colunt possident audaciae praeda est: templa omnia de manubiis, id est de ruinis urbium, de spoliis deorum, de caedibus sacerdotum*. It is contemptible to enslave gods and cults.[163] Later he continues to insult Roman Imperial pride: the Vestal virgins were rarely chaste; there were mighty empires before those of Rome—the Assyrian, Median, Persian, Greek and Egyptian.[164] Tertullian resumes the theme: the Romans, he says, have a contempt for their gods and regard them as chattels;[165] and he mocks ruthlessly at Aeneas and Romulus, accusing the one of cowardice and the other of rape.[166] This contempt for the State religion shows itself particularly in a repudiation of the practice of deifying men which easily leads on to an assault on the practice of deifying Roman Emperors. This aversion to the apotheosis of men can sometimes be found in earlier Greek philosophy. Theocritus of Chios derided the cult of Alexander which was practised during the king's lifetime and remarked after Alexander's death: θαρρεῖτε, ἄχρις ἂν ὁρᾶτε τοὺς θεοὺς πρότερον τῶν ἀνθρώπων ἀποθνήσκοντας.[167] Minucius Felix gives a long list of men who were made gods, including Romulus and Juba,

---

[162] *E.g.*, Or. Sib. Book 8, and especially 37–64; verses 50–64 may refer to the deification of Hadrian's favourite, Antinous (for Christian references to Antinous see below, pp. 175) and may therefore be dated shortly after the Jewish revolt of 135–138 which was suppressed by Hadrian. Contrast 12.28–34, a Christian interpolation quite favourable to the Roman Empire in an otherwise Jewish book.

[163] Octavius 25.1–7, the quotation from 5.

[164] *Ibid.*, 25.10, 11.

[165] Ad. Nat. 1.10.

[166] *Ibid.*, 2.9.

[167] Clement of Alexandria, Protrep. 10.97.1.

alleges that Alexander the Great wrote to his mother that he had frightened a priest into betraying the secret that all gods were originally men, and appeals for support to several historians, including Cornelius Nepos and Diodorus Siculus.[168] He is indignant that the Egyptians worship a man; he gives no names but probably refers to Hadrian's favourite, Antinous, after whose accidental death by drowning in Egypt Hadrian erected a temple in Antinoopolis called after the boy and instituted a cult. Minucius regards the worship of kings and princes as sinful and as conferring no honour upon them.[169] Clement of Alexandria continues the assault upon the cult of Antinous: τί μοι θεὸν καταλέγεις τὸν πορνείᾳ τετιμημένον;[170] he gives a list of people who have made themselves gods, including Ptolemy IV, Mithridates of Pontus and Alexander; they were simply men— only legend and lapse of time (ὁ μῦθος καὶ ὁ χρόνος) have made them gods.[171] Celsus in his book Ἀληθὴς Λόγος deliberately brought up the example of Antinous (whom he calls Hadrian's μειράκιον) in order to disparage the divine honours paid to Jesus. Origen (who supplies the name Antinous) of course indignantly rejects the comparison on the grounds of the immorality of Antinous and of Hadrian.[172] Nearly a hundred years later Athanasius still harps upon this theme. The case of Antinous was the worst example of the bad pagan practice of men worshipping their rulers.[173] He goes on to denounce the habit of the Roman senate of deifying those deceased Emperors whom it admired.[174] Lactantius does not refer to Antinous, but he attacks in trenchant terms the Roman habit of deifying Emperors, and in particular he mocks at the apotheosis of Julius Caesar: *apud Romanos deus Iulius quia hoc scelerato homini placuit Antonio; deus Quirinus quia hoc pastoribus*

[168] Octavius 21.1–10.

[169] *Ibid.*, 29.2–5.

[170] Protrep. 4.49.1–3.

[171] *Ibid.*, 4.54.1–55.6.

[172] Origen, Contra Celsum 3.36–38; Chadwick in loc. gives a full list of Christian references to Antinous.

[173] Contra Gentes 9.45–48.

[174] *Ibid.*, 9.49–66. This passage is relevant to the dating of this work of Athanasius; it suggests that Athanasius when he wrote it did not know whether the Roman Senate would deify Constantine after his death or not.

visum est: cum alter gemini fratris extiterit, alter patriae parricida.[175] It may be that Christian authors choose the case of Antinous not only because his was a notorious example in the eyes of pagans but because nobody after Hadrian's death, apart from local people who had a vested interest in the cult, would be particularly inclined to defend Antinous. But it still must have required considerable courage openly to repudiate Emperor-worship in the late Roman Empire.

The reader will have observed the strategy of the Christian authors of reducing the pagan gods to human proportions, of depriving them of their supernatural authority. It was an ingenious plan, and has an interesting parallel in the similar attempt of the Irish monastic writers of the Middle Ages to reduce the pre-Christian Celtic gods to historical characters, heroes and kings and magicians, to de-divinize them, so to speak, by historicizing them. This particular enterprise on the part of the Christian authors demands special attention, and in particular we must examine the pagan author from whom their example and inspiration was derived, Euhemerus. Euhemerus is a figure who has scarcely been given the credit that he deserves as the leading philosopher of religion in pagan antiquity, almost as the Sir James Frazer of the Greeks, whose thought had almost as much influence upon posterity as that of Frazer has had. He was famous in antiquity as an atheist. Cicero said of him and his school: *quid? aut qui fortes aut claros aut potentes viros tradunt post mortem ad deos pervenisse, eosque esse ipsos quos nos colere, precari, venerarique soleamus, nonne expertes sunt religionum omnium?*[176] Sextus Empiricus describes him as Εὐήμερος ὁ ἐπικληθεὶς ἄθεος.[177] His work was translated into Latin by the poet Ennius and was widely read in the Western as well as the Eastern Roman Empire. A large list of ancient authors who refer to him can be compiled, including as well as those already mentioned Strabo, Aetius (in his 'Placita'), Diogenianus, Athenaeus, Plutarch and Diodorus Siculus in addition to at least ten Christian authors whom we shall cite later.[178] Euhemerus was a

[175] Div. Inst. 1.15.28, 29.
[176] De Nat. Deorum 1.42.
[177] Sextus Empiricus, Adversus mathematicos 9.17.
[178] Much the best source for Euhemerus is F. Jacoby, Die Fragmente der

friend and high official of Cassander, one of the *diadochi* kings after the collapse of the Empire of Alexander the Great (fl. 311–298), in whose service he travelled widely and was enabled to observe a great variety of men and manners. As a result of his travels and experiences, he formed a theory of the origin of religion and gave it to the world in the form of an imaginary journey to a kind of Utopia or Erewhon. He said that he had visited a group of islands beyond the Red Sea and the Arabian peninsula, off the coast of Gedrosia, or as we should perhaps say today in the Gulf of Oman. The most important of these islands was called Panchaia and its inhabitants the Panchaeans. On a high hill in this island was a temple dedicated to Zeus Triphylius built by Zeus when as a human being he was ruling the whole earth from this island. At the middle of the sacred seat (κλίνη) of the god, which was made of gold and skilfully decorated, there was a great golden pillar inscribed with an account, written in Egyptian hieroglyphs, of the activities of Ouranos and Zeus and, after this, those of Artemis and Apollo, composed by Hermes. Diodorus Siculus, reproduced by Eusebius, gives a long extract from this work. It is written in good literary Greek in a simple narrative style a little reminiscent of Herodotus, whom perhaps Euhemerus is imitating. He gives an elaborate description of the geographical position of the islands, their plants and products and their hierocratic social structure. He called his work Ἱερὰ Ἀναγραφή, meaning 'The Sacred Inscription'.[179] Euhemerus' theory was that all gods whose cults can be identified were originally human beings who so impressed themselves on the memory of their contemporaries that on their death they were deified. They made this impression by their benefactions and achievements during their lives and in some instances by instituting cults of themselves during their lifetime. Some examples of this historicizing theory

---

Griechischen Historiker, I, Nos. 1–63, D. Anhang pp. 300–313 (Berlin, 1957, re-ed. of orig. ed. 1922). Euhemerus is variously described by different authors as coming from Cos, from Akragas and from Messene. The last is the most likely as being in or near Cassander's dominions.

[179] Ennius translated this 'Sacra Historia'. Lactantius describes the work by two titles, 'Sacra Historia' and 'Sacra Scriptio'. Diogenianus, Proverbs II.67, calls it Ἱερὸς Λόγος, no doubt mistakenly.

given by Euhemerus can be recovered, and indeed they must have been sufficiently shocking to pious ears when he produced them. The hero, Cadmus, was cook to the King of Thebes who eloped with the King's flutegirl Harmonia.[180] He turned the story of Ouranos, Chronos, Zeus, Hera and the Titans into the history of a single human family extending over three generations, a kind of 'Forsyte Saga'. Ouranos becomes a benevolent and gentlemanly character who could follow the movement of the stars and who first offered sacrifice to the heavenly beings, whom Euhemerus apparently identified with the elements, the sun and stars and sky.[181] The story of Chronos eating his children means that the people of his time were cannibals, and Zeus his son in the next generation suppressed this uncivilized habit. His explanation of the existence of many different dedications to Zeus, *e.g.* Zeus Ataburius, Zeus Labryandius, Zeus Laprius, Molio, Casius, *etc.*, was that wherever the historical Zeus went in the world tours which he made, he concluded alliances and concordats with local kings and rulers, and in order to cement these, he ordered that temples and shrines should be set up to himself in the places which he had visited.[182] When after five world tours Zeus died in Crete the Curetes, Vesta and posterity generally saw to it that he was made a god.[183] Venus was a woman who first practised prostitution for profit, in Cyprus, and persuaded women to follow her example in order to avoid the notoriety of being the only one to follow her trade.[184] Clearly Euhemerus engaged in a thorough historicization of the Olympic pantheon and of many other gods as well. We can admire him as an original and able investigator in the field of the philosophy of religion, but we can easily see that he must have disturbed the piety and upset the conventional outlook of pagan antiquity.

[180] Athenaeus, Deipnosophistae 14.658; Euhemerus attributed this story to the Sidonians.

[181] Jacoby *op. cit.*, pp. 302–303, 311. This suggests that Euhemerus was not really an atheist, but that he regarded the elements as divine, thought not the gods of the myths.

[182] This is from Lactantius, Div. Inst. 1.13.2; 1.22.21–27 (Jacoby 311–312).

[183] *Ibid.*, 1.11.45–46 (Jacoby 312). Lactantius does not tell us what Greek divinity corresponds to Vesta (probably Hestia).

[184] *Ibid.*, 1.17.10 (Jacoby 312).

The Christian intellectuals seized with glee upon the theory of Euhemerus and used it as one of their most powerful arguments against contemporary paganism. They could explain the origin of the gods of polytheism! The gods were men and women of the primitive age deified for various reasons, creditable and discreditable. Minucius Felix states that primitive nations worshipped their dead kings and founders and benefactors.[185] He mentions Euhemerus and links with him the writers Prodicus and Persaeus. Saturn, Janus and Juppiter were all originally men; the last was turned out of Latium by his father, migrated to Crete and died there.[186] We have already seen (see above, p. 172) how firmly Tertullian insists that the gods of the myths, for all the exaggeration of the poets, really were no more than men. Gods who are made gods by popular vote can never be more than men.[187] Saturn was simply a man who at an early period colonized some part of Italy and impressed the bucolic and easily deceived natives.[188] Clement of Alexandria mentions Euhemerus by name as refusing to regard the characters in the myth of Anarcharsis as gods, and later though he does not reproduce Euhemerus' speculations, he uses his theory to reduce several gods and goddesses to human dimensions, ending with a story of the origin of the Muses which he ascribes to Mursilos of Lesbos.[189] Cyprian, in 'Quod Idola Dii Non Sint' (1–3) uses the Euhemerist theory without mentioning its author. Arnobius argues that Euhemerus' theory was right and that the pagan gods were simply men and women of a primitive age. As well as naming Euhemerus he gives the names of several Greek authors of the same school.[190] We have already seen that Lactantius is one of the authors upon whom we rely for information about Euhemerus. Before he actually mentions its author he sets out the Euhemerist argument:[191]

---

[185] Octavius 20.5, 6.

[186] Ibid., 21.1, 5–8.

[187] Ad. Nat. 2.8.

[188] Ibid., 2.12.

[189] Protrep. 2.24.2 and 28.1–31.4.

[190] Adv. Nat. 4.29. Clem. Alex. also names several Euhemerist writers Protrep. 2.24.2. Euhemerus cannot have been alone in his rationalist treatment of religion.

[191] Div. Inst. 1.8, 8; he mentions Euhemerus first at 1.11.33, 34. He mentions

> *quomodo ergo, inquiet aliquis, dii crediti sunt? nimirum quia reges maximi et potentissimi fuerunt, ob merita virtutum suarum aut munerum aut artium repertarum, cum cari fuissent iis quibus imperitaverunt, in memoriam sunt consecrati.*

Then he goes on to try his hand at applying Euhemerus' theory. Juppiter's rape of Ganymede by means of an eagle was an exaggerated account of his capturing the boy with a legion whose standard was an eagle. His rape of Europa was achieved in a ship whose figurehead was a bull . . . *non ergo res ipsas gestas finxerunt poetae, quod si facerent essent vanissimi: sed rebus gestis addiderunt colorem.*[192] Pagan religion, in short, is nothing but ancient history touched up by the poets. Eusebius is the most copious source of information about Euhemerus among the fathers.[193] In the second book of his 'Praeparatio Evangelica' he reproduces long extracts from Euhemerus' own work taken direct from the Sixth book of Diodorus Siculus which has not otherwise come down to us. He historicizes Greek cults and mysteries in accordance with this theory,[194] explicitly stating the Euhemerist argument.[195] Though Athanasius does not mention Euhemerus, he uses his thesis in order to reduce to the dimensions of mere history a long list of divinities: Zeus, Poseidon, Apollo, Hephaistus, Hermes, Hera, Demeter, Athene, Artemis, Isis, Kore, Neotera, Aphrodite.[196] He suggests that proof of the mortality of some of the gods still exists in the cults of Osiris, Horus and Typhon in Egypt, of Zeus at Dodona, and (inevitably!) in Crete.[197] It is no good defending the gods on the grounds that they brought beneficent inventions to mankind: in the first place, they were only imitating nature, and in the second place this plea shows the more convincingly that these so-called gods were only men.[198] Firmicus Maternus

---

him and his translator Ennius again De Ira Dei 11, where he also gives an approving nod to Cicero's 'De Natura Deorum'.

[192] *Ibid.*, 1.11.19, 23 (quotation).
[193] Especially P.E. 2.2, 53.
[194] *Ibid.*, 2.4.1–6.
[195] *Ibid.*, 2.3.3–5.
[196] Contra Gentes 10.1–9, 15ff.
[197] *Ibid.*, 10.30–37.
[198] *Ibid.*, 18.1–40.

operates the Euhemerist thesis in perhaps the most remarkable way of all, though he does not mention Euhemerus himself. He reduces the myths to what one can only call the level of police court news. Liber was the illegitimate son of Juppiter, king of Crete, who was murdered by Juppiter's legitimate wife, Juno;[199] another man of the same name was a dissolute magician of Thebes who was expelled from his country by Lycurgus for corrupting the minds of women and finally (as Homer testifies, Iliad 6.135) thrown down from a high crag into the sea as capital punishment.[200] The story of the rape of Proserpina is explained on not dissimilar lines. Ceres was a woman of the Sicilian town of Henna, Proserpina her daughter, Pluto a rich rustic so-called from his wealth. When Pluto was apprehended in attempting to rape Proserpina, he plunged with his prize to their death in a lake. Ceres wandered to Athens where the place Eleusis was so-called after her arrival there (Firmicus has a weakness for plausible but *ersatz* etymological explanations). Her inculcation of domestic economy in managing grain there resulted in 'the irresponsible Greeks' (*Graecorum levitas*, 6) causing her to be reverenced as a goddess after her death.[201] One of the most ingenious of the Christian applications of Euhemerus' suggestive theory was the claim that the god Serapis, who was represented as having a bushel for a head-dress, was in reality the patriarch Joseph whom the superstitious Egyptians had deified after his death out of gratitude for his supplying them with corn.[202]

A. D. Nock, in a passage devoted to the attitude of Christianity to pagan cults, maintained that within Christianity two views upon this subject prevailed. One was that gods were

[199] De Errore 6.1–5.

[200] *Ibid.*, 6.6–8.

[201] *Ibid.*, 7.1–6. The Euhemerist argument is repeated by an author as late as Gregory of Nazianzus, Theological Orations 2.14.

[202] This brilliant piece of theorizing crops up in Tertullian Ad. Nat. 2.8 and Firmicus Maternus 13.1–3, where he adds one of his characteristic etymologies; Serapis is Σάρρας παῖς. Cumont confirms that Serapis had a crown in the shape of a bushel (Oriental Religions, p. 76); Burckhardt tells us that Canopus, who was associated with Serapis, was worshipped in the shape of a pitcher with human head and extremities in Canopus in the Delta (Age of Constantine, p. 153).

non-existent; this view was derived from ancient writers who believed that gods were either dead men worshipped for their eminence or personifications of the elements and heavenly forces. The other view was that gods did exist but were evil daemons.[203] We have seen enough now to realize that this is a not altogether accurate account of the subject. Most, if not all, Christian writers did not regard these views as mutually exclusive, but combined them. Gods, as described in the myths, were no more than human beings, but the cult of the gods, as operating in their day, was manipulated by daemons. A further inaccuracy is to be detected in the account of the worship of the elements (a subject which we have not yet touched upon). Because the ancients regarded the elements as gods, this did not mean (as Nock implies) that they in effect said that gods were non-existent. On the contrary. It is likely that Nock has been misled by a passage in Diodorus Siculus[204] to the effect that two different explanations are given to account for the worship of gods. One account says that they are eternal and incorruptible, and are such objects as the sun, the moon, the stars, the wind and elements of that nature; others maintain that gods are earthly beings (ἐπιγείους) who achieved eternal honour and glory because of their benefactions to mankind. This last was the Euhemerist view. Diodorus does not in this passage identify Euhemerus' account directly with atheism, far less the other account. In fact the view that the elements were gods appears as early as Plato. In the final phase of his thought, Plato commended very strongly the worship of the heavenly bodies—sun, moon and stars—on the grounds that they were controlled by divine minds; not only did he believe in their divinity (a truism in his day) but in their cult, including sacrifice.[205] This continued to be not only a widespread but a generally accepted view in antiquity. We have already seen that

---

[203] Nock, Conversion, pp. 221–222. Dodds, Pagan and Christian, p. 117 n 3, gives a briefer, more schematized and therefore even more inaccurate account of this subject.

[204] Diodorus Siculus 6.1, reproduced in Eusebius, P.E. 2.2.52, 53.

[205] So Dodds, Greeks and the Irrational, pp. 220–221. He gives references to the 'Apology', 'Cratylus', 'Laws' and 'Epinomis' (which he regards as either written by Plato or composed from his 'remains').

Euhemerus himself may have believed in the worship of the heavenly elements (see above, p. 178, n. 181), thereby showing the compatibility of this belief with his theory of the origin of the myths of the gods. Celsus quotes Euripides in support of the view that the sun and moon were made for man, but disagrees with this view,[206] and later expresses surprise and even disgust that Christians do not worship the sun, moon and the stars.[207]

The Christians were bound to object to this worship of the elements. Tertullian devotes the whole of the third chapter of the second book of his 'Ad Nationes' to a demonstration of the impossibility of regarding the elements as gods. They demand a creator and a *primum mobile*; God cannot be created nor can he be moved by another. Both Origen and Eusebius object to the allegorizing of the myths into pseudo-science (the *physica ratio*) not only because the process is illegitimate but because it results in a deification of the elements.[208] Athanasius declares that it is not sufficient to abandon the worship of creatures on the earth in favour of worshipping the elements and the heavenly bodies, as some pagans do. It is clear from its interconnectedness that the universe as a whole has been created by God.[209] Firmicus Maternus has the curious notion that all forms of pagan cults can be reduced to a worship of the elements: the Egyptians worship water, the Phrygians the earth, the Assyrians and Africans the air, the Persian magi fire.[210] Cumont strangely approves of this impossible schematization on the part of Firmicus: 'all writers agree with Firmicus that the ancients worshipped the *elementa*', he says.[211] Perhaps; but nobody in the ancient or modern world could agree with Firmicus' extraordinary proposition that all the cults of the people of the Late Roman Empire can be identified as or reduced to a cult of the elements. We shall, however, later note that Christian writers on the whole thought the worship of the elements a better and nobler form of worship

---

[206] Origen, Contra Celsum 4.77.

[207] *Ibid.*, 5.6.

[208] Origen, Contra Celsum 5.38; Eusebius, P.E. 3.1–15; in Eusebius' case it is the Neo-Platonists who allegorize thus.

[209] Contra Gentes 27.1–62; *cf.* caps. 28 and 29.

[210] De Errore 1.2–5.2.

[211] Oriental Religions, p. 206.

than the current polytheistic cults of their day (see below, pp. 185–6).

In the course of their attempts towards forming a philosophy of religion we can very occasionally detect the Christian fathers considering religion dispassionately as a human phenomenon. Others before them had, of course, done this. Varro had divided gods into three classes, according to Tertullian; *unum esse physicum, quod philosophi retractant: aliud mythicum, quod inter poetas volutetur; tertium gentile, quod populi sibi quoque adoptaverunt.*[212] This, the reader will observe, is precisely the same as Eusebius' divison of gods into φυσικόν, μυθικόν and πολιτικόν, which we have noted already (see above, p. 161). Cicero made a distinction, supported by dubious etymological evidence, between *superstitio* and *religio*.[213] Tertullian, of course, does not accept Varro's categories of gods as sound, though he considers them. His reasons for rejecting this classification are succinctly stated: *ubinam veritas collocanda? in coniecturis? sed incerta conceptio est; in fabulis? sed foeda relatio est; in adoptionibus? sed passiva et municipalis adoptatio est.*[214] Lactantius comes much closer to a genuinely philosophical examination of religion. Animals, he says, have some sort of reason (*ratio*); what they never have is religion: *ex quo efficitur ut is < homo > agnoscat Deum qui unde ortus sit quasi recordetur;*[215] and again, *religio sit paene sola quae hominem discernat a mutis.*[216] And it is Lactantius who makes the penetrating suggestion which even a modern scholar should not lightly set aside that the Golden Calf which the children of Israel worshipped at Mount Sinai while Moses was absent at the top of the mountain was the Egyptian bull-god Apis.[217]

This interest in religion as a phenomenon worth examining for its own sake emerges finally as an attempt to give a scientific account of the development of religion. Once again, the

[212] Ad Nat. 2.1.

[213] De Nat. Deorum 2.28.

[214] *Op. cit.*, 2, 1. See above, p. 918.

[215] Div. Inst. 3.10.8 (a quotation from Cicero, De Legibus 1.8.24).

[216] *Ibid.*, 7.9.10 (another quotation from Cicero *ibid.*, 1.8.24); *cf.* De Ira Dei 7.

[217] *Ibid.*, 4.10.12, 13.

Christians here were building on foundations laid by the Greek philosophers. There was a virtually universal belief that there had existed a primitive era when religion and cult had been simpler. Plato had conjectured that originally men's worship had been confined to the heavenly elements, sun, moon and stars.[218] Theophrastus had speculated that a very long time ago the inhabitants of the country by the Nile (generally reckoned the most ancient and hieratic civilisation) had sacrificed only fresh green sprays of foliage and similar material to the gods, and had not stained their altars with blood, nor added the elaboration of incense or spiced fumes. They regarded fire as a way of making things immortal for the enjoyment of immortals.[219] Clement of Alexandria agrees that the Egyptians were foremost in religious development, though he puts this agreement in the form of saying that the Egyptians were the first to produce the fantastic idea (ὀνειρώσσοντες) that gods and men appeared together on earth.[220] But he too has the picture of a primitive simplicity and truth. There was an original natural kinship between man and divine things which has never been completely forgotten even among pagans:[221]

ἦν δέ τις ἔμφυτος ἀρχαία πρὸς οὐρανὸν ἀνθρώποις κοινωνία, ἀγνοίᾳ μὲν ἐσκοτισμένη, ἄφνω δὲ διεκθρώσκουσα τοῦ σκότους καὶ ἀναλάμπουσα, οἷον δὴ ἐκεῖνο λέλεκταί τινι τό·.

ὁρᾷς τὸν ὑψοῦ τόνδ' ἄπειρον αἰθέρα
καὶ γῆν πέριξ ἔχονθ ὑγραῖς ἐν ἀγκάλαις;
καὶ τό·.
ὦ γῆς ὄχημα κἀπὶ γῆς ἔχων ἕδραν·
ὅστις ποτ' εἶ σύ, δυστόπαστος εἰσιδεῖν.

Clement then proceeds to give an order of degeneration from this primitive pure religion, running a course first through the

[218] Cratylus 397. Plato went on to derive θεός from the running (θέειν) of these bodies in their courses. Tertullian devotes most of cap. 4 in Book 2 of Ad Nat. to disproving this famous etymology.
[219] Eusebius P.E. 1.9.7–10, quoting Porphyry who is quoting Theophrastus.
[220] Protrep. 1.6.4.
[221] Ibid., 2.25.3. Clement's first quotation is from Euripides' fragment, and the second from Euripides' Troades 884–885.

worship of the heavenly elements (accepting Plato's θεὸς—θέειν etymology), then the fruits of the earth. Next, men gave religious reverence to vendettas and disasters (Eumenides, Erinyes, *etc.*, largely invented by the dramatists). Next, the philosophers made gods out of passions (Phobos and Eros and the Hubris and Anaideia to which Epimenides dedicated altars in Athens). From this, men went on to imagine human deities like Dike and Clotho and Lachesis and Atropos. The sixth degree of error was to number the gods, as Hesiod speaks of the twelve gods. The seventh degree was to apotheosize benefits which God had poured on mankind, imagining the Dioscuri and Heracles and Asklepius as saviours.[222] Observe how high in the scale the worship of the elements is placed. It must not be thought that this account of Clement was meant to be an alternative to the theory of Euhemerus, for shortly afterwards Clement produces a theory which is in effect Euhemerism, though Clement does not name Euhemerus. Clement is giving a speculative account of the development of religion before the practice of deifying men set in. Origen also believed that men originally had a natural knowledge of God which never quite disappeared among the pagans. He takes as a proof of it Zeno's saying (already quoted above, p. 146) that there was no need for men to build temples.[223] Later he says more explicitly that in the early years of the human race there was a closer affinity between God and men than there was later. He suggests that in the early period man had not made so much progress in intelligence as later and he therefore needed more help in the form of miraculous appearances and the presence of angels.[224] Elsewhere he says that the Greeks, the Scythians, the Persians, the Indians, the Ethiopians and the Libyans all have separate and not identical gods because they abandoned 'the pure idea of the Creator of the universe which they had possessed at first'.[225] Lactantius appears to echo this theory of an original pure religion when he says that daemons corrupted the original truth

---

[222] *Ibid.*, 2.25.4–26.8.
[223] Contra Celsum 1.5.
[224] *Ibid.*, 4.79, 80; Origen quotes Hesiod fr. 82 to support his point.
[225] *Ibid.*, 6.39; H. Chadwick's tr.

unius saeculi stultitia.[226] Eusebius sets out the whole development at greater length. The earliest stage of the religous development of mankind (except for the Jews who always knew the one supreme God) was a worship of the elements and an offering of innocuous and simple things like gums and plants. Men knew nothing of gods and goddesses, nor of their names, nothing of daemons nor animal sacrifices, nor of altars nor statues nor temples. These were all inventions, and bad inventions, of later ages, produced first by the Phoenicians and Egyptians, and later spreading to the Greeks. Eusebius' authorities are all, of course, ancient Greek authors.[227] Eusebius has also an interesting theory that before the Mosaic legislation was given, there existed a primaeval religious way of life exemplified by such people as Enoch, Noah, Abraham, Isaac, Jacob and Job illustrated by such passages as Job cap. 31. The Jews had corrupted this pure primaeval religion while they were in Egypt. The legislation of Moses was designed to protect them from this corruption. Moses himself as a boy in Egypt followed this primaeval religion; it dispensed with food-laws, circumcision, and observance of the sabbath. Christ came to restore this primaeval religion. But there were two differences between this primaeval religion and Christianity; the latter allowed no polygamy and no animal sacrifices.[228] The ancient Hebrews certainly did perform animal sacrifices from the earliest period, from an earlier period than the Greeks adopted the practice. The reason for their sacrifices was an offering of animal life in the place of one's own life; but this was deficient in not affecting the 'rational and spiritual substance' (λογικῆς καὶ νοερᾶς οὐσίας) of men,

---

[226] Div. Inst. 4.1.1.

[227] P.E. 1.9.13–19; the rest of chapter 9 and chapter 10 give his accounts of the invention of gods in this period of degeneration.

[228] Demonstratio Evangelica 1.2–6 and 9.1–21. The concept of the Mosaic law as a preservative against idolatry is found in Justin Martyr, Dialogue 20.1; 22.11; 67.10; Tertullian, Adv. Marcionem 2.18.2, 3; Origen, frag. on Leviticus (P.G. 12.397) and frag. on Numbers (P.G. 12.580); in Contra Celsum 1.36 he assigns the same preservative function to the prophets, *cf.* Marcel Simon, Verus Israel (Paris, 1948), pp. 196–203; R. P. C. Hanson, Allegory and Event, cap. 11, and *ibid*, Biblical Exegesis in the Early Church, in: Cambridge History of the Bible I, ed. P. R. Ackroyd & C. F. Evans (Cambridge, 1970), pp. 412–453 and especially pp. 423–426.

only their physical life.[229] It is interesting to find Eusebius apparently conceding a point to the Greeks out of respect for the undoubted fact that the Old Testament recorded animal sacrifice as taking place at a very primitive period. Athanasius produces another account of the order of degeneration from pure primitive religion to idolatry and polytheism. Men first worshipped the sun and moon and stars which they thought to be the originators of the rest of creation (once again we observe the relative innocence of the cult of the heavenly bodies). Then they reverenced the elements and τὰς ἀρχὰς τῆς τῶν σωμάτων συστάσεως, hot and cold, moist and dry substance. Next, they deified men and the shapes of men either during their lives or after their deaths; then stones, blocks of wood, things of the water and the land and irrational wild beasts. They proceeded further to worship things which did not exist, such as dog-headed, snake-headed and ass-headed gods in Egypt and the ramheaded Ammon in Libya, or else parts of the body like head, shoulders, hand and foot. Beyond that they deified their pleasures, Eros and Aphrodite. They also worshipped the rulers and the ruler's sons, witness Zeus in Crete, Hermes in Arcadia, Dionysus in India, and in Egypt Isis, Osiris and Horus. The worst example was Hadrian's deification of Antinous.[230] Firmicus Maternus gives an order of disillusionment with false gods: the false deities used to fill people with fear, then familiarity bred contempt; then the mind, undismayed by wonder or fear, began to enquire rationally about them: *tunc ex assiduis tractatibus latentium ratione collecta pervenit ad causas, ut profanarum religionum miseranda commenta humanum genus primum disceret, deinde contemneret, tertio recusaret.*[231] Clearly Firmicus regards himself as effectively furthering this work of disillusionment, with the wind of Imperial approval filling his sails.

In order to complete this section it only remains to point out that in the course of creating a philosophy of religion the early Christian theologians created a philosophy of history.[232] The

[229] Dem. Ev. 1.10.1–11.
[230] Contra Gentes 9.1–48.
[231] De Errore 17.4.
[232] Momigliano, Pagan and Christian Historiography in the Fourth

pagans in attacking Christianity had always accused it of innovation, and claimed for their religion the advantage of immemorial tradition.[233] Nock remarks that to Celsus Christianity appeared as 'a mass movement of failing away from tradition'.[234] Very occasionally a Christian writer will reply to this charge by rejecting immemorial tradition. Lactantius can declare that the only argument that pagans can produce for their religion is immemorial tradition; it has no concern for morality and inward religion which are more important than tradition.[235] But for the most part the Christian writers, Lactantius among them, choose to claim that Christianity can show an older, more immemorial tradition than paganism.[236] In the course of demonstrating the prior antiquity of Christianity (*i.e.*, Judaism as a precursor to Christianity), the Christian writers not only explored ancient history and comparative chronology with an unprecedented intensity but gave rise to the concept of the philosophy of history.[237]

Century, in *ibid.* (ed.), Conflict, brings out this point, and especially pp. 82–88. But I think that he overstresses the extent to which Christianity was prepared for Imperial support. In certain important respects it was disastrously unprepared. *Cf.* de Labriolle, Réaction Païenne, pp. 44, 45.

[233] See above, p. 924; also Tertullian, Ad Nat. 1.8.1, *divortium ab institutis maiorum*: 'Acta Proconsularia' at Cyprian's trial 1 and 4; Lactantius, Div. Inst. 2.6.7 *hae sunt religiones quas sibi a maioribus suis traditas pertinacissime tueri ac defendere perseverant . . . tantaque est auctoritas vetustatis ut inquirere in eam scelus esse dicatur.*

[234] Conversion, p. 207.

[235] Div. Inst. 5.17.1–33. de Labriolle, Réaction Païenne, p. 345, notes this tendency in Lactantius, and parallels it with passages in Eusebius (P.E. 2.6), Athanasius (Contra Gentes 10), Ambrose and Prudentius.

[236] There are innumerable passages that can be quoted: a very small selection is Justin, Apol. 1.44.8 and 54.5 and 59.1, Theophilus, Ad Autol. 3.16–29; Tatian, Orat. 36–41; Minucius Felix, Octavius 6.3; Lactantius, Div. Inst. 4.5.3–10; Origen, Contra Celsum 6.43 and 7.28; Arnobius, Adv. Nat. 2.72; Eusebius, P.E. 10.4.1–32; 9.1ff.; 10, 1–23. See de Labriolle, Réaction Païenne, pp. 44 and 45. It is interesting to note the same argument in the Jewish Or. Sib. 3.105–161.

[237] The subject of the Christian philosophy of history is explored in depth in such works as A. Luneau, L'Histoire du Salut chez les Pères de l'Église. La doctrine des âges du monde, Coll. Théol. historique 2 (Paris, 1964) and K.-H.

III   Common Ground

One of the largest areas of common ground shared by the religion of the early Church with the religion of paganism was a belief in oracles. The age in which Christianity grew from a Jewish sect to a universal religion was one in which everybody was interested in oracles. The Church writers did their best to represent the Scriptures of the Old Testament, and especially the prophets and the Law-books, as a series of oracles.[238] The fact that both Jews and Christians took the trouble to forge the 'Sibylline Oracles' is eloquent testimony to their admiration of this form of divine communication. Indeed, that the enemies of paganism should find it advisable to imitate the forms of pagan oracular utterance and publish their propaganda ostensibly from the mouth of a pagan inspired prophetess suggests an imitation which is near flattery. The 'Sibylline Oracles' purported to be the utterances of ten inspired oracular priestesses in different parts of the world who lived at a very ancient period, before the siege of Troy. The composition of these 'Oracles' was part of the Jewish and Christian claim to an antiquity for their religion prior to the antiquity of paganism.[239] The Cumaean Sibyl was supposed to have persuaded King Tarquinius Priscus to institute a search for the oracular books and to store them carefully in the Capitol at Rome.[240] The Fathers constantly quote these 'Sibylline Oracles', as often because they regard them as an early witness as because they think that they are a pagan one. Lactantius gives more information about them than any other writer,[241] and lists them as a witness with Hermes Trismegistus, the Old Testament, the early Greek philosophers, Pythagoras, the Stoics, the Peripatetics and the Platonists.[242] He knows that the enemies of Christianity allege that the 'Sibylline Oracles' were invented by

Schwarte, Die Vorgeschichte der Augustinischen Weltalterlehre, Antiquitas I, Abhandlungen zur alten Geschichte 12 (Bonn, 1966).

[238] See R. P. C. Hanson, Biblical Exegesis in the Early Church, pp. 419–422 for evidence and references.

[239] See the prose Prologue to the Or. Sib., pp. 29–50.

[240] Ibid., pp. 51–74.

[241] Div. Inst. 1.6.7–17.

[242] Ibid., 2.8; cf. 4.6; 7.7 and 22.

the Christians themselves, but he denies this.[243] He believes that
Sibylline inspiration has now ceased.[244] There are several other
passages in the Fathers which claim that all oracles are dumb by
the time the writers are writing. Minucius Felix, speaking of
Apollo, says: *cuius tunc cautum illud et ambiguum defecit oraculum, et
politiores homines et minus creduli esse coeperunt.*[245] Clement of
Alexandria makes an even more sweeping statement: all oracles
are now dumb, Claros, the Pythia, Didumaea, Amphiareus'
shrine, Apollo (but the text is corrupt), Amphilochius.[246]
Eusebius says that Delphi, Claros and Dodona are silent.[247] Later
he declares that the oracles ceased and some of the gods were
reported to have died at about the time that the Gospel appeared
and began to spread. He links this with the disappearance at the
advance of the Roman Empire of separate sovereign
jurisdictions, civil wars and continuous national conflicts. The
stage has been reached, he believes, when churches and shrines
to the true God have been set up throughout the Empire in
towns and villages, and oracles everywhere are silent.[248] Strabo
(17.1.43) appears to support this when he says that oracles are
everywhere neglected because the Romans are content with the
oracles of the Sibyls and the Tyrrhenian prophecies (*i.e.*,
Etruscan *haruspicina*).[249] Juvenal writes as if at least Delphi was
no longer functioning in his day.[250]

   In fact, however, it is clear that these writers are giving a false
impression. The brutal sacking of Epirus in 189 B.C. by the
Romans does indeed appear to have put an end to the oracle of
Zeus at Dodona,[251] and probably Clement of Alexandria, in the
last passage quoted from him, was correct in saying that private

[243] *Ibid.*, 4.15.

[244] *Ibid.*, 1.6.

[245] Octavius 26.6.

[246] Protrep. 2.11.1, 2.

[247] P.E. 4.2.8; Eusebius seems to imagine that there is a difference between
the Pythian oracle and the oracle at Delphi.

[248] *Ibid.*, 5.1.2, 4, 5, 7.

[249] H. W. Parke, Greek Oracles, Hutchinson University Library, Classical
History and Literature 89 (London, 1967), p. 133, draws attention to this.

[250] Juvenal, Satires 6.555–556. Lucan, too, apparently echoes this; so Nock,
Conversion, p. 112.

[251] Parke, *op. cit.*, p. 132.

192   CHRISTIAN ANTIQUITY

mediums (ἐγγαστρίμυθοι) had greatly increased in popularity.[252] And no doubt the Greek *mantis* or inspired prophet independent of a fixed oracle had disappeared by the fourth century.[253] But there is no doubt that some oracles were still functioning in the second, the third and even the fourth centuries after Christ. We have unimpeachable evidence from Plutarch that the oracle at Delphi was functioning in the third decade of the second century, where Plutarch lived and where at the end of his life he was the chief priest at the shrine. One of his dialogues deals with the decline of the oracle at Delphi. Μεγάλη γὰρ ἡ παλαιὰ δόξα τῆς ἐκεῖ θειότητος, he says, τὰ δὲ νῦν ἔοικεν ὑπομαραίνεσθαι.[254] He tells us that there are no oracles left in Boeotia, which used to be full of them. Only Lebadeia remains. Several reasons for this are given in this dialogue—the withdrawal of gods as a punishment of men's wickedness, or the depopulation of Greece, or the alteration of the current of the mantic vapour which causes the priestesses to utter.[255] But it is quite clear that the Pythian oracle is still functioning, albeit not so busily as of old, in Plutarch's day. He testifies also that at least until fairly recently the oracles of Mopsus and Amphilochius in Asia were functioning.[256] It is clear that the Delphic oracle in Plutarch's time was no longer consulted on political questions (and this probably accounts for Strabo's remark quoted above, p. 191), and that the priestess no longer gave her answers in hexameter verse.[257] We can be sure, too, that oracles at Claros and Didyma were flourishing and much used during the reigns of Antoninus Bassianus (Caracalla) and Elagabalus. L. Robert has been able to demonstrate this by comparing a document called 'The Theosophy of Tübingen'

---

[252] Dodds notes this: Pagan and Christian, pp. 55, 56; *cf.* also Plutarch's remarks De Pythiae Oraculis 25 (407).

[253] So Johanna ter Vrugt-Lenz, Das Christentum und die Leberschau, pp. 22–23. She notes that the Emperor Julian found no *manteis* left to consult.

[254] Plutarch, De Defectu Oraculorum, ed. Flacelière, 5.411.

[255] *Ibid.*, 7.412, 413; 8.414; 43 and 44 (433–434). The suggestion is also made that the guardian daemon can desert the shrine and render it mute, 15.418.

[256] *Ibid.*, 45.434.

[257] Plutarch, De Pythiae Oraculis, ed. F. C. Babbitt, Loeb (London and Cambridge, 1936), passim, and especially 26.407 and 28.408.

with inscriptions and other evidence.[258] This oracle shared with Didyma the enquiries of the Greek cities of Asia Minor. Delphi had by then lost its influence altogether in Asia Minor; part of the reason must be the prosperity of the cities of Asia and the relative decline of mainland Greece.[259] Porphyry in his 'Philosophy of the Oracles' said that in his time only Apollo at Delphi and at Didyma and at Claros still gave oracles.[260] We have already seen that Diocletian's consultation of an oracle just before beginning the last persecution of the Church is uncertain (see above, p. 157, n. 70); Eusebius quotes Constantine (V.C. 2.50, 51, 54) as saying that Diocletian approached Apollo at Delphi, Lactantius (who is more likely to be right), Apollo at Didyma. Licinius is said to have consulted Apollo at Didyma before the final struggle with Constantine.[261] We know from the history of Constantine that the oracle of Apollo at or near Autun was functioning about 311. If we accept the authenticity of Constantine's letter quoted by Eusebius, V.C. 2.50, 51, 54, it is clear that in his later life Constantine thought that the Delphic oracle was functioning in 303. We know that it had finally lapsed into eternal silence when the Emperor Julian sent to consult it in 362; on the other hand when Julian consulted Apollo at Daphne near Antioch the machinery of consultation was apparently available even though the priest in charge declared that no answer could be given because of the presence of the bones of the martyr, Babylas. We shall probably be wise in concluding that the early Christian writers were exaggerating when they said that all oracles had fallen dumb, but that by

---

[258] L. Robert, Trois Oracles de la Théosophie et un Prophète d'Apollon, pp. 568–569. Robert's excavations at Claros have also added to our knowledge of this oracle.

[259] So Parke, Greek Oracles, pp. 138–140.

[260] Cited by Eusebius, P.E. 5.16.1.

[261] Burckhardt, Age of Constantine, p. 280. Burckhardt, pp. 203–205, gives a long list of oracles which he alleges to have been still functioning in Constantine's day, without producing any evidence to support this list; we should be sceptical about it. Eusebius (H.E. 8.14.8) says that Maximin Daza scarcely ventured to stir without consulting μαντείων καὶ χρησμῶν, and (V.C. 2.4) that Licinius when conflict with Constantine became inevitable asked advice from soothsayers, prophets and oracles.

Constantine's time the oracles were much in decay.[262].

Thoughtful pagans themselves had taken rather diverse attitudes to the oracles. Some had mocked at them and regarded them as fraudulent.[263] Others had regarded them with great respect. Celsus indulged in a eulogy on the benefits which they had brought to mankind,[264] and Porphyry, in his 'Philosophy of Oracles' had attempted to exalt the utterances of the oracles into a doctrinal system. We can gain from Plutarch some idea about how educated pagans thought of the inspiration of oracular priestesses and priests in the early centuries of the Church's existence. It was regarded as absurd and indecent to imagine that the god speaks through the genital organs of the priestess as she sits on the sacred stone. This is to associate the divine too closely and compromisingly with the human.[265] It could be that when the soul is to some extent or for some period free from the body it is able to develop latent predictive powers.[266] Inspiration may be conveyed through the air or by running water in such a way that when the element is absorbed by the body it creates an atmosphere or temperament (κρᾶσιν) conducive to the soul's forseeing the future.[267] Plutarch rather favours a materialistic

---

[262] So Parke, Greek Oracles, pp. 147–148. See also R. P. C. Hanson, The Oratio ad Sanctos attributed to the Emperor Constantine and the Oracle at Daphne, Journal of Theological Studies 24 (1973), pp. 505–511. See also K. Buresch, Klaros. Untersuchungen zum Orakelwesen des späten Altertums (Leipzig 1889, repr. Aalen 1973).

[263] Aristotle and the Peripatetic philosophers and Epicurus had criticized them (Origen, Contra Celsum 7.3); one of the stock charges against them was that the Pythia had commanded that Cleomenes the boxer should be given divine honours and that she had driven away the man who had killed Archilochus the poet in battle, stigmatizing him as a murderer of the servant of the Muses, in spite of the licentiousness of his poetry (Origen, Contra Celsum 3.25; see Chadwick's note in loc.). Lucian had derided oracles in his 'Alexander the False Prophet' and 'Peregrinus'. Eusebius quotes Diogenianus against oracles (P.E. I. 3.1–13), and he gives a long list of accusations against oracles from a book called Γοήτων φώρα (the title of which speaks for itself) by a cynic philosopher called Oenomaus (P.E. 5. 19.1–36.5).

[264] Origen, Contra Celsum 8.45.

[265] Plutarch, De Defectu 9.414. We shall find Origen repeating this story twice; see below, p. 948.

[266] Ibid., 38.431–40.432.

[267] Ibid., 40.432.

explanation. He describes the action of prophetic inspiration on the soul by a chemical analogy which he appears to think is not so much an analogy as an example of the same kind of thing.[268] The earth sends up streams, πολλὰ τῆς γῆς ῥεύματα μεθιείσης, and among them prophetic inspiration (like some sort of natural gas).[269] He even uses the term 'predictive vapours' (τὰς μαντικὰς ἀναθυμιάσεις).[270] It is not adequate either to emphasize the divine inspiration in prophecy, ignoring intermediate causes, nor to explain all by purely physical causes, but we can envisage prophecy as a divine power working on the soul through the body with the aid of daemons. It is obvious that the inspiration of the Pythian priestess is fitful and varying, dependent partly at least upon her physical condition.[271] Plutarch, indeed, produces precisely the kind of defence of the inspiration of the Pythia that modern theologians give when defending the inspiration of the Bible: the god inspiring the priestess accommodates himself to the girl's limitations, capacities and character. She is only a poor uneducated peasant, though pure in body and soul; she could not be expected to speak in grandiloquent hexameters.[272] Most people, says Dodds in a useful discussion of the subject,[273] simply thought of the Pythia as possessed. The theory that she was affected by mephitic vapours from a fissure in the rock or earth is 'a Hellenistic invention' (p. 73). Excavations have shown that there are no vapours and no chasm from which they could have come. It seems likely that the priestess could be heard and even seen while under inspiration and that the responses given were based on her actual words, though an official at the oracle probably edited them before they reached the enquirers.

For the most part Christian writers did not deny the preternatural inspiration of pagan oracles, but they ascribed

[268] *Ibid.*, 41.433. Parke remarks that 'To Greek thought there was always a great difficulty in conceiving the existence of anything completely immaterial. Even the soul was pictured as made of some extremely fine substance'. (Greek Oracles, p. 135).

[269] *Ibid.*, 42.433.

[270] *Ibid.*, 43.433.

[271] *Ibid.*, 48.436, 437; 50.437.

[272] De Pythiae Oraculis 21—22.404–5.

[273] Greeks and the Irrational, pp. 71–74.

them to daemonic instigation.[274] Origen did not attempt to show that the Delphic priestess gave fraudulent oracles, but argued that her inspiration was devilish; he produces the unsavoury explanation that the daemon inspired her by making an entry through her genitals.[275] To Celsus' eulogy of oracles he opposes the predictive oracular power of the Hebrew prophets.[276] Eusebius devotes the whole of the fourth and much of the fifth book of his 'Praeparatio Evangelica' to an attempt to discredit the oracles. He uses every conceivable argument, suggesting both that they were manipulated by daemons to foretell the future accurately and that they were often mistaken and frequently deliberately deceitful and that pagan philosophers had attacked and exposed them. But his chief theme is their devilish inspiration. Eusebius had two motives for his unusually close attention to oracles; he connected the activity of oracles with the prevalence of pagan sacrificial worship very closely, one might say he made a quite unjustifiably close link between them; and he was writing against the book 'The Philosophy of Oracles' in which Porphyry had attempted to give a kind of authoritative doctrinal basis to paganism by expounding the answers of oracular shrines. On the other hand, Minucius Felix's references to oracles appear to be on the whole directed towards proving them fraudulent rather than diabolical. We have already seen how he dismisses Delphi (see above, p. 191) as abandoned by the progressive march of intellect and civilization. Just before this passage he argues that all oracular utterances were either proved by events ignorant of the future or happened on the truth by chance.[277] Even Lactantius, deep as is his respect for the 'Sibylline Oracles', can censure them for their inaccurate prediction of a *Nero redivivus*.[278]

[274] Parke observes this: Greek Oracles, p. 145.

[275] Contra Celsum 3.25 and 7.3; he also, rationalist that he is, objects to her receiving inspiration in a trance, while the rational faculties are not functioning, 7.4. He consistently vindicates the rationality of the prophets while under inspiration (see Hanson, Allegory and Event, pp. 194–196). He also revives the stock philosophical arguments against oracles, 3.25; 7.3.

[276] Ibid., 8.46, 47.

[277] Octavius 26.5–7.

[278] De Mortibus Persecutorum 2.8–9. This incidentally shows that

In spite of all this, we must recognise that in oracular utterance the Christians found a phenomenon of pagan religion that impressed them in spite of themselves. They were impressed by the Delphic oracle's testimony to the wisdom of Socrates.[279] Origen can take the claim of the Pythia to a kind of omniscience as a parallel to the Christian claim that the Logos spoke through the human body of Jesus.[280] In a sense, oracles were prophets. In some shrines there was even an official attached to them called a *prophetes*. The cult of the Christian 'prophet' evident in the first two Christian centuries, culminating in Montanism, was perhaps one form of a much wider cult of the prophet in the Roman Empire.[281] The Christians might repudiate the god who inspired the prophetic priestess. They found it difficult to repudiate the institution. As the 'Sibylline Oracles' put it:[282]

οὐ ψευδοῦς Φοίβου χρησμήγορος, ὄντε μάταιοι
ἄνθρωποι θεὸν εἶπον, ἐπεψεύσαντο δὲ μάντιν.

From the fields of Christian polemic against paganism we can glean a few more grains of actual approval of some pagan practices and some pagan persons. Minucius Felix allows that the Greek philosophers had attained to partial truth, and he points out that both pagan poets and pagan myths agree that hell, a place of eternal punishment by fire for the wicked, exists.[283] We shall find this theme of the philosophers achieving partial truth recurring again and again. Tertullian can point to examples in pagan religion of virginity and chastity in order to encourage Christians to exhibit the same virtues;[284] he spends part of his 'Ad Martyras' referring to pagan examples of heroic endurance, and he can adduce the example of Mithras-

Lactantius genuinely did believe in the authenticity of this work.

[279] Tertullian, Ad Nat. 1.4.5–7; Origen, Contra Celsum 7.6 (though grudgingly accorded).

[280] Contra Celsum 2.9.

[281] So Dodds, Pagan and Christian, pp. 63–68.

[282] Or. Sib. 4.4, 5.

[283] Octavius 34.5: *animadvertis, philosophos eadem disputare quae dicimus, non quod nos simus eorum vestigia subsecuti, sed quod illi de divinis praedicationibus prophetarum umbram interpolatae veritatis imitati sunt*; also 35.1–3.

[284] Ad Uxorem 1.6.3–5.

worshippers to urge Christians to refuse a military crown.[285] It is
well known that Clement of Alexandria believed that pagans,
and especially pagan philosophers, could attain to truth, and at
one point he even suggested that what the Old Testament was
to Jewish Christians the works of the Greek philosophers might
be to the Greeks. The third-century Syrian 'Didascalia'
cautiously advances the example of pagan priesthoods in order
to justify the practice of calling Christian bishops priests.[286]
Cyprian points out that the pagan Hermes Megistus recognizes
only one God.[287] Origen not merely respected the pagan
philosophers. He was the first mind in Christian history to
attempt to provide the Christian faith with a solid philosophical
grounding. We have already seen that he refers with approval to
the words of Heracleitus and Zeno on idols (see above,
pp. 145–6); he thinks that Plato's myth of Ploutos and Penia in
the 'Symposium' may be a garbled version of the story of Adam
arid Eve;[288] and he applauds Euripides for this conviction that the
sun and the moon were made for man.[289] Lactantius has a warm
admiration for Cicero's belief in a universal moral law; when
pagans speak like this, he says, they do not speak like philosphers
but *tamquam divinent spiritu aliquo instincti.*[290] He acknowledges
that many pagan philosophers achieved truth, including the
recognition of monotheism, even though they did not import
this truth into their worship.[291] He will even agree that the poets
received truth, though they corrupted it.[292] We can observe a
tendency among some authors to admire the stern Old Roman
virtues of the Republican period. Arnobius appears to
commend those nations, including the Romans, who would
not recognize mystery cults.[293] Eusebius records that Dionysius
of Halicarnassus congratulated the Romans upon not accepting

---

[285] De Corona 15.3.4.
[286] Didascalia (ed. R. H. Connolly) IX, pp. 90–92.
[287] Qud Idola Dii Non Sint 6.
[288] Contra Celsum 4.39.
[289] *Ibid.*, 4.77.
[290] Div. Inst. 6.8.10.
[291] *Ibid.*, 2.8.23; 4.6.3–9; 7.7.1–14; De Ira Dei 11.
[292] Div. Inst. 2.10.4–13; 7.22.1–19.
[293] Adv. Nat. 5.24.

the Greek myths.[294] Firmicus Maternus thought that ancient Roman virtue was vindicated by the punishment of death inflicted in the consulship of Postumus upon a young man who introduced the rites of Liber (*i.e.*, Dionysus or Bacchus) to Rome.[295] One more curious and interesting piece of information is worth recording. Celsus alleges in his 'True Word' that Christians boast that if they strike an image of Zeus or blaspheme it, the image takes no vengeance on them. Origen replies that well-instructed Christians would not do this, because a text in the Old Testament (Exod 22.8) says, 'Thou shalt not speak evil of gods'.[296] This at first sight surprising remark can be supported by several other pieces of evidence. In Rom 2.22 Paul writes ὁ βδελυσσόμενος τὰ εἴδωλα ἱεροσυλεῖς; This implies that Jews (and no doubt following them, Christians) were forbidden to damage pagan temples or their contents. Among all the accounts of the defiance of the State by Christians up to 313 there are remarkably few stories of even fanatical Christians attacking sacred statues or temples.[296a] They avoided them, of course, but they did not attempt to damage them. A little further light is thrown upon the subject by an article by C. Mango which suggests that in Constantinople at any rate such antique statues as survived were used by the common people of the city for superstitious purposes, as apotropaic or tutelary mascots, and that the intellectuals regarded them rather as works of art than as objects of dislike or attack.[297]

The figures of pagan antiquity whom the Christian fathers discuss more frequently than any other are those of Socrates and of Plato, and their attitudes towards them vary. Justin Martyr can compare Socrates to Christ.[298] Minucius Felix disparages Socrates: his *daemonium* by whose advice he made important

---

[294] P.E. 2.8.1–13.

[295] De Errore 6.6–8; Firmicus' chronology is much confused.

[296] Contra Celsum 8.38.

[296a] The Council of Illiberis (305 A.D., see below, p. 202) in its sixtieth Canon legislates against idol-breakers.

[297] C. Mango, Antique Statuary and the Byzantine Beholder, Dumbarton Oaks Papers 17 (1963), pp. 53–75, especially pp. 59–70.

[298] Apol. 2.10.5.

decisions, was a daemon, and he is dismissed as *scurra Atticus*.[299]
Tertullian has several friendly references to him, on the rather
inaccurate assumption that he repudiated the gods,[300] but cannot
believe that he attained to truth; probably what Tertullian
cannot pardon is that Socrates on his death-bed ordered a cock
to be sacrificed to Aesculapius.[301] Origen, as might be expected,
cannot bring himself to censure Socrates; he regards him as a
fine example of one who was prepared to face death for his
philosophical principles; Leonidas at Thermopylae is another.[302]
Lactantius brings up the sacrifice of a cock against Socrates.[303]
Many Christian theologians pay unconscious tributes to Plato
by absorbing his philosophy, especially Clement of Alexandria,
Origen and Eusebius; Justin says that for a period he was a
serious Platonist, though his knowledge of Plato's philosophy is
not impressive. Plato the man, however, is not well treated
among the early Christian fathers, mainly because he acquiesced
in the pagan cults of his period and society. Origen seldom
denigrates Plato by name; his respect for him was too great for
that. Like Clement his predecessor, he subscribes to the legend
that Plato had visited Egypt and there learnt something of the
lore left behind by Moses. But even he criticizes the
philosophers (he usually cannot bring himself to name Plato or
Socrates) because they went to the Peiraeus to worship Artemis
and sacrificed a cock to Aesculapius.[304] Other authors are not so
nice; Lactantius inveighs against Plato for allowing a
community of wives.[305] Eusebius also holds against him and
against Socrates their taking part in the cult,[306] and Athanasius

---

[299] Octavius 26.9 and 38.5; *scurra Atticus* is the epithet that Zeno is supposed
to have applied to him; see Cicero, De Nat. Deorum 1.34.

[300] Ad. Nat. 1.4, 10; 2.2.

[301] De Anima 1.4; *cf.* Apol. 46.5.

[302] Contra Celsum 2.17; *cf.* 8.8. Other references to Socrates (none
disparaging) at 1.3, 6.8 and 7.6.

[303] Div. Inst. 3.20.16.

[304] Contra Celsum 6.4; in 6.17, however he does blame Plato by name for
taking part in idolatry. In 6.2 he allows that Epictetus' thought has benefited
large numbers of people, unlike Plato's. *Cf.* De Labriolle, Réaction Païenne,
p. 156.

[305] Div. Inst. 3.21.4, 5.

[306] P.E. 2.6.21; 13.14.3–4.

repeats the threadbare charge.[307] Intolerance has here united with a total lack of historical imagination to create an obfuscating littleness of mind in these authors.

When we turn, however, from the works of the Christian theologians up to the time of Constantine, who were almost all intellectuals, and look at the habits and behaviour of ordinary Christian people, we find a different picture. It is quite clear that many pagan religious customs and habits were carried on into the practice of Christianity. For instance, the oracles may have grown dumb, but Christians continued to use various devices to foresee the future. Nicetas, who was bishop of Remesiana, near Naissus (Nish) from 370 to 414, found it necessary to write a book called 'Adversus Genethilogiam' against the practice of casting horoscopes at birth,[308] and the habit of seeking oracular responses from gods was continued when the faithful approached the Christian God along with the invocation of some saint (e.g., St. Philoxenus); the most mundane matters were broached; the theory probably was that the saint invoked would ensure an answer.[309] Magic continued to be practised: the intellectual Origen believed as devoutly as anybody else in the magical power of invoking divine names.[310] Many magical papyri have been found containing the names of God and Christ, angels and saints, the Holy Spirit and the Virgin. The chief quarries supplied by Christianity for magic formulae were Psalm 90, the Lord's Prayer, St. Matthew's gospel, and the book of Proverbs; the symbol of the Cross was thought to have magical efficacy too.[311] John Chrysostom has to warn recently baptized Christians in a homily against belief in omens and wearing of amulets. The council of Laodicea in the mid-fourth century had to forbid Christian clergy to become magicians,

---

[307] Contra Gentes 10.35–37.

[308] See M. L. W. Laistner, Christianity and Pagan Culture, p. 47. See the remarks of Dodds, Pagan and Christian, p. 15, with references.

[309] B. S. Rees, Popular Religion in Graeco-Roman Egypt II. The Transition to Christianity, Journal of Egyptian Archaeology 36 (1950), p. 87.

[310] Contra Celsum 1.6 and 5.47; See Hanson, Allegory and Event, pp. 205–207, for further references; also De Labriolle, Réaction Païenne, p. 159.

[311] B. S. Rees, Popular Religion, pp. 88, 89.

charmers, soothsayers or astrologers or to make amulets.[312] Incubation in a Christian church took the place of incubation in the temple of Aesculapius or of some other healing god.[313] Some Christians must certainly have taken part in pagan sacrificial rites despite all prohibitions, for some even as early as the late second and early third centuries were municipal officials. Cyprian says that the Imperial government in 258 proceeded against Christians who were members of the senatorial and equestrian class and officials.[314] The canons of the Council of Illiberis, held just before 303, lay down penances for Christians who as provincial *sacerdotes* or municipal *duoviri* or *flamines* take part in pagan rites or celebrate games.[315] Christians continued to consult *haruspices* in the West as late as the seventh century.[316] The feast of Christmas was deliberately placed on December 25th to replace the feast of Sol Invictus. The feast of Epiphany was a deliberate replacement or imitation of pagan feasts of the Θεοφάνεια (ἱερά), originally first celebrated at Delphi, when statues of gods were exhibited to the people; and γενέθλια, in pagan usage the birthday of a god or semi-divine personage, was transferred by Christians to the celebration of a saint's birthday or a martyr's death.[317] We cannot exclude the possibility that the first Christian anchorites had pagan

[312] The homily can be found P.G. 49.223–240; so Laistner, Christianity and Pagan Culture, p. 41 and note on p. 128. A. A. Barb, The Survival of Magic Arts, in: Momigliano (ed.), Conflict, p. 106, refers to a similar homily from Chrysostom in P.G. 52.357–358; and see Barb, *op. cit.*, p. 107.

[313] Dodds, Pagan and Christian, p. 46; Rees, Popular Religion, pp. 90–91. Sozomenus (Historia Ecclesiatica 2.3) tells us that Aquilinus the Christian sought a cure for his sickness by spending a night at a Christian church. The Montanists practised incubation at Pepuza, according to Epiphanius, Panarion 49.1–2.

[314] Epistles 81.1; so Laistner, Christianity and Pagan Culture, p. 28; he cites Leclercq in Dictionnaire d'Archéologie et de Liturgie I. 80.

[315] Momigliano points this out in Conflict, p. 21. See E. J. Jonkers (ed.), Acta et Symbola conciliorum quae Saeculo Quarto habita sunt, Textus Minores 19 (Leiden, 1954), Concilium Eliberitanum canons i–iv. Canon lv, however, decrees a milder penance for those who have held these offices without sacrificing or paying for the cult of idols, and this is significant.

[316] Johanna Ter Vrugt-Lenz, Das Christentum und die Leberschau, p. 27.

[317] H. Dörries, Konstantin der Große (Stuttgart, 1967, repr. of ed. of 1958), pp. 134–135; Rees, Popular Religion, pp. 94–96.

predecessors. The word ἀναχώρησις itself was a technical term among Egyptian peasants to describe a retreat or escape from ordinary life into the desert or some inaccessible place under the pressure of the tax-collector. It constituted a kind of strike.[318] Temples of Serapis sometimes had round them devotees living a life permanently immured in little cells.[319] E. Norden suggests that though the cult of the martyrs was no direct successor to the pagan cult of local heroes, the latter probably prepared for the Hellenic consciousness for the former;[320] the pagan Eunapius in a violent attack on monks in his 'Lives of the Sophists' compares the cult of relics to the former pagan polytheism.[321] We have already had occasion to note that in the second half of the fourth century Christians began borrowing extensively from the vocabulary of the mystery-religions. Did space allow, several more examples could be given of direct borrowing by Christians of pagan religious terms.[322]

It has sometimes been asserted that early Christian worship owed something to the influence of the pagan cults.[323] As far as

[318] A.-J. Festugière, Personal Religion Among the Greeks, Sather Classical Lectures 26 (Berkeley, 1960), pp. 58, 66–67. I cannot agree with Festugière that the use of the word by the first Christian eremitics is mere coincidence. Dodds points out resemblances between Cynic and Christian ascetics, Pagan and Christian, p. 60, n. 3.

[319] Burckhardt, Age of Constantine, p. 151; Burckhardt also sees antecedents to the stylite eremitics in two enormous phallic stone pillars at the temple of Astarte in Hierapolis in Syria, up which a man would climb in order to pray sleeplessly for seven days, ibid., p. 145.

[320] E. Norden, Die antike Kunstprosa vom 6. Jahrhundert v. Chr. bis in die Zeit der Renaissance II (Leipzig and Berlin, 1909), p. 470.

[321] So De Labriolle, Réaction Païenne p. 365–366. Retail trade in the bones and relics of martyrs had reached such a pitch by the reign of Theodosius that it had to be forbidden (Cod. Theod. 9.17.6 and 7, for years 381 and 386); so C. N. Cochrane, Christianity and Classical Culture. A Study of Thought and Action from Augustus to Augustine (Oxford, 1940), p. 326.

[322] Cumont, Oriental Religions, pp. 101–102, points out that refrigerium was taken from the religion of Osiris, and Rees, Popular Religion, pp. 93–95, gives several more instances, such a σὺν θεῷ or θεοῦ θέλοντος and θεοῦ βοηθοῦντος. See also W. W. Fowler, Religious Experience of the Roman People, pp. 462–464.

[323] E.g., A. Alföldi, The Conversion of Constantine and Pagan Rome, transl. by H. Mattingly (Oxford, 1948), p. 12; Cochrane, Christianity and Classical Culture, p. 220. Norden, Antike Kunstprosa II, p. 471, is more cautious.

the period up to the reign of Constantine is concerned, there is no satisfactory evidence for this assertion. It is a priori unlikely that Christianity which regarded itself as in constant conflict with diabolic forces represented by the pagan cults should have imitated them, even unconsciously.[324] What happened after the peace of the church, from the middle of the fourth century onwards, is another matter. We may perhaps see some influence from contemporary society on the Christian ministry. Part of Cyprian's picture of the ideal Christian bishop is contributed by the Roman magistrate; the local *ecclesia* is sometimes like the *civitas* and the clergy and people like the *ordo* and *plebs*.[325] It has been suggested more than once that the procedure of church councils, which first began to assemble at the turn of the third and fourth centuries, was modelled on that of the Roman senate. It would be difficult to deny that one contribution to the development of the title *archiereus* (high priest) for the Christian bishop was the existence of influential *archiereis* having some sort of responsibility for all the pagan cults in such towns as Ephesus and Alexandria. We have seen some evidence for this already (see above, p. 198).

On the subject of architecture and art, we are on more debatable ground. There is no evidence at all that early Christian churches were modelled on pagan temples. Such a policy would have been utterly against the ethos of the church about the year 300. The earliest Christian churches were house-churches (*i.e.*, private houses deliberately adapted to receive a Christian congregation from the local area), and when in the second half of the third century free-standing churches began to be built the very scanty evidence that survives suggests that they were of *basilica* shape. Certainly when with the advent of

[324] This negative conclusion is supported by Nock, The Development of Paganism in the Roman Empire, in: Cambridge Ancient History, XII (Cambridge, 1939), pp. 444–446, and Conversion, p. 204, and by Dodd's remarks on Montanism in: Pagan and Christian, p. 63.

[325] Cochrane, Christianity and Classical Culture, p. 219. But it must be remembered that sometimes the reverse movement took place. De Labriolle reminds us (Réaction Païenne, p. 329) that when Maximin Daza was trying to reanimate paganism he organized *archiereis* of all pagan cults in a local centre and other officials higher than they, imitating the Christian organization of bishops and metropolitans.

Constantine to supreme power in the West and later in the East also a vast expansion of ecclesiastical building covered the Roman Empire with churches the *basilica*-shape became enormously popular and was soon the standard, though not the exclusive, form for churches to take. The origins of this *basilica* model are much disputed, but nobody has seriously suggested that it derives from any but a secular building, and the same applies to any other shape chosen for churches, such as the circular *martyrium*. They were on the whole functional buildings adapted from secular models. It has sometimes been supposed that many early churches, especially from the middle of the fourth century onwards, were abandoned pagan temples converted to Christian use,[326] and some actual instances of these have been adduced, such as the action of Joseph, a converted Jew, who in the reign of Constantine, according to A. H. M. Jones, 'Despite violent opposition was able with official backing to convert a derelict temple at Tiberias, the Hadrianeum, into a church, and to build a small church at Sepphoris. The mission, however, was not successful, and Joseph migrated to Scythopolis . . .'[327] It seems to me most unlikely that this kind of conversion was at all widespread until well after the reign of Constantine. In fact Epiphanius, who is the source here, makes it clear that Joseph's church was built upon an unfinished temple whose walls had reached no higher than about seven feet; obviously it had not been used as a temple. The authorities (who must have been overwhelmingly Jewish) would hardly have favoured the use of a pagan temple, and we are told that they were thinking of converting it into a bath-house.[327a] A reading of such a classic work as Gregorovius' 'History of Rome' will make it clear that for some considerable time after the triumph of Christianity and the decay and collapse of paganism the

---

[326] E. G. Cochrane, Christianity and Classical Culture, p. 208, 'In some cases pagan temples were reconsecrated as Christian churches'.

[327] A. H. M. Jones, Constantine and the Conversion of Europe (London, 1948), p. 222. Libanius, Epistles 1364 (363) supplies an example of a temple being converted into private house, but that is not the same thing. See J. H. W. G. Liebeschuetz, Antioch, City and Imperial Administration in the Late Roman Empire (Oxford, 1972), p. 43.

[327a] Epiphanius, Panasiou 30.1.12.2 (P.G. 41.425f.).

Christians left the pagan temples closed and empty but did not convert them into churches. They very often used them as quarries from which to erect churches in the neighbourhood. All over Europe there are fifth-century and sixth-century churches still standing or unearthed by the archaeologist's spade the pillars of whose *basilica*-plan were taken from pagan temples, not only in Rome and Constantinople but in remote places like Canterbury and Northumberland. But the period of direct conversion of pagan places of worship did not arrive until later. The conversion of the Pantheon, of the Temple of Antoninus and Faustina in the Roman Forum, of the Temple of Juppiter Capitolinus, of the Parthenon, of Diocletian's mausoleum at Salona, did not take place until later, in some places until much later. The reason is quite simple. One can imagine the conversion of Christian churches into Marxist museums of atheism; but one cannot imagine the conversion of Marxist museums of atheism into churches. The Christian had learnt to hate and dread pagan temples as places of defilement where filthy daemons were falsely worshipped by their deluded devotees. He would naturally avoid such places. A Christian passage in the (? third-century) 'Sibylline Oracles' says that Christians are not allowed to approach pagan temples: οὔποτε πρὸς νηῶν ἀδύτοις ἐώμεσθα πελάζειν.[328] Gregory of Nazianzus in his funeral oration on his mother, who must have been born early in the reign of Constantine, lists among her other virtues the fact that she never shook hands with nor kissed a pagan and never even looked at a μιαρὸν οἶκον, *i.e.*, a pagan temple.[329] People with a mentality like this would be most unlikely to countenance the direct conversion of pagan temples into churches, no matter what ceremony of reconsecration might be available.

There is one field, however, where the Christians did not hesitate to use the heritage of pagan religion, and that is the field of pictorial art. In what is in other respects one of the best introductory books on early Christian art, F. van der Meer gives

---

[328] Or. Sib. 8.487–495, quotation 487.
[329] Gregory of Nazianzus, Oratio 13.9 (P.G. 35.996, 997). For a fuller treatment of this subject, see cap. 16 in this book.

the impression that the use of pagan myths in early Christian art was confined to the carved decoration on churches in Coptic Egypt.[330] This is far from being the case. There are several examples from the third and fourth centuries of motifs from pagan myths being used and given a Christian meaning in the art of the catacombs. From the catacomb of Domitilla there is Christ as Orpheus with animals from a third-century tomb in a stairway, and another third-century Christ the Good Shepherd as Orpheus on the ceiling of the 'Ancient Chamber'; in the New Catacomb of the Via Latina there is a representation of the goddess Demeter (mid-fourth century) and four more of the same period representing Hercules in other parts of this catacomb, and another showing Hercules bringing Alcestis back from the dead of the same period.[331] These are not the only mythological themes treated in early Christian painting; we could add examples of Cupid and Psyche, Ulysses and the Sirens, and many more from the cycle of Hercules.[332] J. Allenbach has made a convincing case for the theory that one of the contributory causes of the extraordinary abundance of representations of Jonah in early Christian art was the identification of Jonah with the figure of Endymion who was thought to symbolize the state of rest for souls after death.[333] Jocelyn Toynbee has made the attractive suggestion that the mythological themes in mosaics of Roman British villas of the fourth and fifth centuries may, in those villas which we have other reason to regard as inhabited by Christians, be meant to be given a Christian interpretation.[334] We can recall the Christian Gnostic fresco in a third-century tomb near the Viale Manzoni in Rome apparently depicting the return of Odysseus to Ithaca

[330] F. van der Meer, Early Christian Art (E.T. by P. & F. Brown, London, 1967 of original Dutch of 1959), p. 116.

[331] P. du Bourguet, Early Christian Painting (E.T. London, 1965 of original French of 1965), Plates 27, 32, 104, 105–108, 116.

[332] Ibid., p. 24.

[333] J. Allenbach, La Figure de Jonas dans les Textes Préconstantiniens, pp. 96–112; in: La Bible et les Pères (Paris, 1971), especially pp. 109–112.

[334] Jocelyn M. C. Toynbee, Pagan Motifs and Practices in Christian Art and Ritual in Roman Britain, pp. 177–192, in: Christianity in Britain 300–700, ed. M. W. Barley and R. P. C. Hanson (Leicester, 1968).

as a type of the soul's return 'to its own country'.[335] We can illustrate this by a passage from Clement of Alexandria allegorizing the story of the Sirens and Charybdis in the Odyssey into the Christian's journey among the seductive wiles of the world:[336]

ἐὰν ἐθέλῃ μόνον νενίκηκας τὴν ἀπώλειαν καὶ τῷ ξύλῳ προσδεδεμένος ἁπάσης ἔσῃ τῆς φθορᾶς λελυμένος, κυβερνήσει σε ὁ λόγος τοῦ θεοῦ, καὶ τοῖς λιμέσι καθορμίει τῶν οὐρανῶν τὸ πνεῦμα τὸ ἅγιον.

We may conclude that the literature of the early Christian Church probably gives us an unbalanced view of the relation of Christianity to paganism. Intellectually and socially the Christians may have attempted to maintain a complete intolerance and isolation. Culturally, they could not and hardly attempted to do so. It is a most remarkable fact, of which we are reminded in H. Marrou's magisterial work on education in the ancient world, that the Christian Church made no serious effort to create its own educational system but simply accepted that which it found in the society in which it grew up. There was some opposition to the reading of pagan literature in the pre-Constantinian Church, voiced, as one would expect, by Tertullian among others.[337] But even Tertullian could not forbid Christians to attend pagan schools. Christians should not, he says, be teachers because this compromises them with idols. But they have to be pupils because otherwise they would go without education.[338] E. Norden reminds us that in the view of Libanius rhetoric was bound up with the old religion; the art had languished since Constantine had pulled down the temples.

---

[335] Dodds, Pagan and Christian, p. 101, n. 1, citing J. Carcopino, De Pythagore aux Apôtres pp. 175–211.

[336] Protrep. 12.118.1–4 (quotation from 4).

[337] Tertullian, De Spectaculis 7, *quod in facto reicitur etiam in dicto non est recipiendum, etc. Cf.* also Didascalia 12 which warns against reading 'the books of the heathen'. See Laistner, Christianity and Pagan Culture, pp. 50–51. The Christian school at Alexandria associated with Pantaenus, Clement, Origen, Heraclas and later Didymus is a very obscure subject. It has been interpreted as representing a number of educational stages from the Sunday School to the University. But it is clear that whatever it was it had few or no imitators.

[338] De Idololatria 10.

Norden is inclined to agree with him.[339] This may be true of the very much restricted sphere of the *ars rhetorica*. It cannot possibly apply to the culture of pagan antiquity as a whole. When pagan religion died it left a large legacy of culture endowed with which Christianity moved into the Middle Ages.

Many authors have discussed how far paganism had prepared the way for Christianity to succeed, and what were the points of agreement and difference in the two systems.[340] It is easily agreed that the stumblingblocks in the Christian creed for paganism were the doctrine of the incarnation, eschatology, and the doctrine of the resurrection of the body.[341] Norden adds that Christianity lacked the warm cheerfulness of pagan antiquity, its national cultural exclusiveness, and its passionate love of beauty of form. Nock suggests that the two religions differed in their doctrine of salvation: 'The one (Christianity) built on a consciousness of sin and on revelation, the other on a consciousness of goodness and on common sense'.[342] But there were points of similarity. The ancients, Norden points out, were not always cheerful. They could call the body a tomb and the earth a Hades. Stoic philosophy had achieved an ideal of world brotherhood not incompatible with the Christian concept of unity in Christ. Some ancient philosophers shared the Christian contempt for beauty of form and on the other hand Christian writers found themselves impelled to imitate the forms of Classical literature, and Christian artists (as we have seen) adopted the forms and themes of pagan antiquity, even

---

[339] Antike Kunstprosa II, pp. 451–452. His remarks on p. 477 are worth perusing also.

[340] See Norden, Antike Kunstprosa II, pp. 452–460; Fowler, Religious Experience of Roman People, pp. 452–465; H. Mattingley, The Later Paganism, Harvard Theological Review 35 (1942), pp. 171–179; Nock, Conversion, pp. 229–251; Dodds, Greeks and the Irrational, pp. 248–249; *ibid.*, Pagan and Christian, pp. 120–130; Momigliano, Pagan and Christian Historiography, in: *ibid.* (ed.), Conflict, pp. 82 and 83.

[341] But Dodd's statement that Origen's doctrine of the resurrection of the body was his greatest concession to paganism (Pagan and Christian, p. 130 n. 1) is an unsatisfactory way of stating the matter. Origen did not need to make concessions here; his philosophical principles (which were quite as strong as his theological) forced him to modify the current Christian doctrine in order to satisfy his own conscience.

[342] Conversion, p. 249.

though they filled them with a new spirit. Fowler has some interesting things to say about the ways in which Roman religion paved the way for Christianity. The work of the emperor Augustus had firmly established the connection of religion with the state so that when the time came there were a calendar, ritual, and even vocabulary to be taken over, in form if not in content. A certain orderliness, sobriety and decency in religion had already been an established tradition (one thinks of the early Roman liturgy), and something too of the old Roman religious spirit survived into Roman Christianity, a matter-of-factness, an interest in history, a tone which was ethical rather than speculative, legal, and rhetorical more than poetical.

But many writers are agreed that the two most important ways in which paganism prepared for Christianity were in its 'loss of nerve' and in its syncretistic monotheism. By 'loss of nerve' (a phrase originally coined by Gilbert Murray) is meant a retreat from rationalism, a yearning for salvation, flight from the disinterested search for truth, a tendency to rely on authority rather than individual ability, the substitution of the αὐτὸς ἔφα of Pythagoras or Plato or Chrysippus or Epicurus for enquiry, the exaltation of oracles to the status of revelation.[343] This tendency may be regarded as deplorable, as it was by Gilbert Murray, or it may be welcomed, but there is no doubt that it was there in late pagan antiquity and that it prepared the ground for Christianity. That paganism by the third and fourth centuries was inclining more and more towards a kind of monotheism has been remarked by many authorities: Plutarch in his 'De Iside et Osiride' and Maximus of Tyre, an eclectic Platonist of the period of the Antonines, had taught a syncretistic monotheism. Apuleius professes a reverence for the *summus et exsuperantissimus divom*. Celsus professes belief in a single god of many names (Contra Celsum 1.24; 6.41). Egyptian syncretism did not find it difficult to fit into a monotheistic frame. Isis and Osiris had absorbed many deities in Egypt before they moved beyond their native shores and then they were identified with many gods in the Hellenistic world; inscriptions

[343] Norden, Antike Kunstprosa II, pp. 452–460, and Dodds, Greeks and the Irrational, pp. 248–249, take particular note of this.

have been found reading *Isis una quae est omnia* and Εἷς Ζεὺς Σάραπις. The epithets *pantheus* and *panthea* are applied to several deities, including Isis, in inscriptions. We can recall Statius' hymn to Apollo at the end of the first book of his 'Thebaid' and a similar prose rhapsody by the rhetorician Menander at the beginning of the third century. Attempts were even made to include the god of the Jews and Christians in this syncretism by Numenius and (much later) by Macrobius; an oracle from Claros identifies Hades, Zeus, Helios and Iao. Towards the end of the period the most powerful agent for syncretism was the Solar cult favoured by Aurelian and Diocletian, about which more will be said in connection with Constantine.[344] There can be no doubt that this syncretistic monotheism which had been gathering force since the second century had by the year 300 done much to prepare men's minds for the monotheism preached by Christianity.

But when all allowance has been made, it must not be denied that one of the great reasons for Christianity prevailing over its rivals was its intolerance. Christian men and women were not prepared to make any but the most superficial compromises with paganism, whereas paganism was for the most part almost endlessly tolerant. Had Christians been ready even to join in the cult of traditional gods and especially the Imperial cult while at the same time practising Christianity they would probably have encountered very little opposition from the third century onwards. But they refused to compromise and were ready to pay for this refusal with their lives. Christianity, in short, displayed a tougher, more enduring, character, based on a deeper conviction of possessing truth, than the other religions. It paid the price for this strength by the intolerance which it continued to show when it had won.[345] It reached the beginning

---

[344] See Burckhardt, Age of Constantine, p. 578; Cumont, Oriental Religions, pp. 88–90, 134ff.; de Labriolle, Réaction Païenne, pp. 314–315; R. Walzer, Galen on Jews and Christians, p. 45; Nock, Conversion, pp. 136–137, and Parke, Greek Oracles, pp. 146–147. The first few chapters of Burckhardt's book are still one of the best succinct introductions to pagan religion about the year 300.

[345] Norden, however, reminds us that Christianity was not completely intolerant: 'gerade dadurch, daß sie nicht ausschließlich zerstörend vorging,

of the fourth century endowed with more enduring qualities than its rivals: 'Christianity was bound to conquer in the end, because it provided answers which were incomparably simpler, and which were articulated in an impressive convincing whole, to all the questions for which that period of ferment was so deeply concerned to find solutions.'[346]

IV Constantine

When we approach the subject of Constantine the Great we are instantly faced with a conflict between scholars over the value of our sources for reconstructing his religious development. The two sides are set out with a wealth of learning in N. H. Baynes' magisterial but exasperating book.[347] He traces the view of Burckhardt that Constantine was an able politician who used the Church for his own ends and never completely abandoned paganism; the views of those scholars, such as Zahn, that Constantine had an intermediate period after the battle of the Milvian Bridge when he favoured a syncretistic religion of paganism and Christianity united in worshipping a Supreme Power; the views of Brieger and Schwartz which represented a return to the earlier view that 'der Wille zur Macht' was the keynote of Constantine's character and that this Emperor used both Christians and pagans for his own ends; the views of some (such as V. Sesan and Maurice) that Constantine was deservedly regarded by the Eastern Church as a Christian saint; and the

sondern in gegebenen Grenzen Toleranz übte, ist die Katholische Kirche Siegerin über das Pantheon geworden'. (Antike Kunstprosa II, p. 460).

[346] Burckhardt, Age of Constantine, p. 214; see also Momigliano, Pagan and Christian Historiography, in: *ibid.* (ed.), Conflict, pp. 82, 83.

[347] Constantine the Great and the Christian Church, 2. ed. with a pref. by H. Chadwick (London, 1929, new printing 1972), pp. 34–49. This is an indispensable book for the study of Constantine by a recognised authority. Its method and arrangement are inconvenient in the extreme. It consists of a single lecture swollen by a much longer series of notes subsequently written, with an Appendix. It presents the appearance of a notebook or, to use an ancient term, 'Stromateis', rather than a properly planned book. It illustrates both the best in England historical scholarship and the worst in English disinclination to write books. A second edition has appeared (1972), with a useful Preface by Henry Chadwick, but the manifold inconvenience of the work remains quite unamended.

view of O. Seeck who passionately hated Christianity but tried to do justice to Constantine's religious convictions. Several scholars in the past have attacked the reliability and integrity of Eusebius' account of Constantine, and especially his 'Vita Constantini',[348] arguing that the 'Vita' was interpolated later to assist the cause of Constantius II, and Seeck accused Athanasius of forging the imperial documents which appear in his works. Baynes gives a temperate and convincing defence of the basic integrity of these works, though he does not exclude the likelihood of Eusebius having been always biased and sometimes mistaken. The only important document in connection with Constantine about which he expresses reservations and doubts is the 'Oratio ad Sanctos' ascribed to Constantine.[349] Baynes appears to have been followed in these judgements by most of the scholars who have written upon Constantine since his day, *e.g.*, A. H. M. Jones, Kraft, Alföldi, Dörries and MacMullen, and he appears to have been to some extent anticipated by the less known but competent American scholar, C. B. Coleman.

It is difficult, if not impossible, to distinguish between Constantine's religious development and his religious policy. At the beginning of his political career we can assume that he accepted the kind of religion which it was then conventional for members of the Imperial family to profess, the cult of Juppiter and of Hercules as in some way specially associated with the Emperors and Caesars, the cult of the Sun as it had been established by Aurelian and perpetuated by Diocletian (about which we shall say more later), and the cult of the traditional Roman pantheon which was regarded as part of the apparatus of the Roman state. Eusebius (V.C. 2.49) quotes Constantine as saying late in his career that his father Constantius (known as Constantius Chlorus to distinguish him from his grandson

---

[348] Crivelucci, Seeck, Schultze, Mancini, Pasquali, Martroye and Batiffol.

[349] Baynes, Constantine the Great, pp. 50–56. I believe that many clear indications in the text of the 'Oratio ad Sanctos' make it impossible to attribute this work either to Constantine or to Eusebius himself; see R. P. C. Hanson, The *Oratio ad Sanctos* attributed to the Emperor Constantine and the oracle at Daphne, 505–511. Kraft, however, apparently accepted the authenticity of the work; see Rel. Ent. 153 and n. 2.

Constantius II) had been a religious man and had always called on the Redeemer for aid. We may doubt whether Constantine was as explicitly Christian as to pray to Christ; this sounds like a later elaboration of either Eusebius or (more likely) Constantine. Eusebius' account of Constantius' attitude to Christianity (V.C. 1.15–17) probably grossly exaggerates his attachment to the faith. But there is some evidence of Constantius favouring Christianity. He called one of his daughters Anastasia, which he could hardly have done had he been positively anti-Christian. And it is certainly true that the persecuting decrees of Diocletian were not enforced in the territory under the control of Constantius with the same rigour as they were in other parts of the Roman Empire. Unless we are to count Alban and Isaac and Aaron in Britain (who might just as well have been victims of the Decian and not of the Diocletian persecution), we hear of no martyrs in Britain or Northern Gaul. It is therefore reasonable to conclude that Constantine was initially not hostile to Christianity, following his father's example.

We can be sure that not long before Constantine's campaign against Maxentius which ended at the battle of the Milvian Bridge in 312 he was a fervent worshipper of Apollo. There is a reference in a panegyric to some experience encountered by Constantine when he visited a temple of Apollo near Autun, probably in the year 310.[350] The passage runs as follows:

ipsa hoc sic ordinante fortuna, ut te ibi rerum tuarum felicitas admoneret, diis immortalibus ferre quae voveras, ubi deflexisses ad templum toto orbe pulcherrimum imo ad praesentem, ut venisti, deum.

This is generally taken as indicating that Constantine went out

---

[350] C. B. Coleman, Constantine the Great and Christianity (New York, rep. 1968 of orig. ed. of 1924), p. 75, places this incident in 310. Burckhardt (Age of Constantine, p. 293) dates it to 308. Coleman's book is a particularly useful one because it often gives the original text of his authorities. The text quoted is to be found in Galletier 7.21 (72) (P.L. 8.637ff.). Presumably it is to be translated in some such way as this: 'for Fortune herself so arranged that the very success of your enterprises should admonish you to carry out the vows you had made to the immortal gods, on the occasion when you had made a diversion to visit a temple which is the loveliest in the whole world, but more, to visit the god who made himself present for your arrival'.

of his way to consult the oracle of Apollo near Autun and that he received some sort of message there, or at any rate that on his visit he gained somehow enough divine encouragement to cause him to make some sort of vow to Apollo. It is highly probable that he identified Apollo with the deity of the Solar cult. As we shall see, it is significant that long after his death his devoutly pagan nephew Julian should accuse him of deserting the Sun-god. Immediately after his victory at the Milvian Bridge references to pagan deities continued to appear on Constantine's coins, and for some years afterwards. These deities include Mars, Hercules, Genius Populi Romani, Fortuna, Fides, Concordia, Pax, and, in 317, Juppiter Conservator, when the new Caesars, sons of Constantine and of Licinius, were proclaimed. Alongside these the figure of Sol Invictus appears on the coins constantly and prominently. By 320–1 all the other pagan deities have disappeared from Constantine's coins, except Sol Invictus.[351]

It is clear therefore that Constantine began his religious career as a fairly conventional pagan according to the standards of the fourth century. He certainly ended his career as a professed Christian. To discuss adequately how this transformation came about would exceed the limits of this essay, but some elementary points must be made.

It is very difficult to determine exactly how and when Constantine first associated the success of his arms with the invocation of Christ. Lactantius gives one account, involving a dream before the critical battle of the Milvian Bridge (De Mortibus Persecutorum 2.5–6), Eusebius another, suggesting a vision seen by Constantine in the sky, followed by a dream the same night, at some undetermined but lengthy period before the battle (V.C. 1.27–29). Eusebius claims that Constantine was his informant (1.28). But, even if Constantine informed him, he can only have described this experience to Eusebius long after it took place, near the end of his life, and Eusebius was writing after Constantine's death when it was impossible for his story to be checked. Lactantius was writing at a period much nearer to the crucial battle, within Constantine's lifetime, and as one who

---

[351] Alföldi, Conversion of Constantine, p. 54.

was known to the Emperor, since he had chosen him as tutor to his son Crispus. He is the more convincing source on this point. But, however we assess the evidence, it is difficult to avoid the conclusion that Constantine did after the battle of the Milvian Bridge regard himself as in some way committed to Christ as peculiarly his divinity owing to some internal experience which he had had, vindicated as it had been by the outcome of the battle.

If we accept the authenticity of one incident recorded as taking place shortly after the battle, we can be quite certain of this conclusion. Two references, one in a panegyric delivered in Gaul in the year 313, and one in a passage in Zosimus,[352] have been taken to mean that on the day after the battle when Constantine entered the city of Rome in triumph, at the point when, proceeding along the Sacred Way towards the Capitol, he was expected to continue the conventional route onwards to the Temple of Juppiter Capitolinus in order to make the customary sacrifices there, the Emperor suddenly diverged from this route and steered his course directly to the Palatium, deliberately omitting the visit to the Capitol and its sacrificial ritual.[353] Against this it has been objected that the words of the Panegyrist are not conclusive evidence against Constantine's having visited the Capitol, and that Zosimus' passage, coming as it does in association with the author's discussion of Constantine's 'conversion' under the influence of bishop Hosius and as a reaction to the deaths of Crispus and Fausta, about the year 326, refers to Constantine's last visit to Rome, in 326 or

---

[352] Galletier 9.19 (138/9) (P.L. 8.667–668) and Zosimus, Historia Nova 2.29.5.

[353] Zosimus actually says that he refused the sacrifice to Juppiter Optimus Maximus; the Panegyrist in his description of Constantine's entry into Rome omits all mention of the Capitol and of a sacrifice to I. O. M. Further, his words are significant in commenting upon Constantine's going into the Palatium: *ausi etiam quidam, ut resisteres, poscere et queri tam cito accessisse palatium, et, cum ingressus esses, non solum oculis sequi, sed paene etiam sacrum limen irrumpere.* This suggests that objection was raised at the time to Constantine's disappearance into the Palatium, and we can even conjecture that a mob stood outside demanding his reappearance and perhaps his continuing the procession to the Capitol.

327, and not to his visit in 312.[354] The question has been examined at some length by J. Straub.[355] He argues with a wealth of evidence that Constantine on the occasion of his entry into Rome after the battle of the Milvian Bridge did not sacrifice to Juppiter Optimus Maximus on the Capitol. Eusebius in his 'Vita Constantini', he points out, mentions that Constantine omitted the sacrifices at his Decennalia (315) (*cf.* Eusebius V.C. 1.48), his Vicennalia (325), and his Tricennalia (335).[356] Both Nazarius and the Panegyrist of 313 treat the occasion as a triumph, so that the argument that this was not a triumph and that therefore Constantine would not have been expected to sacrifice carries no weight, and there is abundant evidence that Emperors visiting Rome after a victory over their enemies (and not least intestinal foes) went to the Capitol to sacrifice.[357] Constantine conformed on the occasion of his visit in 312 to all the other conventions of a triumphing Emperor; he gave games, he visited the Senate, he distributed donations, and so on.[358] Though Zosimus appears to assign the refusal of sacrifice to Constantine's last visit to Rome, in 326, this historian is notorious for the confused manner in which he presents chronology; he knew that Constantine had omitted the *ludi saeculares* in 312, for he makes a great point of that. Hosius had been in Constantine's train as early as 312. It is therefore quite possible that Zosimus knew that it was in 312 that Constantine refused the sacrifice on the Capitol, and may not even have intended to transfer the incident to Constantine's last visit to Rome.[359] We need have no hesitation in following Straub upon this point and concluding that after the battle of the Milvian Bridge Constantine did deliberately omit the customary sacrifice to Juppiter Optimus Maximus on the

[354] Coleman (Constantine the Great, p. 62) and Alföldi (Conversion of Constantine, p. 62) argue that Constantine sacrificed on the Capitol, Dörries (Konstantin der Grosse, p. 37) and R. MacMullen (Constantine [London, 1969], p. 81) that on this occasion he refused to sacrifice.

[355] Konstantin's Verzicht auf den Gang zum Kapitol, Historia 4 (1955), pp. 297–313.

[356] *Ibid.*, pp. 298–299.

[357] *Ibid.*, pp. 299–301.

[358] *Ibid.*, p. 301.

[359] *Ibid.*, pp. 303–304.

Capitol. We can add that it is in this year, 312, that he began displaying the Chi Rho sign on his coins. We cannot avoid the conclusion that this marks a decision by Constantine that he was in some way obliged to, or an adherent of, Christ as his divinity.

In the year immediately after the battle of the Milvian Bridge, Constantine began openly to bestow favours upon the Christian Church. He proclaimed toleration for it, he persuaded Licinius to adopt the same policy, he secured the return of its property which had been confiscated during Diocletian's persecution, he exempted the clergy from curial duties and gave them various financial subsidies. We need not disbelieve Eusebius' story that he caused a statue of himself to be put up in Rome holding a cross in its hand with an inscription attributing his victory to this symbol (H.E. 9.9.10; 10.4.16; V.C. 1.40). But he did not pay exclusive attention to Christianity. We have already seen that up to 320 he allowed quite a wide range of pagan gods to appear on his coins. In particular he showed no signs of abandoning the Solar Cult, the worship of Sol Invictus.

We have already met the suggestion that Constantine's devotion to the cult of Apollo near Autun was one form of his worship of the Sun-god.[360] A set of magnificent gold medallions was struck to celebrate the meeting of Constantine and Licinius at Milan showing the heads of Constantine and of the Sun-god side by side.[361] Even after 321, by which time Constantine had ceased to put any other pagan gods on his coins, he continued to honour the Sun-god on them. It was only in 324, when his rivalry of Licinius had reached the final stage of open war, that

---

[360] Baynes (Constantine the Great and the Christian Church, pp. 57–58, n. 25) gives an extensive bibliography on the Solar Cult in the Late Roman Empire.

[361] See Alföldi, The Conversion of Constantine, pp. 5–7; Jones, Constantine and the Conversion, p. 95; Dörries, Konstantin p. 25. Dörries shows a medallion on which Constantine can be seen in profile with the Sun-god in the inscription *Invictus Constantinus* (Plate 8, II); MacMullen, Constantine, Plate 3, Inset 1, shows a similar but not identical medallion. Baynes cites G. Costa as suggesting that the Labarum was an adaptation for Christian purposes of a sign which Constantine would have known from childhood in 'the symbolism of the solar religion of the Gauls' (Constantine the Great, p. 60, n. 33). But was there a solar religion among the Gauls? This is to open a large and obscure question.

he abandoned reference to the Sun-god on his coins. In retaliation, Licinius ordered his soldiers to observe the annual cult of the Syrian sun-god with appropriate sacrifices; he was in fact the last Roman Emperor to be portrayed on coins in the act of sacrificing.[362] It has been plausibly suggested that Constantine found it possible to continue the cult of the Sun-god for some time after he had abandoned other pagan cults because this particular cult was rather less obnoxious to Christians than others. Christians had already reverenced Christ in his character as 'the sun of righteousness' (Malachi 4.2) as the sun-god *par excellence*, or, as Clement of Alexandria put it, ὁ πάντα καθιππεύων δικαιοσύνης ἥλιος.[363] More than one author has drawn attention to the curious story called the 'Passio Quattuor Coronatorum'[364] of the four Christian stone-masons in Pannonia who were ready to make a colossal statue of the Sun-god for Diocletian, but who refused to make a statue of Aesculapius and were put to death. They may have thought of the sun as symbolic of Christ. Alföldi, on the other hand, suggests that Constantine did not identify the Sun-god with Christ, otherwise he would have indicated so on his coins, but identified him with the Almighty God of the Christians.[365] It seems likely that we have in this example of the Solar Cult not so much an attempt at syncretism by Constantine in the manner which his nephew Julian was later to apply to paganism, as an attempt to find common ground between Christianity and one prominent pagan cult especially favoured by the Imperial house

[362] Dörries, Konstantin, p. 44.

[363] Protreptikos 11.14.3; for further references see Baynes, Constantine the Great, pp. 99–100, and F. J. Dölger, Das Sonnengleichnis in einer Weihnachtspredigt des Bischofs Zeno von Verona, Antike und Christentum VI, 1940, pp. 1–58. See also the picture of Christ Helios on the ceiling of the pre-Constantinian necropolis under St. Peter's in Rome. Dörries reproduces this, Konstantin, p. 14 of the Plates, and du Bourguet in Plate 130 of his 'Early Christian Painting'. Alföldi, The Conversion of Constantine, pp. 54–56, examines this conception at some length, also Dörries, *op. cit.*, pp. 133–134.

[364] H. Delehaye, Acta Sanctorum, Novembris 3 (Brussels, 1910). Baynes, Constantine the Great, p. 102 and Dörries, Konstantin, pp. 133–134, allude to this story.

[365] Conversion of Constantine, p. 56. *Cf.* Cochrane, Christianity and Classical Culture, p. 216.

in the past. Kraft in more than one passage of his work supports the conclusion that there were Christians who regarded the Sun-cult as legitimate and that Constantine could have counted himself as one of them (Rel. Ent. 15, 16, 158). Jones suggests that one reason for the continuance of dedications to *Invicto Soli Comiti Augusti* was that 'Illyricum was the chief recruiting-ground for the armies, and the Illyrian peasants were devoted sun-worshippers'.[366]

We have further evidence that Constantine tolerated and perhaps even encouraged a certain ambiguity in official statements about religion between 312 and 324. There are references to the deity in the panegyric delivered before Constantine in Treves in 313. The panegyrist says that *divina mens et ipsius urbis aeterna maiestas* deprived Maxentius of counsel just before the battle of the Milvian Bridge.[367] The orator invokes this deity in these terms: *rerum sator cuius tot nomina sunt quot gentium linguas esse voluisti, quem enim te ipse dici velis scire non possumus.* He has earlier said that though this divine mind exercises providence over everything it is Constantine who gives this providence expression. Hence Constantine has no need of human counsel.[368] In accordance with this declaration, the panegyrist calls this deity 'divine spirit', 'godhead', and 'celestial power', but gives him no name. Burckhardt describes this as 'a worthless monotheism', ready to trim its sails to every wind, Jones as 'carefully neutral', and Dörries says that the rhetor and Constantine have tacitly agreed to occupy neutral ground.[369] Another example of the same deliberate ambiguity may be seen in the inscription on the arch of Constantine in Rome, which was erected in the year 315. It reads thus:

IMP. CAES. FL. CONSTANTINO MAXIMO
P. F. AUGUSTO S.P.Q.R.

---

[366] Constantine and the Conversion, p. 131.

[367] Galletier 9.16 (136) (P.L. 8.665).

[368] *Ibid.*, 9.2 (124) (P.L. 8.672). *Habes profecto aliquod cum illa mente divina, Constantine, secretum, quae, delegata nostri diis minoribus cura, uni se tibi dignatur ostendere.*

[369] Burckhardt, Age of Constantine, pp. 202–203; Jones, Constantine and the Conversion, p. 92; Dörries, Konstantin, pp. 29–30; *cf.* Coleman, Constantine the Great, p. 76.

QUOD INSTINCTU DIVINITATIS MENTIS
MAGNITUDINE CUM EXERCITU SUO
TAM DE TYRANNO QUAM DE OMNI EIUS
FACTIONE UNO TEMPORE IUSTIS
REMPUBLICAM ULTUS EST ARMIS
ARCUM TRIUMPHIS INSIGNEM DICAVIT.[370]

Both Baynes and Dörries see this as a deliberately neutral reference to the Deity acceptable to both pagans and Christians.[371] Perhaps we may see the same tendency in the prayer which, as Eusebius tells us, Constantine gave his army to repeat: 'We know that thou alone art God. We acknowledge thee as the king. We call upon thee as our helper. We have received victory from thee. Through thee we were stronger than our enemies. We acknowledge our indebtedness to thee for the gifts we have received and hope for those to come. We all earnestly supplicate thee that thou wilt preserve Constantine, our Caesar, and his sons, beloved of God, sound and victorious for a long life'.[372] If we recollect the movements of thought which were converging to create a vaguely monotheist belief in the minds of the pagans of the time, we will not find it difficult to agree that Constantine was at this stage in his career intending to appeal to a faith which he thought that pagans and Christians would hold in common. It may be that Constantine's

---

[370] Presumably this very carefully constructed sentence should be translated, 'To the Emperor Caesar Flavius Constantinus Maximus, Pious and Fortunate, Augustus, the Roman Senate and People dedicated this arch decorated with trophies, because by the prompting of the Deity and his own lofty design he avenged the state at one blow with his army in a just war both against the tyrant and against all his party.' The panegyrist in 313 speaks of Constantine's *magnitudo animi*. Baynes is clearly right in translating the words *instinctu divinitatis mentis magnitudine* as above and not, as G. Costa suggested, 'by the prompting of a deity, his own great mind' (Constantine the Great, pp. 66–68 and p. 183 n. 1 and p. 216). I do not think that Cochrane ('Christianity and Classical Culture') is justified in seeing in this phrase an echo of Plutarch's words about Alexander διὰ τὸν ἐπὶ τοῖς καλοῖς ἐνθουσιασμόν and the μέγα φρόνημα with which, like Hercules, he confronted fortune and overcame her (De Alex. Magn. Virt. aut Fort. 1.9 and 2.10). Cf. *divino instinctu* Galletier Paneg. 10.17 (180).

[371] Baynes, Constantine the Great, pp. 66–68; Dörries, Konstantin p. 30.

[372] Vita Constantini 4.20; Dörries translates it into German, Konstantin, p. 136.

declaration of the *dies venerabilis solis*, the first day of the week, as a public holiday during this period does not show a desire to profess Mithraism or sun-worship, but a similar move in religious policy that would be acceptable to both pagans and Christians.

Later, however, the evidence suggests that Constantine inclined more definitely to Christianity and took less trouble to find common ground between it and paganism. A letter of his sent to officials in Palestine after his victory over Licinius declares that God has brought him from the extreme western parts of the Empire, the Britains, to the East in order to encourage the whole human race to adopt the cult of the true God (Eusebius V.C. 2.28). Alföldi points out that from the year 317 he began to express his cult of the Solar deity in a new way. There now appears the inscription *Claritas Reipublicae* on coins featuring first his sons and then himself, and this legend sometimes appears round the figure of *Sol*. The suggestion is that the Emperor and his family illuminate the state as the sun illuminates the world; it is perhaps a deliberate attempt to 'disinfect the Solar cult'.[374] In spite of a feeling among some Christians that the worship of 'the elements', and in particular the worship of the sun, was less reprehensible than other pagan cults, sun-worship had been forbidden by the Church and continued to be so during the next two centuries.[375] From 324 onwards, after his overthrow of Licinius, Constantine began to substitute *Victor* for *Invictus* in his inscriptions. His last mention of Apollo occurred in 324. Later, at the end of his life, he was to recall that it was Apollo's 'evil oracle' that had misled Diocletian into persecuting Christians. After his death Julian was to accuse

---

[373] Coleman, Constantine the Great, pp. 33–34; Baynes, Constantine the Great, pp. 101–102. *Cf.* the closing lines of Kraft's book: 'In zweiter Linie allerdings zeigt sich hier noch einmal die leicht gnostische Färbung von Konstantins Christentum, das keinen Anstoß nimmt, den ehamals heidnischen, in der monotheistischen Astralreligion heimischen Attributen einen christlichen Sinn zu geben' (p. 159).

[374] Alföldi, Conversion of Constantine, pp. 58–59.

[375] See Didascalia, cap. 21; Eusebius of Caesarea, Vit. Const. 2.58; Eusebius of Alexandria, Περὶ ἀστρονόμων, P.G. 86.453; Leo the Great, In Nativitate Domini 7, 4 (P.L. 54, 218f.); Patrick, Confession 60.

his uncle of having betrayed the sun-god.[376] In Constantinople Constantine set up a colossal statue of himself with a radiate crown, facing the rising sun, with the inscription. Κωνσταντίνῳ λάμποντι ἡλίου δίκην. The ˌstatue had probably been one of Apollo-Helios on some pagan site, to whose body the Emperor gave another head. It was intended to signify that instead of being a sun-god Constantine gave his allegiance to the God who made the sun.[377] By this time, of course, Constantine had become much more involved in the internal politics of the Christian Church. He had attempted unsuccessfully to interfere in the Donatist Controversy; here he burnt his fingers and gave up intervention in 321. He had inherited the Arian Controversy on becoming master of the Eastern Empire in 324,[378] and had presided at a general Council of bishops. He had deposed, exiled, and recalled bishops on his own initiative; he had acted as a kind of appeal court from local councils, and had fulfilled an ambitious building-programme for the benefit of the Christian Church throughout the Empire.

On one subject Constantine had been intolerant from the beginning of his career as a supporter of Christianity. He had disliked the practice of sacrifice. A reference in the Panegyric of 313 suggests that, though he allowed the auguries to be taken by *haruspicina* at the beginning of the campaign which ended at the Milvian Bridge, he ignored them when they were contrary.[379] When after 312 he began appointing large numbers of Christian officials, and especially governors of provinces, he exempted

[376] Dörries, Konstantin, pp. 133–134.

[377] So Baynes, Constantine the Great, pp. 101–102. *Cf.* Mango, Antique Statuary and the Byzantine Beholder, p. 57.

[378] It is not perhaps widely enough realised by theologians and church historians that the Arian Controversy began in Alexandria in 318, when the Eastern Empire was under the rule of a pagan, Licinius, who, though he had declared tolerance towards Christianity, had shown no particular favour towards it. There was then no apparent prospect of his rule being overthrown. This consideration alone should throw doubt upon the theory that Arianism was designed to facilitate the conversion of multitudes of pagans who were anxious to flood into the Church. Until 324 there were no political incentives in the Eastern Empire for joining the Church.

[379] *Contra consilia hominum, contra haruspicum monita*, Galletier 9.2 (124) (P.L. 8.655/6). *Cf.* Coleman, Constantine the Great, p. 76; Kraft, Rel Ent, p. 83.

them from performing the sacrifices which had hitherto been part of the duty of all officials, and particularly on January 3rd when the sacrifices would have been carried out for the welfare of the Emperor and his family.[380] In 319 he rigorously forbade all consultation of *haruspices* in private houses in a law addressed to the population of Rome.[381] Soon after 324 Constantine prohibited the erection in pagan temples (but not of course elsewhere) of statues to himself and the religious worship of them (V.C. 4.16), and also the participation of state officials at the rites of pagan sacrifice and the actual carrying out of public sacrifices. He did not forbid the rest of the ceremonies customary at festivals.[382] He had not objected earlier to the Panegyrist in 313 describing his father Constantius Chlorus as deified and saying to the Emperor himself: *Merito igitur tibi, Constantine, et nuper senatus signum dei dedit* (i.e., a golden statue).[383] Libanius once asserted that Constantine had pulled down the temples and extinguished all the holy laws, and Jerome (in his 'Chronicle' under the year 335) echoed this statement.[384] But Libanius himself goes far to contradict his own assertion when in his 'Pro Templis' he says that Constantine did not at all change the traditional religion, and even the highly critical Zosimus (2.29.3) declares that Constantine tolerated pagan worship. Constans, in a law of 341 (Cod. Theod. 16.10.2) has been taken to imply that Constantine his father had abolished all pagan worship; but in fact all that he says is that his father had suppressed all sacrifices, a fact which is well attested elsewhere. Further, the frenzied appeals to the Emperors Constantius and Constans which appear in the pages of Firmicus Maternus' 'De Errore Profanarum Religionum' suggest that the

[380] Alföldi, Conversion of Constantine, p. 49.

[381] Cod. Theod. 9.16.12. See Johanna ter Vrugt-Lenz, Das Christentum und die Leberschau, pp. 27–28; she here traces the later history of this prohibition; also Straub, Konstantin's Verzicht auf den Gang zum Kapitol, p. 303.

[382] Alföldi, Conversion of Constantine, p. 89. Eusebius does not support his account of Constantine's laws against paganism in V.C. 2.44.45; 4.23.25, with any citation from official documents; they should be treated with caution.

[383] Galletier 9.25 (143) (P.L. 8.667/8).

[384] Norden, Die Antike Kunstprosa II, pp. 451–452, discussed Libanius' statement. Similar, much vaguer, statements can be found in Eusebius.

practice of pagan religion was at that time still in evidence.[385] Constantine certainly did close or pull down some temples, but in most of the recorded cases he can be shown to have had special reasons: either they encouraged immoral practices or they occupied ground specially holy to Christians, or their treasures were particularly valuable. There was no general policy of closing temples. Elsewhere converted populations were applauded or rewarded for pulling down pagan shrines of their own accord, e.g., Maiuma, the port town of Gaza, was renamed Constantia for such an act, and no doubt regarded itself as having gained a trick from its rival Gaza thereby.[386] It is significant that Gaza was one of the places which indulged in anti-Christian rioting under Julian. It should be noted that Constantine closed or demolished such pagan temples as he did suppress. He did not convert them into Christian churches.

There is some evidence to be placed on the other side, that Constantine at the end of his life tolerated and even in some respects faintly encouraged paganism. Baynes calls attention to an inscription from Egypt by a certain Nikagoras, priest of the Eleusinian mysteries, dated 326, who was permitted by Constantine to use the imperial post in his visit to Egypt, and who thanks the Emperor for this favour.[387] A decree of the year 320–1 permits the exercise of *haruspicina* in the case of an imperial residence or a public building being struck by lightning, though the decree repeats the veto on the private practice of this art.[388] Though Constantine exempted Christian clergy from curial duties and *munera* in 320, he did not withdraw this privilege from priests of acknowledged pagan

---

[385] Coleman, Constantine the Great, pp. 37–39, deals well with this subject; the text of Constans' decree runs thus: *Cesset superstitio, sacrificiorum aboleatur insania. Nam quicumque contra legem divi principis parentis nostri et hanc nostrae mansuetudinis iussionem ausus fuerit sacrificia celebrare, conpetens in eum vindicta et praesens sententia exeratur.*

[386] See Dörries, Konstantin, pp. 135–136; Burckhardt, Age of Constantine, p. 304, who gives a list (though not an exhaustive one) of temples known to have been destroyed by Constantine. See Eusebius, V.C. 3.54–58; 4.38.39; Oratio Tricennalis 8.1–9.

[387] Constantine the Great, p. 83, n. 58.

[388] Coleman, Constantine the Great, p. 35, who gives the Latin text; the reference is Cod. Theod. 16.10.1.

religions and even extended it to the 'patriarchs' and elders of the Jews.[389] There was the well-known case of the little Umbrian town, Hispellum, which late in Constantine's career petitioned to be allowed to erect a temple to him and to his family and to institute priests, and was allowed to do so on condition that sacrifices were not to be offered, though annual games could be celebrated.[390] A decree dated June 29th 326 ordering responsible officials not to begin new building works till those which their predecessors had begun were finished, *exceptis dumtaxat templorum aedificationibus*,[391] not only implies a low rating of temples but reveals that temples were still being constructed. Other evidence, from archaeology, assures us that the building of pagan shrines did not end with Constantine.[392] Constantine certainly continued to employ pagans in his court to the very last. The Neo-Platonist Sosipater was, according to Eunapius, Zosimus and Suidas, employed in an important position by him well after the year 330. Kraft regards Constantine's patronage of Hermogenes and Sosipater and the permission and subsidy which he gave to Nikagoras as a sign that he was ready to favour a paganism which did not indulge in bloody sacrifices and maintained an elevated moral standard (Rel. Ent. p. 125). Sosipater was indeed eventually executed by the Emperor, but we have no clear evidence that this was because he professed paganism. It is more likely that the reason was that he practised theurgy which looked like magic to Constantine. Constantine was not the first Emperor to be sensitive upon this subject; some of his stoutly pagan predecessors had been just as sensitive. In a letter quoted by Eusebius and dating from the latter part of Constantine's life he speaks with the greatest contempt of paganism but obviously does not want to involve himself in persecuting it (V.C. 2.60).

---

[389] Cod. Theod. 16.8.2 (November 29th 330) and 4 (December 1st 331); see Coleman, *op. cit.*, pp. 31–32.

[390] Dörries, Konstantin, p. 135, among others, deals with this case.

[391] Cod. Theod. 15, 1.3; see Coleman, Constantine the Great, p. 39.

[392] *E.g.*, to go no further than remote Britain, the pillar dedicated in the name of the *prisca religio* in Cirencester in the mid-fourth-century and the temple of the Celtic god Nodens restored at Lydney in Gloucestershire about 370.

Burckhardt alleged that Constantine erected temples in Constantinople to the Mother of the gods, to the Dioscuri and to the Fortune (Tyche) of the city. He admits later that the Emperor placed a cross on Tyche's forehead and that Christian prayers were said at the dedication of the temples.[393] Evidence has been produced to show that Constantinople was dedicated with pagan rites.[394]

We cannot go all the way with Burckhardt who envisaged Constantine as a hard-headed manipulator of religion who to the end played Christianity and paganism against each other, committing himself to neither, and who if he at any point favoured Christianity did so simply because as a statesman and politician he admired its organisation.[395] But it is impossible also to see Constantine simply as a Christian champion determined to overthrow paganism, as some in later ages were ready to see him. It would perhaps be wiser to see Constantine as rather more of a product of his age in this respect than has hitherto been allowed. The review of the attitude of Christianity to pagan religions which has been conducted in these pages suggested that much of Constantine's attitude to both systems of religion can be explained if we see him as inheriting the mentality and viewpoint of Christianity as it was about the year 300, not those of the intellectual but of the *homme moyen sensuel*. The point at which most violent repudiation of pagan cults occurred was the practice of sacrifice, and there was a strong tradition of dislike of

[393] Age of Constantine, pp. 302 and 352.

[394] Burckhardt, of course, accepted this; most scholars since then seem to have doubted it; but fairly recently Mango, relying on A. Frolow, said that this assertion, 'had been proved' (Antique Statuary and the Byzantine Beholder, p. 56). Eusebius (V.C. 3.48) directly contradicts this suggestion, writing not long before the year 340.

[395] Age of Constantine, pp. 176, 261, 279, et alibi. Even though scholarly opinion may have swung a little away from the decisive rejection of Burckhardt's views by Baynes, Jones, Alföldi and Dörries, it is impossible to accept them without many qualifications. As Constantine became better acquainted with the organisation of the Christian Church and more involved in attempts to improve it, it is wholly unlikely that he came to admire that organisation more. On the contrary, it must have seemed in many respects very unsatisfactory to him. Yet as he grew older he became more devoted to Christianity.

this feature among pagans themselves. Here Constantine showed his hand unmistakeably at an early point. Even before the decisive battle of the Milvian Bridge he had ignored the traditional auguries. Immediately after the battle he at some risk to his reputation pointedly refused to sacrifice to Juppiter Optimus Maximus on the Capitol. It seems likely that he incurred immediate criticism from the mob for this act, and he must have known that his refusal would annoy the senatorial class in Rome. He continued this attitude of opposition to sacrifice consistently for the rest of his life and later attempted to enforce it upon the whole Empire.[396] But he could not accept the imposition of a total social and cultural *apartheid* between Christianity and paganism, and it is clear that many Christians (probably the majority) had found it impossible to maintain this *apartheid* in practice by Constantine's day. He allowed pagan religion in large part to continue, though there were occasions when he tried to purge or disinfect it. The most obvious common ground between paganism and Christianity was that of monotheism. Paganism had achieved an inchoate monotheistic belief, though not a practice, by Constantine's day. Christians were prepared to allow that the worship of the elements was a less objectionable cult than others and that it had immemorial antiquity behind it. The Solar Cult seemed for some time to express this common ground most suitably. The reverence for holy sites where a special closeness to deity might be available had been a great part of paganism and had not completely died out in Constantine's day. The Emperor and his mother therefore occupied themselves when they could in erecting churches and shrines at the holy places dear to Christians, at the shrine of St. Peter on the Vatican hill and at the traditional site of St. Paul's martyrdom on the Ostian Way in Rome, at the traditional site of the birth of the Saviour in Bethlehem, on the Mount of Olives, site of the Ascension, at Calvary and round the tomb of our Lord in Jerusalem, at Mamre, a spot particularly associated with the patriarch Abraham. The Christian Church had made no serious attempt to produce a rival culture to that of paganism, and neither did

[396] *Cf.* Kraft, *op. cit.*, p. 48.

Constantine. His ecclesiastical buildings derived from no consciously ecclesiastical architecture. Their decoration was almost wholly derived from contemporary pagan art. The mausoleum which he erected for his sister Constantia outside Rome survives largely intact to this day. She certainly was buried with Christian rites but the decoration of Santa Constanza that dates from the fourth century is wholly that of the Late Roman Empire, consisting of charming mosaics of birds and flowers and scenes of vintage and harvest, with no hint of Christian symbolism at all.

Constantine provided the Church with a breathing-space between the experience of violent or latent hostility from the Roman Imperial Government and the experience of embarrassingly close support and favour by that Government. His reign constituted an interval between a crucial struggle with established paganism and the long period during which Christianity was to be closely fused together with European civilization and culture. His mentality and his policy in some ways represent the situation in which both Christianity and paganism found themselves at this period. Constantine was at once a summary and a catalyst.

Part II

Part II
The Fourth and Fifth Centuries

10

THE DOCTRINE OF THE TRINITY ACHIEVED IN 381[1]

I

When we read the Creed of Constantinople of the year 381, which is generally called the Nicene Creed, we gain the unmistakable impression that we have travelled a long way from the opening verses of St. Mark's Gospel. This paper will consist of an attempt to answer the question, Was this journey really necessary? A number of negatives have been given to this question. It has been asserted that the doctrine of this creed was reached because the spirit of useless intellectual curiosity and of metaphysical speculation had gripped the theologians of the Church, so that the creed became only a stage towards 'the bankruptcy of Patristic theology' which was to be reached by the middle of the next century. It has been suggested, perhaps as a variant of the same argument, that this creed represents the capture of the original Judaeo-Christian message or gospel of primitive Christianity by a process of Hellenisation, a gradual approximation to late Greek, mainly Platonic, philosophy. The theory has even been put forward with a wholly misplaced confidence that the doctrine of the Trinity was produced in order to guarantee a celestial order and security corresponding to and supporting the order and security represented by the Christian Emperor himself. These are all explanations of the doctrinal journey which in one way or another see it as a superfluity or a deviation.

This doctrine and the creed which represents the official and dogmatic justification for the doctrine were achieved, as is well known, as the result of a controversy known conventionally but not quite accurately as the Arian Controversy. The version of events connected with this controversy, which lasted from 318 to 381, to be found till very recently in virtually all the text-books runs something like this: in the year 318 a presbyter called Arius was rebuked by his bishop Alexander of Alexandria for

[1] A lecture delivered at the Colloquium in Commemoration of the Nicene Creed at New College, University of Edinburgh, 2nd May 1981.

teaching erroneous doctrine concerning the divinity of Christ, to the effect that Christ was a created and inferior god. When the controversy spread because Arius was supported by wicked and designing bishops such as Eusebius of Nicomedia and his namesake of Caesarea, the Emperor Constantine called a general Council at Nicaea which drew up a creed intended to suppress Arianism and finish the controversy. But owing to the crafty political and ecclesiastical engineering of the Arians, this pious design was frustrated. Supporters of the orthodox point of view such as Athanasius of Alexandria, Eustathius of Antioch and later Paul of Constantinople were deposed from their sees on trumped-up charges and sent into exile. Orthodoxy was everywhere attacked and, as later in the controversy succeeding Emperors joined the heretical side, almost completely eclipsed. But Athanasius resolutely and courageously sustained the battle for orthodoxy, almost alone, until in the later stages of the controversy he was joined by other standard-bearers of orthodoxy such as Hilary of Poitiers, Pope Damasus, and the three Cappadocians, Basil of Caesarea, Gregory of Nazianzus and Gregory of Nyssa. Ultimately by the aid of the Emperor Theodosius right prevailed, the forces of error and wickedness represented by the Arians were defeated and crushed, and the formulation of Constantinople in 381 of the revised Nicene Creed crowned the triumph of the true faith.

This conventional account of the controversy, which stems originally from the version given of it by the victorious party, is now recognised by a large number of scholars to be a complete travesty. To see this it is only necessary to read that weighty and magisterial recent work upon the subject, *La Crisi Ariana nel Quarto Secolo* by M. Simonetti, a Roman Catholic scholar whose integrity is as unexceptionable as his orthodoxy. At the beginning of the controversy nobody knew the right answer. There was no 'orthodoxy' on the subject of 'how divine is Jesus Christ?', certainly not in the form which was later to be enshrined in the Creed of Constantinople. It is *a priori* implausible to suggest that a controversy raged for no less than sixty years in the Church, so that every single one of the original contestants was dead by the time the controversy was settled, over a doctrine whose orthodox form was perfectly well known to everybody concerned and had been well known for centuries past. Arius' particular doctrines, as far as we can reconstruct them, seem to have been almost uniquely calculated to arouse both agreement and dissension without giving any serious prospect of providing ground for a solution of the dispute. That is his main claim to fame. The Creed of Nicaea of 325, produced in order to end the controversy, signally failed to do so. Indeed, it ultimately compounded the confusion because its use of the words *ousia* and *hypostasis* was so ambiguous as to suggest that the Fathers of Nicaea had fallen into Sabellianism, a view recognised as a heresy even at that period. What is conventionally regarded as the key-word in the Creed, *homoousion*, falls completely out of the controversy very shortly after the Council of Nicaea and is not heard of for over twenty years. To regard the bishops and theologians taking part in the controversy as falling simply into two groups, 'orthodox' and 'Arian', immediately after the Council of Nicaea of 325, and to interpret the course of the Controversy as a straightforward struggle between these two points of view, with sub-groups forming themselves from time to time within the two clearly-defined camps, is a grave misunderstanding and a serious misrepresentation of the true state of affairs.

The dispute was indeed aggravated and clouded by a number of extraneous factors and a number of dangerous mistakes and serious faults committed by those who were parties to it. But these mistakes and faults were not confined to the upholders of any one particular doctrine, and cannot all be grouped under the heading of a wicked Arian conspiracy. The most serious initial fault was the misbehaviour of Athanasius in his see of Alexandria. Evidence which has turned up in the sands of Egypt in the form of letters written on papyrus has now made it impossible to doubt that Athanasius displayed a violence and unscrupulousness towards his opponents in Egypt which justly earned the disgust and dislike of the majority of Eastern bishops for at least the first twenty years of his long episcopate. It is of course true that Eusebius of Nicomedia, who had supported Arius, displayed ambition and craft in forwarding the interests of his own party and in his relations with Western bishops, but the depositions of his opponents cannot all be attributed to an

Arian plot. It seems highly likely that Eustathius of Antioch was guilty of some misconduct, because it is only long after his deposition, and perhaps after his death, that he begins to rank as a martyr in the cause of orthodoxy. The Westerners at Sardica in 343 significantly fail to mention him in their roll-call of the innocent injured. Paul of Byzantium/Constantinople appears to have become embroiled in a domestic quarrel unconnected with the Arian Controversy and, like Eustathius, to have been the subject of pro-Nicene hagiography only at a comparatively late date. Julius of Rome was in Eastern eyes irresponsible to the point of mischievousness in championing the deposed Eastern bishops, Athanasius, Marcellus and Asclepas, in assuming that they must have been the victims of injustice and in branding as 'Arian' all those who disagreed with them; and we can sympathise with the Easterners' resentment here. The views of Marcellus of Ancyra were eccentric by any standards of orthodoxy recognised in the fourth century. Marcellus in some respects displayed a discernment in interpreting Scripture which others lacked, but he cannot be acquitted of Sabellianism. The fact that he could sign the baptismal creed of Rome was no proof at all of his orthodoxy, because it constituted no sort of test of Trinitarian doctrine. That Julius and later the Westerners at Sardica should have declared him orthodox was bound to appear to the Eastern theologians to be a condoning of Sabellianism, a doctrine which the anathema of Nicaea against those who maintain that the Son is of a different *hypostasis* or *ousia* from those of the Father and the emphatic identification of the *ousia* and *hypostasis* of the Father and the Son in the Western statement after the Council of Sardica only seemed to support. The repeated confusion caused by the use of the same terms by different writers in different senses, right up to the very end, well after the Council of Alexandria of 362 which on the conventional view is supposed to have cleared up the confusion, added its own exasperation to the whole dispute.

Up to the year 357 the East could label the West as Sabellian and the West could label the East as Arian with equal lack of discrimination and accuracy. In the year 357 Arianism as a relatively clearly thought out doctrinal position emerged for the first time, and for the first time those Eastern theologians who were not Arian were in a position to distinguish their own views and confess them. This is the point at which the solution to the controversy begins very faintly to dawn, though its full realisation was delayed for twenty-four years. The end was at last gained when an Emperor had secured a genuine consensus for one point of view and was able to enforce it. Throughout the controversy everybody with rare and occasional exceptions assumed that the final authority in bringing about a decision in matters doctrinal was not a council nor the Pope, but the Emperor. Several Emperors had attempted to fulfil this role, Constantine, Constans, Constantius, and Valens when in intervals of fussing ineffectively about administrative affairs he began fussing about ecclesiastical matters. All had failed because though the measures which they took might for a time appear to have been successful they in fact were not supported by a consensus in the Church at large. Theodosius succeeded because by the time he came to Imperial power the point of view which he supported was backed by a consensus in the Church. In the past Imperial coercion had been freely applied but had failed. Now it succeeded, not because it was coercion but because it was coercion backed by general assent. But even here we must dissent from the conventional account of the end of the Arian Controversy. The solution did not emanate directly either from Rome or from Alexandria. On the contrary: the opening of the year 375 saw the ironical situation in which the Pope, Damasus, and the archbishop of Alexandria, Peter, were supporting Paulinus of Antioch, a Sabellian heretic, and Vitalis, an Apollinarian heretic, against Basil of Caesarea, the champion of Nicene orthodoxy in the East, later to be acknowledged universally as a great Doctor of the Church, who never during a single minute of his existence was formally in communion with the see of Rome! The direct source of the solution of the Arian Controversy, and the great articulators of the doctrine of the Trinity, were the three Cappadocian fathers whose origins were undoubtedly from that Homoeousian party whom Epiphanius, that unsubtle but useful preserver of the views of others, had the impudence to call 'Semi-Arians'.

II

But we must delve deeper than this if we are to understand the reasons for the formation of the doctrine of the Trinity. We must ask, not what was the immediate occasion of its development, but what was the original urge or need or dynamic which made it seem necessary to those who formed it? The answer lies in the necessity for finding a specifically Christian doctrine of God. The Bible does not give us a specifically Christian doctrine of God, though it gives us the raw material for this. When the N.T. was canonised, in effect by the middle of the third century, even those parts of it which were devoted to a consideration of the person rather than of the function of Christ, such as the first chapters of the Gospel according to St. John and the Epistle to the Colossians and the Epistle of the Hebrews, did not supply anything more than some hints towards the formation of a specifically Christian doctrine of God. Before the writing of the N.T. the Church professed to all appearances the monotheism of late-Judaism with the story of an eschatological Messiah as an addendum. To say that Christians believed in one sole God and in addition that Jesus Christ was a very important person was not to state a specifically Christian doctrine of God. I may perhaps illustrate the point by relating an experience which I had recently. I was invited to a lunch in Manchester along with the representatives of several other religions and after lunch our genial host required of us to state our religious views in two sentences. The Sikh representative (who I do not for a moment believe was capable of giving us the authentic doctrine of Sikhism) said that his fellow-worshippers believed in one God and that Sikhs should not be required to wear helmets when they rode motorcycles. The doctrine of primitive Christianity would have appeared, at least to the non-Jew, not much less disproportionate in its parts than that. The N.T. made some closer approach to an integrated doctrine of God, but was still far from achieving anything more than a subvariant of the Jewish doctrine of God.

There certainly were forces within Christianity even before it emerged from its Jewish milieu or matrix moving towards an integrated doctrine of God. There was the fundamental Jewish urge towards monotheism, its rejection of lesser deities or any qualification or diminution of the concept of God. There was the doctrine of the pre-existence of Christ which can be traced back to a very early period. There was the practice of praying to Jesus Christ as well as praying through him. There were the theological trajectories (to use current theological jargon) pointing to a doctrine of incarnation, in Matthew, in Paul, in Hebrews and above all in John. There was, in fine, the ineradicably Christocentric nature of Christianity, the concept of Christ as the Last Act of God, the eschatological pressure, so to speak, that his figure exerted on Christian thought. But as long as Christianity remained in a Jewish environment none of these factors was strong enough to constitute on its own a movement towards the development of a specifically Christian doctrine of God, the enterprise of determining what difference the career of Jesus Christ must have in forming the Church's thought, not just about what God had done, but what God is.

It was when Christianity emerged during the second century into a non-Jewish largely Gentile milieu that the pressure to produce a specifically Christian doctrine of God became unavoidable. The intellectual world of the Late Roman Empire, enjoying under a series of enlightened Emperors chosen on an adoptive rather than hereditary principle its last St. Luke's summer of peace and prosperity before the storms and disasters of the next three centuries, was dominated by the inheritance and the practice of Greek philosophy. The Greek intellectual tradition had of course altered since its great days in the fifth and fourth centuries before Christ. Its Platonism was not exactly the Platonism of Plato; Stoicism had arisen as a distinct and attractive alternative; Aristotelianism, though studied by some, was under eclipse. Greek philosophy had become more eclectic than in Plato's day, and also much more religious and theistic. What J. B. Bury in all the confidence of Victorian rationalism has called a 'loss of nerve' had taken place. But philosophy was still full of vitality and was actively studied or at least acquired in a general way by the great majority of those who called themselves intellectuals or who had received a higher education in that age. And Greek philosophy required of any religion which aspired to be an universal religion, as Christianity did, that it should give a rational account of itself. If it had a teaching about God, the intellectual tradition of the Late Roman Empire insisted that that teaching should be rational (not necessarily rationalist), consistent, defensible, intellectually acceptable. If Christianity was to be more than an enthusiastic or moralising sect making no pretensions to intellectual respectability, more than an ethnic religion, more than a barbaric cult or a sub-variety of Judaism, in short if it was to capture the mind as well as the heart of the society in which it existed, it was bound to produce a specifically Christian doctrine of God. This was not an unreasonable demand, not the requirement of a futile speculative Greek curiosity, but a plain necessity if Christianity was to be a genuinely missionary religion, a religion capable of sustaining the daring claim that it was a faith for all races and all classes and all minds, a religion for the whole world.

The first attempt at this task was made by the group of writers whom we call the Apologists, and it was made, significantly enough, to a large degree in independence of the thought of the Fourth Gospel. This group had nothing in common, if we except the connection between Justin Martyr and Tatian, apart from a common purpose and a common pattern of thought. They did not all live in the same place or at the same time. But their common aim resulted in a common pattern of theology. They used to great effect several features of contemporary Greek philosophy to enable them to construct their doctrine of God. They identified the pre-existent Christ, thought of as manifesting himself on critical occasions throughout the history of the Jewish people, with the *nous* or Second *Hypostasis* of contemporary Middle Platonist philosophy, and also borrowed some traits from the divine Logos of Stoicism (including its name). They thereby solved for those who accepted their doctrine a difficult contemporary philosophical problem: how was the supreme being, whether conceived as *to on* or *to agathon* impersonally or as a personal mind or deity, to communicate in his immutable, abstract, immaterial condition with our world of change and decay, transitoriness and matter? The answer was, the divine Logos or *nous* identified with Christ both pre-existent and incarnate in his earthly ministry. He was the agent for creating the world of the supreme Divinity and also the means of the Divinity revealing himself in the world, both in the history of the Jews and in the earthly career of Jesus. They felt some obligation to fit the Holy Spirit into this scheme, but were less successful here. They could hardly be said to have developed a recognisably Trinitarian scheme, but they certainly had produced the first specifically Christian doctrine of God. They were writing mostly for non-Jews and non-Christians. Such a public demanded philosophical consistency but no very great attention to historical detail nor to the witness of the Bible.

The theological structure provided by the Apologists lasted as the main, widely-accepted, one might almost say traditional framework for a Christian doctrine of God well into the fourth century, and was, in differing form, the basic picture of God with which the great majority of those who were first involved in the Arian Controversy were familiar and which they accepted. The doctrine was given a better balance and proportion by both Irenaeus and Tertullian. They redressed the tendency of the Apologists to fall into an almost Gnostic doctrine of an unknown, inaccessible High God from whom the lesser god, the Logos, brings communications. They paid much more attention to Scripture, and especially to the Fourth Gospel. They made more room for the Holy Spirit in their doctrine of God, and brought out the significance of the earthly career of Jesus, which all the Apologists apart from Justin had ignored. But their fundamental theological structure was the same as that of the Apologists. The Logos was begotten or produced or put forward by the Father as his instrument or tool for communicating with the world, a subordinate though essential divine agent. Origen produced something like a theological revolution without however completely demolishing this theological structure. He extended and diversified it, but he did not alter most of its main features. In his brilliant search for common ground between Christianity and the kind of philosophy which appealed to him, late Middle Platonism laced with some Stoicism, he introduced some new and enduring features and made some daring speculations. He launched the doctrine of the eternal, not merely the economic, Trinity; he produced a neat and ingenious account of how the

Son/Logos could be, as incarnate, both divine and human. He taught the eternal pre-existence of souls, and a pre-mundane fall, and he demythologised eschatology as radically as ever Bultmann did. But he still envisaged the Son as a subordinate agent of the Father and still treated him as an ingenious philosophical device, indeed he enhanced this feature in his Trinitarian doctrine.

Even when greatly altered and given a much more sophisticated appearance by Origen, this form of the Christian doctrine of God had serious flaws. Its chief flaw was that which the Apologists had regarded as its greatest merit. It made Christ into a convenient philosophical device. He was the means whereby the supreme God, the Father, was protected from embarrassingly close relation to the world. He was, not by reason of his incarnation but by reason of his very nature apart from the incarnation, a defused, depotentiated version of God suitable for encounter with such compromising things as history and humanity and transitoriness. He was the safeguard against a too close acquaintance with our existence on the part of the supreme God. This Logos-doctrine was not the Logos-doctrine of the Fourth Gospel, where the incarnate Logos is the guarantee that the supreme God has in fact communicated himself to and in our world, where the fact that the Son is accessible in the flesh means that the Father is accessible to us too, where the veil or restriction imposed on himself by God is not his Son but the Son's humanity, where the contrast is between sight and faith, not between incorruptibility and the corruptible. Whatever the theological or philosophical effect of the conventional Trinitarian doctrine with which Christianity entered the fourth century may have been, its religious effect, once granted the worship of Christ, was to make the Son into a demi-god. This can be observed by looking at the second-rate or third-rate writers of the period, not at the successors of Origen, Theognostus, Methodius, Eusebius of Caesarea, but at Lactantius, Arnobius, Victorinus of Pettau, Dionysius of Alexandria. They present us unashamedly with a second, created god lower than the High God and capable of incarnation. When Gwatkin nearly a century ago in the last full-scale book written in English on the Arian Controversy branded

Arianism as 'heathen to the core' and as a watered-down version of Christianity suitable for imperfectly converted pagan polytheists, he was writing vague imperfectly substantiated rhetoric, based on an inadequate examination of Arius' background, but he was not talking complete nonsense. The Arianism of Ulfilas, of Palladius at the Council of Aquileia of 381, of Eunomius, does present the Son as in effect a demi-god, even though the antecedents of this doctrine are not to be found in pagan religion nor directly in Greek philosophy but in various theological strands to be detected in Christian theology before the fourth century.

The ancient world did not disdain demi-gods. The word *theos* or *deus*, for the first four centuries of the existence of Christianity had a wide variety of meanings. There were many different types and grades of deity in popular thought and religion and even in philosophical thought. This is a fact which is often forgotten by those who are anxious to read the later doctrine of Christ's divinity incontinently into the N.T. This is why Christians found it quite possible to hold the kind of conception of Christ's divinity which was widespread in Christian thought as the third century gave way to the fourth. Of course Christ was divine. But how divine, and what exactly did 'divine' mean in that context? It was with this question that the Arian Controversy started and it found nobody in a position to give an immediately satisfying answer. But once the question was raised—and Arius' teaching had raised it in such a way that it could not now be ignored—it could only by answered by the formulation of a more detailed and thorough Christian doctrine of God.

The Church of the fourth century after much travail answered this question. The answer was only reached after long controversy, heart-searching, confusion and vicissitude in a manner which can best be described as a process of trial-and-error in which the error was by no means confined to the so-called heretics. Its result in the Nicene Creed was to reduce the meanings of the word 'God' from a very large selection of alternatives to one only, so that today it is part of the bloodstream of European culture. When Western man today says 'God' he means the one, sole exclusive God and nothing else. Even when he denies the existence of God he does not even pause to disbelieve in gods. Even when he blasphemes, he swears profanely by the sole God. This is why the theologians of the Eastern Orthodox Church who use the word 'god' to describe the divinised human nature of Christ and the final state of man in glory can only cause bewilderment and dissent in the minds of Westerners. What the fourth-century development did was to destroy the tradition of Christ as a convenient philosophical device, of Christ, as the Cappadocian fathers put it, existing for the sake of us instead of our existing for his sake. The Cappadocians, following in the footsteps of Athanasius, put a firm 'No Thoroughfare' notice in front of this theological track, a track which must have seemed to many a hopeful and useful one. In this respect at least they fought an example of the Hellenisation of the gospel, they rejected the allurements of Greek philosophy. Indeed if we want a beautiful example of Hellenisation of Christianity we can turn to the most extreme of the Arians, Eunomius, who would have agreed heartily with the title of Toland's famous book, *Christianity not Mysterious*, and who had an unbounded confidence in the capacity of Greek metaphysics to solve all theological problems and to scale all the heights of knowledge of the divine. In the course of refuting his teaching Gregory of Nyssa has quite often to pause and protest against his indiscriminate use of philosophical jargon.

In the place of this old but inadequate Trinitarian tradition the champions of the Nicene faith substituted another which was more in accordance with the pressure towards monotheism that is part of the inner nature of Christianity and that also did justice to the ancient practice of worshipping Christ. They were forced through the exigencies of controversy to realise that Christ is either ultimately irrelevant to Christianity, a paradigm, an example, a supremely obedient and godly man, but no more, or he must be a mediator, and therefore authentically God and not a second-class deity. The dispute was about the necessity, the centrality, the indispensability of Christ. They developed a doctrine of God as a Trinity, as one substance or *ousia* who existed as three *hypostaseis*, three distinct realities or entities (I refrain from using the misleading word 'Person'), three ways of being or modes of existing as God. This doctrine which finally emerged was the result of assimilating the indispensability of Christ to the monotheism which Christianity inherited from Judaism and which it would not abandon.

Of course the theologians of the side which was ultimately victorious included the Holy Spirit in the Trinity. In a sense this was an afterthought, because the theme of the Son occupied the screen, so to speak, right up to the year 360. It was only when the battle for the recognition of the Son's full divinity was in a fair way to being won that the Spirit moved to the centre of the stage. It has been suggested that this pneumatological development was a kind of lame epilogue or unhappy corollary to the development concerning the Son. Napoleon Bonaparte was Emperor of the French, Emperor in fact and in form. His brother Joseph was for a period by a kind of creaking imperial logic king of Spain, in form if not in fact. Was this the kind of process by which the Holy Spirit became deified? It is certainly true that until the middle of the fourth century very little attention had been paid to the Holy Spirit by the theologians. I do not believe those historians of doctrine who tell us that people like Novatian and Victorinus of Pettau were really Binitarians, but certainly nobody for the first four centuries had seen the necessity of working out a theology of the Spirit and when Athanasius in his *Letters to Serapion* set out to do so he was not wholly successful. Further, two of the Cappadocians, Basil and Gregory of Nazianzus, admit silently that the Scriptural evidence for the Spirit as a distinct *hypostasis* within the Godhead is inadequate. Basil in his *De Spiritu Sancto* tries to take refuge in a most unsatisfactory doctrine of secret unscriptural tradition on the subject. Gregory, though he tacitly rejects Basil's device, in effect appeals to the experience and practice of the Church to supplement Scripture at this point. It was not that the Scriptures did not declare the Spirit to be divine, but in the matter of their witnessing to his existence as an *hypostasis*, a distinctly recognisable reality, within the Godhead, they were, not contradictory, but insufficient.

Certain points can, however, help us to understand the Cappadocians' decision that the Holy Spirit must be included in the Trinity and why they wrote of him as they did. In the first place, Christians have always found it difficult to write about the Holy Spirit, just because he is God as we encounter him. It is always difficult to write about our own religious experience, to stand outside ourselves sufficiently to convey what we know to be true in ourselves. In the second place the Spirit is God sovereign over time, God overcoming the limits of history and space and time. He is in the N.T. an eschatological figure. He is Lord of history and his appearance heralds the end of the ages. It is therefore improper or inconsistent to expect the historical witness which we have in the Bible to his advent to be entirely adequate. Historical documents cannot adequately witness to him who is beyond history as well as in it, who makes past history present for us, and who has not yet finished unfolding the history of salvation. Finally when the Cappadocians decided that having been committed to drastic theological conclusions about the Son they could not avoid making theological decisions about the Spirit they were being true to the N.T. The Holy Spirit is bound up with, inseparable from, Jesus Christ, and if we decided that Christ is divine we cannot in the end withhold divinity from the Spirit. The Cappadocians therefore boldly included the Spirit in their Trinitarian theology. They resisted a formidable movement to reject the Spirit's divinity, led not by the shadowy Macedonius, but by that extraordinary and unpredictable character Eustathius of Sebaste. They formulated a full-blooded Trinitarian doctrine and went some distance towards defining the relations of the Persons within the Trinity. The revised Nicene Creed of 381 enshrined the conclusions to which they had come without canonising any one Trinitarian formula.

III

The last section of this paper must be devoted to comment upon the achievement of these fourth-century theologians. It must be noted that the development of the doctrine of the Trinity was carried out in terms which were almost wholly borrowed from the vocabulary of late Greek philosophy. All the technical terms of Trinitarian talk were Greek, *hypostasis, ousia, homoousios, homoeousios, tautousios, heterousios, hyparxis, prosopon, perichoresis,* and so on. In this matter the ancient theologians had in fact no choice. Once the theologians of the early period had, under the influence of the Christian Platonists of Alexandria, abandoned the illusion that Christianity was itself a philosophy rivalling the others, and had realised that their faith needed the aid of philosophy in order to express itself in contemporary and comprehensible terms, then the Church was committed to the necessity of explaining its beliefs in the terminology of Greek philosophy. One of the lessons learnt by the bitter experience of the Arian Controversy was that you cannot interpret the Bible simply in biblical terms. If your intention is to explain the Bible's meaning, then on crucial points you must draw your explanation from some other vocabulary apart from that of the Bible. Otherwise you will be left with the old question in another form still unanswered. The only alternative language available for interpreting the Bible was that of Greek philosophy. Roman philosophy was no more than a pale imitation of Greek. There was no philosophical language available in the tradition of Syriac-speaking Christianity, even had it been comprehensible to the majority of ancient theologians. Indian philosophy, though not wholly unknown, was too remote and too strange to serve their purpose. No other intellectual tools were at their disposal.

This borrowing from Greek philosophy, like all borrowing, exacted a price. The case was not merely that the theologians of the fourth century used Greek words. They thought Greek thoughts. Many of the fundamental assumptions which they made in all their theological writing were those of Greek philosophy not those of the Old and New Testaments. Their psychology and anthropology were, with few exceptions, largely Stoic or (less frequently) Platonist. Their ethics were for the most part not the ethics of the Bible, involved as these are in particular situations and rule-of-thumb expressions, not easily detected or identified. The Stoics had developed a consistent and attractive ethical system, and the Christian theologians found it impossible to resist the temptation (if temptation it was) to read this system into the biblical text. More important was their unanimous assumption that ontological immutability is an essential attribute of God, that under no circumstances could God ever be thought of as coming in contact with the transitory and corruptible or mortal, a concept which is quite alien to the conception of God to be found in the Old and New Testaments. This axiom had far-reaching effects on their theology. It troubled Athanasius when he had to face the undeniable fact that the Bible represents God as acting in history. He had to fall back on the lame explanation that all the events of salvation history had been eternally predestined by God before the foundation of the world. The same axiom produced extraordinary results when the pro-Nicene theologians came to envisage the earthly life of Jesus. Almost all the orthodox theologians say that while the Word of course took human flesh, it was not human flesh like ours, but a different sort of purer, sanctified human flesh. Hilary of Poitiers plunges wildly into Docetism at this point: Christ felt the effect of the blow when he was struck, but not its pain, and so on. Another consequence of this axiom is that very few theologians of the fourth century appreciate the full force of the dynamic, eschatological language which the N.T. uses of Christ and of the Holy Spirit. They flatten and blunt this language, transposing it into ontological categories. For Athanasius, as has frequently been observed, the divinity of Christ means his ontological stability.

But though the fourth-century Fathers thought almost wholly in the vocabulary and thought-forms of Greek philosophy, they were by no means consistent in using them. The study of *ousia* by G. C. Stead in his book *Divine Substance* has shown how large was the variety of meanings which the Fathers attached to that word, and E. P. Meijering has demonstrated that even in so apparently precise a term as 'beyond being', *epekeina tēs ousias*, different writers could attach different meanings to it. In such obviously unplatonic subjects as the resurrection of the body, the creation of matter out of nothing, and the possibility of an incarnation of God, the Fathers recognised clearly that Christianity manifestly diverged from philosophy and said so. Perhaps the best way to express the situation would be to say that in all their theology there is a tension between the ideas of Greek philosophy and those of the tradition of Christian truth which they inherited, a tension sometimes explicitly realised but more often not, and that in none of them is this tension completely resolved. While, for instance, they believe that Christ's humanity could not have been exactly like ours because he was born of a virgin without male human parentage, they also reject the Arian doctrine that incarnation necessarily implies inferiority in the God who is incarnate. Here the tension becomes very visible. It is perhaps worth noting incidentally, on the subject of consistency, that the Nicene dogma does not entail the Chalcedonian dogma with an iron necessity. On the contrary, the two-nature scheme of Chalcedon might be regarded as a drawing back from the full drastic consequences of the Nicene Creed under the influence of a Greek fear of compromising God with human experiences.

How much of faithfulness to Scripture did the Fathers of the fourth century sacrifice? Maurice Wiles has suggested that as far as grotesque misunderstanding of the truth of the Bible goes the pro-Nicenes were as distant from accurate interpretation as the Arians. Certainly all exegetes of whatever colour in that period shared common ideas about the Bible which are impossible for us, Julian the Arian on Job as well as Didymus the Blind on Zechariah. For them most of the Psalms were tape-recordings made by David of conversations held between God the Father, God the Son and the Church. Very large numbers of passages in the O.T. spoke to them directly of Christian doctrine which to us are wholly devoid of such reference, *e.g.* Prov 8.22 which might be called the key-text of the Arian Controversy, and Amos 4.13 which was much adduced by the Macedonians. The Antiochene preference for eschewing allegory in handling Scripture had scarcely yet appeared in the fourth century; the irresponsible use of allegory abounded, perhaps more among the pro-Nicenes than among the Arians. Julian in his Commentary on Job uses it very little. But though in detail Patristic interpretation of the Bible can be utterly different from ours today, in several of the points where what one might call the weight or what Athanasius calls the *skopos*, the main burden or message of Scripture, is concerned they discern clearly enough the true facts. They recognise at least in theory, as an intellectual proposition, the humanity of Christ, they resist Apollinarianism. They know that the O.T. witnesses to God revealing himself in history. They acknowledge consistently that God can only be known in faith. They do some justice to the thought of St. Paul, Augustine almost full justice. Above all, they are deeply influenced by the Fourth Gospel, whereas the Arians are not. This is the crucial point of interpretation where Athanasius has a deeper appreciation of the thought of the N.T. than his opponents. For the Arians, God cannot communicate himself to man, he can only send a well-accredited messenger, because incarnation is a reduction, a diminution of Godhead. Athanasius accepts the full significance of the doctrine of that Gospel, though he expresses it in terms of Greek ontological thought and though, like all the pro-Nicene theologians, he assumes erroneously that St. John is laying out pre-fabricated Trinitarian doctrine in his pages. But here he shows a vitally important insight into the significance of the N.T. which the Arians, preoccupied as they were with the incomparability of God, failed to see.

We must also realise that when the Cappadocian Fathers presented the Church with the doctrine of the Trinity they did not present it with a formula designed to express that doctrine permanently. There is no universally recognised formula expressing the doctrine of the Trinity, for the Athanasian Creed, which has such a formula, is not an ecumenical creed. The theologians of the fourth century, though they were quite ready to countenance creeds, did not have the same intense addiction to precise formulae as later ages had nor the same insistence on precise accuracy as we have. Auxentius of Milan could say that the creed which he had probably met for the first time when he became bishop of Milan was what he had learnt from his youth up; he was referring to the content, not to the words. The fact that the members of the council of Constantinople of 381 could regard themselves as reproducing in the creed which they adopted the original formula of 325, which we would regard as a very different document, speaks for itself. At one point Gregory of Nazianzus, in a letter defending Basil against the charge of refusing to acknowledge openly the divinity of the Holy Spirit, states explicitly that it is not the words that count but the meaning which they convey. The Cappadocians cannot be accused of spinning theological formulations simply for the sake of creating ever new Greek metaphysical constructions.

They were very well aware, as was Athanasius, of the inadequacy of language to express thought about God. It was one of the lessons learnt during the course of the controversy. What the Cappadocians contended for was the shape of Trinitarian doctrine, not for any particular formulation of it. They were emphatically not fighting for a creed, but for a doctrine. That doctrine has since been expressed in different ways by later theologians by, for instance, Augustine, Thomas Aquinas, Gregory Palamas, John Calvin and Karl Barth, but it remains the same doctrine.

Last of all, we must ask whether this doctrine of the Holy Trinity, achieved after so long and trying an experience of controversy, heart-searching and vicissitude, was an interpretation of the Bible, or whether it should rather be regarded as a development. If, as I think, we can answer the question originally asked in this paper by saying that the journey was really necessary, we must decide what sort of a journey it was. Of course the doctrine of the Trinity was in a sense an interpretation of the Bible. It began as an attempt to answer the question, how divine is Jesus Christ?, and went on to decide whether God has communicated himself or not. Neither of these questions lie directly on the surface of the Bible, though they are both raised if the Bible's contents are studied with care and in depth; the Bible does not directly answer either. The question we deal with here is ultimately that which Newman raised, but did not answer, in his *Essay on the Development of Christian Doctrine*. I think that a consideration of the whole history of the gradual formation of this doctrine must convince students of the subject that the doctrine of the Trinity is a development, and a development which in its shape, as distinguished from the diverse formulations of its shape, is true and authentic. Christians can honestly worship Jesus Christ and also honestly declare that they are monotheists, but only if they adopt a concept of God which has a Trinitarian shape. When they profess this doctrine they are not saying precisely what Mark in his first chapter and Paul in the first of Romans were saying, though in different words, just that and nothing more. Time and trial and long thought and ventures into speculation and even into error, both aided and hindered by non-biblical thought, have taught the Church something about the implications of its faith, have assisted towards the gradual unfolding and uncovering of the basic drive and genius and spirit of Christianity here. Development has meant discovery.

THE TRANSFORMATION OF IMAGES IN THE TRINITARIAN THEOLOGY OF THE FOURTH CENTURY

I

This is a restricted study of the development of doctrine, confining itself to a few of the most usual images used in Christian authors of the fourth century to illustrate the relation of the Father to the Son, and also to suggest the relations to each other of the three Persons of the Trinity. It is not exhaustive even in treating of the images which it selects; for instance, it makes no reference to Cyril of Jerusalem. But it aspires to be an adequate account of some part of the remarkable and significant development which took place in the formation of doctrine during the fourth century; and it attempts to draw some conclusions from the evidence assembled here which may not be without interest to scholars of the twentieth century.

The doctrinal activity of the first three centuries of the history of the Christian Church had already brought into prominence several images to illustrate the relation of the Son to the Father, some of them Scriptural and some not. I do not include the word *Logos* in this list, because it is not so much an image as a more or less direct description, which has its own history, not dealt with here. Enough to say that from the theological activity of the Apologists onwards the word had been applied in such a way as to make the pre-existent Christ a convenient philsophical device, a means of solving a pressing contemporary philosophical problem, viz. how the ultimate reality, whether thought of as the Supreme Good or the One or God, could come in contact with the world of transcience and decay which human beings experience. And this employment of the pre-existent Son as a philosophical device was part of the theological tradition which the Christian intellectuals of the fourth century inherited and found themselves obliged to come to terms with. The most important image is of course that of Father and Son; indeed, this is not so much an image as an analogy, and one which caused the writers of the fourth century much thought. The next most important Scriptural images besides Father and

Son and *Logos* which theological thought before the fourth century had used were *icon* (image or reflection) taken from 2 Cor 4.4 ('Christ who is the *icon* of God') and Col 1.15 ('He is the image of the invisible God'); *apaugasma* (brightness, ray or reflection) taken from Heb 1.3; and *character* (impression or stamp) also taken from Heb 1.3. Behind all these images, as behind the use of them in the New Testament, was a single passage from the Old Testament, Wisdom 7.26. To these, however, at least three other images had been added by Justin, by Tertullian, and by others, the image of the stream descending from its source and that of the branch coming from the trunk or from the root and that of sunbeam deriving from the sun. Tertullian indeed had elaborated these into a kind of analogy for the Trinity of Persons, using the image of source-stream-river and of sun-sunbeam-point of light to illustrate his doctrine of the Trinity always potentially within the Father which was extrapolated or unfolded in order to achieve God's purpose of creation, revelation, and redemption.[1]

He used other images as well, and these images in their turn were handled by later writers in the third century. But this paper does not purport to deal with them further than to note Origen's extensive use of the term *icon* and especially the expression derived from him *aparallaktos icon* (unchangeable image)[2] and the unfortunate venture of Dionysius of Alexandria into imagery when, speaking of the relation of the Father to the Son, he had declared that the ship was not greater than the ship-builder nor the vineyard than its planter.[3] It is the business of this paper to trace part of the history of the images already mentioned in the thought of the writers of the fourth century. I

---

[1] Justin, *Dial.* 61.2 and Tatian, *Orat.* 5 (ed. E. J. Goodspeed, *Die Ältesten Apologeten* (Gottingen, 1914) for fire); Justin, *Dial.* 128.3; Tertullian, *Apologeticus* (ed. T. R. Glover, London, 1931) 21.12; *Adv. Praxean* (ed. J. N. Bakhuizen van den Brink, The Hague, 1946) 8 for shoot/branch, sun/ray, source/stream· Hippolytus, *Contra Noetum* (*P.G.* 10.803ff.) 10–11 for sun/ray, source/stream.

[2] See H. Crouzel, *Théologie de l'image de Dieu chez Origène*: (Paris, 1956) for a monograph on this subject. At no point in Origen's surviving work does the term *aparallaktos icon* actually occur.

[3] *Letters and other Remains of Dionysius of Alexandria*, ed. C. L. Feltoe (Cambridge, 1904), p. 190.

will first deal with the relevant authors who wrote before the appearance of the Cappadocian Fathers, and then with the Cappadocians themselves.

II

The first author to be surveyed is Eusebius of Caesarea. Eusebius is not much concerned about the difficulties or limitations of speaking of God in terms of Father and Son. He does not attempt to explain how the Father generated the Son, for he regards this as a subject infinitely beyond human knowledge.[4] He is, however, prepared to say how the Son was *not* begotten: not by division or alienation or emanation or by any *pathos*; not by command or utterance as men utter words; not by regarding or contemplating so as to create out of nothing; not by manipulating or ordering pre-existent substance, but by a peculiar divine way quite incomprehensible to us.[5] And he insists throughout his works that the Son was produced at no point in time, though he does not specifically speak of eternal generation.[6] His vague references to a pre-aeonian production of the Son are indeed at times reminiscent of those of Arius.

On the subject of the Son as the *icon* of the Father, however, Eusebius has much to say. It may be described as his favourite image, at least in his earlier work. His maturest thought in the *Praeparatio* and *Demonstratio Evangelica* seems to conclude that the Son should be described as the *icon* of the Father's *ousia*,[7] or of the ineffable and incomprehensible Godhead,[8] or of the ingenerate nature (of God).[9] In his most carefully defined statement he calls the Son: 'the image of God, in a way ineffable and incalculable in our terms, the living image of the living

---

[4] *Ecclesiastical Theology* (ed. with *Adv. Marcellum* and Fragments of Marcellus, E. Klostermann, rev. G. Hansen (G.C.S.) and 1972) I.12.70–72 and 8.66.

[5] *Ibid.*, III.6.103; *cf. Demonstratio Evangelica* (ed. I. A. Heikel (G.C.S.), 1913) V.1.20.

[6] For example, *Dem. Ev.* V.1.18.

[7] *Praeparatio Evangelica* (ed. K. Mras (G.C.S.), 1954, 1956), VII.15.1, 2; *cf.* XI. 15.1, 6; *Dem. Ev.* IV.3.8.

[8] *Dem. Ev.* IV.2.2.

[9] *Ibid.*, V.1.4.

God, existing in its own right immaterially and incorporeally and without any involvement in its own opposite, but not an image like that which exists among us which is different in its form, but rather himself being the whole identical form, and assimilated to the Father in his own self-existence.[10] He defends Asterius' use of ἀπαράλλακτος εἰκών against Marcellus' criticism of it, declaring, in true Origenist style, that the Son can be 'the animated image of his own Father', and so need not be visible.[11] But in his later works he employs *icon* in this Trinitarian context more sparingly. Generally speaking, *icon* was for Eusebius an expression of the mediatorial status of the Son in the Origenist sense. For Eusebius, the Father is inconceivable, incomprehensible and unapproachable, whereas in contrast the Son is 'he who can draw near to everybody'.[12]

Closely associated in the earlier writings of Eusebius with *icon* is another image, that of scent or perfume; the relation of the Son to the Father is that of a perfume to its source, εὐωδία or ὀσμή.[13] He is the 'most vital perfume of the Father'[14] and the 'perfume of the Father's being'.[15] But, as with *icon*, he qualifies this image to rule out some wrong interpretation to which it may lead; in some respects the relation is not like that of a scent to its source, for the Son does not proceed from the Father by *pathos* or division, nor has he existed along with the Father un-originatedly (ἀνάρχως) since the Father is ingenerate and the Son generate so that the one is subordinate to the other.[16] It is interesting by way of contrast to see the author of the *De Trinitate*, ascribed by some to Didymus the Blind, much later attaching the expression 'a kind of perfume of the Trinity'

---

[10] *Ibid.*, V.1.21, εἰκὼν θεοῦ, ἀρρήτως παὶ ἀνεπιλογίστως ἡμῖν, ζῶντος θεοῦ ζῶσά τις καὶ καθ' αὑτὴν ὑφεστῶσα ἀΰλως καὶ ἀσωμάτως καὶ τοῦ ἐναντίου πάντος ἀμιγῶς, ἀλλ' οὐχ οἷα τις πάλιν ἡ παρ' ἡμῖν εἰκών, ἕτερον δὲ τὸ εἶδος, ἀλλ' ὅλον αὐτὸ εἶδος ὤν, καὶ αὐτουσίᾳ τῷ πατρὶ ἀφομοιουμένος.

[11] *Adversus Marcellum* I.4.24, 25, ἔμψυχος εἰκών.

[12] *Ecc. Theol.* II.17.121, the Father ἄληπτος, ἀχώρητος, ἀπρόσιτος; the Son ὁ τοῖς πᾶσιν ἐγγιῶν.

[13] *Dem. Ev.* IV.3.8–12; V.1.18 (scent of myrrh).

[14] *Ibid.*, V.1.21, ζωτικωτάτη τοῦ πατρὸς εὐωδία.

[15] *Ibid.*, V.1.24 τῆς πατρικῆς οὐσίας εὐωδία.

[16] *Ibid.*, V.1.20.

(εὐωδία τις τῆς τριάδος) to the archangel Michael.[17] Eusebius is also quite ready to use the old image of the ray of light coming from its source, comparing the Son to φωτὸς αὐγή[18] and calling him 'light and the spiritual product of indescribable light'.[19] But he modifies this image in a subordinationist direction even more drastically than he does that of the *icon*. It is proper, he thinks, to use the analogy of a ray coming from a source of light which fills everywhere but is still only one stream of light, but the limits of this analogy must be observed.[20] You cannot seperate ray from source, but 'the Son exists in his own right individually apart from the Father'.[21] A ray of light involves energy, but 'the Son is something different from just a phenomemon of energy, since he had existence in himself'.[22] The ray originates along with the light and completes it and co-exists with it (καθ αὐτὸ συνυφέστηκεν). But the Father originates before the Son and his existence is before the Son's origin, for he alone is ingenerate.[23] In both these statements Eusebius is referring to logical rather than chronological priority. The Father is the cause of the Son's being and is not completed by the Son; the Son is δεύτερος to the Father in that he receives his being from him.[24] Again, the ray does not shine by anybody's choice, 'but in a sense occurs inseparably from the existence' (of the light), whereas 'the Son exists as the *icon* of the Father by his decision and choice'. It is the Father's will which has produced the Son.[25] In short, Eusebius is content to use the traditional sun/ray image, but modifies it carefully to suit his particular version of Origen's subordinationist account of the relation of the Son to the Father,

---

[17] *De Trinitate* (Book I ed. J. Honscheid, Book II ed, Ingrid Seiler, Meisenheim-an-Glan, 1975) II.7.8.

[18] *Dem. Ev.* V.1.18.

[19] *Oratio Tricennalis* (ed I. A. Heikel (G.C.S.) 1902) 12.8; *cf. Theophania* (ed. J. Gressmann (G.C.S.) 104) I.4.

[20] *Dem. Ev.* IV.3.2, 3.

[21] *Ibid.*, 4.

[22] *Ibid.*, 4, ἕτερόν τι ἢ κατὰ ἐνέργειαν τυγχάνει, καθ' ἑαυτὸν οὐσιώμενος.

[23] *Ibid.*, 5.

[24] *Ibid.*, 6.

[25] *Ibid.*, 7. A similar qualification of the sun/ray image can be found in *Dem. Ev.* V.1.19.

being well aware of the theological currents flowing around him which were destined so soon to contribute to the Arian controversy. It should be noted also that Eusebius occasionally uses the image of a source or well, πηγή. In his *Demonstratio Evangelica*[26] he can link the concept of source with that of *icon*, and when much later he writes his *Ecclesiastical Theology*, by which time he has almost dropped his analogies of *icon* and perfume, he can still describe the Son as 'filled by his participation (μετουσίας) in the Father as by a stream poured out upon him'.[27]

It is possible that one of the reasons why Eusebius was less ready to use the *icon* and *euodia* analogy in his later works was because Marcellus of Ancyra, with whom he conducted a lively controversy, had been criticising many of the traditional images, or at least the way in which contemporary theologians were handling them. Marcellus, much of whose work we know only because Eusebius quotes him, certainly accused Eusebius and the Origenists generally of using the Father/Son image too literally (ἀνθρωπικώτερον) so as almost to involve God the Father in *pathos*.[28] He held that the only case to which the terms of a divine begetting could be applied was that of the Incarnation; otherwise it was more correct to speak of the Logos having come forth (προῆλθεν) from the Father; the term 'begetting' was too anthropomorphic to apply to the prolation of the eternal *Logos*.[29] In similar vein Marcellus objected to the use of *icon* by contemporary theologians, Eusebius, Narcissus of Neronias and Asterius, who might be described as traditional Origenists being pushed towards Arianism in the stress of controversy. Asterius had said 'he who was begotten from him (the Father) is distinct (ἄλλος), because he is the *icon* of the invisible God' and that the *Logos* differs from God as much as a man's *icon* differs from himself. Marcellus denied that the Son was the *icon* of the Father in this sense. The pre-incarnate *Logos* could not have been the *icon* of the Father because an *icon* must be a visible representation of an invisible or absent original; yet

[26] VIII.15.1.
[27] *Ecc. Theol.* I.2.63.
[28] Eusebius, *Adv. Marcellum* I.4.18.
[29] Eusebius, *Ecclesiastical Theology* II.8.106–108.

before the Incarnation the *Logos* was invisible. Asterius had, among his other Christological categories, revived the ἀπαράλλακτος εἰκών of Origenist tradition. If Christ were all that Asterius said he was, Marcellus replied, then he would not be the *icon* of God, but himself the original God.[30] He believed that Eusebius' doctrine of the Son as the *icon* of the Father involved believing in 'two beings (*ousiai*) and two things and two powers'.[31] For Marcellus, it was the incarnate *Logos* who was the *icon* of the Father and who alone can properly be called 'Son'.[32] If Moses recorded God as intending to make man 'after our *icon*' (Gen 1.26), this was a reference to the incarnate *Logos* who was to appear later, and so with all those Old Testament passages which the Fathers believed to refer to the pre-incarnate Christ.[33] Indeed according to Eusebius Marcellus identified the flesh of Christ with 'the image of the invisible God',[34] though it would perhaps be more accurate to say that he identifies the *icon* with the *Logos* incarnate. Marcellus was apparently one who had dimly realized how profoundly unsatisfactory was the Christological interpretation of the Old Testament of his day. Though he can hardly be described as having achieved a viable alternative interpretation, his work must have served to make his contemporaries and successors look more carefully at their interpretation of traditional images.

Athanasius can hardly be accused of not using the image of Father and Son to express the relation of the Second to the First Person of the Trinity. It is indeed at the very heart of his theology, and needs no illustration here. He was necessarily, however, even more aware than his predecessors of the dangers and limitations of this image, because he had constantly to face the Arians' insistence upon taking literally and directly the logical consequences of the use of this particular term; sons are produced after fathers and as long as they are sons are inferior to

[30] Eusebius, *Adv. Marc.* I.4.24, 25. This is the point at which Eusebius describes the Son as ἔμψυχος εἰκὼν τοῦ ἰδίου πατρός. *Cf.* Fragments 96, 97 (pp. 206, 207).

[31] *Ibid.*, I.4.26.

[32] *Ibid.*, II.2.35, 36.

[33] *Ibid.*, II.3.47–51; this applied even to the key text Prov. 8.22.

[34] *Eccles. Theol.* II.23.134.

them, therefore the divine Son must have been produced after
the divine Father and be inferior to him. It was in fact this kind
of argument which compelled Athanasius and the
Cappadocians after him to examine the whole status of language
about God.[35] Consequently Athanasius takes a good deal of
trouble to guard himself in his use of the Father/Son image. The
first seven chapters of the fourth of his *Letters to Serapion* (the
only authentic part of that letter extant) are devoted solely to
this theme. In the *Orations against the Arians* he replies to the
Arian objection that if the Son is wholly like the Father then he
must be a father and beget a son; he replies: οὐκ ἔστιν ὡς
ἄνθρωπος ὁ θεός: in the case of the divine Persons the Father is
wholly and only Father (and not Son) and the Son is wholly and
only Son (and not Father).[36] Again, the Arians assert that as sons
do not exist before they are born so the Son οὐκ ἦν πρὶν
γεννηθῆναι. Athanasius answers: 'Architects cannot make
things except out of previously existing material and men
cannot exist except in a place. We do not because of these
obvious truths argue that God, who made the world, made it
out of previously existing material nor that God, who exists, is
spatially bounded'.[37] This is Athanasius' way of protesting
against a wrong use of analogical language. He has sometimes to
steer skilfully between the pitfalls which attend this difficult
subject. Any father, he says in his *Letters to Serapion*,[38] is the
progenitor and not the creator of his son, so, he implies, the
divine Father is the progenitor but not the creator of his divine
Son. He contrasts the shipwright and housebuilder as creators of
ship and house. He means that generation, as distinct from
ordinary creation, implies an impartation of the nature of the
begotten. He probably does not have in mind the remarks of his
predecessor Dionysius about the creative relationship of the
Father to the Son.

Athanasius is quite ready to use the *icon* analogy, and he

[35] See cap 13 below.
[36] I.20; Julian the Arian at least appreciated this. See below note 56.
[37] *Ibid.*, I.22, 23.
[38] 2.6 (C. R. B. Shapland, *The Letters of Saint Athanasius concerning the Holy
Spirit* (London, 1951) and P.G. 26.529ff).

naturally has no such desire to modify it as had either Eusebius or Marcellus. If we regard his two-volume work, *Contra Gentes* and *De Incarnatione* as composed before the Arian controversy, as on the whole I think that we should, we can see the pre-Nicene Athanasius using this image. Man, he says, is the *icon* of the *icon*, that is of the *Logos* who is the *icon* of God.[39] Twice in this work he uses the traditional expression *icon aparallaktos* of the Son.[40] In the *De Incarnatione* he says that men by seeing God's *icon* in Christ could have formed a just conception of him.[41] Here he clearly refers to the preincarnate *Logos*. But he goes on to say that because men had failed to take advantage of what they had originally been given, nothing was left but that God should send his own *icon* to them.[42] Here he is clearly referring to the incarnate Word. Even if Athanasius had heard of Marcellus' theory which confined the *icon* to the incarnate Word, he does not agree with it. But it is not likely that he had heard of it when he wrote the *De Incarnatione*. Otherwise Athanasius uses *icon* as a typical Scriptural image of the relation of the Son to the Father,[43] and as an expression of the full and unqualified resemblance to the Father exhibited by the Son.

The sun/ray image Athanasius finds quite as useful. He accepts 'reflection or brightness' (*apaugasma*) as a satisfactory Scriptural and traditional image to describe the relation of the Son to the Father.[44] But in several places he uses the image for a purpose that is markedly distinct from the purpose for which it had traditionally been used. Tertullian no less than Eusebius had used it to illustrate how the Son could be distinct from the Father while remaining united in Godhead with him. In three different places in the *Orations against the Arians* Athanasius calls in the sun/ray image in order to illustrate the intensely close relationship between the Father and the Son. Once it is a kind of

---

[39] *Contra Gentes* (ed. with the *De Incarnatione*, R. W. Thomson (Oxford, 1971)) 2.8.

[40] 41.2, 3 and 46.52–61.

[41] 11.3.

[42] 13.1–8.

[43] For example in *Letters to Serapion* 1.20, among a list of such images, called παραδείγματα.

[44] *Contra Gentes* 41.5–7; *Letters to Serapion* 1.20.

gloss on the term *icon aparallaktos*.[45] Once it is used to show 'that (the Son) and the Father are one in the particularity (ἰδιότητι) and peculiarity (οἰκειότητι) of their nature, and in the identity (ταυτότητι) of the one Godhead'.[46] Once it is invoked to prove that the Son is not produced only by the will and thought of the Father; nature precedes and transcends will.[47] We must believe, he says elsewhere, in one God, ἕνος ὄντος εἴδους θεότητος ὡς ἔστι τὸ φῶς καὶ τὸ ἀπαύγασμα.[48] If Athanasius can use this image for this kind of argument, one can see why Eusebius, whose doctrine on this subject was very different from that of Athanasius, was not altogether easy in employing the sun/ray illustration. Even so Athanasius' use of it marks a stage in the transformation of this image.

Athanasius of course uses other images. Source (πηγή) is one that is not uncongenial to him. The *Logos* proceeds from the Father (οἷα πηγῆς ἀγαθῆς ἀγαθός.[49] He regards (somewhat inaccurately) πηγή and ποταμός as typical Scriptural images to describe the relation of the Father to the Son.[50] The Father is the source of life (a reference to Jer 2.13 and 17.12), the Son is life.[51] 'Impress' (χαρακτήρ) and 'fruit' (κάρπος) occur in a list of words designed to describe the Son's relation to the Father[52] and χαρακτήρ again in another similar list.[53] It is particularly interesting to note that Athanasius appears to be the first fourth-century writer who attempts to find an analogy for the whole Trinity, not merely for the relation of the first two persons. Eusebius and Marcellus made no such attempt, we can be pretty sure, because neither of them can be regarded as having a Trinitarian theology worth the name. But in his *Letters to Serapion* Athanasius suggests two distinct analogies for the Trinity: one is φῶς, ἀπαύγασμα and ἡ τούτου ἐνεργεία καὶ

---

[45] II.33.
[46] III.4.
[47] III.66.
[48] *De Synodis* (ed. H.-G. Opitz, *Athanasius Werke* II, 1 (Berlin, 1941)) 52.1.
[49] *Contra Gentes* 41.5–7.
[50] *Letters to Serapion* 1.20.
[51] *Orat. adv. Arianos* (ed. W. Bright (Oxford, 1873)) 1.19.
[52] *Contra Gentes* 46.52–61.
[53] *Letters to Serapion* 1.20.

αὐτοείδης χάρις.[54] The other is the common humanity shared by individual men and angelic nature shared by individual angels.[55] The English editor of this work, Shapland, notes that in his *De Decretis* 20 Athanasius had rejected this generic consubstantiality as an analogy for the consubstantial Trinity. But when he came to write his work on the Holy Spirit he returned to it.

In the work of Hilary of Poitiers we see a considerable advance in the process of transforming the traditional images. He is quite as awake as any other writer to the limitations and embarrassments of the Father/Son image. There is a point, he says, at which in considering the divine Fatherhood the human analogy of fatherhood breaks down. 'As far as One being derived from One', he writes, 'and God being born from God, our earthly birth contributes a certain understanding of the meaning'. But for many of the conditions of human birth the analogy collapses, 'intercourse, conception, lapse of time, delivery', so that 'in the case of God being born from God nothing else is to be understood except that God is born'.[56] He accepts the expression *icon*, or rather *imago*, but is careful to define it so as to support his pro-Nicene theology. What those who could perceive saw in the incarnate Word was the *imago Dei*, but we must realize that this image 'does not differ in kind (from the original) but represents the original . . . The Son . . . is the living image of him who is alive, and because he is born from him he has no diversity of nature and, being diverse in nothing, possesses the power of his nature from which he is not diverse'.[57] Elsewhere he says that the incarnate Christ could not be the visible, concrete image apprehensible to the senses, of the infinite, invisible God. What Paul means at Col 1.15 is that he is the image of God as performing the works of God (Jn 10.37).

---

[54] 1.30.

[55] 2.3.

[56] *De Trinitate* (*P.L.* 10.25ff.) 6.9 (163); *cf.* 7.28 (224). In fairness it should be pointed out that the Arian Julian in his *Commentary on Job* (ed. D. Hagedorn (Berlin, 1973)) 245.7–246.7 and 270.12–271.3 makes much the same point not long after Hilary.

[57] *De Trin.* 7.37 (230, 231).

And he is the image of God's *nature*, not of his form.[58] Hilary warns his readers carefully against using the image of fire, though he had no objection to that of light. A certain Hieracas had said that the Son was produced from the Father as a light is lit by a light or a lamp. This illustration had of course also been employed by Justin and Tatian. Hilary strongly rejects this image and denies that it is consistent with the Nicene doctrine. The unity of Father and Son does not consist in the sharing of a common pre-existent material. 'They are not connected together like two lamps or two torches by an external nature. The birth of the only begotten God from God is not a series but a generation (*non series sed progenies*). It is not a process (*tractus*) but light from light'.[59] Later in the same work [60] he issues another warning against the image, and points out that illustrations of divine things are only intended to make our understanding of them easier by thinking of them in earthly terms. Later still he directly rejects two or three traditional images for the relation of the Son to the Father: 'It is not possible . . . that there should be extension or series or emanation (*fluxus*), so that (we should think of) a stream producing a river from a source or a tree maintaining a bough in a trunk or a fire sending out heat into a space. *Haec enim ab se inseparabili protensione manent potius detenta quam sibi sunt*'.[61] Here Hilary is almost anticipating the Cappadocians in his criticism of traditional images. In the same work he directly rejects the kind of image which Dionysius of Alexandria had used, though he does not indicate that he knew that Dionysius had done so, the relation of the painter to his picture, of the smith to the sword which he has made and the architect to the house which he has built.[62] And he explicitly and specifically rejects the well-established and traditional idea that the pre-existent Son should be used as a convenient philosophical device: he calls the idea that Christ was created for the sake of creating the world *hic*

[58] *Ibid.*, 8.48 (272).
[59] *Ibid.* 6.12 (165–167).
[60] 7.29, 30 (224–225).
[61] 9.37 (308, 309).
[62] 12.12 (440).

impiissimus sensus.[63] Athanasius similarly accuses the Arians of teaching that οὐκ ἡμᾶς ἔκτισε δι' ἐκεῖνον, ἀλλ ἐκεῖνον δι' ἡμᾶς,[64] and Pseudo-Didymus of the *De Trinitate* echoes this charge.[65] Hilary then is much more critical of traditional images of the Father and the Son than were any of his predecessors, with the possible exception of Marcellus, and though he does not himself advance any analogy for the Trinity as a whole was inclined to reject any that had been produced by others.

III

I will deal with the Cappadocians as a group, investigating their attitude to each point, instead of surveying the ideas of each on the whole subject, with an occasional reference to the Pseudo-Didymean *De Trinitate*. Basil and Gregory of Nazianzus each discuss the subject of images. Basil points out that the Scriptural writers speak about God's *ousia* only in metaphors and allegories, such as amber (Ezekiel) or fire (Moses), using images which taken literally are often contradictory.[66] Gregory of Nazianzus, describing the Son as *gennema* and *problema*, says that he is at a loss what language to use if we remove images taken from what is visible.[67] Similarly Basil can warn against taking illustrations as more than a shadow of the truth, 'because it is not possible to make what can be seen in an illustration consistent in every detail with that for which the necessity of illustrations arises'.[68] The Cappadocians maintain the practice inherited from their predecessors of qualifying the Father/Son image. Fatherhood, Basil insists, is an analogy implying unlikeness as well as likeness.[69] But we should not despise human analogies,

---

[63] 12.43 (460); see also *Collectio Antiariana* (ed. A. Feder (C.S.E.L.) 1916), 149.6.

[64] *Encyclical Letter to Egyptian Bishops* (ed. W. Bright, *Historical Writings of St. Athanasius* (Oxford, 1881)) 12.

[65] I.8.6.

[66] *Adversus Eunomium* (P.G. 29.497ff.) 1.14 (544–555).

[67] *Theological Orations* (*Orat.* I–V ed. A. J. Mason (Cambridge, 1899), other Orations P.G. 35.396ff.) III.2.

[68] *Letters* (ed. Y. Courtonne (Budé ser., Paris, 1957), and where this fails R. J. Deferrari (London, 1961) XXXVIII.5.1–5.

[69] *Ibid.*, LII.3.1–4.

once we have purified them so as to safeguard God's holiness and impassibility.[70] To the objection of his opponents that to believe in the co-divinity of the Holy Spirit is either to end up with two Sons or with the Spirit as the Father's grandson, Gregory of Nazianzus answers, 'the Son is a son by some higher relationship; even though we cannot demonstrate his being from God and his consubstantiality by any other method, we must not therefore think it necessary to transfer to the Deity all lower names connected with our human kinship'. Otherwise we should have to call God masculine, and end up perhaps in the ridiculous concept taught by Marcion and Valentinus of an hermaphrodite God.[71] He has to answer the Arian objection that any speech about the Son as generated or created must imply some lapse of time, for this applies to all human experiences of generation, even the generation or production of thought. He replies that God's creation by the *Logos* is manifestly different from our thinking, for we do not create a city, for instance, by merely thinking about it. And if God creates differently, then clearly he begets differently. The begetting of the Son is manifestly different from human begetting; the Son was not at one time in the Father and then later begotten from him.[72] Similarly Gregory of Nyssa can assert that, in calling God the Father of the Only-begotten we abandon all the undesirable attributes of the word 'Father'. Not only must all corporeal assumptions be purged away, but also anything suggesting a difference or interval between Father and Son.[73]

Basil has one quite new image for the relation of the Father to the Son, which we shall encounter again when we consider analogies for the whole Trinity, that of the impartation of an art or skill (τεχνή) from one person to another; the giver does not lose but the receiver gains. But even here he warns that the analogy is deficient, because the lapse of time involved renders it imperfect.[74] He is quite content with the *icon* analogy: 'in the

---

[70] *Adv. Eunom.* 2.22 (621).

[71] *Theol. Orat.* V.7.

[72] *Orations* XX.8 (1076).

[73] *Contra Eunomium* (ed. W. Jaeger (*Opera* I) Leiden, 1960) III.77 (*P.G.* 45.593); cf. III (VI).35–39 (45.781, 784).

[74] *Adv. Eunom.* 2.16 (605).

impression the nature of the seal is perceived; through the image knowledge of the original comes about'.[75] Gregory of Nazianzus likes the expression *aparallaktos icon*.[76] Following the example of Alexander of Alexandria, he pushes *icon* beyond the status of an image. In the case of the Son *icon* means something more unchangeable than it means when we say that Seth was the *icon* of Adam: 'This is the nature of simple things (τῶν ἁπλῶν), that they are not like in some respects and unlike in others, but the whole of one is a reproduction (τύπον) of the whole of the other and is an identity rather than a resemblance'.[77] In the employment of the sun/ray image for either Trinitarian or Christological purposes on the other hand, the Cappadocians have no difficulty at all. Eunomius disliked this image, regarding it as either leading to the conclusion that God is compound (which is impossible because he is ingenerate), or as meaningless. Basil, who had earlier declared that this image is the stronghold of the case of the orthodox, is happy to assert that what we see in the Father is ingenerate light and what we see in the Son is generate light.[78] Gregory of Nazianzus extends this image to cover the whole Trinity, in the manner of Tertullian, writing ἐκ φωτὸς τοῦ πατρὸς φῶς καταλαμβάνοντες τὸν υἱὸν ἐν φωτὶ τῷ πνεύματι.[79] Gregory of Nyssa can describe the Spirit as μονογενὲς φῶς διὰ τοῦ ἀληθίνου φωτὸς ἐκλάμψαν, but he adds that these various forms of light do not differ as to distance or nature.[80] We should remember that the ancients had not calculated the speed of light, otherwise the Cappadocians might have wished to qualify this image. Naturally, Gregory has no objection to the Nicene Creed's formula φῶς ἐκ φωτός.[81] The Pseudo-Didymean author of *De Trinitate* finds the same satisfaction in the image of light as something which

[75] *Ibid.*, 1.17 (552).

[76] For example *Oration* XXXVIII.13 (36.325) as well as in the next instance.

[77] *Theol. Orat.* IV.20. Alexander also likes *aparallaktos icon*; see Opitz, *op. cit.*, III i. 14.23, 38 and 27.47, and his remark in 48 πάντων γὰρ εἶναι τὸν εἰκόνα πλήρη δι᾿ ὧν ἡ μειζων ἐμφέρεια δῆλον. The Synod of Antioch of 325 had adopted *aparallaktos icon* also (see *ibid.*, 18.39.10.).

[78] *Adv. Eunom.* 2.25, 28 (629, 637).

[79] *Theol. Orat.* V.3.

[80] *Contra Eunom.* I.378 (45.369).

[81] *Ibid.*, III.85 (45.596).

unites and extends without a temporal interval: 'whatever pre-temporal time or primal impetus (ἀκαριαίραν ῥοπήν) or pre-eternal eternity one may imagine', he says, 'the Word is the inseparable brightness (ἀχώριστον ἀπαύγασμα) of God and no shadow of non-existence attaches to him'. But what impresses this author about the sun/ray image is its power to illustrate the inseparability of source and product:[82] 'as the ray cannot be divorced from the light nor wisdom from the wise man, that is the Son from the Father, so the Holy Spirit (cannot be divorced) from him whose Spirit he is, as is the case with us and the breath we breathe'.[83] It is not surprising that this author virtually rejects the image which brought Dionysius of Alexandria into controversy, when he contrasts man being made in the image of God, which is the *icon* of the maker seen in the thing made, with the Son as the *icon* of the Father. He who has seen the chariot has not seen the coachbuilder, but he who has seen the Son has seen the Father.[84] Gregory of Nyssa makes the same point when he says that nobody would suggest that the architect had 'sired' (ἐτεκνώσατο) the house which he had built nor the vine the 'growth' (γέννημα) of the vinedresser.[85] Gregory of Nazianzus at one point puts forward a new and complex image for the Son's relation to the Father, obviously because he finds all traditional images unsatisfactory. It is the image of water under sunshine producing a moving and dancing image on the wall. He has clearly thought out this carefully but says that it is not his own invention.[86]

We have seen already occasional attempts to produce analogies not just for the relation of one Person of the Trinity with another, but for the whole three in their relations with each other. The Cappadocians, as might be expected from their pre-occupation with Trinitarian, as distinct from simply Christological, doctrine, go further than any of their predecessors in this enterprise. Basil reproduces that analogy

---

[82] *De Trinitate* I.15.20 (the quoted passage) and 15.35.

[83] *Ibid.*, 16.19; *cf.* 6.22, the light does not beget the ray nor the source the stream.

[84] *Ibid.*, I.16.42–45.

[85] *Contra Eunom.* III.95 (45.600).

[86] *Theological Orations* V.32.

which Athanasius had both accepted and rejected, based on his assumption that *ousia* means the universal and *hypostasis* the particular. Just as living being (ζῶον) refers to the general and a particular man to the particular, so God, the Godhead, is the general and Father, Son and Holy Spirit the particular.[87] This is indeed a very unsatisfactory analogy, and Gregory of Nazianzus seems to admit this when he allows that the Greek concept of Godhead as shared by all gods is no more than a notional hypothetical universal (τὸ ἓν μόνον ἐπινοίᾳ θεωρητόν).[88] But he is prepared to admit this concept of the shared Godhead as the generic thing shared by the Persons in contrast to the individual properties of each Person as the particular because it seems to him to guarantee that each Person is God in his own right and not simply by reason of his relation to the others.[89] Gregory of Nyssa also accepts this universal/particular analogy and, as is well known, illustrates it by saying that if we call Peter and Paul and Barnabas τρία πρόσωπα but still see them as having one *ousia*, how little are we justified in seeing three *ousiai* in God just because we can see three πρόσωπα in him.[90] What is less well known is that Gregory immediately qualified this suggestion by pointing out that we deduce that existence of one *ousia* in the three men metaphysically or indirectly or analogically (κατχρηστικῶς) because we can only observe the concept (ὅρος) of 'man' in a multitude of changing instances, whereas we can observe the *prosopa* of the Trinity as always the same and immutable.[91] It should be pointed out, because Gregory had sometimes been given less than his due on this subject, and because the Cappadocians are sometimes contrasted unfavourably with Augustine in the matter of providing analogies for the Trinity, that Gregory of Nyssa elsewhere provides three much more sophisticated Trinitarian analogies,

---

[87] *Letters* CCXXXVI.6. We might add another at *Letters* XXXVIII.5, but this letter may be by Gregory of Nyssa; see note 93 below.

[88] *Theol. Orat.* V.15.

[89] See the complicated argument in *Theol. Orat.* III.14, 15.

[90] *Ad Graecos* (*ex communibus notionibus*) (ed. F. Müller (*Opera* III) Leiden, 1958), 22.

[91] *Ibid.*, 23–27.

of which the first is a particularly interesting one which had been anticipated in part by Basil. The three are:

(i) Two or three different disciplines in the mind of a single man, *e.g.*, medicine, philosophy and similar arts;
(ii) the smell of myrrh mingling with the air in a room so that they seem identical but are in fact distinct; and
(iii) the light of the sun, the air and the wind mingling with each other but still remaining separate.[92]

In another work he supplies another analogy (his fifth), that of two lamps being lit from a third, which revives an old image which had not always commended itself to the writers of the fourth century.[93] If we attribute to him the 38th in the Collection of Basil's *Letters*, we can add a sixth, the colours of the rainbow melting together yet distinct as an analogy for unity and distinction in the Trinity (see n. 87).

But it should be recognized that the Cappadocians, who come at the end of this period of the formation of doctrine, are more uneasy with all images designed to illustrate the relations of the Persons of the Trinity to each other than their predecessors, whether those images are Scriptural, traditional or recent. They are much more aware than their predecessors of the weakness of virtually all images in that they imply a lapse of time or some sort of interval between the Persons, and are anxious to remove that weakness. Except for their distinguishing characteristics, the Persons of the Trinity, says Basil, are inseparably united and no object can intrude between them nor any space exist between them.[94] He allows that there is an order (*taxis*) which constituted a difference between the Persons, as indeed all the Cappadocians do, but no time (*chronos*) nor age (*aion*).[95] The relations and characteristics of the Persons, says Gregory of Nazianzus, are wholly independent of time.[96] If

---

[92] *Adversus Arium et Sabellium: de Patre et Filio* (ed. F. Müller *ut supra*) 83.

[93] *Adversus Macedonianos* (ed. F. Müller *ut supra*) p. 91 (*P.G.* 45.1307).

[94] *Letters* XXXVIII.38–62.

[95] *Adv. Eunom.* I.20 (557); at 3.1 (656) he allows the Spirit a difference of *axioma* as well as *taxis*; it is doubtful whether the two Gregories would have permitted this.

[96] *Theol. Orat.* III.3; echoed in *Poems* I.1 line 27 (*P.G.* 37.403).

we take the word ἀρχή as referring to time and not to origin, then he insists more than once that the Son is ἄναρχος.[97] He describes the Son as 'existing from (the Father) and not after him, or, at any rate, only in the logical sense of *arche*, in that *arche* is his case'.[98] If there was a time, says the author of the Pseudo-Didymean *De Trinitate*, when God the *Logos* did not exist, then there was a time when the name 'Father' was not in existence.[99] The author regards this as a *reductio ad absurdum*, but it is precisely the proposition which Tertullian had propounded in *Adversus Hermogenem* (3; cf. *Adv. Prax.* 7). So Basil could say 'we have right up to this moment never heard of a second god' (δεύτερον θεόν). But Justin and Origen had.[100] Consistent with this anxious monitoring of the images in order to eliminate intervals between the Persons is the firm rejection by all the Cappadocians of the traditional, indeed time-honoured, practice of envisaging the Son as a convenient philosophical device. Gregory of Nazianzus is particularly emphatic here. In his poems he insists that Christ was not made for the sake of creation.[101] In a sermon delivered in Constantinople in 379 A.D. he has this sentence: 'The more worshipful God is than creation so much the more exalted than creation is he by his primal causality, his constituting the origin of deity, and by employing his Godhead as a medium to reach creation, rather than on the contrary the Godhead (*i.e.* of the Son) existing for this reason (*i.e.*, to reach creation), which is the doctrine of those who are too curious and speculative'.[102] And a little later in the same discourse he says that to make the son and Spirit the mere instruments for creating, existing as a means for something else, is to dishonour them.[103] Words such as these sound the death-knell of a lively and at one time popular theological development going back at least as far as Justin Martyr.

[97] *Orations* XX.7 (35.1073); XXXIX.12 (36.348), the maker of times is not subject to time, he is in this respect *anarchos*.

[98] *Ibid.* XX.10 (35.1077); in this passage the Father is called αἴτιος, πηγή, and ἀΐδιον φῶς, but the Son *arche* of the universe.

[99] *De Trin.* I.37.

[100] *De Spiritu Sancto* (ed. B. Pruche (S.C.) 1946) XVIII.45 (*P.G.* 32.149).

[101] *Poems* I.1 lines 51–56 (37.405).

[102] *Orations* XXIII.6 (35.1157).

[103] *Ibid.* XXIII.6 (35.1160).

Indeed the most significant fact about the treatment of images by the later Trinitarian theologians is that they either use them for another, untraditional, purpose, or reject them altogether. We have seen several examples of this employment of images for a different purpose already,[104] but we can add one or two more. Gregory of Nyssa uses the old lamp/ray image, not, as in pre-Nicene times, to establish the possibility of undivided derivation within the Godhead but that of simultaneous necessary existence of the source and that which is derived from it.[105] The Pseudo-Didymean author of the *De Trinitate* compares the generation of the Son to the fruit appearing along with the root at Gen 1.12, events which he assumes to have been simultaneous.[106] This same author, in a manner reminiscent of Gregory of Nazianzus, alters the *icon* analogy for his own purposes. It is not true in the case of God that, as the Arians argue, the image is different from the original. The *icon* of God is not an *icon* in only one respect. That which is true and the archetype and the greater and the self-sufficient and incomparable cannot be manifested by that which is unlike and less and of an inferior nature.[107] Peter at Caesarea Philippi 'recognized the branch (κλάδος) of God which was of the same nature and eternity as he, and honoured in (his utterance) the self-originating and unbeginning (αὐτογενῆ καὶ ἄναρχον) root which was revealing (himself to him)'.[108] In his determination to transform these traditional images he has lapsed into sublime nonsense, for a συναίδιος κλάδος and an ἄναρχος ῥίζα are contradictions in terms.

It is not therefore surprising, in view of the difficulties encountered in this transformation of images, that the two Gregories sometimes advocate the rejection of all images, traditional or not, or nearly all. At one point in his *Fifth Theological Oration* Gregory of Nazianzus rejects *seriatim* virtually all analogies for the Trinity. This rejection includes the analogy of the source (*pege*) and stream, because it might suggest

---

[104] See above, pp. 257, 261.
[105] *Ad Simplicium de Fide* (ed. F. Müller *ut supra*) 63–64.
[106] I.15.47.
[107] *Ibid.* I.16.33–36.
[108] I.30.10.

that the Godhead is in process and not static and because it does not present us with distinct entities but only one, differently shaped. He rejects the analogy of sun/ray because it suggests a composite nature for what is not composite and because one might regard the sun's rays as powers or emanations or essential qualities, and none of these are suitable to describe the Son's relation to the Father. He even finally rejects his own analogy of the moving pattern on the wall reflected by the sun's rays on water. No analogy or image is satisfactory, he concludes, unless the user of it had the good sense to hold onto one point and throw away the rest.[109] He reaffirms this rejection in his *Poems*, precisely and carefully denying virtually all analogies suggested by the pre-Nicene Fathers, source/stream, lamp/ray, even *Logos*, and including his own one of the reflection on the wall.[110] In similar vein Gregory of Nyssa rejects all images involving use of matter or lapse of time. The only common element in the analogy can be nature (φύσις). Even those more refined images derived from material process (ὑλικὴ ἀπορροία), by which he means such images as ἀπαύγασμα δόξης, ὀσμὴ μύρου and ἀτμὶς θεοῦ, involve matter and are liable to be misunderstood. The only images which he finds satisfactory are some of those to be found in Scripture, but not all, for he views, as we have seen, some Scriptural, as some traditional, images with suspicion. He allows *nous* and *logos*, but not as the audible spoken word.[111] He repeats this almost apophatic doctrine in another work. The word 'Son', he says, is used in Scripture without explanation or overt qualification, but we must drastically modify this analogy, leaving once more *physis* as the only common element in the analogy. But he allows the Scriptural images ἀπαύγασμα δόξης and ὀσμὴ μύρου and ἀτμὶς θεοῦ (Heb 1.3; John 12.3; Wisd 7.25), as long as they are purified of the circumstances and conditions of earthly generation and taken to signify simultaneous existence. And once again he commends *nous* (which is probably taken from 1 Cor 2.16) and *logos*.[112] His

[109] *Theol. Orat.* V.32, 33.

[110] I.1 lines 61–69 (37.413). Compare his disclaimer at *Orations* XXIII.11 (35.1161, 1164).

[111] *Contra Eunom.* III (VI).35–40 (45.781, 784).

[112] *Refutatio Confessionis Eunomii* (ed. Jaeger (*Opera* II)) 91–96 (45.508, 509).

ultimate intention here appears to be to suggest that if all the Scriptural images are taken together they correct and balance one another and make a total impression which is the correct one.

IV

This brief survey of the transformation undergone by the traditional images to describe the relations of the Father to the Son and of the three Persons to each other suggest certain observations, with which this paper will conclude. The first observation is that history undoubtedly reflects a development of doctrine, a distinct and unmistakable change of direction. Economic Trinitarianism, that is the doctrine that God unfolded himself into a Trinity for purposes of creation, revelation and redemption, was in the course of this development decisively rejected, even though it had been the accepted orthodoxy of Justin, of Irenaeus, of Tertullian, of Hippolytus and of several lesser writers in the second and third centuries. Indeed direct contradictions of positions which had earlier been regarded as sound are not lacking. The Cappadocians cannot tolerate mention of a δεύτερος θεός, whereas Justin and Origen explicitly accept this term. Gregory of Nazianzus directly denies that God had never been in a condition when he was not Father of the Son, whereas Tertullian had plainly stated that he had. The images which give most trouble to Eusebius, such as sun/ray and *icon*, are those which the Cappadocians find most acceptable, and at least two of the oldest and most favourite images of earlier writers, those of source/stream and root/tree, the Cappadocians virtually reject. The Father/Son image, which is more securely entrenched in the New Testament than any other, causes some uneasiness to almost everybody and undergoes drastic qualifications at the hands of the Cappadocians. Indeed the fact that an image was Scriptural did not emancipate it from criticism. *Apaugasma* was not left unqualified by Eusebius nor *pege* (which on the basis of a passage in Jeremiah was thought to be Scriptural) by the Cappadocians. Whatever lip-service the men of the fourth centry paid to tradition, they were quite ready to reject or alter it if they thought this necessary. Change in doctrine there certainly was.

The contributors to this process of development would of course have claimed that their doctrine was in continuity with the earliest doctrine. And in as much as they used for the most part the same images, we must grant some validity to this claim. But though they used for the most part the same images, they adapted these images to fit a different doctrine. Eusebius' use of *icon* was almost exactly opposite to that of Pseudo-Didymus. The earlier writers in their use of the image of sun/ray stress derivation within unity while the Cappadocians employ the same image to emphasize simultaneous co-existence of the source and that which is derived from it. Perhaps the best that can be said for the view that this process of development preserved a certain continuity in that while using much the same materials in distinctly different ways all the writers who used them had the same intention. The intention was to produce a specifically Christian doctrine of God. It was not enough, they all realised, either to leave the primitive Christian Messianic expectation in a completely undeveloped state not easily distinguishable from the ideas of several other first-century Jewish sects, nor naively to repeat that Christians were monotheists, like the Jews, who also happened to think that Jesus of Nazareth was a very important person. All the writers were equally attempting to contribute to that task which the intellectuals of the Christian Church felt themselves from the mid-second-century onwards bound to undertake, the development of a doctrine of God which should be faithful at once to the witness of the Bible (or at least to what they took to be the witness of the Bible), to the religious experience of the Church and of the individual Christian worshipper, and to common sense or logic. This common enterprise gave to the development a certain continuity, though a continuity which certainly was not without considerable diversity.

We might be inclined to add one more criterion to this list of norms to which the development was attempting to be faithful, the contribution of Greek philosophy, of Stoicism, of Middle Platonism and of Neo-Platonism, but I do not think that Greek philosophy can be regarded as a norm alongside the other norms. Of course all the writers considered in this paper were deeply influenced by Greek philosophy and used it as a tool in their theological work, and allowed it to influence their unexamined assumptions. They were all convinced, Eusebius and Marcellus as much as the Cappadocians, of the necessity of preserving the impassibility of God, and none of those considered here objected to considering or defining the doctrine of the Trinity in the static terms of *ousia* and *hypostasis* given them by Greek philosophy, and they would have repudiated any attempt to consider the doctrine of God in explicitly dynamic terms which might have been more suitable to the thought of the Bible which they were all ostensibly anxious to reflect. We must allow that when they used Greek philosophy as a tool—and we can hardly deny that they had no alternative tool available to them—they were inevitably limited and conditioned in the process of using it. But one fact has emerged from our study of this subject which should cause us to pause before we envisage the Fathers as blind and unconscious devotees of Greek philosophy. The development of the Christian doctrine of God in the fourth century finally and deliberately rejected the practice of using the pre-existent *Logos* as a convenient philosophical device. Instead of regarding the *Logos* as a buffer to protect God the Father from compromising and dangerous involvement in terrestrial, transient and human affairs, Athanasius, Hilary, Basil, the two Gregories and the author of the *De Trinitate* ascribed to Didymus the Blind insisted that on the contrary the *Logos*, both pre-existent and incarnate, was the guarantee that God had involved himself in this peculiarly intimate way with our experience and the circumstances of our existence. This was a remarkable rejection of Greek philosophy, the putting of a 'No Thoroughfare' notice to a theological tradition which had had a long and not dishonourable history, one which had gained lustre from the genius of Origen, and which had seemed to many to represent the happiest combination of Christian doctrine and Greek philosophy. All this rejection was carried out largely as a result of the witness of the one book of the New Testament in which the deeply philosophical word *Logos* had been applied to Christ in a highly theological context. This interesting and almost startling repudiation of tradition should remind us further that a process of development of doctrine can very well include a movement of pruning, almost of reformation, as well as a positive evolution into something new.

Last of all, we may consider a charge which has been levelled against the Cappadocians. What is the significance of the tendency which we can see beginning in Hilary and completed in Basil and the two Gregories of rejecting all images and analogies, or at least of reducing them to a minimum? Is this one more proof that they are guilty of reducing the Godhead to a condition in which the Persons are so alike that they are virtually indistinguishable? This is an accusation which has been made against the Cappadocians in recent English Patristic study. It is certainly true that the Cappadocians insist that we do not experience the Persons of the Trinity separately and that their account of the relationship and peculiar characteristics of the Persons within the Trinity is halting, tentative, uncertain, and, in the case of the Holy Spirit, so negative as to be almost meaningless. Is their lack of confidence in handling traditional images used to illustrate the relations of the Persons to each other an index of the incoherence and fragility of their Trinitarian doctrine?

I do not think that this is a fair accusation. I believe that it may rest upon a certain confusion between religious experience and theological analysis. It would be in any circumstances mistaken to imagine that we could experience the Persons of the Trinity separately; this would inevitably result in a lapse into blatant tritheism. We experience God in God the Holy Spirit; indeed we experience God as God the Holy Spirit. We do not have direct experience of God the Father or God the Son independently of God the Holy Spirit; God the Holy Spirit is God as we experience God, though of course we experience him as the Spirit of Jesus Christ who reflects and expresses the act and character of God the Father. The Holy Spirit would not be the Holy Spirit if he did not bring us to the knowledge of God in Christ. Then again we must realize the situation in which the Cappadocians found themselves and what they were attempting to do. They had inherited a tradition, enshrined above all in the Bible, of what we today call 'salvation history' (*Heilsgeschichte*) in which first Israel and then the Christians came to a knowledge of God as he gradually disclosed himself, first in the history of the Jews and then in the career of Jesus Christ and the experience of the Church. They were attempting to see what all this meant for the doctrine of God, a specifically Christian doctrine in which what the Christian knows of Jesus Christ should be incorporated and integrated into a consistent and rationally defensible doctrine of God. Of course this argument will not impress those who believe either that the Church does not need and should not seek a consistent and rationally defensible doctrine of God, or that such a doctrine cannot be achieved. But in these circumstances it is not surprising that the Cappadocians should have laid such emphasis upon the unity of the Trinity, upon the one Godhead as distinct from the three Persons. They were not, like Augustine, in a position in which they had inherited a securely established Trinitarian faith. They were, on the contrary, in the process of developing such a faith in the face of tendencies to abandon or reduce the significance of one or other of the Persons, and their response to these tendencies was to emphasize strongly the ontological co-divinity of the Persons while leaving inevitably a certain vagueness about their relations within the Trinity. They recognized and honestly accepted the necessity of that vagueness. Nobody can seriously doubt that they were confident that knowledge of God through his revelation in Jesus Christ is open to everybody.[113] It was ultimately in order to safeguard this truth that they built their superstructure of Trinitarian doctrine.

[113] Out of hundreds of possible references one could make this brief selection: Basil, *De Sp. Sanct.* XXII.53 (32.168); *Letters* XXXVIII.4; CCXXXIV.1, 2 ; CCXXXV.1–3; *Adv. Eunom.* 1.17 (552); 2.8 (552); 2.8 (585); 24.1 (628). Gregory of Nazianzus, *Theol. Orat.*II.5; XXIII.11 (35.1164). Gregory of Nyssa, *Con. Eunom.* I.498 (45.404); II.13 (45.913, 916), 93–102 (941–945); III (i).108 (45.604); III (viii).7–12 (45.829, 832); *Ref. Conf. Eunom.* 17 (45.473); *Catechetical Discourse* (ed. L. Meridier, Paris, 1908) XV.1.

12

THE FILIOQUE CLAUSE

I

The following essay was written for the Anglican/Orthodox Joint Doctrinal Commission, and is published with their permission. The subject is, however, of interest to theologians generally and should be of use to those Anglicans who may have to explain to their people why many today are anxious to remove the *Filioque* from the Nicene Creed. For those to whom these terms with initial capitals are incomprehensible it must be briefly explained that when the original Greek of the Nicene Creed which is recited in their eucharistic worship by all Anglicans and all Roman Catholics and all Orthodox was originally drawn up in the year 381 at the Council of Constantinople held in that year, the article dealing with the Holy Spirit in one of its clauses simply ran 'Who proceeds from the Father', not 'who proceeds from the Father and the Son'. The words 'and the Son' (*Filioque* in Latin) were added by the Western, Latin-speaking Church gradually over the next six centuries or so, and were finally approved by the Pope in the year 1014 (though one of his predecessors early in the ninth century had refused, even under pressure from the Emperor Charlemagne, to add them). This addition to the original words of the Creed has from an early period been a bone of contention between the Western Latin-speaking and the Eastern Greek-speaking Churches. In 1976 the Anglicans on the Anglican/Orthodox Joint Commission during a meeting in Moscow formally agreed that the words 'and the Son' ought to be removed from the Creed by Anglicans, and the Lambeth Conference of the same year endorsed this decision. Several references to this Commission will be found in the pages below. The essay is, however, as readers will soon learn, concerned not with the question of whether the *Filioque* should be in the Creed or not, but with whether the *Filioque* is a true and valid doctrine which Anglicans, among others, should hold, even though it may not appear in the Creed.

The subject of the *Filioque* Clause can be regarded as

important for several different reasons. It can be regarded as the material for heresy,[1] or its rejection can be regarded as a heresy, as Anselm of Canterbury all but states.[2] Apart of these extreme views, the subject of the *Filioque* introduces the question of whether the Western Christians were canonically justified in introducing this clause into the Nicene Creed (finally in 1014), and it can open to us a long and interesting history of debate and controversy, involving the Athanasian Creed, Photius, Damiani, Gregory Palamas, the Councils of Lyon and of Ferrara/Florence, the Old Catholic Church, Vladimir Lossky, and many others.

I shall say a little more later about the views of Anselm and of some others. But first I must explain that I shall not here refer, except incidentally, to the history of the Filioque Controversy. Nor shall I say more about the canonical questions except that in our Athens Meeting in 1978 the Anglicans affirmed that we do not think that Western Christians are any longer justified in retaining the clause in the Creed, that the Lambeth Conference later that year endorsed this opinion, and that I have seen no reason to change my view since then.

The reasons for taking the question of the *Filioque* Clause seriously which seem to me weighty are that we are in this subject dealing with the content of, or at least an interpolation into, the Nicene Creed, and this Creed is of lasting and supreme importance. It is early dogmatic tradition which has formed the minds and life of all those contemporary denominations who accept it, even of those who do not repeat it in their worship. It forms an important bond between Orthodox, Roman Catholics and many non-episcopal bodies. It is the doctrinal basis upon which the Ecumenical Movement has lived; it is not simply the Bible which forms a bond between the participants in the Ecumenical Movement. There are thousands of Christians who devoutly respect the Bible but who execrate the Ecumenical Movement. It is the Nicene Creed and the dogmatic tradition represented by it that form the true bond of

[1] See J. Romanides, 'The Filioque', in *Kleronomia* (Thessalonica, July 1975), VII.5, pp. 285–314; and 'Participation in the Grace of the Holy Trinity', presented to a Sub-Commission of the A/OJDD.

[2] Migne, *Patrologia Latina* 158, XXVI (321).

unity in the Ecumenical Movement. Lastly, consideration of the *Filioque* Clause may not bring us face to face with an article by which the Church stands or falls, but it is impossible to discuss the *Filioque* in any depth without being led into deep waters of Trinitarian theology, and this gives the theme a special importance.

I approach this subject in no controversial spirit. I want to offer the opportunity for Christians of the Eastern and of the Western traditions to understand each other upon a point of doctrine which the men of the Eastern tradition at least regard as most important, without requiring either tradition to surrender entirely its assumptions and usual approach.

II

We cannot seriously regard the doctrine of the *Filioque* as a heresy. Vladimir Lossky heaps upon its head every major defect or evil tendency in Western theology since the year 1000. Others see it as the sign of an unnecessary preoccupation with philosophy and a dangerously wrong doctrine of how we know God. On the other side, Anselm in his *De Processione Spiritus Sancti*[3] claims that if you deny the doctrine of *Filioque* you destroy the whole Christian faith. Utterances as extreme as these on either side make the honest reader wonder if he is inhabiting the same universe of discourse as those who utter them. Ideas are not things. We are not living in a world where ideas work out their consequences with unerring doctrinaire logic and precision, and where the slightest deviation in orthodoxy will produce vast and century-long results. The doctrine of *Filioque* is concerned with a point which ordinary common sense must describe as recondite, abstruse, even hypothetical. To attach enormous weight to it, either in championing or denouncing it, is to betray the fact that one's thinking has begun to lose a proper grasp of proportion. If we are to understand each other, we must avoid extreme positions such as these. With these positions I group the argument in defence of the *Filioque* which has in the past been advanced (*e.g.*, by E. J. Bicknell in his *Introduction to the*

---

[3] *Op. cit.*, XXVI (321).

Thirty-Nine Articles) that the clause was useful in refuting the Arian heresy. We know so little of how and why the *Filioque* doctrine first rose into favour in the West that historical arguments can hardly help us here. I find it difficult to imagine, in fact, how the *Filioque* could have assisted the struggle against Arianism in Spain, or anywhere else. The Arians held what might be called their own verison of a *Filioque* doctrine. They believed that the Spirit was the first creation of the Son. I do not see how the doctrine that the Holy Spirit proceeds from the Father and the Son could have been either relevant or helpful here. And finally, I must dissent from the argument of Professor Romanides' brilliant and forceful paper, 'Participation in the Grace of the Holy Trinity'. It requires us to abandon all ontology, to reduce Christianity to an analysis of religious experience and to desert the whole Western tradition of theology. Anglicans who want to be honestly faithful to their own tradition cannot possibly do that.

III

Let us now remind ourselves of what the doctrine of the Trinity, of God as three Persons but one God, actually is. It cannot be described as a private opinion nor as a doctrine of minor importance; it is a dogma. But it is a dogma which only very gardually came to be understood and accepted during the history of the Church of the first four centuries. We cannot uncritically read this dogma back into the New Testament, and even less are we justified in doing so for the Old Testament. The Apologists of the second century did not know of the doctrine of the Trinity as it was fully developed in the fourth century, neither did Tertullian nor Irenaeus nor Hippolytus, all of whom believed that God unfolded himself into a Trinity for the purpose of creation, revelation and redemption. Even Origen, who first unequivocally taught that God always had been a Trinity, who first articulated the doctrine of the eternal generation of the Son, subordinated both Son and Spirit to the Father in a manner which later upholders of the doctrine of the Trinity could not have accepted, and he did so because this subordination was inevitably necessitated by the basic assumption of his thought. I do not believe the evidence that he applied the term *Homoousios* to the Son, and I have given my reasons elsewhere in this book, reasons with which some eminent scholars have agreed.[4] The doctrine of the Trinity as we accept it today emerged as the result of the Arian controversy and the impetus which that controversy gave to the theologians of the Christian Church. The controversy compelled the defenders of orthodoxy to ask themselves searchingly how they could reconcile belief in the divinity of Christ with monotheism, and the answer was not achieved without strife, uncertainty on all sides, long-lasting confusion in the use of terms, and the aid of late Greek philosophy called in as an essential though perhaps eclectically used companion. The full doctrine of the Trinity was developed as the conclusion of a search, and the end was not fully understood while the search was continuing. Those who were most influential in bringing it to its final form, Athanasius, Basil of Caesarea, Gregory of Nazianzus, and Gregory of Nyssa, were most emphatic in emphasizing that we ought to appreciate in handling this doctrine particularly the inadequacy of not only the human language but of human thought to understand and to express the deepest things of God.[5] This fact alone should warn us against doctrinaire insistence upon the exclusive validity of the more abstruse expressions associated with the doctrine of the Trinity.

The doctrine of the Trinity was in fact developed as a safeguard for our belief in the divinity of Jesus Christ the Son of God. This doctrine alone, the Fathers of the fourth century believed, could guarantee that our belief in the divinity of Jesus Christ was not corrupted, reduced or misunderstood. Only this doctrine could ensure that Jesus Christ was not regarded as a demi-god, the incarnation of some lower deity sent as a messenger of the incommunicable and unknowable high God. This doctrine alone could assure us that the career of Jesus Christ did not represent a mere *epiphany* of God, a temporary

---

[4] See cap 4.
[5] See chapter 13 of the present work.

appearance followed by a withdrawal, like some powerful American president paying a quick flying visit to a small European state, but on the contrary meant the permanent and decisive intervention of God himself, the authentic Godhead, into human affairs and human history.

This being so, the doctrine of the Trinity must be regarded as a necessary inference from the data of revelation, from salvation history. The terms in which the doctrine was ultimately expressed by the great theologians of the second half of the fourth century were almost entirely drawn—and drawn for good reasons—from the vocabulary of late Greek philosophy, but the content expressed and the necessity to express it came from the Biblical witness and Biblical record, and arose out of the fundamental drive and genius of the Christian faith. The Christian doctrine of the Trinity arises out of an argument concerning God as he must be in himself drawn from what we know about God in his revelation of himself. In discussing any aspect of the doctrine of the Trinity we must not lose contact with this important truth. For our knowledge of what God is in himself we have no other source except our knowledge of God as he has revealed himself, and the rules of logic.

We must apply this principle to the case of the *Filioque*. If we can know whether the Spirit proceeds from the Father or from the Father and the Son, we can only achieve this knowledge by inference from the relations of Father, Son and Spirit in revelation. If the evidence in Scripture appears to suggest that the Spirit proceeds from the Father and the Son, or from the Father without mention of the Son, we cannot cancel out this inference by reference to abstract relation between *ousia* and *hypostasis* or to a doctrine of God as known only in his *energeia* and not in his *ousia*, useful though such terms may be in their proper contexts. The economic Trinity, God as known in the history of salvation, is our only source of knowledge for the immanent Trinity, God as he is in himself. In constantly recurring to this point Karl Barth in his dealing with the subject, was certainly right.[6] But is the witness of salvation history on

---

[6] Karl Barth, *Church Dogmatics* (E.T. Edinburgh, 3rd imp. 1955) III, Cap. II, Part I, § 12 (pp. 513–560).

this point entirely clear, as clear as Barth, in the sweep of his argument which sometimes brushes aside too readily difficulties and uncertainties, assumes that it is? The Scriptural evidence is fragile and difficult of interpretation. Its two main texts have always been Jn 14.26 ('For the Comforter, the Spirit whom the Father will send in my name') and Jn 15.26 ('when however the Comforter will come, whom I shall send you from the Father'). They have been interpreted with equal confidence in different directions by those who defended and those who rejected the *Filioque*. If we are to invoke the witness of Scripture, we must do so from a larger basis in the Bible than this one.

But at this point we strike one of the major controverted points in the subject of the *Filioque*. Can we argue from the temporal mission of the Holy Spirit to his eternal procession? The Eastern tradition of theology strongly denies that we can, asserting that the mission of the Holy Spirit to created things can be no clue to the eternal procession of the Spirit in the uncreated Trinity, even occasionally going so far as to suggest that to handle the subject in this way approximates to the Arian error of regarding the Holy Spirit as himself created. The Western tradition teaches that we can and must move from the Spirit's temporal mission to his eternal procession. Anselm and Barth are even ready to argue from the activity of Father, Son and Spirit in creation to their relation within the Trinity, and Barth adds his own peculiar idea that we can determine the procession of the Holy Spirit by arguing from the 'communityness' brought about by the Holy Spirit between man and God to the 'communityness' (as it were) of the Holy Spirit within the Godhead. Gerald Bray, in a very interesting and able paper given as the Tyndale Fellowship Historical Theology Lecture in 1982, entitled 'The *Filioque* Clause in Historical Theology', has a not dissimilar argument (p. 23) to that of Barth, though perhaps with a special slant to it, which we shall consider later. I can see no serious objection to arguing from the temporal mission of the Holy Spirit, even though that mission was indeed to mortal creatures. To say that this implies that the Holy Spirit is created is absurd. More than this, I have already indicated, I do not see what other source of knowledge we have about the relation of the Spirit within the Trinity to the Father and the Son except what is called the economic Trinity. The statement on this subject by the Anglicans (including myself) in Moscow in 1978 now seems to me equivocal and not easily defensible. Of course the language of our Lord in St. John's Gospel is concerned with the economic Trinity, but where else shall we learn of the immanent Trinity? On the other hand, I think that we must interpret the evidence of the economic Trinity cautiously and discriminately, and consequently I do not like arguing from the role of the Spirit in creation to his relation to the Father and the Son within the Trinity because this role is by no means clearly set out in either the Old Testament or the New Testament and I distrust the too frequent habit of theologians of seeking *obscurum per obscurius*.

IV

But the subject of the *Filioque* plunges us into an even more fundamental question: How do we know God in revelation? Eastern Orthodox theologians answer this with a doctrine to which I have already slightly referred. We cannot know God as he is in himself, in his *ousia*. We can only know him through his uncreated *energeia* which encounters us as we are by the Holy Spirit brought into his redeeming act in Jesus Christ, and as we so respond to him. The procession of the Spirit from the Father is concerned with God as he is in himself, with his *ousia*, and therefore we cannot infer from our encounter with God in revelation what the relation of the Spirit is within the Trinity, from the economic to the immanent Trinity. I have never been able to find a satisfactory answer to the question which this doctrine raises in my mind: how do we know that the *energy* of God as we meet it in revelation is a clue to the authentic nature of God himself? Eunomius, the Neo-Arian of the fourth century, readily accepted this distinction, but believed that the *energeia* of God was different from his *ousia*. How are we to know that he was wrong? The Orthodox answer appears to be, we know this in some act of inspiration or mystical vision. I have always thought it unsatisfactory to defend the doctrine of the Trinity on the grounds that it alone can ensure that in Jesus Christ we have knowledge of the authentic God and of nothing less than he, and then to maintain that this knowledge is not in fact knowledge of God as he is in himself, but of his uncreated energy. This doctrine seems to undermine the whole basis for believing in the doctrine of the Trinity. Furthermore, it seems to rest on a distinction taken directly from late Greek (and particularly Platonic) philosophy, and I do not see the necessity of introducing ancient philosophy quite so centrally into our theology here. Much more can of course be said on this subject, and several misapprehensions (not least my own) can perhaps be cleared up, and I am not so bold as to ask our Orthodox brethren to abandon nor even to modify their doctrine. I only ask that they should appreciate some of the reasons of Westerners' hesitations and reservations about this doctrine.

Some of the expressions used, by non-Orthodox, I must admit, about this point in that admirable and informative series of essays *Spirit of God, Spirit of Christ*[7] I find positively shocking. An Old Catholic Scholar, Herwig Aldhoven, can use the expression 'the not-directly knowable Father',[8] on the grounds that we know the Father through the Son and in the Spirit, and Garrigues (a Roman Catholic) in his essay[9] constantly speaks of 'the mediation of the Son in the procession of the Spirit'. But if God is not directly knowable in Christ, what is the point of the doctrine of the Trinity? The Son, as Irenaeus said, is the knowability of the Father. And there can be no mediation within the Godhead, or we are back into Arianism again. It is as he is incarnate that Christ is a mediator, not as he is the Son within the life of the Trinity. And while we can and must distinguish the Persons of the Trinity in our thought and discourse, and must perceive that those distinctions are given us in Scripture and in tradition, it is in my view a mistake to conclude that we can separately and distinctly experience the Persons, so that now we experience the Father, and now the Son and on another occasion the Holy Spirit.[10] We experience God

[7] ed. Lukas Vischer (WCC Faith and Order Paper 103) S.P.C.K. London, 1981.

[8] Vischer, p. 128.

[9] *Ibid.*, pp. 149–163.

[10] Aldhoven seems to me to come close to saying this (Vischer, pp. 121, 122).

the Holy Spirit, and in him we experience the Father through the Son, simultaneously, in a single experience, not separately. Our experience of God must be in this sense Trinitarian. Of course we can only experience God in faith, and we can never in this life or the next grasp him, master him, comprehend him, even though we can hope for an increasing knowledge of him beyond this life. In this sense he is incomprehensible. But he is never unknowable.

V

As we tentatively progress in our investigation of the doctrine of God, like pot-holers cautiously moving on to a further subterranean cave, we must next face the most difficult question of all raised by the subject of the *Filioque*: what is a Person (*persona, hypostasis*)? *Persona* and *hypostasis* are not entirely identical in their meaning and even these terms were only reached by the theologians of the fourth century after a long period of confusion and misunderstanding. The inability of both Athanasius and Hilary, as well as a number of minor writers, during the middle years of the Arian controversy, to state precisely what God is as Three which he is not as One, contributed considerably to lengthen the controversy. The Cappadocians achieved the feat of confining the word *hypostasis* to denoting the Persons and *ousia* to mean the substance, and succeeded in establishing this distinction permanently in the Eastern theological tradition. But they were not called to determine with great precision what *hypostasis* means, that is to say, not what is each Person that the other Two are not, but what does *hypostasis* mean in itself not merely as distinct from *ousia*. This was a question which much troubled Augustine; it is almost possible to say that if baffled him.[11] My reading of the *De Trinitate* suggests that Augustine never decided what was meant by *persona* in a *Trinitarian* context. Logically, he thought, God

---

[11] At *De Trinitate* V, 9.1 occur the famous words about the Persons: *Magna prorsus inopia humanum laborat eloquium. Dictum est tamen: tres personae, non ut illud diceretur, sed ne taceretur; cf.* VII, 4.7: *verius enim cogitatur Deus quam dicitur, et verius est quam cogitatur.*

should only be regarded as one *persona*,[12] though he of course admitted the distinction of Father, Son and Spirit and carefully avoided Sabellianism. He regarded the Persons as relations, real, subsistent relations (whatever that means), but no more. Bray in his paper defines the ancient concept of Person as 'an objective reality capable of acting' (p. 6) or 'which is an active subject' (p. 9); for Augustine, the Persons 'were not objective realities in their own right, but expressions of real relations which are subsistent in the divine Being' (p. 11); hence presumably the 'subsistent relations' of Aquinas and of later traditional Western theology. I find this last term incomprehensible. The modern age has introduced a new and dangerous complication to this tricky question. The emphasis on the subjective experience of the individual and the advance in knowledge of human psychology which has been evident in European thought ever since the Renaissance have imported into the word 'person' all sorts of meanings and associations which were not present to the mind of the ancients when they used the words *hypostasis* and *persona*. Today 'person' inevitably involves the concept of an experiencing mind, a conscious subject, and if we emphasize that *hypostasis* or *persona* means an individual reality, then 'person' today must mean an individual conscious subject of experience. These ideas were not attached to the words *hypostasis* or *persona* by the ancients. To them the central element in a 'person' was existence as a distinct objective reality. In consequence very many people today when they learn that God is three Persons assume that this means three minds or three distinct conscious individuals. And the rise of idealist philosophy in the last century enabled some theologians (among them many Anglicans such as William Temple and Leonard Hodgson) to suggest a theory of a 'Social Trinity', of God as actually consisting of three 'persons' in the modern sense, or at least as possessing three minds or consciousnesses.[13] It seems to me to be verging dangerously towards tritheism. To cut a long and complicated story short, I shall here assume that 'Person'

[12] *Ibid.*, VII, 4.8.

[13] This tendency has now appeared in Lutheranism with Pannenberg and, in an extreme form, with Moltmann.

when applied to the Trinity means a distinct objective reality within the being of God but not a distinct mind or consciousness and not simply a relationship. God has three ways of being his Self, three modes of subsisting as God (Karl Rahner), or three ways of being the One God, but he is not three 'persons' in our modern sense of the word.

The relevance of this discussion becomes clear when we consider briefly some aspects of Augustine's doctrine of *Filioque*. He maintained that the Spirit was the bond of love (*nexus amoris*) between the Father and the Son, and this doctrine has been characteristic of Western theology ever since. The Father loves the Son and the Holy Spirit is the love with which they love each other. God's love is expressed by a lover and a loved within the Trinity eternally. Attractive though this doctrine is in some respects, it seems to me to have the fatal defect of assuming unconsciously that each distinct Person is a mind or personality capable of feeling and expressing love, except in the case of the Spirit who is an affection joining the other two Persons. This will make some sort of sense if we assume that the Persons of the Trinity are 'persons' in our modern sense, though even in that case I do not see at all clearly what it means to say that the Spirit is the *nexus amoris*. but if we reject this dangerously tritheist assumption Augustine's doctrine leaves us in an impossible situation: God in one mode of subsistence loves himself in another mode of subsistence and in a third mode of subsistence is the love with which he loves himself! Anyway, what is the point of saying that God loves himself? We have no example in our experience of good and proper self-love (though we have of self-respect). And if I am asked what object of love did God (who is eternal love) have before the creation of the universe I am inclined to give the traditional reply that he was occupying himself making places of punishment for people who ask foolish questions. Barth can in one breath deny that the Persons are separate 'I's' or 'persons' in the modern sense, and in the next maintain that the Spirit is *nexus amoris*, without, of course, explaining the apparent inconsistency.[14] Augustine's *nexus amoris* theory therefore seems to me to land us in

---

[14] *Op. cit.*, pp. 537–538.

difficulties which are inextricable and throws no light on whether we should accept the doctrine of *Filioque* or not. Bobrinskoy in Vischer's symposium suggests interestingly that the Orthodox can achieve all that the *nexus amoris* is meant to achieve without incurring its unfortunate consequences, by teaching that the Spirit has no 'prerogative' to be the link between Father and Son, but that 'Each *hypostasis* gathers together and unites the others in himself, the Father as source in the monarchy, the Son as the One in whom the Father and the Spirit find their resting place'.[15]

Augustine, of course, was impelled towards the *Filioque* doctrine by two of his fundamental assumptions about the Trinity. He assumed that the Persons derive from the *essentia* of the Godhead, of the Trinity, and not from the *hypostasis* or Person of the Father, and this assumption partly at least arose out of his uncertainty as to what was meant by 'Person',[16] and he noted that since God is a Spirit the Father and the Son are Spirit also. The Holy Spirit, as Spirit *par excellence*, must therefore unite Father and Son. Now, I do not underestimate Augustine's greatness as a theologian. His was one of the greatest intellects that has ever existed on this planet. Augustine realized that the Cappadocians had confessed that they could not give any meaningful description of how the Spirit subsists as an *hypostasis*. The Father subsists ingenerately, the Son filially, and these are words which have some analogy in their experience. But to say that the Spirit either just is, or is between ingenerate and generate, or subsists 'procession-wise' (*poreutikōs*) is to say nothing at all. And this was as far as the Cappadocians could go. Augustine made a highly intelligent suggestion that the Spirit exists as Gift (*donum* immanently, *donatum* economically). I do not think that this was in the end a successful theory, but it was a most ingenious one.[17] To any eager theological mind the doctrine of the Spirit as it was handed on to Augustine by the Cappadocians had gaps in it. These he attempted to fill. When

---

[15] Page 142 Garrigues, in the same book (p. 162 n. 1) quotes St. John of Damascus to the same effect.

[16] Anselm, of course, followed Augustine in this doctrine; and for him 'Person' certainly meant nothing but relation.

[17] Barth, of course follows Augustine; *op. cit.*, p. 537.

all is said and done, however, I do not think that Augustine was
wise in suggesting that the Son and the Spirit derive from the
substance or *essentia* of the Trinity and not from the Father's
hypostasis. In Augustine's theology the theory did not produce
happy results and in Anselm's hands it constantly threatened to
fall into absurdity and could only be prevented from doing so
by the application of arbitrary philosophical brakes on his part;
there is no reason on his premises why the Son should not
proceed from the Spirit or the Spirit originate from himself,
except that Anselm does not choose to believe this.[18]

VI

We must therefore conclude that the Son and the Spirit as
Persons derive not from the substance or Godhead of the
Trinity simply but from the *hypostasis* of the Father, in the case
of the Son, or in the case of the Spirit either from the *hypostasis*
of the Father or from the *hypostasis* of Father and Son. Before I
attempt to determine whether the Spirit derives from the Father
or from the Father and the Son—a decision which I have
deliberately postponed to the end of this paper—it must be
pointed out that even if it were decided that the Spirit derived
from the Father and not from the Son, or, in Photius' phrase,
from the Father alone, it is undeniably significant that the Spirit
proceeds from the *Father*, not from the Godhead considered
apart from its distinctions, and unless we are to distinguish the
First Person as Father from the First Person as Source or Origin,
which I do not think that we are justified in doing, though
Anselm in fact did it, this means that the Spirit's procession
cannot be wholly separate from and unrelated to the *hypostasis*
of the Son who is the Son of the Father. Moltmann's essay in
Vischer's symposium emphasizes this, so much so that he
proposes to substitute for the *Filioque* the formula 'from the
Father of the Son' (*a Patre Filii*).[19] Garrigues says that 'the
procession of the Spirit depends upon the generation of the

---

[18] *De Processione* VIII (298, 299); XV (308); XVIII (311, 312); XXVII (321,
322).
[19] Vischer, 164–173.

Word in the bosom of the Father' and maintains that the *Filioque* is thus far a legitimate doctrine but disavows 'any desire to turn into a dogma one of the theological explanations of *how* this dependence works'.[20] and elsewhere declares, 'The Holy Spirit proceeds from the Father inasmuch as the latter is Father of the unique Son'.[21] An Orthodox contributor to the same work, Bobrinskoy, does not of course subscribe to the *Filioque* doctrine, but in an eirenic spirit gives what he regards as the proper Orthodox alternative to it. The Spirit does not merely proceed from the Father and the Son, or through the Son, but rests upon the Son from all eternity so that there is a reciprocity between the two in their manifesting and giving themselves.[22] And earlier in the book Kurt Stadler an Old Catholic contributor, had reminded his readers of the valuable dictum of the Old Catholic bishop Urs Küry that the Spirit only exists because the existence of the Son is presupposed.[23]

These views seem to bring the Eastern and Western doctrines about the procession of the Spirit closer to each other. But the main Orthodox objections to the *Filioque* remain: it is the peculiar property (*idioma*) of the Father's *hypostasis* to bring forth, therefore the procession of the Spirit can only derive from him and not from the Son. There cannot be two origins, two *archai*, in the Trinity. The Father does not share with the Son his status as Source (*pēgē*).[24] Augustine attempted to meet these objections by saying that the Spirit derived from the Father and the Son, but from the Father *principaliter* (presumably not meaning 'mainly' but 'as the *principium*').[25] The Son can be called *principium* in relation to creation, but with the Father in this relation he is not two *principia* but one; so the Spirit can also

[20] Page 152

[21] Page 156

[22] Pages 144, 145

[23] Pages 105, 106. *huparchontos tou huiou*; his thought was borrowed from the Russian Orthodox theologian Bolotov. Staniloae's essay (p. 178–179) touches on the same point.

[24] These arguments are repeated over and over again in the papers already submitted to the Sub-commission. A. de Halleux, a Roman Catholic contributor, gives a very clear statement of the Orthodox point of view in Vischer, p. 71.

[25] *De Trinitate* XV, 17.9, 26, 27.

be called *principium* in relation to creation, and again with the Father and Son he is one *principium*, not three. This is the ground in the action of God upon created things on which Augustine bases his doctrine of the *Filioque*.[26] In the procession of the Spirit the Son is also a single *principium* along with the Father.[27] He explains this double procession thus (the subject is the Father): *Quidquid unigenito Verbo dedit gignendo dedit. Sic ergo eum genuit ut etiam de illo Donum commune procederet, et Spiritus sanctus esset amborum.*[28] Anselm firmly rejects the Augustinian concept of the Spirit proceeding *principaliter* from the Father on the grounds that it suggests an interval or space interposed between the Father and the Son.[29] *Spiritum sanctum asserimus suo modo, non quasi de duobus fontibus sed vere de uno fonte procedere* (310). To conclude that the Spirit proceeds *principaliter* from the Father would be to admit a variety in the essences of God, an imbalance;[30] all that he can allow this Augustinian term to mean is: *quia ipse Filius, de quo est Spiritus sanctus, a Patre habet hoc ipsum, ut Spiritus sanctus sit de illo; quonium id quod est habet a Patre* (319). If Augustine's *principaliter* means that the Spirit proceeds 'mainly' from the Father (but a bit from the Son!), this is a ridiculous doctrine; if it means 'from the Father as *principium*', then the case for the *Filioque* collapses. Later Western theology took up a phrase of Anselm and taught that the Spirit proceeded from the Father and the Son *quasi de uno principio*.

Photius criticized the *Filioque* as in effect admitting two causes into the Godhead, the Father and the Son. Augustine in the *De Trinitate* does not speak about causes, and Anselm in his work is very chary of doing so. He does not like applying the word 'cause' to God, though he apparently is compelled to do so. *Principium* suggests something beginning to be and having previously not been; and a cause cannot be without an effect. Neither of these conditions apply to God. But he reluctantly admits a kind of order in the Trinity.[31] Later theology, however,

[26] *Ibid.*, V, 13.14.
[27] *Ibid.*, V, 14.15.
[28] *Ibid.*, XV, 17.29, *cf.* 26.47; 27.49.
[29] *Op. cit.*, XVI (319, 340).
[30] *Ibid.*, XXIV (319, 320).
[31] *Ibid.*, XVIII (311, 312).

did not shrink from describing the Son as a joint-cause of the Holy Spirit.

It must be obvious to any fair-minded investigator that theologians of the Western tradition have never intended, no matter how they may have juggled with words, to envisage two sources or *archai* in God. I think that we can legitimately share Anselm's reluctance to speak of *causes* within the Godhead. If we believe in God as one God who exists in three distinct Persons who have existed from eternity and whose relations with each other are equally eternal, it seems that to speak of causes within the Godhead is to stray into a realm in which words begin to lose their meaning—a fault to which exponents of the doctrine of the Holy Trinity are peculiarly liable. Even if we wish to teach that the Spirit proceeds from the Father and Son, we must allow that it is from and owing to the Father that this state of affairs prevails.

At this point in the argument, however, I am like Augustine, overcome by the insufficiency of thought or language to guide us. It is admitted on all sides that we do not know what 'procession' means. It was a term taken indeed, from the Fourth Gospel and used by the Cappadocian Fathers to denote, but not to define or describe, the peculiar mode in which God exists or subsists as Holy Spirit. They candidly admitted that they did not know what it meant, that it was a blank cheque, and it cannot be said that later generations of theologians have written anything significant upon that cheque. We are speaking of the 'procession' of one of the Persons of the Trinity. We find this concept of 'Person' within the Godhead very difficult if not actually impossible to define, though we can be sure that these 'Persons' exist. In these circumstances to say with dogmatic certainty either that the Holy Spirit does not proceed from the Son as well as from the Father or that he does proceed from the Father and the Son appears to be unjustified, to be unpleasantly like an attempt to rush in where angels fear to tread. It is an option which should be left entirely open.

To this three more points only will be added here. First, we must take seriously the Christo-centric arguments which flow so constantly from the pen of Karl Barth. In all his treatment of the Holy Spirit Barth insists that we must not separate him from

Jesus Christ. The Spirit does not illuminate nor sanctify us apart from Jesus Chrust. He acts with the Son, and, in the Son's incarnate life, on the Son. Secondly, Professor Eugene Fairweather in his paper submitted to the Sub-Commission [32] shows how for the Western doctrine of salvation the indissoluble unity of the Spirit and the Son is an essential element. It is the Spirit who brings us to the Son, who operates in the Incarnation; who, poured into our hearts, arouses us to respond to the love of the Father manifested in the Son. If we are to argue from the economic to the eternal Trinity, there is no point at which we can separate (though we can distinguish) the Spirit from the Son. And finally Dr. Bray, in a striking argument drawn from the work of Calvin, suggests forcefully that as we are remade in the image of the Person of the Son so the Holy Spirit who actually carries out the work of regeneration cannot be in his *hypostasis* divided from the *hypostasis* of the Son.[33] In the whole drift of this argument we return to the Bible. But we do not now dispute about single texts, moving perilously from a few words attributed to Jesus Christ to a vast range of Trinitarian thought. Whatever Jesus did or said in his earthly ministry, he did not walk the lanes of Galilee and the streets of Jerusalem laying down direct unmodified Trinitarian doctrine. Our Biblical base here is much broader and deeper. It consists of the whole weight of the New Testament doctrine of salvation, supported by the religious experience of regenerated men and women. The doctrine of the *Filioque* has solid ground beneath it.

In conclusion, I suggest that, with Garrigues,[34] we should insist neither upon the ancient philosophical doctrine of a distinction of *ousia* and *energeia* within God, nor on the ancient philosophical doctrine of subsistent relations within God, but recognize that both Eastern and Western Christians in their diverse approaches to the origin of the procession of the Holy Spirit have at heart legitimate Scriptural and orthodox interests and that, as each group pursues its own tradition while honestly

[32] 'The Filioque Clause in Ecumenical Perspective', pp. 21–22.
[33] *Op. cit.*, pp. 16, 22–24.
[34] Vischer, p. 151.

attempting to understand that of the other, neither is justified in accusing the other of veering dangerously away from true doctrine and sound faith. As St. Gregory of Nazianzus once said in a letter defending St. Basil of Caesarea, it is not the formula that matters but the doctrine behind the formula.

13

DOGMA AND FORMULA IN THE FATHERS

Anglicans belong to a creed-repeating denomination. More than any other Christian body they have laid down in their formularies the injunction to repeat creeds. If an Anglican priest were to take all the rubrics of the Book of Common Prayer *au pied de la lettre*, he would find himself repeating the Apostles' Creed twice every day of his life, the Nicene Creed at every celebration of the eucharist and, if he belonged to the Church of England, the Athanasian Creed thirteen times a year. One of the motives of the founding fathers of Anglicanism in giving birth to such a passionate addiction to creeds was no doubt a desire to associate their church with the ancient Church by ordaining the repeating of creeds which the ancient Christians repeated. If they give the impression that they are devoted adherents of the practice of repeating doctrinal formulae, it is because they thought that the ancient Christians were great repeaters of formulae also.

But in fact the evidence on this point is far from convincing. The origin of the interrogatory baptismal creed can only be traced with any confidence to the middle of the second century. There is no satisfactory evidence that anything that could be called a creed—that is an invariable formula expressing the essence of Christian belief—was used earlier than that. There are of course plenty of doctrinal formulae to be discovered in the New Testament and in the sub-apostolic literature and in the Apologists which were used for teaching or for exposition,[1] but these are not invariable formulae and are not treated as formal summaries of the Christian faith and are not handed down to succeeding generations. The earliest approach to a creed which we can find is the formula attributed to the Ethiopian eunuch in the 'Western' textual tradition at Acts, 8.37; he is here represented as saying at his baptism: Πιστεύω τὸν υἱὸν τοῦ

---

[1] *E.g.*, Rom 1.3, 4; 4.24, 25; 8.34; 1 Cor 8.6; 1 Tim 2.5; 3.16; 2 Tim 2.8; 1 Pet 3.18; Ignatius, Eph 18.2; Trall 9; Smyrn 1.1, 2; Polycarp, Phillipians 2.1; Aristides, Apol 15.1–3; Justin Martyr, Apol 1.6.2, 21.1, 42.4, 46.5, 67.2; Dial 85.2; 132.1.

θεοῦ εἶναι τὸν Ἰησοῦν Χριστόν. I have given reasons elsewhere[2] for thinking that this revision or series of interpolations should be dated about 120. It is understandable that in the earliest period of the Church's life, filled with eschatological expectations, no invariable credal formula should have established itself. And perhaps it is understandable that once Christology replaced eschatology as the main intellectual interest of the Church a credal formula should appear. But even when it does appear it is a long time before it achieves any but the most skeletonic form or is regarded as of great importance. Even in the third century, in the second half of which the declaratory, in contrast to be interrogatory, baptismal creed was to develop, Christian theologians speak of the creed in terms which suggest that they regard it as a brief summary of the Christian faith, of relatively minor importance. Irenaeus had called it an 'abridgement' of the Christian faith in his *Demonstration*.[3] Tertullian had called it 'a rather larger formula than the Lord laid down in the gospels'.[4] Clement of Alexandria called the creed 'the main points'[5] and Origen used a rather similar expression[6] and also called it 'the most important summary of the faith', and 'holy seeds'.[7] There is no satisfactory evidence that this interrogatory baptismal creed, even though it was the only form of creed known until the second half of the third century, was ever regarded as a test of orthodoxy. Quite apart from the existence of some evidence that heretics, and not least Gnostic heretics, were ready to use the form of creed used by the Church, a consideration of even the relatively developed form of creed found in Hippolytus' *Apostolic Tradition* will show that there were no expressions in the creed calculated to exclude heresy, *i.e.*, no expressions which most of the leading heretics of the second and third centuries, let us say Valentinus,

[2] Cap 3.

[3] Demonstration, 6; another translation of the Syriac is 'drawing up'.

[4] De Corona, 3.3—*amplius aliquid quam dominus in evangeliis determinavit*.

[5] Clement, Stromateis, vii. 15 (P.G. 9.525), τὰ μέγιστα.

[6] Origen, Peri Archon, 1, Praef. 2, *in magnis et maximis*, in Rufinus' translation.

[7] τῷ μεγίστῳ τῆς πίστεως κεφαλαίῳ, Comm. on John 32.3; τὰ σπέρματα τὰ ἅγια, Hom. on Jeremiah 4.3.

Marcion, Praxeas and Sabellius, could not have repeated with an easy mind. The interrogatory, baptismal creed was a formula indeed, but as a heretic-repelling formula it was quite inefficient. It clearly was not intended for this purpose. Perhaps it was worth observing that a situation in which you are asked to repeat a formula during a ceremony when water is being poured over your head in considerable quantities as you stand in a tank or trough is not the best situation for the nice enunciation of dogmatic formulae designed to safeguard the faith. Generally speaking the pre-Nicene Church did not express dogma in a fixed credal formula. Its fixed credal formula, what we call the Apostles' Creed, the interrogatory baptismal creed, even at its most developed stage in the fourth century, did not mention the Incarnation, the Atonement or the doctrine of the Trinity. Before the second half of the third century nobody appears to have connected the enunciation of dogma with a fixed formula. Once the declaratory creed, as opposed to the interrogatory, had emerged and had very soon been used for the statement of dogmatic formulae, the place and purpose of the earlier, interrogatory creed became uncertain and in many respects otiose. We today inherit this interrogatory creed which we call the Apostles' Creed. It is a curious and rather useless, though venerable relic. It is impossible to imagine it as a symbol round which divided Christians can be united. It has a strange, incongruous air; it rather resembles a doctrinal washing line, and as a summary of the Christian faith it has as much consistency, coherence and logic as a washing line.

When the pre-Nicene fathers wanted to express dogma they did not produce the creed. They produced the rule of faith. This expression and concept first appear with Irenaeus. Indeed, E. Molland may be correct in his conjecture that Irenaeus invented the expression, though Irenaeus can hardly have invented the concept. It is widely used by writers at the end of the second and during most of the third centuries, and is used in both fourth and fifth centuries, though naturally in a different sense. In its early use it means the teaching of the Church as it is known to the writer who uses the expression, assumed to be in continuity with and to be identical with the teachings of the Church from its earliest days. The rule of faith can be, and often is, divided into subjects or articles of faith; complete or partial lists of these can be reproduced or deduced from Irenaeus, Tertullian, Hippolytus, Origen, Cyprian, Novatian, Dionysius of Alexandria and the 'Didascalia Apostolorum' that survives in Syriac. The content of this rule of faith is broadly the same wherever it appears, but it exhibits local differences. Irenaeus introduces into it his 'recapitulation' doctrine; Tertullian includes the idea that Jesus Christ preached a 'new law'; Origen sees it as covering authority to allegorize the Scriptures. It cannot possibly be regarded as a formula, for there occurs in all the examples of it no invariable form of words to be handed down to posterity intact. Several ancient writers seem to assume that the interrogatory, baptismal creed is a short summary of the rule of faith; it seems wholly probable that catechetical instruction in preparation for baptism was based on the rule of faith. The rule of faith, which is also described in several other similar terms, such as 'rule of truth', 'definition of faith', 'rule of piety', is emphatically a means of expressing and teaching dogma, such dogma as the Church of the second and third centuries had achieved, *i.e.* some Christological statements about the person of Christ, some statements of the incarnation and some about the function of the Holy Spirit in redemption. It would have been correspondingly much more difficult for heretics to assent to the rule of faith, and indeed it is the rule of faith to which writers of this period refer in refuting the opinions of heretics. We can therefore with confidence say that though the writers of the second and third centuries knew something of dogma and also in their baptismal creed possessed a fixed doctrinal formula, they showed no inclination to associate dogma permanently with an unchanging formula.

The change from a creed which has an interrogatory form and is used at the rite of baptism to a declaratory creed which is used to test orthodoxy and to express orthodoxy in an invariable form is difficult, if not impossible, to trace. There are some hints that in the second half of the third century statements like reproductions of the rule of faith, or of parts of it, are beginning to be used as tests of orthodoxy. At the Council of Nicaea in 325 Eusebius of Caesarea tells us that he produced the creed which he had been taught in his youth in Caesarea in

Palestine, and it is not an interrogatory baptismal creed in the form of question and answer, but a single statement, beginning, 'We believe'.[8] But whether we accept Eusebius' account of his creed as accurate in all its details or not, it is certain that the Council of Nicaea did adopt a formula of faith in the form of a declaratory creed, not in an interrogatory form, beginning 'We believe', and that it deliberately introduced into this creed a number of expressions, of which the best known is the term ὁμοούσιον τῷ πατρί applied to the Son, intended to act as a formula to test orthodoxy and presumably to be repeated without variation thenceforward. Dogma was now expressed in an invariable formula. This was a new experience for the Church and it opened a new era in its history. We shall for the rest of this essay consider the attitude to this phenomenon of some of the leading minds in the Church in the fourth and early fifth centuries.

Perhaps we should first notice that the Council of Nicaea did not succeed in its main object, which was presumably to settle a controversy by means of a formula. The controversy continued for more than fifty years. Many scholars have observed that during the opening stages of the controversy it almost looks as if the Nicene Creed had been forgotten. Nobody refers to it until early in the fifth decade of the fourth century moves are made to produce an alternative creed, moves which meet a surprising amount of support in the East. It is not to be thought that we can attribute the support given to the 'Dedication' Creed of Antioch of 341, and to several of its successors, purely to the machinations of politically-minded Arian ecclesiastics. However, it is obvious that the attempt to find an alternative formula did not succeed, and when this attempt was overtaken, in what might be called the intermediate stage of the controversy, between 357 and 362, by the attempt to reach agreement upon evading a testing formula, this enterprise did

---

[8] See J. N. D. Kelly, Early Christian Creeds, pp. 39–52, 88, 95; H. J. Carpenter, 'Creeds and Baptismal Rites in the First Four Centuries', Journal of Theological Studies 44 (1943), pp. 1–11; R. P. C Hanson, Tradition in the Early Church, pp. 69, 74, 82, 83. Eusebius' creed is to be found in Socrates, Ecclesiastical History, 1.8; it is a more elaborately doctrinal creed than any known before it.

not succeed either. It is difficult to determine with confidence the springs and motives of the Arian controversy, but we may reasonably conclude that by the time the Emperor Theodosius came to power in the Eastern Empire, most responsible Christians had come to the conclusion, after nearly sixty years of debate and vicissitude, of trial and error, that the formulae enshrined in the Creed of 325 were the best expression of the Church's doctrine of God and best declared what the Church believed. But it is worth noting that the Council of Constantinople of 381, in drawing up a creed which is usually reckoned as having settled the Arian controversy, did not exactly reproduce the Creed of 325; in fact the Council took as its basis a different creed, though they reproduced the controversial testing formulae of 325. This does not suggest a passionate addiction to formulae, rather perhaps a recognition that formulae have their uses in maintaining the true faith.

Certainly some of the leading minds between the years 330 and 430 took a cautious and minimizing attitude towards the formation of the Nicene dogma. Athanasius, the great champion of the Nicene doctrine, has certainly no idea that he is laying the foundation of a vast development of dogma. The Arians of his day constantly contended that the pro-Nicene party were anxious to involve the historic faith in complicated and unnecessary dogmatic subtleties, and Athanasius, instead of replying 'A formidable superstructure of dogma is necessary', invariably argued that the Nicene formulae did not complicate the faith but merely safeguarded the original meaning of the faith. He calls the term *homoousion* 'a rampart against every unorthodox interpretation'.[9] He declares that the fathers of Nicaea knew well both Scripture and the views of the earlier fathers, but 'they rightly wrote in this way (*i.e.*, in the Creed of Nicaea) so that those who examined the writings of others (*i.e.*, previous authors) should be able to recall by their means orthodox belief in Christ as it is proclaimed in the divine Scriptures'.[10] Basil of Caesarea was a great supporter of the

---

[9] De Synodis, 45: ἐπιτείχισμα κατὰ πάσης ἀσεβοῦς ἐπινοίας.

[10] De Synodis, 6: ἀλλὰ καὶ ἔγραψαν οὕτω καλῶς, ὥστε τοὺς γνησίως ἐντυγχάνοντας τοῖς ἐκείνων γράμμασιν δύνασθαι παρ' αὐτῶν

divinity of the Holy Spirit, but he was not at all anxious to create dogma for the sake of creating dogma. He wanted only to add to the Nicene Creed a formula on the Holy Spirit because the status of the Spirit in the Godhead was in dispute in his own day; it had not been a matter of controversy when the Nicene Creed was drawn up, and hence in that creed the Spirit had been passed over cursorily. But Basil did not want to involve himself in any project for adding to the creed in order to exclude Apollinarianism, little though he favoured that deviation.[11] According to his brother Gregory of Nyssa, to Basil the Nicene Creed was something accepted in a general council as interpreting ambiguities (ἀμφιβολίας) concerning the faith (περὶ τοῦ δόγματος) at various crises (κατὰ καιρούς τινας) and handed down in the churches as written traditions (παραδόσεις ἔγγραφοι).[12] For Gregory of Nyssa himself the Nicene dogma is also something inherited from the past to be maintained; 'It is sufficient to demonstrate our argument', he says, 'that the tradition has come to us from the Fathers handed down like an inheritance in continuity from the apostles through the holy men who succeeded them'.[13] He seems to think that before Nicaea traditional doctrines implicitly handed down the *homoousion*.[14] It should be noted also that Gregory of Nyssa, like most of the theologians of the second half of the fourth century, was aware of the danger incident to the formation of dogma of transposing biblical language into purely Greek philosophical terms. In his great writings against Eunomius he is facing an adversary who has no qualms at all about this danger. Eunomius will readily plunge into a sea of technical philosophical language to expound his doctrine of the Trinity, whether it is energies reacting upon each other[15] or the

ὑπομιμνήσκεσθαι τὴν ἐν ταῖς θείαις γραφαῖς καταγγελλομένην εἰς Χριστὸν εὐσέβειαν.

[11] Basil, Letters (ed. Y. Courtonne), cxxv 3.1–49; cclviii 2.

[12] Gregory of Nyssa, Contra Eunomium (ed. Jaeger), I, 158.

[13] Gregory of Nyssa, III (II), 98: ἀρκεῖ γὰρ εἰς ἀπόδειξιν τοῦ ἡμετέρου λόγου τὸ πατρόθεν ἥκειν πρὸς ἡμᾶς τὴν παράδοσιν, οἷόν τινα κλῆρον δι' ἀκολουθίας ἐκ τῶν ἀποστόλων διὰ τῶν ἐφεξῆς ἁγίων παραπεμφθέντα.

[14] *Ibid.*, III (II), 112.

[15] *Ibid.*, I, 223.

inseparability of *prosegoria* and *ousia*,[16] or the relation of ingenerateness to substance.[17] Gregory protests more than once against this habit,[18] and at one point ironically bursts out, 'Just look at his dialectical demonstration! With what technical perfection his argument progresses towards its target!'[19] If we are to decide which of these two controversialists is dedicated to a Hellenization of Christianity in the course of developing doctrine there can be no uncertainty; it is Eunomius. It is notorious how reluctant Augustine was to plunge into dogmatic definitions about the Trinity, and we shall revert to this later. He recognises with the others that Trinitarian terms are only justified as a defence against error. 'What can we do therefore', he says, 'except confess that these terms were produced by the need to speak when an elaborate controversy was required against the wiles or errors of the heretics?'[20] Vincent of Lérins, who had had more opportunity to meditate upon the development of dogma than any of the others just quoted, expresses the Fathers' attitude to dogma magisterially when he writes:

In short (the Catholic Church) attempted nothing else in the decrees of councils except that the same doctrine which had previously been believed in simply should be believed in more carefully; that what had previously been preached more loosely should henceforward be preached more strictly; that what had previously been worshipped more unreflectingly should henceforward be worshipped with greater attention ... that what it had received before from our forefathers by tradition alone it should then later register through the record of writing, by summarizing in a few letters a great amount of material, and often for the sake of illuminating the understanding by marking

---

[16] *Ibid.*, III (V), 18.

[17] *Ibid.*, III, 67.

[18] *Ibid.*, 188–9; III, 67.

[19] *Ibid.*, II, 306: βαβαὶ τῆς διαλεκτικῆς ἀποδείξεως, ὡς τεχνικῶς ὁ λόγος αὐτῷ πρὸς τὸν σκόπον συμπεραίνεται.

[20] Augustine, *De Trinitate*, 7, 4, 9: *quid igitur restat, nisi ut fateamur loquendi necessitate parta haec vocabula cum opus esset copiosa disputatione adversus insidias vel errores haereticorum?*

the meaning of the faith which is not new by the appropriate use of new vocabulary.[21]

It seems clear that during the period when the dogma of the Trinity was reaching its final expression and finding formulae for that expression which were to become traditional, some of the best minds which assisted that process were well aware of the danger of smothering the faith in technical philosophical language and placing a distance between the language of the Bible and the language of the Church's doctrine. This problem raised itself in a peculiar way during the Arian controversy because the Arians' manner of conducting that controversy caused those who were defending the Nicene doctrine to examine the whole question of how we can use language about God at all. The Arians had inherited from somewhere in their intellectual ancestry a conviction that we must accept the words of Scripture at their face value and were distrustful of allegory or any tendency to explain away the meaning of the text. They insisted that the statement of the Bible about the Son of God must be taken directly, unequivocally, as far as possible literally. If the Bible called Jesus Christ the Son of God then there must somehow follow for his situation the consequences which normally follow for sons in situations known to us; he must have been at one point non-existent, at another existent, and so on. If the fourth Gospel calls the Son 'only-begotten' then there must follow for him all the consequences of being begotten, *e.g.* that he should be later in time than the Father who begat him. When Solomon at Prov 8.22 apparently said that God created Wisdom, this could only mean that the Father created the Son; when at Amos 5.13 the prophet describes God as 'he who creates the Spirit', this could only mean that the Father—or possibly the

---

[21] Vincent of Lérins, Commonitorium (ed. R. S. Moxon), xxiii (32), 95: *denique quod umquam aliud conciliorum decretis enisa est, nisi ut quod antea simpliciter credebatur hoc idem diligentius crederetur; quod antea lentius praedicabatur hoc idem postea instantius praedicaretur; quod antea securius colebatur hoc idem postea sollicitius excoleretur . . . ut quod prius a maioribus sola traditione susceperat hoc deinde posterius etiam per scripturae chirographum consignaret, magnum rerum summam paucis litteris comprehendendo, et plerumque propter intellegentiae lucem non novum fidei sensum novae adpellationis proprietate signando. Cf.* xxix (41), 120.

Son acting for the Father—created the Holy Spirit.

This kind of argument troubled the pro-Nicene theologians. It was not the crude literalism such as Origen had occasionally encountered in the third century. It was an appeal to the Scriptures, to what looked like the plain sense of text, which they found difficult and embarrassing to counter. We can see them groping towards an answer and gradually finding one. It is, we must allow, the right answer, but it is not one that permits us to put great confidence in the unalterable validity of formulae for expressing dogma. It replies to this difficult argument by pointing out, in the first place, the inadequacy of all language about God, and in the second the equivocal and analogous nature of any language about God.

In illustrating what the Fathers said about the inadequacy of language about God I am not touching upon the allied question of their ideas concerning our knowledge of God, and in particular the concept which can be abundantly illustrated from the fourth century Greek Fathers that we can know God's activity (ἐνεργείαι) but not his essence (οὐσία). This is a question which has caused no little debate in our own day, and I am not going to introduce it here, however interesting it may be. It is Athanasius who first becomes conscious of the fact that the Arian controversy raises the whole question of our language about God, and it is only at a relatively late stage in the debate that this conclusion dawns upon him. In his *Letter to the Monks* prefixed to his *History of the Arians* he says 'I could not even express in writing what I thought I was thinking; indeed what I was writing was less than even the briefest shadow of the truth which was in my mind'.[22] And he goes on to say that though it is not possible for us to know what God is, we can know what he is not, and can see that heretical accounts of the status of the Son of God are false.[23] In his *Letters to Serapion on the Holy Spirit* he declares that after a certain point speculation about the Godhead is futile; the cherubim cover with their wings.[24] Basil of

---

[22] Athanasius, Hist. Arianorum, 1: καὶ γὰρ οὐδὲ ὃ ἐδόκουν νοεῖν, ἠδυνάμην γράφειν ἀλλὰ, καὶ ὃ ἔγραφον ἔλαττον ἐγίνετο τῆς ἐν τῇ

[23] *Ibid.*, 2.

[24] Letters to Serapion, 1, 17, 18.

Caesarea is even more vividly aware of the limitations of language about God: 'All theological utterance', he says in one of his letters, 'is less than the thought of him who speaks it, and less than the intention of him who is conducting the discussion, because language is somehow inadequate to represent our thoughts'.[25] Elsewhere he reminds his readers that the divine writers only speak of God in metaphors and symbolic language (τροπολογίαις καὶ ἀλληγορίαις), and in images which are often contradictory when taken literally,[26] and that if we believe only in that which can be fully expressed in words the Christian faith and the Christian hope have vanished.[27] Hilary of Poitiers uses much the same language: 'Every analogy, therefore, must be thought useful to man rather than suitable to God'.[28] God is beyond all description in language and makes nonsense and contradiction of language: 'Perfect knowledge is, so to know God that you may know him to be, though not unknowable, still indescribable'.[29] It is impossible to conceive of God clearly, says Gregory of Nazianzus, far more to speak of him[30]: even notions like 'light' and 'love' and 'righteousness' are bound up with our existence in space and time which we find it impossible to eliminate when we try to think directly of God. Even if we put a number of images together we are trying to understand something that is simple by means of something that is composite.[31] We can only faintly conceive of God, we cannot name him: 'Faintly sketching God's character from what is known about him, we gather a dim and weak and patchwork

---

[25] Basil, Letters, vii 44: πᾶσα θεολογικὴ φωνὴ ἐλάττων μέν ἐστι τῆς διανοίας τοῦ λέγοντος, ἐλάττων δὲ τῆς ἐπιζητοῦντος ἐπιθυμίας, διότι ὁ λόγος ἀσθενέστερόν πως πέφυκε διακονεῖσθαι τοῖς νοουμένοις.

[26] Adversus Eunomium, 1.14 (P.G., 29.544/545).

[27] Ibid., 2.24 (P.G. 29.628).

[28] Hilary, De Trinitate, 1.19: Omnis igitur comparatio homini potius utilis habeatur quam Deo apta.

[29] Ibid., 2.7: perfecta scientia est sic deum scire ut licet non ignorabilem tamen inenarrabilem scias.

[30] Gregory of Nazianzus, Theological Orations (ed. A. J. Mason, 1899), V, 4: ἀλλὰ φράσαι μὲν ἀδύνατον, ὡς ὁ ἐμὸς λόγος, νοῆσαι δὲ ἀδυνατώτερον.

[31] Ibid., II, 13.

conception'.[32] Gregory of Nyssa echoes the sentiment that it is otiose to name God.[33] He objects to Eunomius' rationalist assertion that everything concerning God can easily be known by anyone and that nothing is beyond expression.[34] Gregory believes, of course, as do all the Fathers, that we know God sufficiently to be saved[35], but he states expressively that 'what the hollow of the hand is compared with the whole sea, that is what any capacity of words is compared with this inexpressible and incomprehensible Nature'.[36] Augustine has much the same feeling of helplessness when he comes to articulate the doctrine of the Trinity:

> At the outset we are undertaking to speak of subjects which cannot by any means be stated as they are thought either by anybody, or certainly by us, even though this thought of ours itself when we consider God as Trinity feels itself very far from equal to that which it is considering.[37]

And later he has the famous sentence:

> However when the question is asked, 'What are the three?', human speech, immediately suffers from a great incapacity. Still it has been said, 'three Persons', not in order to make this statement but to avoid saying nothing.[38]

and after a disquisition on the different ways of saying

---

[32] Gregory of Nazianzus, IV. 17: ἐκ τῶν περὶ αὐτὸν σκιαγραφοῦντες τὰ κατ' αὐτὸν, ἀμυδράν τινα καὶ ἀσθενῆ καὶ ἄλλην ἀπ'ἄλλου φαντασίαν συλλέγομεν.

[33] Gregory of Nyssa, Contra Eunomium, II, 149.

[34] Ibid., I, 460–461. It is worth noting also that Gregory objects to Eunomius' naive and literalistic handling of early passages in Genesis (e.g., Gen 1.3ff.) and laughs at his lack of sophistication here, Ibid., II, 205, 212.

[35] E.g., ibid., III (viii), 7–12.

[36] Ibid., III (v) 55: ὃ γάρ ἐστι χειρὸς κοτύλη πρὸς πέλαγος ὅλον, τοῦτο πᾶσα δύναμις λόγων πρὸς τὴν ἄφραστόν τε καὶ ἀπερίληπτον φύσιν.

[37] Augustine, De Trinitate, 5. 1. 1: Hine iam exordiens ea dicere quae dici ut cogitantur vel ab homine aliquo vel certe a nobis non omnia modo possunt: quamvis et ipsa nostra cogitatio, cum de deo trinitate cogitamus, longe se ille de quo cogitat imparem sentiat.

[38] Augustine, De Trinitate, 5. 9. 10: Tamen cum quaeritur quid tres, magna prorsus inopia humanum laborat eloquium. Dictum est tamen tres personae non ut illud diceretur sed ne taceretur.

'substance' and 'person' in Latin and Greek—*loquendi causa de ineffabilibus ut fari aliquo modo possemus*—he declares that finding a name for these three is really beyond human capacity and he echoes the old conviction 'because the transcendence of the Godhead outstrips the power of normal speech. For God is conceived of more truly than spoken of and exists more truly than he is conceived of'.[39]

This conviction of the inadequacy of language to convey the reality of God often develops into a rather more detailed discussion of the analogous and equivocal nature of the language which we use about God. Athanasius realises that in the matter of fatherhood God is not like man; he is Father without being also Son and Son without being also Father[40], and he grasps that the Arians make a wrong use of analogy.[41] 'It is not right', he says, 'to measure generation from God by man's nature'.[42] Hilary of Poitiers understands that there is a point at which the human analogy of fatherhood breaks down: 'Where one person comes from another and God is born from God, earthly birth can bring an understanding of its meaning to some extent'. But the analogy breaks down at *coitus, conceptus, tempus, partus*, because 'when God is born of God no other meaning should be accepted than "born" '.[43] Hilary even warns against pressing too far the analogy of fire produced from fire.[44] Basil is even more aware of this problem. He warns us that when we use the expression 'to know God' the word 'know' is multivocal (πολύσημον).[45] There is nothing wrong, he thinks, in using earthly and humble analogies for our understanding of God as

[39] *Ibid.*, 7, 4, 7: the last quotation runs: *quia excedit supereminentia divinitatis usitati eloquii facultatem. Verius enim cogitatur Deus quam dicitur et verius est quam cogitatur.*

[40] Orat. contra Arianos, I, 20.

[41] *Ibid.*, I, 22, 23.

[42] *Ibid.*, I, 26.

[43] De Trinitate, 5.37; the passages translated here run: *ubi enim unus ex uno est et Deus natus ex Deo est, affert tantum significationis intelligentiam terrena nativitas,* and *cum Deus ex Deo natus nihil aliud intelligendus sit esse quam natus. Cf.,* 7.28.

[44] *Ibid.*, 7.28, 30: *Non utique ut aliquod naturae Dei satisfaceret comparationis exemplum.*

[45] Letters, cxxxiv. 1.

long as we apply them with caution.[46] The analogy of human fatherhood involves unlikeness as well as likeness.[47] And in a much more detailed statement, he writes:

> I beg you to accept my analogy as a copy and shadow of the truth, not as the actual truth of the matter itself: for it is not possible for that which is considered in analogies in all respects to fit that for which the necessity for analogies is accepted.[48]

Gregory of Nazianzus, as might be expected, presents the same argument with greater sophistication.[49] The Arians produce the objection that if we say that the Son is generated or even created then we have to do with passibility (πάθος) and with time (χρόνος), for all our experience of any sort involves these, even the generation of thought.[50] Gregory answers this by saying that God's creation by the Word is manifestly different from our thinking of it. If this were not so, when anyone thought of a city he would thereby build it. Consequently man creates in one mode but God in another. And if God creates differently then he begets differently. The generation of the Son is clearly different from human generation: the Son was not at one time in the Father and then begotten from him, nor at one time complete and then incomplete. Gregory of Nyssa goes into the subject much more fully and comes closer to defining what is left when we have removed the wrong associations involved in the analogical use of language. There is, he declares, no analogy between human life and the divine life, it is impossible for the human mind to conceive or grasp that which is beyond time and createdness for it has nothing to measure itself by.[51] He warns the reader that the words of Prov 8.22 do not constitute a

---

[46] Adv. Eunomium, II, 24 (P.G. 29. 621).

[47] Letters, li. 3. 1–4.

[48] Ibid., xxxviii. 5.1–5 καί μου δέξασθε τὸν λόγον ὡς ὑπόδειγμα καὶ σκιὰν ἀληθείας, οὐχ ὡς αὐτὴν τὴν τῶν πραγμάτων ἀλήθειαν· οὐ γὰρ δυνατόν ἐστι διὰ πάντων ἐφαρμοσθῆναι τὸ ἐν τοῖς ὑποδείγμασι θεωρούμενον τοῖς πρὸς ἅ ἡ τῶν ὑποδειγμάτων χρεία παραλαμβάνεται.

[49] Orations, IX (P.G. 35. 1076).

[50] Gregory uses the phrase ἡ τοῦ νοηθέντος ἀθρόως εἰς τὸ κατὰ μέρος ἐξάπλωσις, 'the successive and continuous articulation of that which is thought'.

[51] Contra Eunomium, I, 365.

straightforward statement, but are parabolic and enigmatic.[52] The word used about God and about men may be the same, but this identity hides an important difference. The word 'Father' applied to human nature and to the divine nature conceals an alteration of meaning.[53] We speak analogically about God, giving a higher meaning to the words which we use about him.[54]

It is not enough to say that the term 'Son' as used of the Word in the Bible is metaphorical (as Eunomius is in some sense willing to admit); the term is used to convey something deeper, vaster, grander, diviner than ordinary sonship.[55] When God in Scripture uses the term 'Son' he does so in order to assist us and accommodating himself to our understanding, and he uses it without condition or qualification or explanation, not assuming distance or material or such things. The only common element between the divine Son and human sons is the concept of nature (φύσις).[56] Similarly in calling God 'Father' we must abandon all the undesirable attributes of the word; not only must all corporeal association be purged, but also anything suggesting a difference or interval between Father and Son; all that is left is sonship (γνησιότης).[57] So too the concept of origin (γένεσις) must be purged of all corporeal or spatial assocations when applied to the Son, leaving only nature (φύσις). Even more refined images such as 'material emanation', 'reflection of glory' and 'scent of myrrh' and 'vapour of God' are only analogies and involve matter and must not be misunderstood.[58] Elsewhere Gregory of Nyssa repeats the last three of these examples and reminds his readers that they only serve to convey the truth that the Son 'must be thought of as identically from him (*i.e.*, the Father) and with him'. And finally, God graciously added two

[52] *Ibid.*, III (i), 21–26.

[53] *Ibid.*, I, 622.

[54] *Ibid.*, III (vi), 32.

[55] *Ibid.*, III, 131–134 and 135–138.

[56] Refutatio Confessionis Eunomii (ed. Jaeger), 91–96.

[57] Contra Eunomium, III, 77.

[58] *Ibid.*, III (vi.), 35–39; the phrases quoted are ὑλικὴ ἀπορροία, ἀπαύγασμα δόξης, ὀσμὴ μύρου, ἀτμὶς θεοῦ. See Heb 1.3; John 12.3 and Wisd. 7.25.

more images to refine and correct the others, Word (λόγος
John 1.4) and Mind (νοῦς, presumably 1 Cor 2.16).[59] Few
theologians of the fourth century can rival Gregory of Nyssa in
the care which he gives to this difficult subject.[60]

When therefore we examine the Fathers whom we have
already considered in order to discover how far they insisted
upon formulae in their defence of the Nicene faith, we shall not
be surprised to find that their attitude is flexible. We can detect
no hint of doctrinaire rigidity in it. Athanasius gives the
impression that he is fighting for a doctrine much more than
that he is fighting for a formula. Of course there are many places
where Athanasius insists upon the *homoousion* and refuses even
the *homoiousion* as an alternative; we have quoted one already.[61]
But in all the first three books of his *Orationes Contra Arianos* he
does not mention the *homoousion* (the fourth book, which does
treat of the word, is generally reckoned not to come from the
pen of Athanasius), and in this work he does commend the term
εἰκὼν ἀπαράλλακτος, an expression which was borrowed
from Origen and which had been used not long before
Athanasius was writing in the 'Dedication' Creed of Antioch
(341).[62]

Similarly, Basil of Caesarea will defend the application of the
homoousios to the Son[63] and to the Holy Trinity,[64] and according
to his brother Gregory of Nyssa he refused to abandon the term
when pressed to do so by an emissary from the Emperor Valens
himself.[65] But he is reluctant to apply this adjective to the Holy

---

[59] Refut. Cont. Eunom. 91–96; the words quoted run τὸ δεῖν ἐξ αὐτοῦ τε
καὶ μετ' αὐτοῦ κατὰ ταὐτὸν νοεῖσθαι.

[60] Certainly Augustine cannot rival him. In his De Trinitate he speaks much
of *vestigia trinitatis in creatura* but scarcely considers the subject of the analogous
nature of our language about God. At one point indeed he treats of it, but with
a curiously uncertain touch, *hoc et de bonitate et de aeternitate et de omnipotentia
Dei dictum sit, omnibusque omnino praedicamentis quae de Deo possunt pronuntiari,
quod ad se ipsum dicitur, non translate ac per similitudinem, sed proprie; si tamen de
illo proprie aliquod dici ore hominis potest; 5.10.11.*

[61] De Synodis, 45; see above p. 303.

[62] Orat. Contra Arianos, II, 33; III, 5 and 11.

[63] Letters, li. 1.24–27 and xc. 2.19–24.

[64] De Fide, 4 (P.G. 31, 688).

[65] Gregory of Nyssa, Contra Eunomium, I, 135–137.

Spirit, however deeply he believes in the divinity of the Spirit.[66] And in one of his early letters, written about 361, he agrees that he could accept the formula ὅμοιον κατ᾽ οὐσίαν provided that the adverb ἀπαραλλάκτως is added to it, because he thinks the expression equivalent to ὁμοούσιον.[67]

Gregory of Nazianzus was, of course, one of the most stalwart defenders of the Nicene dogma, not least in his *Orations*, and during his short tenure of the see of Constantinople he suffered for his convictions. But he is also the most candid of all the Fathers considered here about disavowing rigid addiction to formulae. Gregory can attack the Councils of Seleucia and Constantinople (359 and 360) on the grounds that they opened a door to assail the *homoousion* and in its place offered a formula of deliberate vagueness (μεσότης, ambiguity), a formula which was a statue facing in all directions, a boot to fit either foot.[68] But in the same work he can give a careful account of wrong interpretations of the doctrine of the Trinity, followed by a summary of the doctrine without once mentioning the word *homoousios*,[69] and his own theological vocabulary is fairly fluid. As has been recently observed by J. Daniélou,[70] Gregory, as an outstanding man of literature himself, did not take kindly either to the atmosphere or the jargon of theological controversy. Like his friend Basil, he appears deliberately to refrain from applying *homoousios* to the Spirit,[71] he can use φύσις of the individual characteristic of the Father and of the single Godhead of the Trinity in the same sentence;[72] and he says of the choice of ὑποστάσεις or πρόσωπα to describe the Persons, 'we shall not make nice

[66] For instance when he gives a formal statement to Eustathius of Sebaste of his doctrine of the Holy Spirit Basil does not use the adjective *homoousios* (Letters, ccxxvi. 3), and in another letter he writes πιστεύω εἰς θεὸν πατέρα and εἰς θεὸν υἱόν, but εἰς τὸ θεῖον (not θεόν) πνεῦμα τὸ ἅγιον (CCXXXVI. 6).

[67] Letters, ix. 3.1–18.

[68] Orations, XXII (xxii) (P.G. 35. 1108).

[69] Ibid., XX (vi) (P.G. 35. 1072).

[70] The Pelican Guide to Modern Theology, ed. R. P. C. Hanson, Vol II, pp. 98–99.

[71] Orations, XXXII (v) (P.G. 35. 180).

[72] Ibid., XXXII (xxi) (P.G. 35. 197).

distinctions about words as long as the syllables come to the same meaning.[73] The most striking example of this undoctrinaire attitude towards formulae is to be found in one of Gregory's letters. This is one written by Gregory to his friend Basil while Basil was bishop of Cappadocian Caesarea. It describes the reply which Gregory made during an after-dinner discussion with a friend. The friend challenged Gregory to defend the refusal of Basil directly to call the Holy Spirit 'God'. Gregory defended Basil on the ground that Basil, as bishop of Caesarea, had a responsibility to the whole church to see that he says nothing that might lead to his expulsion from his see (presumably by Imperial order), and so to the ruin of the orthodox cause. Obviously both Gregory and Basil believed in the full divinity of the Spirit, but Gregory takes this opportunity to say plainly that dogmas are not a matter of mere formulae. 'There is no harm', he says, 'in our saying in effect that the Spirit is God, even if we use other terms (for truth does not lie in sound but rather in meaning)'.[74] Gregory of Nyssa also played a valiant part in defending the *homoousios*, what at one point he called 'this ridiculed doctrine' (τὸ καταχλευαζόμενον δόγμα)[75] against Eunomius, but he too can express a very flexible attitude to formulae. He declares this in a passage which is worth quoting:

> Since then it is orthodox to believe that he who is the cause of everything does not himself have any underlying cause, once this has been fixed in the mind, what further controversy about words does there remain for sensible men, because every word by which such a concept is expressed comes to the same thing? Whether you say he is beginning and origin of everything or declare that he is unoriginate or that he exists ingenerately or subsists from eternity or is the cause of everything or alone has no cause, all these expressions are virtually equivalent to each other

---

[73] *Ibid.*, XXXIX (ii) (P.G. 35. 336): οὐδὲν γὰρ περὶ τῶν ὀνομάτων ζυγομαχήσομεν ἕως ἂν πρὸς τὴν αὐτὴν ἔννοιαν αἱ συλλαβαὶ φέρωσιν.

[74] Letters (ed. P. Gallay), lviii. 9, 10, 11: the quotation is from 11 and runs ἡμῖν γὰρ οὐδὲν βλάβος καὶ ἀπ'ἄλλων λέξεων τοῦτο συναγουσῶν θεὸν τὸ πνεῦμα γινσώκειν (οὐ γὰρ ἐν ἤχῳ μᾶλλον ἢ διανοίᾳ κεῖσθαι τὴν ἀληθείαν).

[75] Contra Eunomium, III (v), 18.

as far as the force of the things signified goes and the words have
the same value, and it is futile to dispute subtly about one kind of
vocal utterance or another, as if orthodoxy consisted in syllables
and sounds and not in meaning.[76]

One other point should be noted in connection with this
consideration of dogma and formula in the Fathers. Many
Fathers do emphasize very strongly the baptismal formula as
something to be preserved inviolate and appear to attribute to it
an almost magical or incantatory value, especially Basil in his *De
Spiritu Sancto*.[77] Those theologians who are concerned towards
the end of the Arian controversy to maintain the full Godhead
of the Holy Spirit very often appeal to the baptismal formula.
But this is not precisely an appeal to a formula as unalterably
enshrining dogma. It is a conservative-minded appeal to an
ancient form of words handed down by tradition and usually
ascribed to the Lord himself as evidence for dogma. An almost
superstitious reverence for the formula of baptism was no new
phenomenon in the Church. We can find the same reverence in
as rationalist-minded a theologian as Origen. But this is not the
same as a rigid and doctrinaire approach to doctrinal formulae.
The difference is usefully illustrated in one passage in the *Contra
Eunomium* of Gregory of Nyssa. Eunomius *does* take a
doctrinaire approach to doctrine; he has the rationalist's
unlimited confidence in verbal definition. What matters
supremely to him, he tells us himself in a passage from his works
quoted by Gregory, is not fine-sounding titles nor customs nor
mystic symbols but accuracy of doctrine (τῇ τῶν δογμάτων

---

[76] Contra Eunomium, II, 137: ἐπειδὴ τοίνυν εὐσεβές ἐστι λογίζεσθαι
τὸν τοῦ παντὸς αἴτιον αἰτίαν ὑπερκειμένην μὴ ἔχειν, ταύτης ἡμῖν
ἐρηρεισμένως τῆς διανοίας μενούσης τις ἔτι περὶ τὰ ῥήματα τοῖς νοῦν
ἔχουσιν καταλείπεται μάχη, πάσης φωνῆς, καθ'ἣν τὸ τοιοῦτον
ἐξαγγέλλεται νόημα, τὸ αὐτὸ παριστώσης; εἴτε γὰρ ἀρχὴν αὐτὸν καὶ
αἴτιον τοῦ πάντος εἶναι λέγοις εἴτε ἄναρχον αὐτὸν ὀνομάζοις εἴτε
ἀγεννήτως εἶναι εἴτε ἐξ ἀϊδίου ὑφεστάναι εἴτε τοῦ παντὸς αἴτιον εἴτε ἐξ
οὐδενὸς αἰτίου μόνον, πάντα τὰ τοιαῦτα ἰσοστάσιά πως ἀλλήλοις ἐστὶ
κατὰ τὴν δύναμιν τῶν σημαινομένων, καὶ ὁμοτίμως ἔχει τὰ ῥήματα, καὶ
μάταιος ὁ ζυγομαχῶν περὶ τὸν τοιόνδε τῆς φωνῆς ἦχον, ὡς οὐχὶ τῇ
διανοίᾳ ταῖς δὲ συλλαβαῖς καὶ τοῖς φθόγγοις ἐγκειμένης τῆς εὐσεβείας.

[77] De Spiritu Sancto (ed. Pruche), X, 26.113 a–c & XII, 28.117a; *cf.* Letters
clxxxviii. 1, 41, 42. Compare also Athanasius, Letters to Serapion, 1.28–30.

ἀκριβείᾳ).[78] Gregory in reply asserts strongly the importance of traditional litergy and sacraments (which are in fact the subject of the contention), and in particular the confession of the Triple Name, and says boldly that doctrines may be of no use. He has known some people who have often attained the truth but have still remained alienated from faith; he apparently means intellectual pagans.[79] He is here contrasting participation in the life and worship of the Church with the bare formal acceptance of doctrine, to the disadvantage of the latter.

This brief survey of the period when the most venerable and earliest dogmas of the Church were reaching their final form, therefore, suggests that the theologians who were most responsible for fixing these dogmas in their traditional form had an undoctrinaire and flexible attitude to formulae, were well aware of the inadequacy and limitations of language in expressing propositions about God, and were more concerned with the doctrine expressed by the language than the language itself; what interested them was not the formula expressing the dogma but what might be called the shape of the dogma itself, as we can say there is a shape of the dogmas of the Trinity and of the Incarnation apart from any particular expression of them in words.

These theologians lived and worked at the beginning of the history of the development of dogma, during what might be called the Golden Age of Patristic thought. Cardinal J. Daniélou, in an essay already quoted, has suggested that this Golden Age ends with the fourth century and that the theologians of the fifth century, able men though many of them were, represent a less spontaneously fruitful and creative period, for Eastern and Greek theology at any rate.[80] Perhaps we can see the same tendency illustrated in the increasing interest in formulae, in the exact definition of doctrinal niceties, which the fifth century witnesses in the East. This is evidenced by the careful construction of an eirenic formula (δύο γὰρ φύσεων ἕνωσις γέγονε, in Cyril of Alexandria's letter to John of

---

[78] Contra Eunomiu, III (ix), 54.
[79] Ibid., 55–60.
[80] Op. cit., Cap. 7, pp. 104–115.

Antioch in 433, the *Laetentur Caeli*. We can see it also in the much more elaborate formula produced by the Council of Chalcedon in 451, a formula which we cannot but respect for its combination of subtlety and solidity, but which can hardly be said to have settled the dispute with which it deals, even to this day, and which gives modern theologians considerable trouble just because it is at once so expansive and so magisterial. And we can see the same characteristic in the West in the production later in the century of the 'Athanasian' Creed, a formula which is in many ways admirable in its lapidary conciseness, but which has apparently given way to the error of thinking that gaining heaven or being relegated to hell depends upon the acceptance or rejection of theological formulae. This is an error into which the Fathers of the fourth century would not have fallen. We, standing at a point where most Christian theologians seem more inclined to criticize and modify the long doctrinal development which unrolls behind them than add to it by articulating further dogma, may perhaps gain encouragement from contemplating the experience of these great men of the fourth century.

14

THE RULE OF FAITH OF VICTORINUS AND OF PATRICK

I

The resemblances between the doctrinal formulae in Victorinus of Pettau, *Commentary on the Apocalypse*, chapter II, and in Patrick, *Confession*, chapter 4, have long been noticed.[1] For ease of reference it is convenient to set out both formulae in parallel columns:

VICTORINUS[2]

[4]*'mensura'* autem *fidei est mandatum*/[5] *domini nostri, confiteri omnipotentem, ut didicimus*/[6] *et huius filium dominum nostrum Iesum Christum ante ori*/[7] *ginem saeculi spiritaliter apud patrem genitum, factum homi*/[8] *nem, et morte devicta in caelis cum corpore a patre receptum,*/[9] *sanctum dominum et pignus immortalitatis, hunc per prophetas*/[10] *praedicatum, hunc per· legem conscriptum, hunc per manum dei et*/[11] *per verbum patris omnipotentis et conditorem orbis*

PATRICK[3]

quia non est alius Deus nec umquam fuit nec erit post haec praeter Deum patrem ingenitum, sine principio, a quo est omne principium, omnia tenentem, ut didicimus; **et huius filium Iesum Christum,** *quem cum patre scilicet semper fuisse testamur,* **ante originem saeculi spiritaliter apud patrem** <*et*> *inerrabiliter* **genitum,** *ante omne principium, et per ipsum facta sunt visibilia et invisibilia,* **hominem factum, morte devicta in caelis ad patrem**

---

[1] First apparently by A. Hahn. A bibliography of this subject must include: *Victorini Episcopi Petavionensis Opera*, ed. J. Haussleiter (C.S.E.L. XXXXIX, Vienna, 1916); also review in *Göttingische Gelehrte Anzeigen* 160. Jahrgang, Bd. 1 (Berlin, 1898), pp. 369–371; E. Kattenbusch, *Das Apostolische Symbol*, Vol. 1 (Leipzig, 1894), pp. 188, 212–214, 395; E. Norden, *Agnostos Theos* (Stuttgart, 1956, repr. of ed. of 1923), pp. 263–276; J. E. L. Oulton, *The Credal Statements of St. Patrick*, (Dublin, 1940); L. Bieler, 'The "creeds" of St. Victorinus and St. Patrick', *Theological Studies* 9 (1949), pp. 121–124; R. P. C. Hanson, 'Patrick and the *Mensura Fidei*', *Studia Patristica X* (ed. F. L. Cross, Berlin, 1970), pp. 109–111, an article of which this is a correction and an enlargement.

[2] Haussleiter's ed., p. 96. In future this edition will be referred to as *H*, with page and line given. Patrick's scriptural quotations are indicated in roman type, his reproductions of Victorinus in bold type.

[3] L. Bieler, *Libri Epistolarum Sancti Patricii Episcopi* (Dublin, 1952), pp. 58, 59.

totius mundi/,[(12)] *haec est arundo et mensura fidei, ut nemo adoret ad aram sanc/*[(13)] *tam, nisi qui haec confitetur: dominum et Christum eius.*

receptum, et dedit illi omnem potestatem super omne nomen caelestium et terrestrium et infernorum et omnis lingua confiteatur ei quia Dominus et Deus est Iesus Christus, *quem credimus et expectamus adventum ipsius mox futurum,* iudex vivorum atque mortuorum, qui reddet unicuique secundum facta sua; *et* **effudit** in nobis habunde Spiritum Sanctum, **donum et pignus immortalitatis,** *qui facit credentes et oboedientes ut sint* filii dei *et* coheredes Christi, *quem confitemur et adoramus unum deum in trinitate sacri nominis.*

It should be noted that in cap. 14 of his *Confession* Patrick describes this formula as *mensura fidei trinitatis*; also that Bieler's reading *didicimus* in Patrick's *Confession* 4 is not the best one; it is better to take the *dicimus* of the majority of MSS.

Next, we must note that we have another version of Victorinus' formula, in the recension of Victorinus' *Comm. on the Apocalypse* made by Jerome (as Oulton calculated) about the year 406. It runs thus in *H* (the odd pages of the text being devoted to Jerome's recension, while the even pages show the original of Victorinus), p. 97:

> '*mensura*' *autem filii dei mandatum domini nostri, patrem confiteri omnipotentem; dicimus et huius filium Christum ante originem saeculi spiritalem apud patrem genitum, hominem factum et morte devicta in caelis cum corpore a patre receptum effudisse spiritum sanctum, donum et pignus immortalitatis, hunc per prophetas praedicatum, hunc per legem conscriptum, hunc esse manum dei et verbum patris et conditorem orbis. Haec est arundo et mensura fidei, et nemo adorat aram sanctam, nisi qui hanc fidem confitetur.*

It must also be observed that none of these formulae are creeds. They are all rules of faith, *i.e.,* longer, ampler, looser statements than creeds, but historically related to them. Creeds were first regarded as bare, skeletonic summaries of the rule of faith, but later, in the fourth century, creeds began to be enlarged so much as to become in the end indistinguishable from the rule of faith, and gradually came to take its place.[4] We should also note that Jerome admits in his Prologue to his recension of Victorinus' work that he made three kinds of alteration to it: *correxisse* (*i.e.* he had emended readings corrupted by the carelessness of scribes), *sociavisse vel addidisse* (*i.e.* he had interspersed matter taken from earlier commentators), and *abstulisse* (*i.e.*, he had removed objectionably chiliastic or literalist interpretations of Victorinus).[5]

The general resemblance in form and vocabulary between Victorinus' formula and that of Patrick is obvious, and perhaps most striking is Patrick's calling the formula by the unusual name *mensura fidei* and his echo of Victorinus' *ut didicimus* in the phrase *ut dicimus*. His only noteworthy resemblances to Jerome's version of the formula are in this phrase *ut dicimus* (J *dicimus* without *ut*, V *ut didicimus*), and in his words *et effudit in nobis habunde spiritum sanctum, donum et pignus immortalitatis*, apparently echoing Jerome's *effudisse spiritum sanctum, donum et pignus immortalitatis*. But it should be noted that Patrick places his *ut dicimus* in the same construction as Victorinus places his *ut didicimus*, differing thereby from Jerome, and that he puts his reference to the Holy Spirit at the end of his formula, thereby differing both from Jerome and (at least as far as the position of the words *donum et pignus immortalitatis* goes) from Victorinus.

II

It must now be observed that there are some readings in H's version of Victorinus' formula which are impossible and should never have been allowed to stand. The tenth and eleventh lines of Victorinus' formula contain the words *hunc per manum dei et per verbum patris omnipotentis et conditorem orbis totius mundi*. No verb whatever is supplied for this construction, whereas it is

---

[4] See R. P. C. Hanson, *Tradition in the Early Church* (London, 1962), caps. 2 and 3 and bibliography, and 'Patrick and the Mensura Fidei', pp. 109, 110.
[5] See *H*, pp. XXXVI–XLV.

supplied for the similar construction *hunc per prophetas praedicatum, hunc per legem conscriptum* in lines 9 and 10 above. Victorinus' Latin (as Jerome condescendingly observed) was far from elegant, but it was not execrable; it was much better than Patrick's. Victorinus could not have written a totally ungrammatical and indeed obscure sentence such as that from *hunc per manum* to *totius mundi*. But much more striking is the fact that if we retain the *per* in lines 9 and 10 before the words *manum* and *verbum* we ruin the theology of Victorinus' formula. Much has been made of Victorinus' confusion of the pre-existent Christ with the Holy Spirit, and much of his 'Binitarian' faith in apparently omitting the Holy Spirit altogether from his formula. But nobody appears to have noticed that if we keep Haussleiter's reconstruction of the formula here we have a pre-existent Christ begotten as Son of God before the origin of the age (who was led or appointed or in some way dealt with) *through* the hand of God and *through* the Word of God and (the construction demands it) *through* the founder of the world. What does this imply? Two pre-existent Sons of God or Words? This would be absurd. Clearly the passage must be amended, and if we are to amend it the best authority to fall back on is Jerome's recension. Jerome added to and abstracted from Victorinus' original, but he did not completely re-write it and he tells us that in places he corrected corruptions in the text. We need not assume that all Jerome's variations from Victorinus were derived from Jerome's free fancy or from other authors. For that matter, we need not assume that the text which Jerome had before him was precisely the text which Haussleiter has reconstructed as the original. Jerome is indeed a witness (though an uncertain and biased witness) to Victorinus' text much earlier than the earliest MS of that text (which in fact is of the fifteenth century and very late). When Jerome reproduces Victorinus' text here as *hunc esse manum dei et verbum patris et conditorem orbis*, he not only recalls an early Patristic title of Christ ('hand of God', to be found in Irenaeus *Adv. Haer.* 4.20.1; 5.6.1; 16.1) but also makes good sense of a passage which is otherwise nonsense both grammatically and theologically. Allowing for some stylistic tidying up on the part of Jerome, we can with some confidence reconstruct the original word of Victorinus as *hunc manum dei, et verbum patris omnipotentis et conditorem orbis totius mundi.*

Emboldened by this example, we can now look at the extraordinary expression in line 9 of Victorinus' formula in *H*, *sanctum dominum et pignus immortalitatis.* In fact, the *apparatus criticus* tells us that the MS A, the most important of the three,[6] does not read *sanctum dominum*; it reads *s̄cm d̄m̄.* Haussleiter assumed, not without references to justify the assumption, that *s̄cm* was an abbreviation for *sanctum* and that *d̄m̄* meant *dominum*, though he curiously saw no need to justify this much more difficult assumption. First, the expression *sanctum dominum* as applied to Christ is wholly unparalleled in any doctrinal formula and is peculiarly unsuitable here, as Christ has already been called *dominus* in line 6 above and the word is to be used for God the Father, not Christ, five lines below in line 13. Second, it is wholly unlikely that the expression *pignus immortalitatis* should be used in a doctrinal formula for anyone except the Holy Spirit. For parallels to these expressions Haussleiter adduces Apoc. 6.10, *domine sanctus et verus* (which clearly refers to God the Father), and Eph 1.14, *signati spiritu promissionis qui est pignus hereditatis nostrae.* In Latin here the *qui* can only apply to the Holy Spirit, but some MSS of the Greek read ἐσφραγίσθητε τῷ πνεύματι τῷ ἁγίῳ ὅς ἐστιν ἀρραβὼν τῆς κληρονομίας ἡμῶν though others read ὅ, and the evidence is pretty evenly balanced. Victorinus certainly knew Greek, yet if we assume that he here wrote *sanctum dominum* and applied to Christ the expression *pignus immortalitatis* we are assuming that he was applying to the Son an expression which all his readers who did not know their Greek New Testament would have associated with the Holy Spirit. Indeed in view of the fact that there is good evidence for the reading ὅ and the likelihood that even those readers who saw ὅς in their texts would take it as attracted into the masculine by ἀρραβών after it and not as referring to Χριστῷ several lines above it, perhaps most of the readers of Eph 1.14 who knew Greek would refer the expression

---

[6] For the MSS attestation of Victorinus' *Comm. on Apocalypse*, see *H*, XXX–XXXV.

to the Holy Spirit and not to Christ.[7] Elsewhere in his *Commentary* Victorinus shows that he certainly thinks of the Spirit as a gift and as given or poured out by Christ: cf. 26.9, *spiritus sanctus septiformis virtutis datus est in potestatem eius (Christi) a patre*; 26.12, a quotation of Acts 2.33, *dextra igitur dei exaltatus acceptum a patre spiritum effudit*; 46.7, (Christ) *statim spiritum sanctum effudit qui ferturus est hominem in caelum*; 76.1 *acceperunt, inquit, stolas albas, id est donum spiritus sancti*. I believe that we must be influenced here primarily by Jerome, and more indirectly by Patrick, and assume that the original reading here was *sanctum donum et pignus immortalitatis*, and that the words *effudisse spiritum* have dropped out before *sanctum*. This is either what Jerome read in his copy of Victorinus or what he restored if he found the text as corrupt as it is in Haussleiter's reconstruction. This emendation of the text has the added advantage that it places rather further apart the very difficult but apparently necessary switch in the meaning of *dominum* = Christ in line 6 to *dominum* = God the father in line 13. Oulton (*op. cit.*, p. 17) suggests that we should conclude that Jerome introduced the words *effudisse spiritum* because this would account for the difficulty of the sentence as he has it, changing awkwardly from *donum immortalitatis* to *hunc*, referring back to Christ. But it is just as likely that the corruption (if we accept that Haussleiter's text represents a corruption) first began because of the awkwardness of the original sentence as that Jerome emended it in such a way as to make it awkward. Elsewhere Jerome's text runs smoothly, all too smoothly. The scribe of MS A (Ottobonianus latinus 3288A, which is the chief, indeed in a sense the only MS for this work) intended the reader to read *sanctum donum et pignus immortalitatis*, the words *effudisse spiritum*, as has already been argued, having fallen out before *sanctum*.

I therefore conclude that Jerome's version here, as in lines 10 and 11, represents the correct original of Victorinus, and that what we have to do with here is a rule of faith which is 'Binitarian' in form but not in content. This is, after all, highly

[7] The likelihood of the relative pronoun being attracted into the masculine has been drawn to my attention by my colleague Prof. F. F. Bruce, D.D., F.B.A. The evidence of the MSS stands thus: ὅς-ς D° 1739 al lat ς; ὅ-𝔓46 A B G pm d; R. In 2 Cor 1.22 and 5.5. *pignus* is certainly used of the Holy Spirit.

probable in an author such as Victorinus who was writing at the very end of the third or the beginning of the fourth century. Jerome left it in its 'Binitarian' form (which incidentally suggests that the form was not as obsolete in his day as some scholars have made out). But Patrick received it in a different form approximating closer to the Trinitarian one. This argument also removes the main point of agreement between Jerome and Patrick against Victorinus. Further it means that Victorinus must be removed from the list of those Patristic writers who attest the reading of ὅς rather than ὅ at Eph 1.14.

III

When we come to determine the relation of Patrick's formula to that of Victorinus, we are now left only with Patrick's *ut dicimus* as evidence that he derived his formula through Jerome's recension. This is not a weighty piece of evidence. It is possible, but on the whole unlikely, that *dicimus* is the original reading in Victorinus preserved in Jerome's recension. Oulton[8] refers *ut didicimus* to the incident commented on in *H* 88.18–90.3 when a great angel, whom Victorinus identified with Christ (88.1–7), tells the prophet John to announce *omnipotentis dei verba*. The phrase in 96.5 would then mean that the formula is the words of God, duly announced. Even though Patrick has *dicimus* and not *didicimus*, he places *ut* before it and uses the expression in precisely the position in his formula in which Victorinus put it, viz at the end of the article dealing with God the Father, as a kind of transition between that and the Christological article, whereas Jerome's syntax attaches his *dicimus*, without an *ut*, to the Christological article. It is better to assume that if Patrick's formula derives indirectly from Victorinus, during the course of transmission Victorinus' *ut didicimus*, which became meaningless once the formula was taken out of its context, was reduced to *ut dicimus*.[9]

We can therefore be pretty confident that there is no

---

[8] *Op. cit.*, p. 13.

[9] There are some parallels for the use of *dicimus* in doctrinal formulae of the fifth century and later. See Oulton, *op. cit.*, p. 27 n. 1.

connection at all between Patrick's formula and the formula of Jerome's recension of Victorinus' *Commentary*. Oulton's arguments in favour of a connection between Patrick and Jerome had already been seriously damaged by Bieler's treatment of the subject.[10] But the resemblances between Patrick's formula and that of Victorinus have been increased if the argument of this article is accepted, and make it impossible to deny that there was some connection between them. What that connection was is not easy to determine. It should be noted that Victorinus' *Comm. on Apoc.* was well known and widely read in the ancient Christian world, as Haussleiter makes clear in his Introduction to *H*. Tyconius, the Donatist in Africa, knew it before the end of the fourth century, and Jerome's friend Anatolius as well as Jerome himself in Bethlehem knew it at least as early as the opening years of the fifth century, and the presbyter Beatus of Liebana in Spain knew it in the eighth century. The fact that its author had died as a martyr in the Diocletian persecution no doubt helped its circulation. The very fact that Jerome thought it necessary to issue a revised version of it suggests that it was popular, too popular to suppress or ignore, too chiliastic to leave untouched. And Haussleiter traces two later recensions of it besides that of Jerome.[11] It is not surprising that a copy should have found its way to the British Church of Patrick's day. We need not assume any further connection between the Christianity of Britain and that of remote Pannonia where Victorinus' see of Poetoevium lay, than simply that this popular work by a Pannonian martyr bishop made its way to the British Church. It is a little surprising that there appears to be no evidence that Victorinus' work was read in Gaul. In the lack of evidence we can draw no firm conclusions, but this may indicate that the British Church was not wholly ruled in its tastes and choices by the Gallic.

There is, however, plenty of material in Patrick's formula which does not derive from Victorinus. The most valuable part of Oulton's monograph is that in which he supplies the documentation for this.[12] He finds several points in common

---

[10] For Bieler's article see the bibliography in note 1 above.

[11] See *H*, Introd. pp. XLV–LXVI.

[12] See Oulton, *op. cit.*, pp 17–31.

with formulae associated in one way or another with the creed
produced by the Council of Ariminum of 359, and several
points which recall expressions in the work of Hilary of Poitiers
(ob. 369). He states his general conclusion thus: 'But I do not
claim to have in any sense proved that Patrick read Hilary ...
What does emerge is that Patrick was acquainted with the
theological phrases current in Gaul in the fourth and fifth
centuries and to be met with in Gaul's most eminent
theologians'.[13] This is what might be expected of someone who
was trained to be a priest in Britain. Victorinus' formula has
been enlarged by expressions which reflect the theological
controversies and interests of the fourth century, though not in
any sharp or emphatic way. Though some of Patrick's
expressions echo phrases to be found in some fifth-century
writers, no fifth-century controversy is reflected in any term
used in Patrick's formula. Again, this is what we should expect
from one whose ecclesiastical formation had taken place in a
church remote from the centres of sophisticated theological
activity, a church probably conservative and perhaps even
archaic in its customs, and since Patrick was resident in far-away
Britain and Ireland when the great councils of 431, 449 and 451
took place he would have been unaffected by them. One
resemblance, however, in Patrick's formula demands notice. It
shares two expressions with a creed of Auxentius of Milan; they
are *ante omne principium* and *per ipsum facta sunt visibilia et
invisibilia*. We know this creed because Hilary of Poitiers in his
Contra Auxentium quotes a letter of Auxentius in which he
professes this creed.[14] Auxentius says of it: *ex infantia
quemadmodum doctus sum sicut accepi de sanctis scripturis.*[15] There is
nothing specifically Arian in this Creed, though Auxentius was
Arian bishop of Milan when he uttered it. The year in which he
wrote the letter quoted by Hilary was 364. Auxentius had been
bishop of Milan since 355. He was a native of Cappadocia;
Hilary says that he received his theological education in the
church in which the Arian bishop Gregory of Alexandria had

[13] *Ibid.*, p. 30.
[14] Migne, *Patrologia Latina* 10: 617, 618 (14).
[15] *Ibid.*, 10: 617.

presided.[16] Auxentius himself in his letter says that he had never known Arius and never laid eyes on him and that he did not know his doctrine.[17] There is no reason to suppose that any of these statements are false, except that it is hard to believe that Auxentius did not know Arius' doctrine.

Where did Auxentius' creed come from? From Cappadocia? From Alexandria? Or from Milan? Auxentius' native language was Greek; apparently he only learned Latin when he was appointed bishop of Milan by the Emperor Constantius in 355. But before we rush to the conclusion that Patrick's rule of faith was influenced by a formula from the Eastern Church, we should consider the attitude of the theologians of the early Church, at least till the end of the fourth century, to formulae. The early Christian fathers were not wedded to nor deeply concerned with the actual verbal form of doctrinal formulae. The *homoousion* of Nicea drops out of sight for twenty years after 325. The people who composed the 'Nicene' creed of 381 regarded themselves as exactly reproducing the doctrine of 325, but they appear to have adopted a formula the basis of which was not the creed of 325 and one which by no means exactly reproduced all the terms of that creed. What the theologians of that period were concerned with was not to secure a formula but to secure a doctrine, and this doctrine could be expressed rather differently in different places and times and circumstances, and still remain the same doctrine.[18] Everybody who presented a doctrinal formula in the fourth century, be they pro-Nicene, Arian, Semi-Arian, or anything else, protested that they were not adding to the traditional faith but merely stating it in other words. It would therefore be perfectly possible for somebody brought up in one church to declare his faith in the words of another church and still to protest that this was the faith which he had known from childhood. Marcellus of Ancyra was quite willing to declare in the presence of Pope Julius in 330 his traditional belief in the words of the Roman

[16] *Ibid.*, 614 (8).
[17] *Ibid.*, 617 (14).
[18] For a more elaborate exposition of this point, see cap 13.

creed. It is therefore unnecessary to imagine that in this
document given by Hilary in which Auxentius declares his
creed we are dealing with a creed of Cappadocia or Alexandria.
No doubt Auxentius is quoting a creed of Milan, and declaring
that this expresses adequately the faith that he has always held.
Hilary never attacks this creed as Arian; his only objection to it is
that it is not capable of bringing to light Auxentius' Arianism.
Patrick's formula incorporates expressions from a creed which
was known in Milan in 364. This is as much as we should infer
from the elements common to the formulae of Patrick and of
Auxentius.

It may be asked whether this was a personal formula of
Patrick. Kattenbusch warns against mistaking a private
document for a definite creed and then drawing a conclusion
about the verbal form of the creed of the area where the
theologian in question was a native or functioned as an official of
the Church.[19] But it may be doubted whether this distinction
between a private formula and a formula of the Church is a
realistic or useful one. If by a private formula is meant an
interpretation of the Christian faith wholly confined to the
individual who expresses it, setting out an idiosyncratic list of
beliefs that happen to appeal to him, no such thing existed or
was thought of in the ancient Church. The nearest approach to a
private formula would be some statement covering selected
points of Christian doctrine which either a writer particularly
wishes to emphasise or which have been presented to him by
others who suspect his orthodoxy. Such are the statement that
opens the *Dialogue with Heracleides* of Origen, and perhaps the
Letter of Hymenaeus presented probably to Paul of Samosata,
about 268, and the formula submitted by Auxentius of Milan to
his judges when in 364 his orthodoxy was impugned by Hilary
of Poitiers: *deum verum filium ex deo vero patre.*[20] Even formulae
such as these can scarcely be called personal rules of faith,
because they were all probably known and used by others.

But anyway there is no evidence that Patrick's doctrinal
formula in *Confession* 4 is in any sense a personal declaration of

[19] *Das Apostolische Symbol*, p. 395.

[20] *P.L.* 10: 614 (8), 617 (14). It appears in his creed, but may have been
specially inserted by Auxentius.

faith. He calls it *mensura fidei*, using Victorinus' unusual phrase; he does not claim that it is peculiarly his but suggests rather that its doctrinal content is what everybody should believe. Patrick, we may well agree, was not the sort of person to be, or to set himself up to be, a connoisseur of doctrine.

There are a few faint indications in chapter 4 of the *Confession* that Patrick is retailing here a traditional formula which was regularly handed on to neophytes. The first is the expression *ut dicimus*. Even if this is (as has been suggested above, p. 325) a reduction or corruption of Victorinus' *ut didicimus*, it would still suggest to those who heard it for the first time a formula expressing the Church's faith. The other is a subtler point, but an interesting one.[21] Towards the end of his formula, Patrick quotes in his own version the words of Titus 3.6 *effudit in nobis* (Vulgate, *effudit in nos*). The reading of the MSS is not certain here. D has *effudit in vobis*, the rest *infudit in nobis*. Bieler has chosen to follow D for *effudit* and the rest for *nobis*. This seems an inconsistent and unjustifiable choice, for we should surely choose the whole phrase in D or in the rest. If we are to choose, D will clearly be preferable, and we are therefore faced with the statement *effudit in vobis habunde spiritum sanctum*. There is apparently no precedent for *vobis* in MSS of the Latin New Testament. It is possible that the change from the *nobis* of the Latin Bible to the *vobis* of D reflects a deliberate alteration designed to impress the truth concerning the Holy Spirit upon those who were receiving for the first time this version of the Church's rule of faith, that doctrinal standard upon which, it is reasonable to believe, instruction leading up to baptism was usually based.

We can therefore recognise in Patrick's formula one reasonably reliable account of the rule of faith of the British Church in the first half of the fifth century. It is an adaptation of the rule of faith of a Pannonian martyr bishop as he gave it in a widely read work at the end of the third century. By the beginning of the fourth century the British Church had become

---

[21] This point I owe to the perspicuity of Mr. D. R. Bradley, Senior Lecturer in Greek and Latin and Classical Philology in the University of Manchester, a colleague of mine in a seminar in the University.

firmly, though modestly, established and had been organised into a number of sees.[22] It is likely that this is the period in which Victorinus' formula was adopted as a basis of catechetical instruction. The later material in Patrick's formula reflects the history of Christian doctrine during the fourth century as it was filtered to the distant and conservative British Church through the influential churches and theologians of Italy and Gaul. This rule of faith helps us to place Patrick in the context to which most of the other evidence points, that of a Christian bishop in a remote outpost of the Christian Church in the West in the first half of the fifth century.

[22] See R. P. C. Hanson, *St. Patrick: his Origins and Career* (Oxford, 1968), caps. 1 and 2; M. Barley and R. P. C. Hanson, *Christianity in Britain 300–700* (Leicester, 1968).

15

THE CHURCH IN FIFTH-CENTURY GAUL:
EVIDENCE FROM SIDONIUS APOLLINARIS

There are several reasons why the study of the works of Sidonius Apollinaris should be of particular interest to ecclesiastical historians. He represents in a peculiar way the end of the old *régime*, under which Christianity had taken root and had begun to spread, and the beginning of the new period which we call the Middle Ages. He was a devoted admirer of the Roman imperial system, a devotee of the Muses of Roman poetry and prose, but also, in the second part of his life, a bishop of the Christian Church. He was born about 430, when the emperor Valentinian III, who could be reasonably represented as the scion of a legitimate dynasty, was apparently in secure possession of the imperial throne. He died about 480, bishop of a see in a barbarian kingdom, a few years after the last Roman puppet-emperor had been dethroned. He has left us not only poems and panegyrics but also letters dealing, among other things, with the day-to-day problems of his see. His contribution to our knowledge of the Gallic Church of the mid-fifth century—a dark period by any standard of measurement—must be of great value, and perhaps a fresh survey of certain aspects of it may not be unfruitful.[1]

We can gain interesting glimpses of ordinary church life in Sidonius's works. Imitating Mamertus of Vienne, he instituted regular Rogationtide processions. He describes the ceremonies which had prevailed before this as 'undisciplined, half-hearted, infrequent, and, if I may say so, boring periods of intercession, often reduced in their effect by the incidence of midday meals that interrupted them'.[2] The new processions were more rigorous observances, characterised by fasts, psalm-singing and weeping. Elsewhere he gives an interesting description of the

[1] References to Sidonius's works are taken from the Loeb edition by W. H. Semple and E. H. Warmington, London and Cambridge (Mass.), i, 1963; ii, 1965.

[2] *Vagae, tepentes infrequentesque utque sic dixerim oscitabundae supplicationes quae saepe interpellantum prandiorum obicibus hebetebantuur: Ep.*, v. 14.2; *cf.* vii. 1.1–7.

feast-day of St. Justus observed in Lugdunum in August each year. The festivities began with a *processio antelucana* to the church, where a service of vigils was held. The church was packed and airless. Then the congregation separated, intending to return for the Mass, to be celebrated by the bishop, at 9 a.m. Some of the ways in which they whiled away the time were the dice-board and the ball-game. A crowd of students (*turba scholasticorum*) was present. Sidonius does not carry on the description beyond the point at which they are all going to join the bishop in the church for Mass.[3] We also hear of a week's festivities on the occasion of the dedication of the church at Lugdunum built by bishop Patiens.[4] Bishop Faustus of Riez delivered a sermon on this occasion. We hear of land belonging to the church being let to a refugee deacon to cultivate;[5] and we hear of the famous *contestatiunculae*[6] which Sidonius composed for bishop Methegius. We find Sidonius urging a certain Vettius to persuade his friend Germanicus (whom Sidonius mentions elsewhere), who is the father of a priest and the son of a bishop, to confess his sins publicly and amend his life.[7]

There are a few (but tantalisingly few) references to church buildings. The tenth letter in the second book is concerned with a request made to Sidonius to compose some verses to be inscribed upon the wall of the new church built at Lugdunum by bishop Patiens.[8] Two other poets, Constantius and Secundinus, had already written poems on the walls on either side of the altar (which was perhaps in the middle of the oblong-shaped basilica). Sidonius's poem was to be inscribed on the 'west' wall. The church is hard to reconstruct from the description given in Sidonius's poem. It is full of light; it has a gilded ceiling; it probably has mosaics and perhaps coloured glass in the windows. Sidonius mentions a triple colonnade and

[3] *Ep.*, v. 17.1–9.

[4] *Ibid.*, ix. 3.5.

[5] *Ibid.*, vi. 10.1, 2.

[6] *Ibid.*, vii. 3.1. I do not here examine the question, which is one for the attention of liturgical experts, of what these *contestatiunculae* were, whether 'proper prefaces' or actual masses composed by Sidonius.

[7] *Ibid.*, iv. 13.3, 4.

[8] *Ibid.*, ii. 10.2–4.

another enclosing an *atrium*, and yet another 'clothing the middle section' (*vestit . . . campum medium*). Anderson thinks that this last colonnade represents the columns in the 'nave' of the church, but this seems to me unlikely. It is more likely that Sidonius means that there are three colonnades outside the 'west' front of the church, one in front and two on the wings, a fourth to make a fourth side of the square enclosing a space in front of the church, and a fifth to make a covered way across the square.[9] There are also two interesting references to private family chapels, in the houses or on the estates of friends of Sidonius, the *sacrarium* at Consentius's estate [10] and the *templa dei qui maximus est* at the 'Castle' of Pontius Leontius.[11] We are reminded of the Christian chapel discovered at Lullingstone in Kent not long ago.

The vocabulary used by Sidonius in referring to ecclesiastical persons and offices is of some interest. He restricts the title *pontifex* to bishops, but uses *sacerdos* sometimes for priests and sometimes for bishops, though more often for the latter. He uses the word *antistes*, which later came to be restricted to bishops, in a variety of ways, and more as a complimentary title than as a formal description of an office. It can denote a bishop, an abbot or a priest, and sometimes it describes a bishop as distinguished from an abbot.[12] This means that we cannot assume that the interesting British ecclesiastic Riochatus, to whom Sidonius refers in the ninth letter of his ninth book, is a bishop. On the whole it seems rather more likely that he is an abbot or a monk in priest's orders. Sidonius also uses the phrase *summus sacerdos* for bishops, and occasionally produces the vague and impressive-sounding *protomystes* to indicate some important ecclesiastic.[13] He sometimes uses *presbyter* for priests and more than once he describes deacons as 'levites'.[14] He never once in the

---

[9] Compare the space enclosed by colonnades in front of Constantine's church of the Anastasis at Jerusalem.

[10] *Ibid.*, viii. 4.1.

[11] *Carm.*, xxii. 218.

[12] Examples of its varying meanings can be found in *Ep.*, iv. 11.6; vii. 5.3, 13.1 and 17.1; ix. 2.1, 9.6 and 11.5 and 8; *Carm.*, xvi. 113.

[13] E.g., *Ep.*, ii. 9.4; iv. 17.3.

[14] *Ibid.*, v. 1.2; vi. 10.1; ix. 2.1.

whole of his works mentions the pope of Rome; the nearest he gets to this is when, in describing a journey which he made from Gaul to Rome in 467, he tells us that he visited '*triumphalibus apostolorum liminibus*' in Rome and thereby rid himself of a fever.[15] On the other hand, he sometimes applies to Gallic ecclesiastics titles which we to-day would associate with the bishop of Rome. He calls Lupus of Troyes '*pater patrum et episcopus episcoporum*' and '*primas omnium, qua patet, orbe pontificum*',[16] and describes Agroecius, bishop of Sens, as '*pontificatu maximo dignissimus papa*'.[17] This is partly an indication of the lengths to which Sidonius's rhetorical fulsomeness will go and partly a sign of the isolation of Gaul from Italy that had been evident in other spheres of life also since the beginning of the fifth century. Sidonius regularly describes his own calling as a bishop as '*professio*'.

Sidonius's works throw considerable light on the choice and the function of bishops in fifth-century Gaul. Perhaps the most interesting point for ecclesiastical historians is that he gives strong grounds for concluding that episcopal consecration in Gaul in his day was effected by two, and not by three bishops. This seems to be the case in the two examples of consecration of bishops that Sidonius was concerned in or to which he refers in any detail.[18] In neither of these cases does it seem at all likely that a third bishop could have taken part in the rite, in spite of the canon of Nicaea directing that three bishops shall consecrate, nor does Sidonius betray any consciousness that a third ought to have been present. It is interesting, perhaps, to note that the clerical tonsure (*corona*) has already been introduced into Gaul.[19]

On the system whereby bishops were chosen, Sidonius gives us full and valuable information. His letters tell us in considerable detail of at least two occasions upon which bishops

---

[15] *Ibid.*, i. 5.9.

[16] *Ibid.*, vi. 1.1, 3.

[17] *Ibid.*, vii. 9.6.

[18] *Ibid.*, iv. 25.1–5, Patiens of Lugdunum and Euphronius of Augustodunum consecrate a bishop for Châlons-su-Sâone; vii. 5.1–4 and 9.5–25, Agroecius of Sens and Sidonius of Augustonemetum consecrate a bishop for Bourges.

[19] *Ibid.*, vi. 3.2; viii. 8.1.

were chosen, on one of which he himself played, rather unwillingly, the central part. A bishop was chosen for the see of Châlons-sur-Saône in the year 470. The choice was made by bishop Patiens of Lugdunum and bishop Euphronius of Augustodunum. They did not consult either the *plebs* or the presbyters. They chose an archdeacon, called John, and incontinently consecrated him bishop. But, presumably, the people and presbyters must have accepted him.[20] The other occasion was the choice of a bishop for Bourges. Sidonius gives us a very full description in three letters of the circumstances attending this choice.[21] Apparently it fell to his lot to choose the man, though he shows himself very anxious to associate the metropolitan of Lugdunensis IV, Agroecius of Sens, in the decision.[22] Bourges was in Aquitania II and, indeed, its bishop was metropolitan of that province. On his first visit Sidonius found the town buzzing with rival candidates—clergy, secular and religious, and laymen.[23] In a letter he says that two benches would not hold all the candidates.[24] Some were freely offering money for support. In one place Sidonius's words may imply that there were three stages in the process of election: '*nullus a me hactenus nominatus, nullus adhibitus, nullus electus est*', he writes,[25] and, later, another phrase of his suggests that nomination at least was a formal stage before election.[26] Agroecius apparently failed to respond immediately to Sidonius's call to assist him in finding a suitable candidate for Bourges. Sidonius then found a man whom he considered suitable, and appealed to Euphronius, bishop of Augustodunum, to assist him in having this man, Simplicius, accepted by the people of the see and, one conjectures, consecrated. Sidonius was moved to choose Simplicius because many of the '*boni homines*' (? wealthy men) were in favour of him, and nobody alleged anything against

---

[20] *Ep.*, iv. 25.1–4.
[21] *Ibid.*, vii. 5.8, 9.
[22] *Ibid.*, 5.1, 4.
[23] *Ibid.*, 5.1.
[24] *Ibid.*, 9.2.
[25] *Ibid.*, 5.4.
[26] Neque nominato, licet nedum nostrae professionis, inlicitum opponi: *ibid.*, 8.3.

him, not even the Arians (? the Goths).[27] Evidently Euphronius did not answer this appeal, but eventually Agroecius of Sens agreed to co-operate in the matter. In a long letter to Perpetuus, bishop of Tours, Sidonius described the scene when he formally chose Simplicius and justified his choice in an address or sermon (*contio*) to the clergy, monks and laity of Bourges assembled in the church in the presence of Sidonius and Agroecius. We may presume that after the address Agroecius and Sidonius directly proceeded to consecrate Simplicius, who was a layman. Before giving us the text of his address, Sidonius remarks that the *plebs* of Bourges, now mollified (*lenita*), had agreed to hand over the choice to the bishops (presumably Agroecius and Sidonius). This involved an abandonment of the people's own judgment (*iacturam iudicii*). Some presbyters murmured, twittering like sparrows in corners (*paucis angulatim fringultientibus*), but the majority accepted the choice.[28] The address itself, whose text Sidonius gives us, is a most interesting document. Sidonius lays aside all his episcopal unctuousness and much even of his rhetorical complexity, and describes with appalling frankness the difficulties of choosing a bishop, difficulties which, we may conclude, must have attended any such choice in those days. He had been formally requested by the citizens of Bourges to assist in electing a bishop.[29] But he did not deceive himself into thinking that the choice would thereby satisfy all parties. Were he to choose a monk, even of the strictest asceticism, the cry would go up that this man would be fit for an abbot's duties, but not for those of a bishop, capable of interceding for people's souls, but not of caring for their bodies, and the presbyters and people would submit with an ill grace to '*monasterialibus disciplinis*'.[30] If he were to choose a *clericus*, the other clergy would envy him and would demand as bishop the man who was senior in age, even though he was negligent in preaching and vacillating in administration.[31] If he chose a layman from the

[27] *Ibid.*, 8.1–3.

[28] *Ibid.*, 9.1–3.

[29] *Biturigas decreto civium petitus adveni: ibid.*, 5.1; *paginae decretalis oblatu pontificis eligendi mandastis arbitrium: ibid.*, 9.6.

[30] *Ep.*, 9.9–11.

government service, then the accusation would be made that Sidonius wanted to choose a bishop from men of his own class and was influenced by class-consciousness.[32] However, finally Sidonius announced that he had chosen Simplicius (who was a man of his own class), described his virtues, achievements and qualifications,[33] and asked for the support and acclamation of all those present.[34] Clearly, this approval was given.

It has been worth while going into this election in some detail because the whole process illustrates the relatively free and almost democratic spirit that prevailed on such occasions. Manifestly, Sidonius and Agroecius must obtain popular support for their choice, not by counting heads but by sounding opinion and exercising persuasion. This can, perhaps, give us a glimpse into the motives which cause so many able and intelligent men during the fourth and fifth centuries to abandon the service of the empire for that of the Church. The atmosphere of despotism, repression and immobility that characterised the administration of the empire did not extend to the administration of the Church.

We can gather quite a full picture from the pages of Sidonius of what were generally thought to be the functions of a bishop in fifth-century Gaul. We have two lists of episcopal activities. In one, Sidonius lists the various ways in which Claudianus Mamertus, brother of Mamertus of Vienne, virtually stood in for his brother, though Claudianus was only a priest. Sidonius describes Claudianus as 'a counsellor in judicial decisions, a representative in dealing with the churches, an agent in business matters, a steward for his estates, an accountant for his revenues, a collaborator in reading, an interpreter in his exposition of Scripture, and a companion in his travels'.[35] In one of his poems also Sidonius gives an account of the bishop's duties and

---

[31] *Ibid.*, 9.12, 13.

[32] *Ibid.*, 9.14.

[33] *Ibid.*, 9.16–24.

[34] *Consonate:* 9.25.

[35] *Consiliarium in iudiciis, vicarium in ecclesiis, procuratorem in negotiis, vilicum in praediis, tabularium in tributis, in lectionibus comitem, in expositionibus interpretem, in itineribus contubernalem:* ibid., iv.11.5.

functions. They comprise championing the lesser people, caring for the sick, strangers and prisoners, seeing that the dead are decently buried and preaching to the people.[36] We find other references to the bishop's political duties. Sidonius represents the people of Bourges as objecting to the choice of a monk on the grounds that he could not adequately '*intercedere ... pro corporibus apud terrenum iudicem*',[37] and he reminds his audience that Simplicius, '*si necessitas arripiendae legationis incubuit, non ille semel pro hac civitate stetit vel ante pellitos reges vel ante principes purpuratos*'.[38] Indeed, Sidonius's own career as bishop of Augustonemetum is a better illustration of these ideals than any quotation of his works could be, in that he spent much energy in attempting to defend the independence of his see from Gothic rule, and in procuring assistance for it from the central imperial government, and when that government ruthlessly handed over the Arvernian territory to Euric, Sidonius suffered exile for his zeal on behalf of his people.

The episcopal function to which Sidonius refers most often is that of providing charity to the poor and relief to as wide an area as possible in times of invasion, famine and distress. He refers more than once to the generosity of Patiens of Lugdunum in bringing relief to starving people, not only in his see but widely beyond it.[39] *Humanitas* was a requirement in a bishop, as Sidonius says when speaking of Simplicius.[40] We are reminded of the efforts made to relieve the miseries of this period of invasion and famine, of economic and political dislocation, by such figures as bishop Deogratias of Carthage in the year 455 and bishop Epiphanius of Ticinum, a younger contemporary of Sidonius. Once again we find here a kindlier and more flexible role than that of the Roman official. Some of Sidonius's letters dealt with cases of arbitration in which he was involved.[41] Other activities of his illustrated in his letters were the writing of

[36] *Carm.*, xvi. 116–126.
[37] *Ep.*, vii. 9.9.
[38] *Ep.*, 9.19.
[39] *Ibid.*, ii: 10.2; vi. 12.5, 6, 7; *cf.* iv. 2.3, where Claudianus Mamertus alludes to Sidonius's open-handedness in this respect.
[40] *Ibid.*, vii. 9.19.
[41] *E.g.*, *ibid.*, iv. 24, and vi. 2.

commendatory letters for clergy who were moving from one see to another,[42] and the overseeing of the public confession by those who had sinned and desired to be reconciled to the Church.[43]

It is interesting to observe that there is plenty of evidence that bishops in Sidonius's time were married and lived openly and respectably with their wives. Sidonius himself certainly did so; indeed, his letters show great concern for his children's characters and careers.[44] In his commendation of Simplicius he alludes to the eminent suitability of the candidate's wife to be the consort of a bishop, if only because she was the daughter of a bishop and was descended from other bishops.[45] The couple are bringing up their two boys well.[46] But there are limitations to the connubial bliss of bishops. They must not marry again if their wives die. Two possible candidates for the see of Bourges are eliminated because they have married second wives.[47] And, we may conclude, by the argument from the case of a layman, that bishops were expected not to have sexual intercourse with their wives. In one letter Sidonius urges one of his flock, who is about to abandon a mistress and marry a rich wife, to beget one or two children and then refrain altogether from intercourse.[48] Finally, monks who were made bishops would certainly have no women companions of any sort. This is why it is difficult to believe that Faustus of Riez really did have his aged British mother living with him at Riez, in spite of the words in Sidonius's well-known poem which suggest that he did.[49] Elsewhere Sidonius, commending a converted Jew to Nunechius, bishop of Nantes, can write *'quibus agnitis adventantem Abrahae nunc filium veriorem maternis ulnis spiritalis Sara suscipiat'*,[50] referring in this maternal metaphor either to the

---

[42] *Ibid.*, ix. 10.

[43] *Ibid.*, iv. 13.3, 4.

[44] *E.g.*, *ibid.*, v. 16.4, 5.

[45] *Ibid.*, vii. 9.24: *constanter adstruxerim respondere illam feminam sacerdotiis utriusque familiae vel ubi educta crevit vel ubi electa migravit.*

[46] *Ibid.*, 9.21, 24.

[47] *Ibid.*, 9.18.

[48] *Ep.*, ix. 6.3, 4.

[49] *Carm.*, xvi. 78–82.

[50] *Ep.*, viii. 13.4.

church of Nantes or to *mater ecclesia* generally.

Monks figure quite prominently in Sidonius's work. Once he refers to 'three orders of life',[51] meaning the monk, the cleric and the penitent, and once to '*utriusque professionis ordinibus*', which probably refers to clergy and monks,[52] and once to presbyters being afraid of '*reliquos ordines*', apparently meaning monks and laity.[53] It seems clear that in Sidonius's day there are two sorts of monks. There are monks who live in coenobitic monasteries in relatively remote and unpopulated places, not particularly connected with a bishop's *cathedra*. There is, for instance, the monastery at Lérins, off the south coast of Gaul, which Sidonius mentions several times, and always with great respect and admiration.[54] There are monasteries in the Jura mountains.[55] There are the monks at Grincy, on the Rhône, near Vienne.[56] Among monks such as these some may be of peculiar holiness who practise a solitary asceticism which Sidonius calls '*sectata anachoresis*'.[57] There is an interesting account in one of Sidonius's letters of the monk Abraham, who earlier in his life had been imprisoned in Persia for his confession of Christianity and had later found his way to some place within Sidonius's see and had there founded a monastery.[58] When Abraham died, Sidonius wrote a charming little obituary poem for him, but he also ordered one of his clergy, Volusianus, a presbyter but not (as far as we know) a monk, to re-order Abraham's monastery, and to adapt the '*fluctuantem regulam fratrum destitutorum*' to the rules prevailing either at Grincy or at Lérins.[59] Perhaps the monks were following the traditions of Eastern monasticism. Volusianus is, moreover, to support the new abbot Auxanius,

---

[51] *Vitae tribus ordinibus: ibid.*, iv. 24.4.

[52] *Ibid.*, vii. 5.1, though Anderson (in loc.) may be right in saying that it refers to clergy and laity.

[53] *Ibid.*, vii. 9.3; *cf.* '*sacerdotibus popularibus*' meaning clergy and laity: vii. 8.

[54] *Ibid.*, vi. 1.3; viii. 14.1; ix. 3.4: *Carm.*, xvi. 104ff.

[55] *Ep.*,iv. 25.5.

[56] *Ibid.*, vii. 17.3.

[57] *Ibid.*, vii. 9.9.

[58] *Ibid.*, vii. 17.

[59] *Ibid.*, 7.3.

'*ut abbas sit frater Auxanius supra congregationem, tu vero et supra abbatem*'.[60]

But we also find evidence of another kind of monk, that is, of monks living near to the bishop's *cathedra*, apparently as part of the bishop's *familia*, who hold services in his cathedral church and live a less strictly enclosed life. Claudianus Mamertus, brother of the bishop of Vienne, appears to have been such a monk. As well as performing all the functions that he could as a substitute for his brother, he was choir-master at the cathedral church and teacher at the cathedral school. Sidonius's epitaph for him runs thus: '*antistes fuit ordine in secundo|fratrem fasce levans episcopali|nam de pontificis tenore summi|ille insignia sumpsit, hic laborem*'.[61]

We also hear of monks singing psalms antiphonally with the secular clergy in the cathedral church at Lugdunum on the occasion of the festival of St. Justus.[62] Both the clergy and the monks of Troyes respect bishop Lupus.[63] The monks of the cathedral church of Bourges provide some of the candidates for the vacant see, and Sidonius contemplates the possibility of a monastic candidate being the kind of man who enjoys food and entertains (*eum qui prandendo pascit*).[64] It seems to me that in these monks who appear to be associated with the bishop's *familia*, whose ascetic practices seem to be less rigorous than those of the others, and who seem to be rather less strictly bound to their monastery, we have the type of monk with which the monasticism of Patrick most closely corresponds. The monks whom Patrick mentions are not easy to fit into any category, but they could fit into this one. Further, it seems to me that it was in such a monastic bishop's *familia*, or monastic group attached to a bishop's *familia*, that Patrick is most likely to have received his ecclesiastical formation in Britain about the years 420 to 430.[65] It is clear from Sidonius's pages that the letter

---

[60] *Ibid.*, 7.4.
[61] *Ep.*, iv. 11.6.
[62] *Ibid.*, v. 17.3.
[63] *Ibid.*, vi. 1.3.
[64] *Ibid.*, vii. 5.1 and 9.10.
[65] See my *St. Patrick: his Origins and Career*, 140–158.

addressed by pope Celestine about the year 430 to the provinces of Gallia Narbonensis and Gallia Viennensis, objecting to the choice of monks as bishops,[66] has had no permanent effect. Many bishops in Gaul in Sidonius's day were monks, and Lérins was particularly fertile in producing monastic bishops.

Finally, a brief attempt will be made to estimate Sidonius's own attitude to his episcopal calling and status. Once he is made a bishop, he constantly refers to his own unworthiness and his former sins. It is difficult to envisage what are the precise sins to which he may be alluding. He appears to have been a faithful husband and a good family man before his ordination. It is possible that he had an inordinate love of chariot-racing, because in one of his poems there occurs a graphic, detailed and knowledgeable account of a chariot-race.[67] He appears, also, to have been not devoid of superstition. When, finding robbers desecrating his grandfather's grave at Lugdunum, he laid them over the grave and flogged them then and there (afterwards seeking and gaining the approval of bishop Patiens), he remarks that he punished them '*quantum sufficere posset superstitum curae, mortuorum securitati*'.[68] And he can write an epitaph for a Christian lady which does not breathe the slightest Christian sentiment.[69] Perhaps it was a sense of the worldliness of his previous life that oppressed him when he became a bishop. Some of his protestation about his sin is overdone and conventional, no doubt, but some of it rings true. He calls himself a '*novus clericus, peccator antiquus, scientia levi, gravi conscientia*',[70] and says that he is '*miser ante compulsus docere quam discere et ante praesumens bonum praedicare quam facere*'.[71] He renounced the writing of secular poetry when he received holy orders,[72] though he did not keep this resolve entirely intact. He refused to interpret some biblical passages when a friend asked

---

[66] *Epistola* iv. Praef. 1, 2: P.L., l., 430, 431.
[67] *Carm.*, xxiii. 307–427: cf. *Ep.*, i. 11.10: *postridie iussit Augustus ut epulo suo cirensibus ludibus interessemus.*
[68] *Ep.*, iii. 12.1–3.
[69] *Ep.*, ii. 8.2.
[70] *Ibid.*, ix. 2.3.
[71] *Ibid.*, v. 3.3.
[72] *Ibid.*, ix. 12.1.

him to do so, on the ground of his incapacity.[73] Though his letters are often couched in religious *clichés* and clothed in episcopal unctuousness, he can on occasion drop this and achieve sincerity, as when he addresses the people of Bourges in their cathedral at the election of a bishop, or in the bitter letter which he writes of Graecus, bishop of Massilia, over the betrayal of the Arverni by the emperor Julius Nepos.[74] He has some refreshingly unclerical characteristics: a liking for, and sympathy with the Jews,[75] and a preference for a good layman rather than a conventional cleric.[76] Generally, it is clear that what moved Sidonius to accept the offer of the see of Augustonemetum was a sense of duty. 'As the public welfare must override the shameful sense of one's personal guilt', he writes, 'I will disregard any aspersions cast upon my zeal by some malign critic of my good faith, and under the evil eye of vanity I shall not fear to proclaim the cause of truth'.[77] Sidonius's resolute championship of his adopted people, the Arverni, as well as his performance of his episcopal functions, amply bear out the justice of this statement.

But it would be wrong to conclude that Sidonius saw the Church as a kind of substitute for the Roman Empire, which had collapsed, or regarded his office as bishop as a compensation for the loss of the office of Praetorian Prefect of the Gauls, which his forefathers had held and which he would dearly have liked to hold himself. There is no evidence for this view at all. Sidonius is genuinely attached to, and loyal to, the Christian Church, but it does not occur to him that the Church might take the place of the Roman Empire, and he only becomes a prelate because he realises that this is the best way, in the circumstances, in which he can preserve the interests of *Romanae res*. There is certainly no romantic transference of loyalty from the Romans to the

[73] *Ibid.*, iv. 17.3.

[74] *Ibid.*, vii. 7.

[75] *Ibid.*, iii. 4.1; vi. 11.1, 2.

[76] *Ibid.*, iv. 9.5: *plus ego admiror sacerdotalem virum quam sacerdotem.*

[77] *Ibid.*, vii. 6.3: *sed quoniam supereminet privati reatus verecundiam publica salus, non verebor, etsi carpat zelum in me fidei sinister interpres, sub vanitatis invidia causam prodere veritatis.* The translation in the text is that of Anderson modified by Semple.

barbarians with him, any more than there is with Salvian. In spite of some reluctant admiration for a young Gothic prince, dressed in his best,[78] and some calculated flattery of Euric,[79] and of his minister, Count Victorius,[80] Sidonius loathed the barbarians, and continued to loathe them to the end. He disliked their lack of literacy,[81] and of culture;[82] he disliked their dress (he frequently refers to them as *pelliti*), their speech,[83] and their smell.[84] He complained that they turned Lugdunum into Germany,[85] he declared that he avoided even good barbarians,[86] and once he described them as 'public enemies'.[87] He sees no future for the Roman state in the hands of barbarians; on the contrary, they are sapping Rome's resources.[88] He preserves to the end, almost beyond the end, a pathetic faith in the destiny of Rome. Others may think that the twelve ages portended by the twelve vultures which appeared to Romulus are now nearing their end, but not Sidonius.[89] He is capable of criticising the Roman Empire. It is deplorable that usurpers should act tyrannically.[90] It is deplorable that imperial power should sometimes be wielded by boys like Valentinian III.[91] But Sidonius never gives up hope. He still writes not entirely despondently to the last Praetorian Prefect of Gaul, Polemius, in 475; he has great hopes of the penultimate emperor Julius Nepos; he still believes the Republic capable of bringing forth new Brutuses and Torquatuses.[92] This paper may perhaps most appropriately end with the list of the features of the Gallic town

[78] *Ep.*, iv. 21.1–3.
[79] *Ibid.*, viii. 9.5.
[80] *Ibid.*, vii. 17.1; earlier Sidonius had spoken more distantly of Victorius, *ibid.*, iv. 10.2.
[81] *Ibid.*, ii. 12.
[82] *Ibid.*, iv. 8.5; v. 5.3.
[83] *Ibid.*, iii. 3.2, 3.
[84] *Carm.*, xii. 1–22.
[85] *Ep.*, v. 7.7.
[86] *Ibid.*, vii. 14.10.
[87] *Ibid.*, vii. 7.2: *hostium publicorum*.
[88] *Ibid.*, iii. 8.2.
[89] *Carm.*, vii. 55–56, 357–358.
[90] *Ep.*, iii. 12.5: v. 9.1.
[91] *Carm.*, vii. 359, 533, 597–598.
[92] *Ep.*, iv. 14.1; v. 16.1–4; iii. 8.1.

of Narbo which Sidonius enumerates lovingly in one of his poems, as if the town was for him a visible memorial of Roman civilisation and Roman achievement:[93]

> 'muris, civibus, ambitu, tabernis,
> portis, porticibus, foro, theatro,
> delubris, capitoliis, monetis,
> thermis, arcubus, horreis, macellis,
> patris, fontibus, insulis, salinis,
> stagnis, flumine, merce, ponte, ponto'.

[93] *Carm.*, xxiii. 39–44.

16

THE TRANSFORMATION OF PAGAN TEMPLES INTO CHURCHES IN THE EARLY CHRISTIAN CENTURIES

Anyone who has visited Rome and seen the Pantheon and the Temple of Antoninus and Faustina might be pardoned if he concluded without further investigation that as soon as Christianity was given Imperial approval and support it began the task of taking over the temples of the various cults of dying paganism and transforming them quickly into Christian churches. And if he did jump to that conclusion, he could cite several eminent names in favour of this view. Gregorovius[1] dates the earliest example of this procedure to the year 391. C. N. Cochrane suggests that during Constantine's reign 'in some cases pagan temples were reconsecrated as Christian churches'.[2] A. H. M. Jones thought that he had found an example, which we shall examine later, in the middle of the fourth century.[3] And the late M. Avi-Jonah claimed that as early as the reign of Julian pagan temples 'had been rededicated as churches'.[4] It will be the aim of this paper to show, among other things, that no transformation of a pagan temple into a Christian church can be safely dated as early as the fourth century and that the earliest date which we can assign to this process is about the middle of the fifth century.

It is *a priori* unlikely that in the first flush of their triumph over paganism the Christians should have taken over and merely reconsecrated with a few alterations pagan temples wholesale, for they regarded these temples as the abodes of filthy devils, the

[1] F. Gregorovius, *History of the City of Rome in the Middle Ages* (ET, 2nd edn, London, 1902), 11, 109 n.1.

[2] C. N. Cochrane, *Christianity and Classical Culture* (Oxford, 1940), p. 208.

[3] A. H. M. Jones, *Constantine and the Conversion of Europe* (London, 1948), p. 222.

[4] M. Avi-Jonah, *The Jews of Palestine: A Political History from the Bar Kochba War to the Arab Conquest* (Oxford, 1976), p. 186. F. Homes Dudden, on the other hand, in his book *Gregory the Great* (London, 1905), seems to suggest that almost no transformations were made in Rome at least till the early seventh century after Gregory's death (p. 58); he is here following Duchesne (see below, p. 354).

inveterate enemies of Christianity. Christians would naturally avoid such places. A Christian passage in the *Oracula Sibyllina* declares that Christians are not even allowed to approach pagan temples.[5] Gregory of Nazianzus counts it a virtue in his mother, who must have been born early in the reign of Constantine, that she never shook hands with nor kissed a pagan and never even laid eyes on a 'house of defilement', *i.e.* a pagan temple.[6] Emile Mâle confirms that, as soon as Christianity became dominant, pagan temples, holy sites and statues were regarded with horror and repugnance and avoided.[7] A. M. Schneider takes the same view: 'Heidnische Tempel und sonstige öffentliche Baute hat man nur ungern kirchlichen Zwecken dienstbar gemacht'.[8]

That the first impulse of Christians was to pull down and destroy pagan temples, and that this was the earliest policy followed towards them, there can be no doubt. The original *temenos* area might be preserved, and some of the out-buildings, such as flights of stairs with propylaea, might be adapted, but the temple area itself, and particularly the altar, was given to destruction. This is the clear verdict of what is apparently the most authoritative article on this subject to date,[9] and of almost all the other evidence. When Constantine built his church of the Anastasis, he not only completely destroyed the temple of Aphrodite which had occupied the site, but he removed the foundations and went so far as to carry the débris away elsewhere.[10] Similarly when Constantine built a church at Mambre the existing temple buildings were completely destroyed before any church was built, and also at Aphaka in the Lebanon.[11] George, the Arian bishop of Alexandria in the mid-fourth century, had begun to 'cleanse', *i.e.* to despoil of its

[5] Ed. J. Geffeken (Leipzig, G. C. S. Ser., 1902), 8.487–495.

[6] Oration 13.9 (Migne, *PG* 35.996,997).

[7] *La fin du paganisme en Gaule et les plus anciennes églises chrétiennes* (Paris, 1950), p. 66

[8] Article 'Afrika', in *Reallexicon für Antike und Christentum* (Stuttgart, 1950), I, 178.

[9] F. W. Deichmann, 'Frühchristliche Kirchen in antiken Heiligtümern', *Jahrbuch des Deutschen Archaiologischen Instituts*, LIV (1939), 105–136.

[10] Eusebius Caes., *Vita Const.*, III 26–29, quoted by Deichmann, p. 107.

[11] Deichmann, pp. 107–108.

ornaments and pull down, an ancient and deserted Mithraeum when he was stopped by a riot.[12] It was this sort of conduct which caused him later to be lynched by a pagan mob. At about the same time as George was lynched a certain deacon Cyril, who had in the reign of Constantine distinguished himself by his zeal in burning and destroying cult objects, met the same fate in Heliopolis.[13] Mâle reminds us that, according to Sulpicius Severus, St Martin in Gaul in the West took a great part in destroying pagan temples and sanctuaries during the last two decades of the fourth century.[14] The incident at the Temple of Apollo at Daphne, near Antioch, when the Christians revenged themselves on the emperor Julian for removing the bones of their martyr Babylas by surreptitiously burning the Temple, is famous.[15] At Apamea in 389 a Christian mob, led by the bishop, axe in hand, destroyed the temple of Zeus, and the same treatment was accorded to a temple at Edessa. In both these cases, a church was probably built on the ruins.[16] In 402, by a special edict procured by the Bishop of Gaza, Porphyrius, from the empress Eudoxia, the Marneion in that town was pulled down, against the wishes of the local population, and a church was built on the ruins.[17] The most famous and best reported case of all is the destruction of the Serapaeum in Alexandria in the year 391. About this time a general destruction of temples and statues was taking place in Egypt, with imperial approval.[18] As far as we can piece together the events from the accounts of Rufinus, of Sozomenus and of Socrates,[19] the trouble started

[12] Socrates, *Hist. Ecc.* (ed. W. Bright, Oxford, 1893) III.2 (141), 3 (142–143).

[13] Theodoret, *Hist. Ecc.* (ed. L. Parmentier, G. C. S. Ser., Leipzig, 1911), III.7.3.

[14] *Op. cit.*, pp. 34–35; Mâle particularises only a temple near Amboise, a pagan sanctuary with its statues at Levroux, near Bituriges, and another in the territory of the Aeduani.

[15] Deichmann mentions it; *op. cit.*, p. 116.

[16] Deichmann, pp. 108–109; Mâle, p. 48.

[17] Deichmann,. *loc. cit.*

[18] Rufinus, *Hist. Ecc.* (PL 21.528ff.), II.26.535–536; Sozomenus, *Hist. Ecc.* (ed. Bidez-Hansen, Berlin, 1960, G. C. S. Ser.), VII.5.11–15; Zosimus, *Historia Nova* (ed. L. Mendelssohn, Leipzig, 1881, repr. Hildesheim, 1963), 4.37.

[19] Sozomenus, *Hist. Ecc.*, VII.15.2–10; Rufinus, *Hist. Ecc.*, II.22, 23; Socrates, *Hist. Ecc.*, V.16. Socrates said that it was a Mithraeum that was first

when the Bishop of Alexandria, Theophilus, asked from the emperor Theodosius possession of the Temple of Dionysus, and on gaining his request he caused the cult-objects found in the temple, and especially the *phalloi*, to be paraded in derision round the city. The result was a riot between Christians and pagans during which the pagans took refuge in the Serapaeum. This then was for several days besieged by the Christians. It was finally taken and destroyed, and a few years later a church was built on the spot which was called the *Arcadia*. Many other similar acts in which the temple was destroyed and a church built on its ruins could be recorded.[20]

It is because of this evidence all the more important to examine with care those cases in which there is apparently reported a transformation of a temple into a Christian church, not its destruction but rather its preservation in an altered form and use, as early as the fourth century.

The first two churches to claim our attention are the churches of St Menas and St Mocius in Constantinople. Our source here is a late and not very reliable one, the author preserved in the second volume of Preger's *Scriptores Originum Constantinopolitanarum*, who was writing in the seventh century. He tells us that Constantine 'found that they were temples of idols. He left the holy Menas as it was, but he removed the

---

attacked and that the *phalloi* came from the Serapaeum. Sozomenus gives different officials as governing in Egypt from those given by Socrates. I have chosen to follow in almost every particular the account of Sozomenus, which is more convincing. Theodoret refers to the incident (*Hist. Ecc.*, V.22.16), and Ammianus Marcellinus also (*Römische Geschichte*, ed. Wolfgang Seyfarth (Berlin, 1970), III, Book 22.16. 12, 13). The destruction is also mentioned by Prosper, Malalas, Cassiodorus, Georgius Monachus, Theophanes, Bede, Nicephorus Callistus, Suidas and the author of the *Apophthegmata Patrum*. See also Gregorovius, *op. cit.*, II. 67, A. Calderini, *Dizionario dei nomi geografici e topografici dell Egitto greco-romano*, I. i (Cairo, 1935, repr. Milan, 1972), *sub voc.* Alexandreia, Serapeion, pp. 140–145; E. Amélineau, *La géographie de l'Egypte à l'époque copte* (Paris, 1893), pp. 34–37 (Coptic sources, not very accurate); Deichmann, p. 110.

[20] Deichmann lists Corfu, dated 362 (p. 134), Gerasa, dated 565 (p. 118) and Cuma in Italy, dated before the end of the sixth century (p. 135), among others, *cf.* Constantine's Church of the Mother of God, later called St Thekla, at Kovítaria in Constantinople (T. Preger, ed, *Scriptores Originum Constantinopolitanarum* (Leipzig, 190), II.66 (187)).

statues and gave it its present name'. Later in the middle of the fifth century Pulcheria and Marcian built the whole church with its approaches and holy furniture.[21] It seems likely that the death of the martyr Menas had been in some way associated with this temple; perhaps he was buried in its *temenos*. Constantine therefore, if we can trust this author, as it were cleaned it out, divesting it of pagan associations, out of respect to the martyr, but did not actually make it into a church. Pulcheria and Marcian erected a church on the site. The writer has more to say about the church of St Mocius: 'But the holy Mocius [*i.e.* the building now called by that name] was twice as long as it now is, but Constantine the Great and his mother cut away half of the Temple and erected the altar. Because the holy Mocius was executed there, for that reason he erected the church, as belonging to him, and brought his body there'.[22] In another part of the collection the same writer tells us that 'The holy Mocius was first built by Constantine because many pagans lived in that area; it used to be the Temple of Zeus, and accordingly the church was built out of the same stones'.[23] This is a fairly straightforward case of a pagan temple being half pulled down and a church being built on the ruined part; part of the temple was apparently left still standing but not used for the Church.

The next case is the one referred to by A. H. M. Jones, in which a converted Jew called Joseph is alleged in the reign of Constantine to have transformed a derelict temple in Tiberias in Palestine into a church. If we look up Epiphanius, the source of this information, we find that the temple, a Hadrianum, was not just derelict, it was unfinished; its walls had not reached higher than seven feet; clearly it had never been a temple.[24] It is not

---

[21] Preger, *op. cit.*, II. 3 (214–215). 2.

[22] *Ibid.*, II. 3 (215).3.

[23] *Ibid.*, II (209). 110. The church had a varied history later. I have omitted mention in the text of the Christian church on the Capitol at Constantina in modern Algeria, which was certainly a transformed temple, because, though Dupuch and Raversié in the nineteenth century had assigned its date to the reign of Constantine, Gsell places it with more probability at a much later date. See S. Gsell, *Les monuments antiques de l'Algérie* (Paris, 1901), II.121.192–194.

[24] Epiphanius, *Adverus Haereses*, XXX.1.12.2 (*PG*, 41, 425f.).

surprising, even so, that Joseph's attempts at evangelising failed, because not only would the local Jews have discouraged him but probably the local Christians as well, who would not relish the idea of a Christian church built on even the beginnings of a pagan temple. The next example is the Temple of Didymean Apollo in front of the town of Miletus. When the emperor Julian arrived within reach of it he learnt that Christians had established some sort of worship in the *temenos*. But investigation of this case shows that what the Christians had done was to erect some building near or next to the temple. Julian ordered that if the building had a roof and a holy table it was to be burned; if the buildings were half completed, they were to be demolished from the foundations.[25] Had this been the case of the transformation of a temple, it is wholly improbable that Julian would have ordered its burning or demolition.

Gregorovius states that the Temple of Baal at Heliopolis, converted to a church about 391, is the first instance of a transformation of this kind.[26] Investigation, however, shows that this is not a true example of transformation or conversion of a temple. Gregorovius did not have access to the results of archaeological research, and he may have been misled by the entry dealing with this event in the *Chronicon Paschale*. In fact this entry relates that Theodosius 'destroyed [κατέλυσεν] the Temple of Heliopolis, the Temple of Balanios, the great and famous Trilithon, and made it a Christian Church. Similarly he made the Temple of Damascus a Christian Church'.[27] Archaeological excavation has now shown that the temple itself was demolished, so that the old altar was buried several feet below the floor of the central aisle. Part of the steps leading to the temple-area were preserved, though part was turned into a presbytery, and three portals of the eastern façade of the temple court with a flight of steps leading to them were also left. But the temple itself was destroyed and its materials used for building the church.[28]

[25] Sozomenus, *Hist. Ecc.*, V.20.7. A large church was later erected on the site, see Deichmann, *op. cit.*, pp. 111,129.

[26] *Op. cit.*, II, 109 n. 1

[27] *Chronicon Paschale*, ed. L. Dindorf (Berlin, 1832), I, 561.

[28] Deichmann, *op cit.*, pp. 109, 115, 116.

The last and most apparently impressive evidence for the early transformation of a pagan temple into a church is alleged to have occurred about the year 399 when the Bishop of Carthage, Aurelius, consecrated a temple of the god Caelestis as a church.[29] Our evidence for this is to be found in the narrative of Quodvultdeus, friend and correspondent of Augustine and later Bishop of Carthage, writing at the end of his life in exile from Africa in the middle of the fifth century.[30] The author says that he was present at the incident himself, and there is no reason to doubt his veracity nor his memory. Aurelius caused the road to the temple to be cleared by enthusiastic Christians, *ea facilitate . . . qua templum suo vere caelesti regi et domino consecrarent.* Then the bishop entered the temple, accompanied by a large crowd of clergy and laity, and *cathedram illic posuit in loco Caelestis et sedit.* All were amazed at finding shortly afterwards an ancient inscription in the temple which ran *Aurelius pontifex dedicavit.* At first sight this looks very like a direct taking over of a temple, but second thoughts should give us pause. Quodvultdeus tells us that the temple was outside the city walls at the end of a two-mile path in a deserted and neglected estate. This does not appear the best place to institute a church to be used regularly. It was also surrounded by other temples which were not converted. Further, Quodvultdeus proceeds to tell us in the same passage that several years after, about the year 418, the tribune Ursus razed to the ground all the temples on the site and turned the place into a cemetery. It seems extremely unlikely that he could have done this had the Temple of Caelestis been positively transformed into a church. It is much more probable that Bishop Aurelius about 399 made a single visit to the temple in order, so to speak, to meet the pagan challenge and show that Christ was more powerful than Caelestis. Quodvultdeus does not even say that he celebrated Mass in the temple. I think it most improbable that he did. Quodvultdeus is telling this story not in order to show how pagan temples are being transformed into Christian churches but to relate what he believes to be the wonderful prediction inscribed in the temple. This case cannot therefore be regarded with any confidence as disproving the claim made in this paper that no pagan temples were transformed into churches in the fourth century.[31]

When, then, did the practice of transforming pagan temples begin? It seems likely that the movement was initiated by a law of the year 435. Hitherto the emperors both in the East and in the West had been reluctant to encourage the destruction of pagan monuments and had even forbidden the practice, more persistently in the West than in the East.[32] But in that year a law of Theodosius II officially ordained the prohibition of all pagan cults and encouraged the destruction and transformation of temples and shrines by the Christians, their walls being purified by the sign of the Cross.[33] 'Destruction' in this context may mean no more than removal of furniture, decorations, statues and paintings. We may reasonably assume that this was the period from which began the practice of converting or transforming pagan temples into Christian churches.

It seems impossible to determine with any accuracy which was the first clear example of this type of transformation. Archaeology and literature, however, as has already been intimated, combine to give us plenty of instances. The Lararium attached to the Templum Sacrae Urbis at Rome was turned into the Church of St Cosmas and St Damian in the reign of Pope Felix VI (526–530),[34] the Pantheon was similarly rededicated in the reign of Pope Boniface VI (608–615),[35] the Parthenon in Athens some time between 431 and 595.[36] The

[31] Mâle, pp. 46–47, seems largely to support this view.

[32] For the details of Imperial legislation on this subject, see Gregorovius, I, 64–65, 75–76; Deichmann, pp. 105, 106.

[33] Cod. Theod. XVI. 10. 25 (14 November 435) Isidoro P. P. (Orientis) Constantinopoli; Gregorovius (I, 76) places this law in 425 and attributes it to Valentinian III as well as Theodosius II.

[34] Liber Pontificalis, ed. L. Duchesne, I (Paris, 1886), LVI, 279; Homes Dudden, I, 58; Deichmann, pp 113, 134, 135.

[35] Duchesne, Lib. Pont. I, LXVIII, 317; Homes Dudden, p. 58; Gregorovius, II, 105–113; Deichmann, p. 135; Duchesne reckons this as the first known example of such transformation.

[36] Deichmann, pp. 112, 131.

Theseion and the Erechtheum in Athens were similarly converted at an unknown date, the outsides being left untouched, and only the insides altered.[37] The Cathedral at Syracuse is a transformed temple.[38] The taking over and adaptation of the Temple of Hercules at Agrigentum can be approximately dated to the very end of the sixth century from the description of this event in the life of St Gregory of Agrigentum; it is perhaps worth noting that Bishop Gregory ensured that some considerable time elapsed between his first praying in the temple and exorcising it and the actual dedication to SS. Peter and Paul.[39] Procopius in the middle of the sixth century refers to two temples in Comana in Cappadocia, one dedicated to Artemis and one to Iphigeneia, originally supposed to have been founded by Orestes 'which however the Christians have made into Churches for themselves, scarcely changing the building at all'.[40] Ennodius tells us of the transformation not long before the year 500 of a pagan temple, with very little change, into a church dedicated to SS. Peter and Paul in Novara in Italy.[41] That the building remained substantially unchanged is conveyed to us clearly by Ennodius' words, *in alium statum, inconcussis migraverint fundamenta culminibus et, cum ad structuram parum humanus sudor adiecerit, quaecumque fuerunt innovata sint, dum persistunt* (I, p. 121). Cagnat and Gauckler give a list of a few more temples converted into churches in Tunisia, and Gauckler

---

[37] Deichmann, *loc. cit.*, and p. 132. One scholar, Orlando, thought that he could detect traces of a fifth-century apse in the Theseion, but this is far from certain.

[38] Deichmann, pp. 112, 135 (see Abbild 19).

[39] *Vita S. Gregorii Agrigentini, PG*, 98, 549–716; Deichmann, p. 134. I do not know why Deichmann calls it the Temple of Concordia. It should, however, be noted that recent scholarship has tended to suggest that this particular *Vita* is late and unreliable. See I. Croce, 'Per la cronologia della vita di S. Gregorio Agrigentieno', *Bollettino della Badia di Grottoferrata*, n.s. IV (1950), 189–207; V (1951), 77ff.; E. Patlagean, 'Les moines grecs d'Italie et l'apologie des thèses médiévales', *Studi Medievali* Ser. 3, v (Florence, 1964), 579–562.

[40] Procopius, *History of the Wars* (ed. H. B. Dewing, Loeb ser., London, (1914) I. xvii. 18, 19.

[41] Ennodius, *Opera*, ed. F. Vogel (Berlin, 1885, Mon. Germ. Hist. Auct. Antiquiss, VII), XCVIII. 2, pp. 121–122; Deichmann, p. 134.

alone in a later book some more, none of which can be dated.[42] It is well known that Pope Gregory the Great at the turn of the sixth to the seventh century encouraged Augustine at Canterbury to transform pagan temples into churches rather than to demolish them.[43] Moreover, Mâle points out that in many places a Christian family chapel replaced the family's traditional *lararium* where on certain occasions the workers on the estate would gather for the cult. Paulinus of Nola in the early years of the fifth century built a church in his villa, the *Primuliacum*, on the Garonne, and Mâle gives several other examples of churches being built on the site of *lararia* on estates in Gaul.[44] But these are not precisely the same as transforming shrines into churches. Perhaps the Roman villa at Lullingstone, near Otford in Kent, where the Christian chapel was built one storey above the still-used pagan shrine, represents a half-way stage to this situation. However, none of the examples reviewed here suggests that the process of transforming pagan temples into Christian churches started as early as the fourth century, or that it was widely put in hand even after the year 435. Deichmann points out that pagan temples were not really suitable for such a purpose. The Christian church signified a change from cult-image to cult-space ('von Kultbild zum Kultraum'), and observes that when the Church began to create painting and plastic arts it took its inspiration and models, not from the Graeco-Roman aesthetic tradition, but from the East.[45] The whole of Mâle's book is a testimony to the same truth.

Several instances can be found of secular buildings being taken over in order to transform them into churches. Parts of the porticus system in the Forum at Aelia Capitolina were included in the atrium of Constantine's Church of the Anastasis

[42] R. Cagnat et P. Gauckler, *Les monuments historiques de la Tunisie* (Paris, 1898), I, 121–122, and P. Gauckler, *Basiliques chrétiennes de Tunisie* (Paris, 1913), Plates III and IV and p. 10. Schneider, *op. cit.* p. 178, has a useful comment on one of these; in that part of his article he gives a list of ten examples of such a transformation in Roman Africa known to him.

[43] Bede. *Hist. Ecc.*, I.XXX; Gregory, *Epistles*, xi. 56.

[44] Mâle, pp. 61–64.

[45] Deichmann, p. 114.

at Jerusalem.[46] If we are to believe Mâle, an imperial palace at Trèves was transformed into the Cathedral there as early as 364–378.[47] In the fourth century a secular hall was partly preserved in order to build a church at Deir es-Smēdj in Syria.[48] At some time between 471 and 483 Pope Simplicius transformed a private building originally erected by the consul Junius Bassus in 317 and later owned by somebody called Valila into the Church of St Andrew in Rome.[49] The mausoleum which Diocletian built for himself at Aspalathos (Split) near Salona early in the fourth century was in the seventh or eighth converted into a cathedral.[50] In the sixth century the Church of St Maria Antiqua in Rome was converted from a secular building.[51] It seems as if the Christians were ready to take over secular buildings as churches rather earlier than they felt themselves free to adapt pagan temples.

One other point deserves mention in connection with this subject. Deichmann is very cautious about concluding that Christians when they transformed pagan temples chose the dedications of these churches to suit the deity which had once inhabited them, e.g. that they dedicated to the Blessed Virgin Mary temples which had been sacred to female goddesses. The only examples which he can muster are the Parthenon at Athens, dedicated to the Virgin Mary instead of the Virgin Athene, as a kind of 'reinterpretation', and the Pantheon at Rome, dedicated not only to the Virgin but also to all martyrs.[52] He could, however, have added at least one more, the Temple of Rhea, mother of the gods, at Cyzicus rededicated in the second half of the fifth century during the reign of Zeno

[46] Deichmann, p 120.

[47] Mâle, pp. 127–128.

[48] Deichmann, p. 117.

[49] See Lib. Pont. I. XLVIII, 249, 280, and Duchesne's note there; Homes Dudden, p. 58; D. M. Hope, The Leonine Sacramentary (Oxford, 1971), p. 52, is mistaken in thinking that this is the earliest known instance of a secular building being converted into a church.

[50] See E. Dyggve, Salonitan Christianity (Oslo, 1951), pp. 85, 125–126; a small temple near the mausoleum was made into a baptistery at about the same time.

[51] Deichmann, p. 113.

[52] Deichmann, p. 114 n. 3.

(476–491) to Mary Mother of God.[53] Gregorovius indeed suggests several more instances in Rome: the Lararium with the Templum Sacrae Urbis, associated with the twins Romulus and Remus, dedicated to the twin physicians Cosmas and Damian; S. Sabina taking over the dedication to Diana on the Aventine; Mars the war god replaced by SS. George and Sebastian, military tribunes. He even suggests that the Pantheon must have been dedicated to Cybele mother of the gods because Pope Boniface dedicated it to Maria Deipara; but this is sheer guesswork.[54]

No doubt this principle of 'like to like' did sometimes influence those who chose the dedications of temples converted into churches, but other motives certainly operated also. The biographer of St Gregory of Agrigentum, for instance, in the passage already referred to, says that Bishop Gregory chose to dedicate his church changed from a temple to SS. Peter and Paul because these were the chiefs of the apostles, capable of dealing with the powerful demons who had inhabited the temple. It is perhaps significant that Ennodius reveals in the narrative adduced above that the church converted from a temple at Novara was dedicated to these two saints, Peter and Paul, also.

---

[53] John Malalas, *Chronographica*, ed. L. Dindorf (Bonn, 1831), IV. 77–78 (p. 78). Cedrenus, *Historiarum Compendium*, ed. I. Bekker (Bonn, 1838), pp. 209, 210, repeats the story in almost the same words.

[54] Gregorovius, II, III.

17

THE REACTION OF THE CHURCH TO THE COLLAPSE OF THE WESTERN ROMAN EMPIRE IN THE FIFTH CENTURY[*]

About a century before the collapse of the Western Roman Empire took place the Church had been taken completely unawares by the decision of the Roman Imperial Government to recognize, tolerate and finally patronize it. The Church was taken just as much by surprise by the collapse of the Western Empire. We can hardly blame the church for the first surprise and as far as the second is concerned we can at least say that though the signs of coming collapse were evident enough, nobody at the time, pagan or Christian, recognized them. On the contrary, about the year 400 the average Roman citizen who knew anything of the history of Rome would probably have said that the Empire was in a flourishing and secure state, likely to last for many more centuries. It had indeed survived a severe and menacing time of troubles rather less than two centuries before, when between 249 and 272 it did look very much as if the Empire was breaking up under the stress of internal strife and external attack, economic chaos and serious epidemic. But that danger, everybody knew, was now past. A succession of strong Emperors, culminating in Diocletian, had reunited the Empire and restored order, security and confidence. Economic stringency, particularly in the form of immobility and the disappearance of the small farmer and steady increase of taxation, was indeed a constant threat. But stability had been restored to the currency by Diocletian's and Constantine's gold *solidus,* even though inflation seriously affected smaller, copper, denominations. Theodosius I had recently been successful in suppressing Imperial usurpers and reuniting the Empire. The brilliant general Stilicho was at the disposal of Theodosius' two sons, Honorius and Arcadius, and a very complex and solid, albeit inefficient and bureaucratic, civil

[*] This paper was given to a conference of the Dublin Mediaeval Society held in University College, Dublin (of the National University of Ireland), on January 20th 1971.

service was apparently guaranteeing the indefinite continuance of the Empire. Nobody expected its demise, and certainly nobody wanted it. There were no nationalist movements, no spirit whatever of anti-Imperialism. The barbarians themselves, whose presence within the Empire was now much more apparent than it had been a century before, were not particularly anxious to end Imperial rule. Least of all did the Christian Church, still basking in the sunshine of a patronage the short withdrawal of which by the Emperor Julian forty years before had only served to make the enjoyment of it sweeter, desire such a dismal event as the collapse of the Roman Empire. Even long after the dreadful calamity had taken place, Christian writers could not dissociate membership of the Christian Church from Roman citizenship. To Salvian, writing his *De Gubernatione Dei* in Marseilles about 440, the two are identical; he cannot really envisage barbarians as Catholic Christians. Patrick, as is well known, on the extreme verge of Christendom, evangelizing a country which he believes to be the very last on earth, has his famous phrase *Consuetudo Romanorum Gallorum Christianorum.*[1] In the mind of Sidonius Apollinaris, writing later in the century in Gaul, the Roman Empire and the Christian Church are indissolubly intertwined; the two support each other, but on the whole the Church exists to support the Empire rather than vice versa.

And yet the Empire collapsed. The invasion of Italy by Radagaesus in 405 gave everybody a bad shock. But the true moment of collapse, the moment of irreversible disaster, came with the enormous invasion of barbarians westward across the Rhine over the Belgian, Gallic and finally Spanish provinces which began in 407 and never really finished, for these invaders were never effectively removed and most of them finally settled permanently within the borders of the Empire, acknowledging the rule of the central Imperial Government either only formally or not at all. In 410 came the frightful blow of the capture of Rome by Alaric and his Goths. Thereafter almost every single province of the Western Roman Empire was successfully   wrested   from   the   grasp   of   the   Imperial

---

[1] *Epistle to Coroticus* 14; *cf.* his use of *civibus* at *Ep.* 2.

Government, the German, Belgian, Gallic and Spanish provinces, the African provinces, the Illyrian, and Danubian provinces, and finally Italy itself, after a long period of rule by puppet Emperors supported by barbarian war-lords, was subjected formally and without pretence to the rule of the Herulian Odoacer in 476. Britain alone had revolted of its own accord in 408 and Britain alone remained for a very long time immune from barbarian invasion, though not from barbarian raids. In all his lament for Roman lands whose corruption had entailed their subjection to barbarian rule, Salvian does not mention Britain once. The silence is significant, Britain was the interesting exception, and continued to be an exception, even when the barbarian invaders arrived, by holding up their advance much longer than any other part of the Roman Empire had succeeded in doing.

The shock created by these events was tremendous; we have all read the words of St. Jerome as he deplores the taking of Rome by Alaric in the language of the prophets and of the book of Revelation. Among pagans it roused angry accusations that the Roman Empire had collapsed because the Christians had caused the withdrawal of worship from Rome's ancestral gods. Among the Christians it produced bewilderment and dismay. How could God allow an empire which had recently espoused the cause of Christianity in so signal a manner to be destroyed? Among the uneducated and the semi-educated apocalyptic ideas became widespread, the cry *totus mundus perit* was in the mouths of many. Such calamities must portend the end of the world.[2] Through the two works of Patrick, who must, I fear, be classed on his own confession as semi-educated, runs the conviction that he is in the last period of the world's age evangelizing the last race upon earth. But among intellectuals the disasters occurring to the Western Roman Empire were diversely evaluated, and it is worth while glancing at a few of these different interpretations.

Ammianus Marcellinus, the very able pagan historian of the

---

[2] The expression occurs in the first of *Eight Pelagian Epistles*, edited by Caspari and reprinted in Brussels in 1964, 1.1.(7), *Dices mihi illam vulgi sententiam: Ergo totus mundus perit*. But very similar sentiments can be found in Vincent of Lerins, *Commonitorum* (ed. Moxon, Cambridge, 1915) 1.3.

late Roman Empire, writing in the last decade of the fourth century, has, of course, no inkling of coming disaster. He does in one place remark that the Roman Empire is now in its old age,[3] but we would never have agreed that it had actually reached the hour of death. Rufinus, writing a little later his *Ecclesiastical History*, a conventional, uninformative and over-rhetorical affair ending with the death of Theodosius in 395, can only have seen the very beginning of the end; but he prepares for disasters which his account does not reach by saying of the battle of Hadrianople (378), *quae pugna initium mali Romano imperio tunc et deinceps fuit*.[4] He does not, however, elaborate any particular philosophy of history. Paulus Orosius, on the other hand, wrote his work *Historia adversus Paganos in* 417 or 418 in order, as the title indicates, to counter anti-Christian propaganda disseminated by the pagans as a result of the disasters which had befallen the Western Roman Empire. By this time it was all too obvious that things were going very wrong indeed; and Christians were finding it necessary to explain why things were going wrong under a Christian government. One would expect—and Christian publicists had in the previous hundred years constantly led people to expect—that with firmly Christian, and firmly orthodox, Christian Emperors nothing

[3] *Rerum Gestarum Libri* (ed. Garthausen, Teubner series, Leipzig, 1873) 14.6.3. Contrast the attitude of the pagan historian Zosimus, writing in Constantinople nearly a hundred years later. He is as pessimistic from the pagan point of view as Salvian is from the Christian. He wrote to show how the divine power had withdrawn its support from the Roman Empire because of its Government's defection to Christianity and his date for the origin of the evil is 308, when Constantine should have celebrated the Secular Games and failed to do so (*Historia Nova*, ed. Mendelssohn (Leipzig, 1887, repr. Hildesheim, 1963) 2.7 [65]). He shows peculiar antipathy to Constantine (*ibid.*, 2.8.9 [65–66], 29 [86], 34 [91, 92]). The *daemon* was guiding events (*tyche*) to bring about the ruin of the Roman Empire at the death of the Emperor Julian and at the battle of Hadrianople (*ibid.*, 4.4. [161] and 24 [179]). The Emperor Gratian was punished with early assassination for refusing the title of Pontifex Maximus (*ibid.*, 4.39 [192]). Another landmark of apostasy was Theodosius' closing of the pagan temples (*ibid.*, 4.59 [216]). And the daemon was not gorged with exacting vengeance for the abandonment of the traditional cults by the death of Stilicho (*ibid.*, 5 35 [262]).

[4] *Continuation of Eusebius' Ecclesiastical History*, ed. T. Mommsen (*G.C.S.* series, Leipzig, 1908) 11.13.

serious could happen to the Roman Empire. So Orosius, encouraged by his master Augustine, became the first—and by no means the last—Christian propagandist writer of history. He made a very silly, inconsistent and crude hand at it. For him disaster and calamity are signs of God's wrath when they happen to pagan Emperors and pagan Imperial armies. Similar occurrences experienced by Christian Emperors and armies are the machinations of the devil. The disaster of Hadrianople struck indeed a Christian Emperor, Valens, but as he was an Arian heretic, this does not count; he was punished because he persecuted the orthodox.[5] The murder of the able and loyal Gothic general Stilicho, with his totally innocent son Eucherius, by the inept Honorius, Orosius hails as the act of a religious and liberty-loving Emperor done for the benefit of the Church.[6] The sack of Rome by Alaric should not cause anyone disturbance because the Christians were well-treated by the Goths and only the pagans (deservedly) suffered.[7] His repulsive sycophancy towards the worthless Emperor Honorius is only matched by the idiotic optimism which he displays about the future of the Roman Empire. The barbarian invasions are perhaps regrettable, but they have given the opportunity for the conversion to Christianity of thousands of Huns, Suevi, Vandals and Burgundians.[8] He regards the Empire, in the year 417 or 418, as in a flourishing and peaceful condition under the wise and able Honorius.[9] The Imperial general Constantius had just driven the Goths out of the southern Gallic provinces into Spain where they were occupying themselves most satisfactorily in either killing each other or making peace with Honorius. No circumstances could be happier that these.[10] Shortsighted ineptitude in an historian could scarcely go further than this.

Very different was the attitude of Orosius' master Augustine. Here was one fully capable of formulating an impressive

[5] *Historia adversus Paganos* (Migne, *Patrologia Latina* 31) 23 (1147).

[6] *Ibid.*, 38 (1162).

[7] *Ibid.*, 39 (1163–1165).

[8] *Ibid.*, 41 (1168). Orosius does seem to possess a genuine concern for the conversion of the barbarians, lacking in other authors.

[9] *Ibid.*, 42 (1169–1171).

[10] *Ibid.*, 43 (1171–1174).

philosophy of history, and in his *De Civitate Dei* that is precisely what Augustine did. His approach was at once thorough, realistic and profound. He has no faith in the continuance of the Roman Empire. He surveys it in all its long history; he does his best to render it justice; he recognizes the virtues of its founders and of its great men, even while he is conducting a polemic against its traditional religion. But he tries to view it *sub specie aeternitatis*, and in this perspective it must be condemned. It had placed its whole hope and trust in success—*gloria*—and by that wordly standard it had at last failed, as it was inevitably destined in the end to fail. Even the Christian Emperors could not save it, though Augustine is not above special pleading of their behalf. In contrast to the city of this world, the Roman Empire, Augustine draws a parallel history of the *civitas Dei*, the chosen people of God, whose destiny is beyond this world, whose standards, values and objectives are quite different from those of the wordly city. So hugely superior is Augustine's handling of this subject to that of any other ancient author, Christian or pagan, who dealt with it that it is no wonder that the *De Civitate Dei* became one of the most influential books in the history of Europe for the next thousand years. One could say with only a little exaggeration that the history of the Church in the Middle Ages is the history of the attempt to build Augustine's *civitas Dei* on earth—an attempt which Augustine himself would have strongly deprecated.

Two authors in Gaul later in the fifth century next claim our attention. Salvian was writing in Marseilles a little after the year 440. He, like Orosius and Augustine, is concerned to answer the murmurs of Christians, who now, after nearly forty years of uninterrupted and mounting disaster to Roman power, are asking awkward questions: 'Why should the situation of the barbarians be so much better than ours?' they ask.[11]. But pagans are asking similar questions, and Salvian is concerned primarily to vindicate, not the Roman Empire nor the Christian Church in the Empire, but God's providential ordering of the universe,

[11] *De Gubernatione Dei*, ed. Pauly (C.S.E.L. series, Vienna, 1883), 3.1.2, *cur multo melior sit barbarorum condicio quam nostra? cf.* 4.12.54. God allows us to become conquered by barbarians, to be subjected to the authority of our enemies.

which concerns pagans as much as Christians. Salvian answers precisely the questions which Orosius and Augustine set out to answer, but instead of arguing that only pagans and heretics have suffered and that all is basically well, or that the Roman pagans were responsible for their own collapse because their apparent virtues were only glittering vices, he declares that it is the vices of the *Christian* Romans that have destroyed the Empire, by bringing God's wrath on it. He contrasts the pure and moderate barbarians with the corrupt, incorrigible and lascivious Romans. He harks back, not to the golden age of the early Church, but to the golden age of the early Roman state. He believes deeply in the civilizing mission of the Romans. What he deplores is the Christian Romans' failure to implement and live up to this mission. In spite of his contrast between the relatively innocent barbarian and the sophisticated wickedness of the Romans, and in spite of a remarkably tolerant and large-minded attitude to Arian heretics, Salvian does not like the barbarians. There is not the slightest sign in his writings that he is anxious to pave the way for the Church to come to terms with the barbarians. He is very far from believing that the Church can turn its back on the corrupt Roman past and face a bright future with the barbarians. His outlook is purely pessimistic; he sees no future for the Romans at all, and he is not interested in the future of the barbarians: *illi crescunt cotidie nos decrescimus, illi proficiunt nos humiliamur, illi florent et nos arescimus.*[12] It is the Christians' fault that the barbarians are heretics.[13] The oppression of the Roman Government has driven many Romans to take refuge with the barbarians, in spite of their heresy.[14] Others have taken refuge with the Bacaudae, the irregular armies of bandits recruited from dispossessed peasants, and it is the fault of the Christians that the Bacaudae are formed.[15] One by one the Roman provinces of the West have succumbed to the invaders, but God cannot be blamed for this.

[12] *Ibid.*, 7.11.49

[13] *Ibid.*, 5.3.14.

[14] And in spite of their smell! *Ibid.*, 5.5.20. Sidonius Apollinaris similarly comments upon the barbarians' smell.

[15] *Ibid.*, 5.5.22, 23. Orosius witnesses to the same tendency of Roman citizens to desert to the barbarians, *op. cit.*, 41 (1168).

The misconduct of the Roman Christians has incurred his just wrath.[16]

The other Gallic author is Sidonius Apollinaris. He spent most of his life as a cultured member of the Roman upper classes at his properties in Lugdunum and Avitiacum near Augustonemetum, but in 470 became bishop of Augustonemetum and died some time after 485; he left several letters and some works more interesting for their references to contemporary history than for their literary merit. He was a wholehearted admirer of the Roman Empire; his father and grandfather had held high positions in the Imperial civil service and he was proud to follow in their footsteps even in the twilight period of the puppet Emperors after the death of Valentinian III in 455. He did not abandon hope for the Empire until almost after the last hour. In 456 he declares that he still expects Roman rule to last for centuries.[17] Less than two years before the total extinction of the Western Roman Empire, under the second-last of the puppet Emperors, Julius Nepos (474–475), Sidonius still hopes for a glorious future for the Empire.[18] He sees no future whatever for Romans living under barbarian rule, and actively dislikes the barbarians, even the best of them.[19] He sneers at their lack of culture.[20] He is startled and annoyed when he learns that a Roman friend is learning Gothic or Burgundian.[21] He bitterly describes Lyons under the Burgundian Chilperic II as *Lugdunensem Germaniam*,[22] he refers to Visigoths generally as 'the pact-breaking race',[23] and when Julius Nepos betrayed Auvergne, the very area where Sidonius was bishop, to the Gothic king Euric, Sidonius called the Goths

---

[16] *De Gubernatione Dei* 7.12.50, 52; 13.55, 56.

[17] *Carmina*, ed. W. B. Anderson and E. H. Warmington (Leob series, Vol I. 1963, Vol II. 1965, London and Cambridge Mass.) 7.55–56, *cf. Epistulae* 3.8.112.

[18] *Epistulae* 4.14.1 and 5.16.1.2.

[19] *Epistulae* 2. 1.2; 7.14.10; *Carmina* 12.1 22, the Burgundian billetted on him by the system of *hospitalitas* in his estate at Lugdunum *c*. 462 are unfortunately within smelling distance!

[20] *Epistulae* 4.8.5.

[21] *Ibid.*, 5.5.1–3.

[22] *Ibid.*, 5.7.7.

[23] *Ibid.*, 6.6.1, *foedifragam gentem*.

'public enemies'.[24] Apart from one vague statement that the present era is sinking in old age,[25] he has no philosophy of history. One gains the impression that he consented to become a bishop, not because he perceived that the future lay with the Church, but because he saw this as the best way in which he could serve *Romanae res*. He proved an excellent and conscientious bishop, who even incurred temporary exile by the king Euric for his championship of his flock. As far as he could he no doubt continued to the end his opposition to all things barbarian. It is ironical that his son is found fighting for Euric's successor king Alaric II at the battle of Vouillé in 507 when Alaric was defeated and killed by Clovis King of the Franks. The boy's great-grandfather had served the usurper Constantine III. The family evidently had a penchant for lost causes.

It cannot be said, then, that for the most part the Church foresaw or prepared for the part it was to play in the coming centuries as far as the judgment of the intellectuals is concerned. We have, however, seen some evidence that the bishops found themselves sucked into the new state of affairs without particularly planning to take part. into new political and administrative activity. There had already in the fourth century and in the early years of the fifth existed a tendency for able men to find in the Church a sphere of responsible and constructive action which they could not find elsewhere, *e.g.* in the civil service or the army or just in the administration of their estates. Ambrose is one example, Augustine perhaps another and Synesius a third. The letters of Popes Innocent and Siricius during this period show that many people in high positions in the Imperial civil service were attempting to leave the service in order to get ordained, and although the Popes co-operated with the Emperors to prevent this tendency it is unlikely that they were entirely successful.

As one sees the day to day life of the mid-fifth century Church reflected in the letters of Sidonius Apollinaris one realizes that the Church as a community offered a freedom

[24] *Ibid.*, 7.7.2.
[25] *Ibid.*, 8.6.3.

which was absent from the immobile, totalitarian and bureaucratically stifled Late Western Roman Empire. A sense of justice and of the need to represent all interests prevailed. Local government in a secular sense had long been strangled by the centralized military dictatorship into which the Augustan Principate had developed. But local ecclesiastical government existed and was free, lively and almost, in a 'co-operative' sort of way, democratic. This impression is particularly strong in the accounts which Sidonius gives of the election and ordination of bishops.

One of the most striking examples of the attraction offered by the Church in the fifth century was the life of Germanus who left a good career in the civil service to become bishop of Auxerre in 418, yielding to popular clamour, and who did not hesitate during his episcopal career to add political activities to his episcopal duties. He appears to have felt a particular responsibility for the people of Armorica, and it was while he was visiting the Imperial court at Ravenna to intercede for these people after they had staged some political commotions that he died in 448. He also, like so many bishops at that time, was successful in dissuading, at least temporarily, a Gothic king from invading the territory containing his see. We are reminded of the famous embassy from Rome, of which by far the most important and influential member was Leo I bishop of Rome, which dissuaded Attila and his Huns from attacking the city in 452,[26] and of Ammianus bishop of Orleans who was the life and soul of the resistance to the Huns during their siege of that city in 451.[27] The Goths themselves used Catholic bishops as intermediaries with the Romans according to Salvian,[28] and Sidonius tells us that bishops were used to negotiate treaties with Euric, among them Epiphanius, bishop of Ticinum/Pavia.[29]

[26] Leo also was the chief negotiator with the Vandals when they captured Rome in 455.

[27] This kind of episcopal activity was not confined to the West. We can recall Eunomius bishop of Theodosiopolis who defended the city stoutly when it was besieged by the Persians $c.$ 405. Synesius in Cyrene found himself forced into much the same role in 410–414.

[28] De Gub. Dei 7.9.39.

[29] Epistulae 7.7.10.

Sidonius himself took a prominent part in attempting to preserve the territory in which his see was situated for the Roman Empire, and thereby earned exile from king Euric for his pains. Bishops of course continued throughout the Roman Empire to arbitrate in civil suits when they were asked to do. One reason for the employment of bishops in secular activities was that the barbarian rulers when they gained possession of territories formerly belonging to the Roman Empire found themselves very short of trained and experienced administrators. They found it advisable to make little alteration in the existing system of taxation. They naturally turned for help to the bishops of the Church who were well educated and trained in administration and not inexperienced in financial affairs. Further, with the barbarian invasions the educational system of the Roman Empire broke down completely; the threefold structure of *ludus, grammaticus* and *rhetor* ceased to exist. The Church, which had hitherto entirely relied on the existing system, was forced to improvise its own system, based on the bishop's *familia*, in order to educate its ordinands. By the second half of the fifth century, therefore, clergy were increasingly the only educated, certainly the only well-educated, people in the community, and the barbarian ruler had no option but to employ them in his civil and diplomatic service.

In a quite contrary direction, there can be no doubt that one of the reactions of the Church to the collapse of the Western Roman Empire was an increased impulse towards monasticism. Monasticism had been a slow growth in the West. But even before the collapse came many people were deliberately forsaking society in the West and living voluntary lives of withdrawn asceticism in small groups, as the examples given in the eighth book of Augustine's *Confessions* show and the careers of people like Martin and Paulinus of Nola. Rutilius Namatianus early in the fifth century describes the solitary ascetics who can be seen inhabiting islands and remote places on a journey from Rome to Gaul. It is not surprising that a number of people determined to opt out of a society which appeared to be collapsing around them and to have no future. No doubt economic motives played their part in the movement also. One of Salvian's letters commends a young man to some fellow-monks; his indigent mother has been provided for, and apparently Salvian hopes to have her son provided for in a monastery.[30] There must have been many such cases. There is, however, no reason to doubt the sincerity of the monks whose lives we find pictured in Cassian's *Institutes* and *Conferences* nor of those who formed the monastic communities at Lérins and Grincy, mentioned with respect and admiration several times by Sidonius Apollinaris, nor of the individual ascetics such as Severinus of Noricum and Benedict of Monte Cassino who by their austerity and philanthropy deeply impressed their contemporaries even in that time of chaos and calamity. It is in the fifth century too that there appears the phenomenon of monks forming part of a bishop's *familia* such as we find in the case of Augustine, of some Gallic bishops mentioned by Sidonius and probably in the remote British Isles in the case of Ninian and of Patrick. It is in the fifth century too that there appears that phenomenon of which Martin appears to be the sole representative in the fourth century, the monk chosen to be bishop. We can compile a list of such Gallic bishops including Honoratus and Hilary bishops of Arles, Eucherius of Lyons, and Maximus and Faustus of Riez. Certainly the disasters of the fifth century gave a renewed impulse to monasticism in the West, even though it was not as great as the extraordinary ascetic movement which swept across Europe in the next century and which gave its monastic structures to the Celtic Church. But this increased impetus towards monasticism was not accompanied by any missionary impulse. On the contrary, the missionary expansion of the Church in the West almost came to a stop in the fifth century. This is not surprising, because a period of social collapse and economic chaos and dislocation is not at all likely to be one of missionary expansion. But even the desire to evangelize seems to be lacking. Orosius, it is true, looks forward to the conversion of the invading barbarians, but Orosius was unrealistic to an almost fatuous degree and was writing before it was unmistakably clear that the Empire would not recover from its disasters. Salvian has no expectation of

---

[30] *Epistulae*, ed. Pauly (*C.S.E.L.* series, Vienna, 1883) 1.

converting either pagans or barbarian Arian heretics. It does not enter the head of Sidonius Apollinaris that the barbarians might be converted. Severinus and Benedict live and labour heroically, but they do not attempt to convert either pagans or heretics, though there was no lack of either in the neighbourhood of both men. It is only at the very end of the century, in 496, that the Franks are converted to Catholicism. Only at the very beginning of the century before the troubles have started do we find missionary zeal, with the work of Victricius, and in remote places untroubled by barbarian invasions, such as Britain and Ireland, with the work of Ninian and Patrick. Indeed the evangelistic work of these two is a striking confirmation of the view that Britain in the fifth century was a remarkable exception among the successor states of the former Western Roman Empire, untroubled by invasions, able to develop in relative tranquillity its own social and political life.

We may well ask whether the fifth century, as a time of peculiar misery and wretchedness for masses of people, a period of wrecked houses, displaced persons, enforced movements of populations, economic decline and widespread insecurity and despair, brought out in the Church that which ought to be its characteristic note, and as it were, signature, a sense of compassion. This had not been much in evidence ever since the state had begun patronizing the Church. Constantine's so called humane legislation did not amount to much, and the Church appears to have made no serious protest at the ferocious punishments which the Christian Emperors were wont to mete out, including that of burning to death. Valens, a pious Arian, was particularly addicted to this punishment and it is only poetic justice that he apparently met his end by being burnt to death in a little hut after the calamitous defeat of Hadrianople. It was indeed the humble lower class Christians who made to the best of their ability any protest that was made. Ammianus Marcellinus (27.7.5) tells us that when two Christian officials called Diodes and Diodorus were unjustly condemned to death by burning by Valentinian, the local Christians set up a *memoria* in the place where they were buried and called the place, which was near Milan, *Ad Innocentes*. It is true that the Church had always opposed gladiatorial combats because of their cruelty. Theodoret records the story of the monk Telemachius whose protesting death in the arena ended gladiatorial combats in the arena at Rome in Honorius' reign.[31] Salvian makes it clear that they still existed in Gaul in his day, and stoutly condemns them.[32] One suspects that these displays disappeared in the course of the fifth century not because they were too cruel but because they were too expensive; in fact, Salvian says as much.[33]

But it does seem likely that the enormous dislocation of the fifth century gave Christian compassion an opportunity to function in an atmosphere less restricted than before by conventional barriers of class or bureaucracy. To some degree the universal collapse was seen to reduce all men to an equal level of needy humanity. Salvian says of slaves, *quos etsi nobis servitutis condicio inferiores humana tamen sors reddit aequales*.[34] The function of the bishop as a champion of the weak and helpless did stand out in strong relief in this century which rendered so many people weak and helpless. There are outstanding examples such as old bishop Deogratias of Carthage who succoured the wretched destitute people brought to Carthage in 455 after the Vandal sack of Rome and died during his ministrations to them, or Epiphanius of Ticinum/Pavia who was famous not only as an ascetic and a diplomat but also as a helper of the helpless, or Patiens of Lugdunum, who was a pattern of compassionate concern during all his episcopate and spend a great deal of his own money on distributing food and other supplies over a very wide area during a severe famine brought on by the invasions.[35] One of Sidonius' correspondents praises Sidonius himself for displaying a similar openhandedness when bishop of Augustonemetum.[36] More impressive even than this perhaps is the evidence that generosity to the poor and concern for strangers, the sick and prisoners was expected of any

---

[31] *Ecclesiastical History*, ed. Parmentier (*G.C.S.* series, Leipzig, 1911) 5.26.1–3.
[32] *De Gub. Dei* 6.2.10.
[33] *Ibid.*, 6.8.39–44.
[34] *De Gub. Dei* 3.7.28.
[35] Sidonius Apollinaris, *Epistulae* 2.10.2. and 6.12.5.
[36] *Ibid.*, 4.2.3.

fifth-century bishop in the West. The monk Constantius who wrote the life of Germanus of Auxerre tells us that when Germanus was made bishop he distributed his property to the poor and embraced poverty himself.[37] In one passage Sidonius gives us a poetical summary of the duties and functions of a bishop: they are, to champion the lesser people, to care for the sick, strangers and prisoners, to see that the dead are decently buried, and to preach to the people.[38] Elsewhere he makes it clear that it is the duty of the bishop to be a kind of political champion of the community over which he presides, and he commends a candidate for the see of Bourges on the grounds not only that he has experience of conducting negotiations with barbarian kings and Emperors clothed in purple, but that he possesses the quality of compassion (*humanitas*), which is a requirement in a bishop, and which includes feeding the poor.[39] To these pieces of evidence we may add the practice of ransoming prisoners which became a specially Christian activity in the fifth century when it was specially called for. Paulinus of Nola made the greatest possible personal sacrifices for this purpose early in the century. Patrick in the middle of the century tell us of the regular practice of the Christians of Gaul in ransoming prisoners from the Franks, and regards the British followers of Coroticus as scarcely civilized and barely Christian because they have no such custom,[40] and the ascetic Severinus in the second half of the century is said to have been constantly occupied in ransoming prisoners captured by the barbarians, and to have shown very great care in feeding and clothing the poor, raising supplies for them throughout Noricum.[41] The impression given, therefore, in A. H. M. Jones' magisterial *Later Roman Empire*[42] that the Church's activity did little to mitigate the harshness of existence during the period covered by

[37] Constantius, *Vita Germani Episcopi*, ed. Borius (*Sources Chrétiennes* series, Paris, 1965) 2 (p. 124).

[38] *Carmina* 16.116–126.

[39] *Epistulae* 7.9.9, 19.

[40] *Epistle to Coroticus* 14.

[41] Eugippius, *Vita Sancti Severini*, ed. Sauppe (*Mon. Germ. Hist.* series, Auct. Antiquiss. Tom. I. Pars II, Berlin, 1887 repr. 1961) 9.1 (12) and 17.1–4 (16, 17).

[42] Oxford, 1964. (3 Vols.).

his book is not altogether true for the fifth century. Christian compassion did manage to make itself felt during the misery caused by the break-up of the Western Roman Empire.

There is even a little evidence for the appearance of a new concern for the social justice during the fifth century. The Pelagian works edited by Caspari and recently reprinted certainly exhibit a lively concern for justice, and especially for the fair distribution of income, and even in one place deplore the ferocious punishments inflicted by magistrates.[43] The suggestion recently made that Pelagianism carried with it so lively a concern for social justice and so unconventionally levelling an ethos that this accounts for its violent and unexpected condemnation by Honorius in 418 against the wishes of Pope Zosimus seems a well-founded one.[44] Sidonius in a letter to Riothamus King of Armorica, written some time before 469, asks the King to enquire into the case of a poor man whose slaves have run away 'at the secret instigation of the British'[45] (who were occupying part of Armorica after a recent transmigration thither). It is possible that these British were influenced by Pelagian egalitarianism, because it is known that Pelagianism was particularly strong in Britain. Salvian in many passages displays a genuine zeal for social justice. He really does think that selfishness in the use of wealth and lack of concern for the needy is a more serious sin than fornication, and he has one particularly fine passage declaring that Christ is poor with the poor, needy with the needy and starving with the starving.[46] But of course we must not overemphasize this strain in the thought of the fifth century. Towards the end of the century we can see the Church beginning to fit more comfortably into the new society produced by the barbarian invasions and settlements. It has been observed, for instance, that the fifth century sees the beginning of the process whereby powerful families annexed bishopricks for themselves. In the time of Gregory of Tours all bishops of that see except five had come

[43] Caspari, op. cit., III (Tractatus de Divitiis) 6.2–3 (31–33).
[44] The suggestion has been made by J. Morris, Pelagian Literature, Journal of Theological Studies 16 (April 1965) 40–57.
[45] Britannis clam sollicitantibus, Epistulae 3.9.2.
[46] Ad Ecclesiam 4.4 (21–23).

from Gregory's family since the time of St. Martin, who died in 397. And nobody who has read E. A. Thompson's book, *The Goths in Spain*,[47] could doubt that from the sixth century onward the Church in that century was deeply concerned with preserving and increasing its own property.

Finally, we may note that the fifth century still left a good many pagans in the territories of the former Roman Empire for the Church to cope with. Martin had toiled among rustic pagans in Gaul and Victricius in Belgium before the collapse began, and Germanus later campaigned against paganism in the country round Auxerre. Priscillian's *Liber Apologeticus* written in Spain before the last decade of the fourth century contains a strong attack on idolatry and evidences the existence there of much paganism. The Spanish bishops were still warring against paganism in the sixth and even the seventh centuries. Salvian witnesses to the existence of much paganism in what had formerly been Roman North Africa in the middle of the fifth century, especially the worship of a god Caelestis.[48] Nobody who has read such a book as Zwicker's *Fontes Historiae Religionis Celticae*[49] could doubt that paganism in one form or another flourished for long after the fifth century throughout Western Europe. It is quite likely that the enormous upset caused by the barbarian invasions not only introduced a great deal more paganism but made it an impossible task for the Church entirely to eradicate it. The Emperor closed the temples, and the Church in many cases used their materials for building churches; one has only to look at the earliest chapel below Hexham Abbey and the bases of the pillars of the earliest chapel of St. Martin in Canterbury to see that. Its policy was not at first to take over the pagan sanctuaries as places of Christian worship; there is no evidence, as far as I know, for this being done anywhere before the sixth century. Where it did not rifle the temples for building materials it left them severely alone. But it could not entirely stamp out paganism. By the time the confusion caused by the break up of the Roman Empire had settled down it was too late to tackle this task.

[47] Oxford, 1969.
[48] *De Gub. Dei* 8.2.9–13.
[49] Bonn, 1935.

The Church, then, stumbled unawares into the collapse of the Western Roman Empire, as it had stumbled unawares into the Constantinian era of state patronage. Many of its most faithful sons believed firmly that they were living in the very last days not only of the Roman Empire but of all sublunary things at the very moment when they were most solidly building the mediaeval future. Patrick was one of them. This is a phenomenon which has occurred more than once in Christian history. The activity of Gregory the Great, for instance, exemplifies it. But though it was formally unprepared for the appalling and unprecedented collapse of the society in which it had grown into maturity, when the crisis came the Church found powers within itself to deal with the crisis, to endure, to survive and finally to go far towards permeating and controlling the new state of affairs which the barbarian invasions and settlements had brought about. In these days in which we live of social and economic planning and forecasts, most of which prove mistaken, we can perhaps conclude that this is the best way, and best condition, in which to meet major crises.

INDICES

1. ANCIENT NAMES

377

2. MODERN NAMES